New Directions In Sentencing

Edited by
Brian A. Grosman, Q.C., B.A., LL.B., LL.M.

BUTTERWORTHS Toronto

CANADA: BUTTERWORTH & CO. (CANADA) LTD.
                       TORONTO: 2265 Midland Avenue, Scarborough, M1P 4S1

UNITED KINGDOM: BUTTERWORTH & CO. (PUBLISHERS) LTD.
                       LONDON: 88 Kingsway, WC2B 6AB

AUSTRALIA: BUTTERWORTH PTY. LTD.
                       SYDNEY: 586 Pacific Highway, Chatswood, NSW 2067
                       MELBOURNE: 343 Little Collins Street, 3000
                       BRISBANE: 240 Queen Street, 4000

NEW ZEALAND: BUTTERWORTHS OF NEW ZEALAND LTD.
                       WELLINGTON: 77-85 Custom House Quay, 1

SOUTH AFRICA: BUTTERWORTH & CO. (SOUTH AFRICA) (PTY.) LTD.
                       DURBAN: 152/154 Gale Street

Canadian Cataloguing in Publication Data

Main entry under title:

New directions in sentencing

Papers presented at a conference held in Saskatoon, May, 1979.

ISBN 0-409-83460-2

1. Sentences (Criminal procedure) — Canada — Congresses. 2. Sentences (Criminal procedure) — United States — Congresses. I. Grosman, Brian A., 1935-

KE9355.Z85N49   345.71´0772   C80-094001-6

Contents

Contributors

BRIAN A. GROSMAN

is a partner in the Toronto law firm of Greenglass and Grosman. At the time of the conference he was Professor of Law at the College of Law, University of Saskatchewan, and Chairman of the conference, "New Directions in Sentencing." Mr. Grosman is the Founding Chairman of the Saskatchewan Law Reform Commission and has also contributed to the work of the Law Reform Commission of Canada. Prior to teaching in Saskatchewan he was a member of the Law Faculty at McGill University in Montreal. Mr. Grosman has written key works on the administration of justice in Canada. He is well known for his books on police and prosecution practices: *Police Command: Decisions and Discretion* (1975) and *The Prosecutor: An Inquiry into the Exercise of Discretion* (1969).

J.C. BALL

is Professor of Psychiatry and Sociology at Temple University, Philadelphia. He is a past President of the American Society of Criminology. Professor Ball authored *Social Deviancy and Adolescent Personality* (1962), and co-authored *The Epidemiology of Opiate Addiction in the United States* (1970).

D.R. CRESSEY

is Professor of Sociology at the University of California, Santa Barbara. He has been Visiting Professor at many academic institutions, including Cambridge University. Professor Cressey has authored ten books, including

Justice By Consent: Plea Bargains in the American Courthouse (1976) (with Arthur Rosett) and *Diversion from the Juvenile Justice System* (1973) (with R.A. McDermott), as well as the classic text *Criminology* (with Sutherland).

THE HON. E.M. CULLITON

is Chief Justice of Saskatchewan. He was elevated to the bench of the Saskatchewan Court of Appeal in 1951 after a distinguished legal career. Chief Justice Culliton received his legal education and training is Saskatchewan. He received the D.C.L. Honoris Causa from the University of Saskatchewan in 1962 and was Chancellor of that University from 1963 to 1969.

TANNER ELTON

is Director of the Policy Planning and Research Branch of the Federal Ministry of the Solicitor General, Ottawa. Mr. Elton has also served as a researcher for the Law Reform Commission of Canada. He is a lawyer who has contributed substantially to research in the area of the administration of criminal justice.

E.A. FATTAH

is a Professor in the Department of Criminology at Simon Fraser University, British Columbia. Formerly he was Chairman of that Department. Professor Fattah has been much involved in the sentencing project of the Law Reform Commission of Canada, producing a study paper on deterrence (1974), and has written extensively on the topic of capital punishment: *The Deterrent Effect of Capital Punishment* (1972), and *The Canadian Public and the Death Penalty: A Study of a Social Attitude* (1975).

ALEX D. GIGEROFF

is a graduate of Victoria College and the Faculty of Law, University of Toronto, Osgoode Hall, with a Ph.D. in Criminology from the London School of Economics. Dr. Gigeroff has spent a major portion of his career in research in the area of sex offences at the Clarke Institute of Psychiatry in Toronto. He is best known for his important book, *Sexual Deviations in the Criminal Law* (1968).

E.L. GREENSPAN

is senior partner in the Toronto law firm of Greenspan,

and Moldaver. The Editor of *Martin's Criminal Code* and Editor-in-Chief of *Canadian Criminal Cases,* he also teaches in criminal procedure and criminal law at Osgoode Hall Law School, York University, and at the University of Toronto Law School.

J.C. HACKLER

is Professor of Sociology at the University of Alberta. He is a past President of the Canadian Association for the Advancement of Research in Criminology and Criminal Justice. Professor Hackler has also produced a key work on juvenile delinquency in Canada: *The Prevention of Youthful Crime: The Great Stumble Forward* (1978).

THE HON. E.M. HALL

is a retired justice of the Supreme Court of Canada and holder of the Companion of the Order of Canada. Prior to his appointment to the Supreme Court of Canada, he was Chief Justice of Saskatchewan. He is the National Honorary President of the Canadian Civil Liberties Association and President of the Canadian Section of the International Commission of Jurists. From 1971 to 1977, he was Chancellor of the University of Guelph.

K.B. JOBSON

is Professor of Law at the University of Victoria, British Columbia, and Director of the Law Centre there. Previously, he was a member of the faculty of law at Dalhousie University and Director of the Sentencing Project of the Law Reform Commission of Canada. He is the author of several articles relating to sentencing and imprisonment, one of the most recent being, "Dismantling the System."

N.N. KITTRIE

is Professor of Law and Dean of the American University Law School in Washington, D.C. Former Counsel to the United States Senate Judiciary Subcommittee, Dr. Kittrie is also past President of the American Society of Criminology. He is the author of several books, including, *The Right to be Different: Deviance and Enforced Therapy* (1971), and was instrumental in bringing the *In re Gault* case before the United States Supreme Court.

J.M. KRESS

is a graduate of Columbia Law School and Cambridge University, England. Since 1973, Professor Kress has been teaching at the Graduate School of Criminal Justice at the State University of New York, Albany. From 1969 to 1973, he was an Assistant District Attorney in New York County. Professor Kress is the author of nine books relating to the courts and sentencing, and is best known for developing and implementing the original sentencing guidelines' systems in the United States.

MORRIS MANNING, Q.C.

is in private law practice in Toronto. Mr. Manning practices criminal law, and was formerly Crown Counsel for the Ministry of the Attorney General. Former Editor of *Canadian Criminal Cases, Dominion Law Reports* and *Criminal Law Quarterly,* he has also authored several books: *Protection of Privacy Act* (1974), *Wiretap Law in Canada: A Supplement to Protection of Privacy Act* (1978), and *Criminal Law* (1978) (with Mewett).

J.W. MOHR

is a Professor at the Faculty of Law at Osgoode Hall Law School and at the Department of Sociology at York University. His was a member of the Law Reform Commission of Canada. Professor Mohr was the Chairman of the Working Group on Federal Maximum Security Institutions Design which reported in 1971. He has had a long-standing interest in sex offenders and has published widely in this area, including the authoritative Canadian work on pedophilia: *Pedophilia and Exhibitionism* (1964).

G.O.W. MUELLER

is the Chief of the United Nations Crime Prevention and Criminal Justice Section and Professor of Law and Criminal Justice at the National College of the State Judiciary and at Rutgers University. In the past he has been a Special Consultant to the United States Senate Subcommittee on Improvements in Judicial Machinery. A prolific author, Professor Mueller's book on sentencing, *Sentencing: Process and Purpose,* appeared in 1977. His other works include, *Crime, Law and the Scholars: A History of Scholarship in American Criminal Law* (1969), and *Comparative Criminal Procedure* (1969) (with Le Poole-Griffiths).

THE HON. C.F. TALLIS

is Justice of the Supreme Court of the Northwest Territories. Prior to his appointment he practised law in Saskatoon, Saskatchewan and served as a bencher of the Law Society as well as Vice Chairman of the Provincial Police Commission.

A.R. VINING and CORY DEAN

A.R. Vining is Assistant Professor of the Policy Analysis Division, Faculty of Commerce and Business Administration, University of British Columbia.

Cory Dean is a law student at the University of British Columbia.

Preface

During the last week in May of 1979, a distinguished group of participants attended a conference "New Directions in Sentencing" held in the attractive western City of Saskatoon. Ideas were exchanged in a congenial, yet intellectually stimulating atmosphere unlike that prevailing in most courtrooms across the land where exchanges are of a more adversarial nature. In addition, courtroom battles tend to concentrate on immediate problems rather than the long-term implications of the process. Busy people, from time to time, have to set aside a few moments to re-examine goals and objectives in a broader context than that available on a day-to-day basis in individual professional contexts. The conference provided such a forum.

This gathering was organized in co-operation with Dean Clark and the College of Law of the University of Saskatchewan, with the assistance of the Law Foundation of Saskatchewan. It was structured in order to be self-financing, an important principle in times of increased economy. Universities and governments are less able or willing to sponsor such conferences. The interest in the topic itself brought together 200 participants, who, by their individual subscriptions made the meeting, for the most part, financially independent of funding agencies.

The assistance of Margaret Sarich, the conference co-ordinator and my secretary, Debbie Feader is gratefully acknowledged. My wife, Penny-Lynn, lent her gracious charm and competence to the overall organization of the program activities. The success of the conference was largely due to the co-operative efforts of these people as well as friends and colleagues who wished to make the participants feel welcome in Saskatchewan.

Good friends with great expertise travelled many miles to join us. Their presence added an important international perspective to a problem which is not changed by crossing a border. They provided insights into developments in their own jurisdictions which were directly relevant to our discussions.

On a more personal note, these materials have been assembled and edited at a time when I have just left the contemplative life available in the groves of the academe for the legal skirmishes that are part of a busy barrister's practice in the

City of Toronto. More important, I have exchanged my role as Professor of Law for that of a full-time practitioner of those theories which I propounded to captive law students. The judges before whom I now appear are not always sympathetic to legal theories attractive in a classroom setting, because sentencing is not merely an intellectual exercise, but is the practical "lawyer-stuff" of day-to-day courtroom contact. To some extent this volume attempts to reflect the best of both these worlds, that of the academic and of the practitioner.

No one understands the inherent dichotomies between lawyer and academic more than my law partner and friend, Morton Greenglass, Q.C. who must cope with my dual loyalties. I express my thanks to him for the time made available to me from our law practice in order to complete this book. Thanks are also due to Judith Osborne for her editorial assistance.

Brian A. Grosman
October, 1979
Toronto, Ontario
Canada

INTRODUCTION

Brian A. Grosman

The criminal justice process is not logical or systematic but is a valiant attempt to combine a wish to control crime with a concern for the protection of individual rights. That combination, to some minds, represents an impossible dream. Impossible because of a lack of consensus about strategies and goals. Each actor on the criminal justice stage carries with him attitudes and viewpoints which are particular to his training and which tend to isolate him from those working within the system who do not share those views. Different attitudes about the values and ends to be promoted in the system leads to problems in communication and understanding between different professional groups dealing with the same situation — crime and its aftermath, sentencing.

Prosecutors fight crime by convicting offenders most efficiently. Defence lawyers ensure that their clients are acquitted or only convicted if the evidence establishes every ingredient of the charge beyond a reasonable doubt. The police wish to see the streets free of crime and of those who they believe criminal. Police have difficulty when they have made a professional judgment that a person ought to be arrested and charged, in understanding that the evidence available may be insufficient to justify a conviction. Those police and prosecutors, who see their central role as that of fighting crime and convicting the guilty have a particular perspective with regard to the role of the criminal justice system which often differs from that of the defence lawyer, and even the Judge.

These differences are, for the most part, invisible to the general public, yet they persist and influence each stage of the process from the arrest through to the conviction and sentence. When the sentencing stage of the process is reached, one's orientation becomes critical and most obvious. It is during the sentencing process that, for the first time these disparate viewpoints coalesce in a determination which vitally affects both the offender's and the public's interests.

Debate has raged for centuries about the appropriateness of a sentence, whether it be for a man convicted of stealing a loaf of bread to feed his hungry family, a vicious gangland killer, or a murderer of a prison guard or policeman. Apart from these dramatic examples, there is the everyday ongoing sentencing of thousands of individuals in courts across the land by judges who are attempting to cope, often on the basis of their own experience, attitudes and approaches with a most difficult exercise of judicial discretion.

The conference titled "New Directions in Sentencing," held in Saskatoon in May of 1979, was an attempt to bring together professional persons who are major actors in the criminal justice system to exchange ideas and perspectives in order to break down parochial viewpoints by subjecting them to careful consideration and criticism by others. The conference brought together law professors, criminal defence lawyers, prosecutors, psychologists, psychiatrists, criminologists, sociologists, prison administrators, senior police administrators, parole and probation officers, governmental policy planners, legislators, and judges from every level of the courts in Canada. The papers presented a variety of viewpoints. They illustrate professional perspectives sometimes as much by way of what is left unsaid by a particular contributor as by the contribution itself.

It was felt that a collection of presentations given at the conference would provide readers with insights into the thought processes and viewpoints of those who play key roles in this most sensitive area of the administration of criminal justice. The papers may also highlight some of the controversies which surround sentencing by pointing up themes raised by social scientists and law teachers which may be unfamiliar to the general reader. Hopefully, some of the contributions also indicate the kind of thinking which is proceeding on the frontiers of the criminal justice community and thus provide some insight into the directions which may be taken in the future. There are those contributors who decry present directions and argue that the present tide is misdirected and ought to be reassessed.

Part 1 of the book deals primarily with new directions as viewed by the leading writers and commentators in the field of sentencing in North America. Part 2 deals with sentencing reform by those who have been most deeply involved in the reform of sentencing laws. Part 3 considers sentences in the past and the controversy surrounding capital punishment as well as new kinds of sentences which seem to be part of a future trend. The sentencing of specific offenders like juveniles and sexual offenders is treated in Part 4. Part 5 provides some insight into the viewpoints of the defence lawyer, and the final Part is devoted to the practice of sentencing in the criminal courts.

A number of the contributors react to what they view as the excesses exhibited by the pursuit of the treatment philosophy in sentencing, to the open endedness and the kinds of sentencing disparities it produces. That reaction has been characterized by a resurgence of a call for deterrence and the reassertion of fundamental principles of punishment and security rather than the ephemeral adjustment of sanctions to meet the particular "needs" of the individual. Currently there seems to be a consensus among the public and the legislators that there is a need to eliminate wide variations in the sentences handed down by the courts. In order to do so, fixed or mandatory sentences, "flat sentencing," are being advocated and introduced. These are sentences which proceed on a tariff basis, oriented to the seriousness of the crime committed without any major consideration of the individual, his particular background or suitability for rehabilitation. Another aspect of this movement results in making the length of confinement more certain by way of legislation, and argues for the abolition of parole boards. Overall, this new direction in sentencing encourages the elimination of much of the discretion currently involved in the sentencing process.

Those contributors who addressed themselves to this development are unanimous in their condemnation of it. Dr. Cressey asserts that inflexible sentences produce more injustice than is present in the current process. Dr. Kittrie argues that "flat" or "tariff" sentencing is for the most part, in the hands of the legislature, and, accordingly, is in danger of becoming more overtly political. This means less flexibility as the political system cannot respond to unique and difficult situations as can an informed judiciary. Both argue that once sentences are fixed the courts are unable to respond to changing societal expectations; rigid sentences offer no incentives to the inmate to rehabilitate himself and will, eventually, denigrate the important role of judicial discretion and expertise in the criminal justice system.

These and other contributors feel that a fixed sentence appropriate to the crime is an unattainable ideal. It cannot be achieved, not merely because of the peculiar circumstances of a particular case which may demand mitigation or aggravation of the penalty, but also because judges are not automatons. The judiciary make it clear in their presentations that they value the exercise of their discretion as an essential sentencing component. Unless their role in the criminal justice system is to be radically redefined, the judiciary are unlikely to co-operate in the reduction or elimination of their exercise of discretion in sentencing.

A variation on this same theme is reflected in the concern about sentencing disparities which are seen as a product of wide judicial discretion. These complaints about unstructured judicial decision-making have led to the call for sentencing guidelines. These proposals start from the premise that discretion cannot be effectively eliminated, that some measure of flexibility is still desirable, but that the judiciary cannot continue along their present path, exercising wide discretion often on the basis of very particularistic or idiosyncratic attitudes. The argument is that judicial discretion needs to be more structured and better controlled by the legislature.

This theme is developed by Professor Kress, in his contribution, where he draws attention to the myriad sentencing practices in the United States. In his view, these wide ranging practices need some common factor to bind them together, to provide a common reference base and some measure of consistency. He argues that this can be done by providing some general form of sentencing principles or guidelines. Professor Jobson views the enunciation of sentencing guidelines as being the only way to get the Canadian judiciary to halt their questionable practice of sending vast numbers of minor offenders to prison. He feels that without this impetus, they are unlikely to change their habits which rely, for the most part, on outdated concepts and traditions. Some of the judiciary themselves would probably agree in some measure with Professor Jobson that their role has to be readjusted so that sentencing reform can become a reality. Judges can be innovative in an individual case, depending upon the circumstances, but they are reluctant to adopt innovative general policies. Chief Justice Culliton of the Saskatchewan Court of Appeal points out that judges must act within the current legislative framework. They can interpret and apply, but they cannot legislate.

Dr. Mohr argues that the "new directions" may all be just a tempest in a tea pot, that in reality there are no new directions in sentencing. Instead we are moving in a circular pattern from deterrence to rehabilitation and then back to an emphasis upon deterrence once more. Certainly the flat sentencing approach, which is offence and not offender related, does smack of a reassertion of a "just desserts" philosophy. For those who reach the formal sentencing stage, and this represents only a small proportion of those persons actually involved in crime, the attempt to deter does prevail. This is so much so that we are seeing a reawakened interest in the imposition of the death penalty. At the same time there is an increasing emphasis on keeping as many people as possible out of the formal criminal justice system by diverting them to probation officers and social welfare departments where the emphasis is on rehabilitation. Thus, there exists here at least two major philosophical approaches based upon different ideals, values, practices and consequences.

Currently, considerations relating to the need for more deterrence or more rehabilitation are not the major shaping forces in sentencing policy. More pragmatic considerations are affecting sentencing policy as the public becomes more aware of the economic factors involved in the cost to the community of imprisonment. Prosecution and incarceration are both extremely expensive in terms of time, manpower and taxpayer's money. In times of economic restraint, the courts and the corrections system cannot operate on the basis that moneys will always be found to do the job. New ways to reduce expenditures in these areas are being sought. There are two immediate ways in which this can be accomplished: screen out of the system a number of people who might otherwise come to trial; and utilize lower cost alternatives to imprisonment. Thus, as Dr. Cressey points out, there are financial limitations on the enforcement of criminal law and on sentencing which may provide the catalyst for innovative approaches. Although the social scientists seem to be concerned with the financial limitations of the system and the development of the "flat sentencing" principle combined with the public attitudes calling for more deterrence in sentencing, the judiciary represented in this collection still see the rehabilitative principle as paramount in their own courts.

Public loss of confidence in the sentencing process, in its sufficiency or severity, may result in a number of by-products. Police may resort to their own sanctioning system when dealing with juvenile and other offenders who they feel will be inadequately punished by the courts. Pre-trial detention is an obvious way in which an individual who police feel may face inadequate punishment can at least suffer some deprivation and sanction in advance of any assessment of his guilt or innocence by the courts. An accused who is remanded into custody so that he is subjected to detention prior to trial is indeed, at this early stage, being sentenced. Deprivation of liberty is a severe sanction, whether it is imposed pre-trial or post-trial. Punishment before conviction is particularly heinous in a situation where an individual may never suffer the conviction but is punished nonetheless.

It is the exception rather than the rule for there to be special, separate facilities for holding pre-trial detainees. In general, people remanded in custody spend the period before trial in a local jail alongside those serving short prison sentences. Many of the provincial institutions used to house those awaiting trial in custody are old and poorly equipped. Sanitation and living conditions are primitive; segregation is difficult and the security provisions, designed to meet the requirements of the most difficult inmates, must apply to all.

Although public safety demands that some dangerous or itinerant persons must be confined before trial, the effects of pre-trial punishment should be minimized. Although they often share the same facilities, the conditions of incarceration applicable to convicted prisoners and those merely accused of crime should be differentiated. There should be parity, not between convicted and unconvicted prisoners, but between those released on bail and those remanded in custody. The basis for according different treatment, as between those awaiting trial in prison and those doing so without restraint, is that maintaining the custody of the former is felt to be necessary to ensure their appearance at trial or to avoid danger to the public. Many of these persons detained prior to trial, on whatever basis, suffer a sentence in advance of trial, which is only compensated for if the accused person is found guilty and his pre-trial detention is applied to reduce his post-trial sentence.

Another area where sentencing takes place without the necessity of a trial is in those situations where an individual has pleaded guilty as a result of a plea bargain. Plea bargaining is not strictly the imposition of a sanction without trial, but represents a sentence imposed by short circuiting the formal criminal justice system. There has been, in recent years, a lively debate about the merits and utility of plea negotiation and the resulting diversion of offenders from the trial process by the encouragement of the entry of guilty pleas in return for a reduced charge.[1]

There is an assumption that those who plead guilty will be subjected to more lenient sentences because it is felt they have saved the taxpayer money and the court time by avoiding a lengthy trial. Accordingly, accused persons may feel, either by way of explicit promises by police or prosecution or implicitly, that if they plead guilty they will gain some consideration leading to a reduced sentence. The question remains whether accused persons plead guilty, through a sense of remorse, guilt, or because they feel they will obtain a better deal giving up rights which they might otherwise have asserted. How many of those who have entered guilty pleas for some imagined or practical benefit would have been acquitted if they had gone to trial? In a plea bargaining situation, the effective sentencing power is often transferred from the judge into the hands of the police and prosecution. This is the case because on a plea of guilty many judges simply endorse the prosecutor's recommendation, which in large part is based on police information. The accused person may not fully understand the implications of his plea of guilty to a lesser charge. In fact his sentence may be very much the same as that which he would have received if convicted in due course. The guilty plea speeds up the process while limiting the alternatives available to the judge and to the accused.

Another form of sentencing ought to be considered which is provided for by special legislation and which reverses the onus of proof in certain criminal charges. In the usual criminal case, every ingredient of the charge alleged by the prosecution must be proved beyond a reasonable doubt before the accused can be properly convicted. This is now no longer true with an increasing number of the criminal offences. For example, under the Narcotic Control Act,[2] once the prosecution has established possession of a narcotic, the onus then shifts to the accused to establish that the possession was not for the purposes of trafficking. If the accused cannot establish this fact, then he will be convicted not only of possession but possession for the purposes of trafficking. That kind of reverse onus situation combined with minimum mandatory sentences gives the judge very little discretion in situations which may require more individual judicial discretion than the law grants.

Sentences imposed by criminal courts, whether pre-trial or post-trial, stigmatize and label the individual accused as someone who is an offender and is being appropriately demeaned by imprisonment. If, in fact the individual is ultimately acquitted, the stigma or label often remains. A conviction alone without imprisonment, may constitute a most effective sanction in those cases where rehabilitation or deterrence is not required. Prison is probably the worst environment in which to attempt the rehabilitation of an offender. The difficulties which face the judge are assessing when the conviction alone or a fine is sanction enough, and when the public interest demands that imprisonment be imposed even though it likely serves no individual rehabilitative or even deterrent function.

Recently, five prominent business executives were convicted of defrauding the public by rigging bids on dredging contracts. They were given jail sentences ranging from two years less a day, to five years. In imposing the sentences, Mr. Justice Parker of the Supreme Court of Ontario said that his guiding principle was general deterrence and that he was imposing exemplary sentences so that "individuals will know that the risks (of defrauding the public) are not worthwhile."[3]

Whereas in Quebec a different result prevailed when, through a scheme involving fictitious sales, the accused businessman defrauded his own company of about $500,000 over a 3-year period.[4] When the company went into liquidation the shareholders suffered substantial losses. He was convicted on charges of fraud, conspiracy to commit forgery, forgery and uttering, was sentenced to four years imprisonment and to a fine of $75,000. He appealed his sentence and the appeal was allowed. The Quebec Court of Appeal reduced the sentence to two years and to a $10,000 fine on the basis that the original sentence was excessive, having regard to the accused's lack of previous record and the gravity of the offense.

In the recent case of *R. v. McEachern,*[5] the accused pleaded guilty to theft from a bank of which he was the Assistant Manager. Over a 1-year period he stole $87,000 by signing official bank cheques using moneys held by the bank in term deposits for customers. He was previously "of good character." At trial, sentence was suspended and the accused placed on probation, two of the terms being that he make restitution for the amount still outstanding and that he perform 240 hours of community service. The Crown appealed from the sentence imposed, the appeal was upheld and a sentence of 18 months imprisonment substituted.

Chief Justice Howland of the Ontario Court of Appeal said:

> In our opinion, the gravity of the offences called for the imposition of a custodial term, and there were no exceptional circumstances which would justify a lesser punishment. The trial Judge placed too much emphasis on restitution, and on community service work as an alternative to imprisonment, and did not attach sufficient importance to general deterrence. The public interest requires that it be made very clear to one and all that in the absence of exceptional circumstances a person holding a position of trust who steals from his employer must expect a term of imprisonment.[6]

The foregoing cases indicate a different approach in the sentencing of businessmen employers, employees in a position of trust, and other offenders. The principles involved in the sentencing of white collar criminals as illustrated in the above examples become even more vague when one adds the political component that sometimes surrounds sentencing. The recent trial of Jacques and Louise Cossette-Trudel in Quebec provides a useful example of that process. Chief Justice Mayrand of the Sessions Court in Montreal had pondered the verdict since the former FLQ terrorists pleaded guilty to three charges on May 30, 1979. In handing down the sentence, he also ordered them not to talk to the press, give interviews, make public statements, or participate in public demonstrations for three years "solely to protect their private lives and facilitate their re-entry into society."[7]

They were given three concurrent sentences of two years less a day for the charges to which they entered guilty pleas and given three years probation for a fourth charge, for which they were summarily convicted. The minimum they must serve behind bars before becoming eligible for parole is eight months.

The Cossette-Trudels also will come under the jurisdiction of the Quebec Parole Board rather than the National Parole Board. Judge Mayrand noted that the provincial board is "more flexible" and better suited to looking after them upon their release.

The judge emphasized that the major criterion for his decision was the public interest, and, although there was little doubt in his mind that the Cossette-Trudels were truly rehabilitated and were good parents, the public interest, however, required that their sentence serve as an example to others. The judge said that the usual sentence for kidnapping is about ten years. (Kidnappers of bank managers have been getting between five and ten years in Montreal in recent months because the courts are handing down stiffer sentences to discourage this particular crime.)

The judge said that if he had sentenced the couple to a 10-year term, eight years after the crime had been committed, "it would have been clearly disproportionate and would look like vengence." He noted that the other kidnappers had received eight years, but they had pleaded not guilty, whereas the Cossette-Trudels had pleaded guilty, which saved the taxpayers considerable money by eliminating the need for a long trial. He said further that although their freely chosen exile certainly was not the same as a jail term, it was, in a way, a sort of chastisement. The eight years in exile were surely the equivalent of four years in jail, their defence lawyer had argued. He said that since the couple had returned to Canada they had avoided staging any of the "ungracious incidents" that marked the FLQ terrorist trials in the early 1970s. They had "scrupulously respected their bail conditions showing themselves worthy of the confidence of the Court."[8]

The reaction to the sentence in English-speaking Canada was typified by the editorial in the Toronto *Globe and Mail* of August 8, 1979, which said "Jacques and Louise Cossette-Trudel have been asked to pay an unacceptable small price for a heinous crime."[9] On the other hand, the Quebec press seems to feel that the sentence was adequate and possibly even a bit harsh under the circumstances. Two different political contexts view the sentences imposed as either appropriate or inappropriate to their particular constituency.

The foregoing problems in sentencing are for the most part traditional in the sense that generations of judges have had to cope with them. There are, however, on the horizon, new forms of sentencing which will require a new response from the judiciary. One of these is illustrated by an informal *ad hoc* policy without firm guidelines and is called "diversion." This process is to provide an informal way of dealing with minor crimes, particularly those committed by juveniles without subjecting them to the rigours of the criminal justice system. Diversion is seen as an appropriate way in which minor offenders can be dealt with outside the normal adversary process. There are, however, inherent problems due to the lack of due process involved in such procedures and their potential for coerciveness.

There is an attempt to increase the role of the community in sentencing by providing work programs which are useful to the community and by attempting to reintegrate the offender into the community rather than isolating him by way of imprisonment. There are many problems associated with diversion which are yet to be explored, particularly its bureaucratic nature and the lack of protection for individual rights. It is promoted as a less expensive way of dealing with offenders. The economic argument has not yet been established as a new bureaucracy may be required to handle a wide variety of these programs. Although the concept of diversion is theoretically attractive, in practice, it breeds increasing governmental control over a new population not previously subjected to the rigors of state control and supervision because imprisonment has been, until recently, the only alternative available to a judge who wished to impose some control or penalty upon an offender. Contrary to the claims of those who support diversion, there is no evidence available that indicates that an expansion of diversionary programs results in a reduction in the number of those incarcerated in prison. Nonetheless, diversion has become one of North America's growth industries.

One of the most publicly controversial areas of sentencing relates to delay. Delay lengthens the period of pre-trial incarceration and may lead to added pressure upon the accused to plead guilty in order to expedite the disposition of his case. Excessive delay between the charging of a criminal offense and its disposition by way of sentence after numerous delays waiting for a case to come on for trial results in the punishment of the offender being divorced from the original criminal act which took place some considerable time before conviction. The unpleasant consequences of a prolonged period before trial becomes the punishment for guilty and innocent alike, and the penalty, when it is finally imposed, seems to be more like a gratuitous infliction of harm rather than "just desserts" for a crime committed.

In certain western provinces such as Saskatchewan and Alberta, although natives represent less than 15% of the population they account for over 70% of the admissions to provincial prisons. Even more disconcerting are the figures for native women, since they account for 90% of the female prison population in these provinces. A minority group is being subjected to imprisonment for reasons not yet clearly understood or documented. The cultural and legal implications of this over-representation of those of native ancestry in our prisons presents a critical problem in need of immediate attention. There is justification in the criticism directed at sentencing practices that too often those who are incarcerated are there, not so much because of the nature of the offence committed, but rather because they are poor and culturally maladjusted to the demands of the legal and social system controlled by the majority. The question remains whether the future of sentencing holds more of the same for these disadvantaged groups.

Analysis of judicial predispositions and individual personality characteristics has led to the placement of judges on a political spectrum ranging from conservative-retributive to liberal-permissive. This pseudo-scientific attempt to categorize individual judges and thereby predict approaches to legal issues and to the sentencing of offenders is little more accurate than the trial lawyers' educated hunch which he utilizes in order to bring his client before a sympathetic judge. Personalities under a microscope give rise to broad characteristic tendencies and little additional enlightenment. It is an impersonal and statistically de-humanizing approach.

The judges themselves are most concerned about their collective predilections, standards and goals in sentencing. As a result they spend considerable time together at sentencing conferences engaged in increasing their awareness and expanding their learning. It is that conscientious commitment to understanding and competence that ought to be encouraged among the judiciary. Sentencing remains a human process and as such, a sensitive art rather than an objective science.

Some of these issues and other problems relating to sentencing are considered by the distinguished participants at the conference, ''New Directions in Sentencing.'' These contributors who bring with them a wide variety of professional and intellectual backgrounds, debated and attempted to formulate new ideas about the sentencing process. The aim of the conference was to explore the frontiers of change in the sentencing system and to re-evaluate the present practices in order to consider appropriate adjustments which might ultimately result in a better approach to one of the most difficult problems bedevilling the administration of criminal justice in Canada. Before change is undertaken, such difficulties must be understood, problems identified and alternatives carefully considered. This was a conference of concerned people who play a central role in the implementation of the principles of sentencing. It is hoped that this volume will improve the quality of information available to those interested in the sentencing process and its implications for the fair administration of justice.

NOTES

1. B. Grosman, *The Prosecutor: An Inquiry Into the Exercise of Discretion* (1969) University of Toronto Press, 2nd ed., 1977.
2. R.S.C. 1970, c. N-1, s. 35.
3. *Globe and Mail,* Toronto, June 12, 1979, p. 1.
4. *R. v. O'Bront,* (1979), 43 C.C.C. (2d) 524 (Que. C.A.).
5. (1979), 42 C.C.C. (2d) 189 (Ont. C.A.).
6. *Ibid.,* p. 191.
7. *Globe and Mail,* Toronto, August 8, 1979, p. 1.
8. *Ibid.,* p. 2.
9. *Ibid.,* p. 6.

Part 1

NEW DIRECTIONS

CHAPTER 1

The Future of Sentencing: Back to Square One

Gerhard O. W. Mueller

In a single human life span, sentencing and corrections have gone through four distinct eras: from the era or retribution, which was marked by relatively fixed, severe, although not necessarily brutal, sentences there was a passage to the so-called era of utilitarianism. During this latter period there was a spirit of unbounded optimism which created the conviction that the crime rate could be controlled by manipulating sentencing and correctional schemes, whereby the behavior of individual perpetrators or of whole potential offender groups could be redirected. There followed, well into the 1970s, an era of humanism which aimed at a more equitable and more liberal recognition of the human rights of those caught in the meshes of the criminal justice system. Sentencing and corrections then entered a fourth phase, preceded by pointed research which aimed at examining what does work and what does not, which concluded that nothing does work as expected, and thereby initiated the era of nihilism.

Sentencing nihilism has had a tremendous impact. On the legislative side, bills are being introduced, and some have passed, virtually abolishing the existing sentencing model and returning to various forms of the fixed sentencing schemes in operation around the turn of the century, often demonstrating equal, if not greater, rigor. On the executive-administrative side, the uncertainty over the future of sentencing has had a profound impact on management, on parole board actions, and on staff morale, especially in view of the consequent over-crowding of correctional institutions. On the judicial side, constructive optimism on the part of judges has led to frustration and anger over what is interpreted to be an attack on the judiciary in an effort to deprive them of an important judicial function, namely, sentencing (indeed, judicial confusion and frustration are so great that during the last two years in the United States, practically no judges have signed up for any of the sentencing courses of the National Judicial College, whereas in preceding years, hundreds of judges would sign up annually). Finally, on the academic side, which has always been extremely fad oriented, it is now customary to flog the dead sentencing horse and to demonstrate the evil that comes from all horses.

The not-quite dead horse of sentencing, as it had evolved and stood virtually unchallenged until a few years ago, was marked by a spirit of optimism and hope: crime is not inevitable; offenders can be re-integrated into society; the crime rate can be manipulated by what legislators and judges do with sentencing policies; harsh and retributive sentences are not necessary; imprisonment is to be avoided whenever possible. Surely, such postulates are not by themselves offensive. *Per contra,* they symbolize a humanitarian outlook and commitment. Then why did they come under attack, why did they crumble?

The critics of the utilitarian-humanitarian sentencing system have several points of attack of both a theoretical and pragmatic nature. They argue that the rehabilitative model is *useless* because: (1) Many offenders need not be rehabilitated since they are well-adjusted members of the community and a judgment of conviction by itself does not make it otherwise; (2) Inasmuch as rehabilitation requires manipulations of the human personality, sometimes the brain, often the psyche, it constitutes an impermissible invasion of the most intimate last reserve of the personality; (3) Rehabilitation efforts require variations differing from one human being to another, thus making for inequality in sentences inconsistent with the principle of justice which requires equal treatment of all persons convicted of the same offence. The rehabilitative approach moreover, is said to be useless because it yields no results. In fact recent studies appear to indicate that no perceptible differences were found among those undergoing treatment and those not.

Without entering into methodological controversies as to what evaluative studies prove or do not prove, whether the type of research conducted was appropriate to the occasion or not, etc., the more important point in this regard simply is that, probably, the rehabilitative model was never put into practice. It has always remained a model, like a plastic toy ship, a model which was never translated and constructed into reality. Or does a prison ward become a rehabilitation centre by putting a sign on a cage which reads "rehabilitation centre?" And who says that prison is the place at which to practice rehabilitation my way?

Let me, for the time being, take up the issues of justice and equality, in other words of human rights which the critics have argued. Of course, I am fully in accord with them when it comes to the issue of protecting the integrity of the human personality from invasions by the state. The Universal Declaration of Human Rights and national constitutions bar such invasions, and I trust that with vigilance the advocates of civil liberties can use the courts to stop any conceivable infringements of that sort. In my opinion, even participation in routine prison education and socialization programs should be made to rest on the consent of the convict, and be subject to court supervision. But concern about whether we can get the courts to control abuses effectively is a poor reason for throwing out the idea of socialization. And so it is with the other civil liberties issue, that of egalitarian treatment. It is undoubtedly true that the needs and capacities of human beings vary. While children go through public school at basically the same speed, class by class, year by year, there are slow learners and fast learners, and teachers have to adjust their method accordingly. And so it is with correctional practice which rests on theories not fundamentally different from those governing public education. Surely, gross deviations from a set standard, determined to be "just" by basically agreed upon values, are not tolerable, but within that frame, a modicum of individualization is not only necessary but indispensable. As Mr. Justice Holmes once put it, "there is no greater injustice than to treat unequals as equals." Quite frankly, our penal codes, with their broad reach, catch all kinds of different human beings with different capacities and motivations, different needs and different deeds under the same provision. The idea of establishing and working with guidelines — based on judicial sentencing patterns, developed by the judiciary — is quite attractive and surely deserves greater attention and further study. But, return to totally fixed sentences is a turn to nihilism and to injustice.

Let me now turn to the utilitarian arguments. It would be ludicrous to contend that sentencing policies have no impact at all on the crime rate, e.g., if judges were to set the standard fine for illegal downtown parking at $2, motorists would cheerfully park their cars illegally, because it costs $7, to place the car into a garage. Obviously, it must be readily conceded that most criminal action does not rest on such rational considerations. We know that the greater the psychopathological content of criminal action, the less is the impact of rational considerations. And that makes it very difficult to manipulate crime rates in the short run, especially for offences like homicide or rape. The critics may have something here then. We, in the United Nations, have had frequent occasion to point out that national crime rates are rather more dependent on national, social, educational and economic policies than on the sentencing attitudes of judges, or, indeed, the zeal of police departments. Countries with low crime rates have low crime rates because their primary social control organs, families, extended families, clans and villages are still intact, and strong values are being transmitted and preserved. The as yet not industrialized nations of the Third World prove that point with a crime rate which is less than half as big as that of industrialized or developed countries, as a whole. The point is also proven by the fact that with industrialization and urbanization of those countries, crime increases. The point is lastly proven by the fact that highly developed and rapidly developing countries which recreate or retain social controls, internal and external, also keep the crime rate low, *vide* such widely divergent societies as the socialist countries, Saudi Arabia, Japan, Switzerland, and a host of others.

We now have to return to the real bone of contention regarding sentencing policies, namely, whether re-integration of the offender into society is beyond the capacity of sentencing and correctional policies. One must admit, of course, that a large number of offenders need no re-integration, because they never were excluded and that, moreover, where re-integration is necessary, it is largely due to the fact that imprisonment itself has caused the need for easing the offender back into society after a long period of "prisonization" and "infantilization" in the "iron womb." Perhaps "resocialization" should mean little more than that. It should mean giving an alienated or a never integrated human being the necessary wherewithall to make it in the competitive world. Rehabilitation, therefore, at least in our society, must largely be a *socioeconomic process,* which aims at capacitating the offender to function in the socioeconomic life of his or her society. And if we insist on retribution and on restitution, that too can be accommodated in the scheme I envision, namely by the widest possible use of community service as both a sanction and as a learning process.

Talking about the future of sentencing is a dangerous business. Ten years ago none of us could have predicted the current cry for return to fixed and severe sentences; for imprisonment, incapacitation and retribution. It is, however, not quite as dangerous to predict the next stage of development. The shortcomings of neo-retribution are so apparent, that its life span is bound to be limited. Indeed, in a relevant and recent Delphi study, concerned primarily with the future of parole, the "sages" of the profession predicted that by 1985, "mean" inmate participation will be voluntary and not used as a basis for parole release, that by 1985, "mean" offenders convicted of the same offence will be given "similar" sentences whereby the variability of judicially imposed sentences will be reduced by 50 per cent; that parole supervision will never be restricted solely to public protection, but, rather, will always entail the delivery of social services; that by 1990, prison will be reserved for the most serious felonies, and community treatment will be used for the remainder; but that it will be the year 2000 before we can predict the future criminality of prisoners with 50 per cent more accuracy.

The year 2000 is also our millenium at the United Nations, the target year of the United Nations International Plan of Action for Crime Prevention and the Treatment of Offenders, which envisions a more fair, more effective, more humane system of crime control, but one in which, ultimately, crime will be largely controlled by socioeconomic policies, rather than the criminal justice system acting alone. As part of that International Plan of Action, the Crime Prevention and Criminal Justice Branch will assist the Committee on Crime Prevention and Control and other UN policy-making bodies in working out a more effective and humane sentencing policy as well. And what will that policy look like? It may be presumptious for me to anticipate what the Committee will do, but I can already see a plan emerge which will emphasize a more perfected model of judicial sentencing, with less judicial discretion; more guidelines, but a strong emphasis on the avoidance of imprisonment and prisonization; greater emphasis on community service — along the lines of Canada's experimentations; and far more emphasis on the integration of the whole correctional process with the socioeconomic life of nations. In order to implement this plan, there will be very important occasions during which the international community can help in developing such guidelines and standards. The first one will be the 6th UN Congress on the Prevention of Crime and the Treatment of Offenders, to be held in Sydney, Australia, in 1980.

The concern of the United Nations with issues related to the administration of justice can be traced back to the very beginning of its history. The Universal Declaration of Human Rights refers to the protection of human rights in criminal justice in its articles 7, 8, 9, 10 and 11. The principles proclaimed in those articles have been set forth, *inter alia,* in the International Covenant on Civil and Political Rights (articles 9, 14 and 15), in force since 23 March 1976 and now ratified by a great number of countries.[1] Moreover, the Standard Minimum Rules for the Treatment of Prisoners;[2] the draft principles on freedom from arbitrary arrest and detention;[3] the draft principles on equality in the administration of justice;[4] the Declaration on the Protection of All Persons from Being Subjected to Torture and Other Cruel, Inhuman or Degrading Treatment or Punishment;[5] the draft convention on Torture and Other Cruel, Inhuman or Degrading Treatment or Punishment;[6] the Draft Code of Conduct for Law Enforcement Officials,[7] to be submitted for adoption to the General Assembly in 1979; the body of principles for the protection of all persons under any form of detention or imprisonment,[8] to be presented to the General Assembly in 1980; and the Draft Guidelines on the Expeditious and Equitable Handling of Criminal Cases,[9] can all become central in future efforts towards developing national and international standards and guidelines on sentencing and on the administration of justice. Obviously, the mere development of instruments of this kind is not enough; it must be accompanied by a change in attitudes and conceptions on the part of all those who are involved in the process: judges, correctional officers, and people in general. If we want to effectively change the attitudes and behavior of our offenders, we have to change our own attitudes, namely to a humane and rational approach for dealing with crime prevention and all issues of criminal justice.

NOTES

1. Adopted by G.A.Res. 2200 A(XXI), annex.

2. 1st UN Congress on the Prevention of Crime and the Treatment of Offenders: Report by the Secretariat (UN publications, Sales No.56.IV.4).

3. Study of the Right of Everyone to be Free from Arbitrary Arrest, Detention and Exile (UN publications, Sales No.65.XIV.2).

4. Study of Equality in the Administration of Justice (UN publication, Sales No.E.71;XIV.3).

5. Adopted by the 5th UN Congress on the Prevention of Crime and the Treatment of Offenders and by the G.A. in res. 3452(XXX), annex.

6. Commission on Human Rights, Report on the 35th session, E/1979/36.

7. See A/33/215 and Add.1.

8. See E/CN.4/1296 and the recent ECOSOC res. on the subject.
9. See E/AC.57/34 and E/CN.5/558.

CHAPTER 2

New Directions in Sentencing

J.W. Mohr

THE BOUNDARIES OF DISCOURSE

To speak of "New Directions in Sentencing" implies that sentencing is an activity capable of progress and new positions. In common sense terms the title is obvious. But this very common sense may hide the fact that the promise of new directions has characterized discourse on sentencing for at least 200 years, in which *progress* (direction) and *neo-philia* (love of newness) have determined most activities in our culture. What discourse of this kind further tends to hide is what remains substantially the same — and in sentencing this factor is substantial.

The combination of *new* and *directions* impels us to look forward. Our data, however, can only come from looking backward and even a cursory examination of the history of sentencing shows us that much of what is called new today has already been here before. Reading the literature and accounts of conferences, one is impressed by the repetitiveness of proposed solutions, as if there was no memory of days before yesterday. Even where memory is called upon in the form of history it is often falsified to establish new claims.

There is, to be sure, no absence of claims and counterclaims. Sentencing, after all, is the pivotal point in the criminal law process: judges agonize over it; the prosecution, although reticent in stating its claims, does have expectations which are more clearly expressed in appeals; defence counsel, although far less sure about his role in sentencing than in the trial, knows that for the accused the sentence is the bottom line on the balance sheet; police tend to see the sentence as a measure of the importance of their work — and there is never enough recognition for one's work; the corrections industry lives off the sentence although it does not really know what to do in most cases. And all this happens in a community context where there is not only a great variety of assumptions and expectations but also a basic notion that crimes and criminals should just go away, or that crimes will go away if criminals are put away.

Most of the actors in the drama do not claim great expertise and those who do, such as criminologists, sociologists and psychiatrists and even statisticians are strenuously kept from making decisions, and where they do have some impact such as in release procedures, they have not inspired general confidence. There is nevertheless an abundance of literature on the topic and if one follows it one discovers a remarkable circularity which can only be converted into a direction by a massive forgetfulness of where we have been before.

We have said that sentencing can be seen as the pivotal point of the criminal process. It directs itself both to past and future. The very word expresses this quality. Although it comes from Latin *sentire,* to feel and to preceive, it appears in English as judgment, first on doctrinal questions and then as a term for all authoritative statements in law — ecclesiastical, civil and criminal.[1] The first use denoting *consequences* was in the sentence of excommunication. Sentencing thus shifted its focus from clarification and settlement of disputes to a focus on control. Excommunication was, in fact, the first indeterminate sentence and release from it could only be achieved by submission to doctrinal dicta. In our present trinity of punishment, deterrence and rehabilitation, only the first one directs itself to the past, the just desert evening out the score; the other two are clearly future oriented and later additions. And since deterrence has remained an illusive goal and rehabilitation has been repeatedly pronounced to be illusory, we are, at this point, again being driven back to punishment. This is a direction we can identify although it would take massive forgetfulness to call it new; which does not prevent a number of people from doing so.[2]

In the reaction against the rehabilitative ideal and forms of prevention, the main point which is made is that a man should be punished for what he has done and not for what he is or might do. It can be readily observed that we have come full circle back to the position of the classical school of criminology. The *right to punish* is also pretty well left where Beccaria put it: "Let us consult the human heart, and we shall find there basic principles of the true right of the sovereign to punish crimes."[3] He justified it with the Hobbesian notion, which is still widely accepted: "Weary of living in a continual state of war, and of enjoying a liberty rendered useless by the uncertainty of preserving it they sacrificed a part so that they might enjoy the rest of it in peace and safety."[4] This also echoes Rousseau's social contract which appeared two years previous to *On Crimes and Punishment.*[5] Justifications given today, if they are given at all, fluctuate between Kant and Bentham, hardly contemporary thinkers.

It is already evident in Beccaria's writing that the language of due process is also the language of control and cannot be dichotomized in the way Herbert Packer has attempted to do.[6] Beccaria, and the new legalists, addressed themselves to what they perceived as misuses of the criminal law through arbitrary discretion based on questionable assumptions. The one blamed medieval obscurantism, the others, in very similar tones, blamed developments like the medical model, the very model which the positive school of criminology hailed as the new approach to crime. So Ferri stated: "The 19th century has won a great victory over mortality and infectious diseases by means of the masterful progress of physiology and natural science. But while contagious diseases have gradually diminished, we see on the other hand that moral diseases are growing more numerous in our so-called civilization."[7] Seventy years later, Kittrie and others are warning us against the enforced therapy of deviance and the tyranny of treatment.[8]

What is continuously overlooked and indeed curiously forgotten in the claims of improving humanity and the counterclaims of letting the certainty of justice prevail is that this unacknowledged dialectic, and hence ambiguity and ambivalance, is deeply imbedded in the criminal law itself. If we look at the description of a charge it starts simply enough with "everybody who . . ." and then goes on to describe the prohibited act and to set out the punishment. But then there are small words inserted such as "intentionally," "wilfully," "negligently," "recklessly" and we all know that the very nature of the criminal law hinges on those words. There is a further dilemma: acts cannot be punished, only persons. We do not sentence acts, only persons — consequences fall on the person and are, in the main, not directed to the act.

Even an astute observer of the history of treatment and punishment such as Michel Foucault glosses over this dilemma when he says:

> Legal justice today has at least as much to do with criminals as with crimes. Or more precisely, while, for a long time, the criminal had been no more than the person to whom a crime had been attributed and who could therefore be punished, today, the crime tends to be no more than the event which signals the existence of a dangerous element — that is, more or less dangerous — in the social body.[9]

This now common historical assumption is contradicted by the forms of indictment which were used well into the 19th century. Chitty's Practical Treatise of 1816 (well after Becarria and at the height of Bentham's work) suggested the following examples as standard forms:[10]

For murder:

> . . . the jurors for our lord the king upon their oath present, that A.B. on the day of————, in the place of————, in the county of————, labourer, (this is the standard occupation inserted in almost all indictments) not having the fear of God before his eyes, but being moved and seduced by the instigation of the devil, on the———— day of————

and so on and so forth.

Facts were not quite as important as we are told in the following footnote:

> (i) A day must be stated when the assault was made, though a variance from the real time is immaterial.[11]

For Deceits and False Pretences:

> That L.P. late of, etc. being an evil disposed person, and not minding to get his living by truth and honest labour, according to the laws of this realm, but compassing and devising how he might unlawfully obtain and get into his hands and possession, the moneys of the honest liege subjects of our said lord the King, for the maintenance of his unthrifty living —

and so on and so forth.[12]

Or, against Justices for Oppression:

> And that he, the said T.M. being such justice as aforesaid, and being a person of a wicked and malicious mind and disposition, and having no regard to justice, nor to the duty of his said office of such justices of the peace, but unlawfully, wickedly, and maliciously devising and intending to discredit, disgrace, aggrieve and oppress one M.M. —

and so on and so forth.[13]

Granted all this was asserted without the aid of psychiatrists or social workers, but it was asserted on indictments; and only after the character statements came the specification of acts and this was repeated not only in the wording but in the nature of sentences. It is salutary to remind ourselves when we again talk about the superiority of punishment over treatment what punishments were really like. To give details would, however, offend against the obscenity section of the Criminal Code of Canada.[14] Punishments were, and Foucault depicts them impressively, what we would today call successful degradation ceremonies.[15] We will come back to this later because of the very practical problem we have in making punishments visible and believable.

The point here is that the demonstration of moral inferiority of the accused has always been central to the criminal law and did not have to wait for modern psychology to find expression.[16] The opposite, superior social standing, has equally served as an excuse or at least as a modification of punishment as numerous exceptions such as the benefit of clergy show. This particular excuse was based on a rather simple test, the ability to read, which divided the worthy from the unworthy ones, not unlike our more sophisticated psychological tests today. (Some accused were able to cheat by learning a given judge's favourite passage by heart; this is more difficult with tests which have lie-scales attached to them.)

Although it must be remembered that the scenario of the morality play has been — and still is — the heart of the criminal law and particularly of sentencing, religious justifications have been largely replaced by justifications in the name of utility.[17] (Religious justifications were as questionable then as utility is now.) Bentham, of course, is closely connected with the calculus of the greatest good for the greatest number although interestingly enough we can already find it in Beccaria.(*La massima felicità divisa nel magior numero.*)[18]

The need of modernity to give a rational base to human actions and institutions is well summarized and still upheld by Nigel Walker who significantly calls his treatise "Sentencing in a Rational Society."[19] He identifies five aims of the penal system:

(1) To protect offenders and suspected offenders against unofficial retaliation (Montero's aim);
(2) To reduce the frequency of the types of behaviour prohibited by the criminal law (Reductivism);
(3) That the penal system should be such as to cause the minimum of suffering (whether to offenders or to others) by its attempts to achieve its aims (Humanitarianism);
(4) That the penal system should be designed to ensure that defendants atone by suffering for their offences (Retributivism); and
(5) To show society's abhorrence of crime (Denunciation).

Nigel Walker favours reductivism tempered by economic and humanitarian considerations. He can be seen as a straight descendant of Bentham. We could analyze these aims very differently but in any case we have to see that Bentham, in spite of his monumental work, has had little impact on the criminal law and sentencing except for the idea of the Panopticon which remains the crucial metaphor for the watcher and the watched.[20] The attempts of Bentham and of Walker to rationalize and scientize criminal law and sentencing cannot hide the basic political fact which Foucault put at the center of his attention: Surveillance. Walker, for instance, said: "No society can afford a policeman at everybody's elbow. The number of people willing or suitable to be psychiatrists, probation officers or custodial staff, under present or foreseeable conditions of service, is already insufficient for our *present* penal system."[21] In other words, if we could afford it, it would be a desirable state and our present penitentiary policy-makers seem to think that we not only can afford it, but that it is even good for the economy if we only do it in a big way.[22]

Rationality and formalism have been severely attacked and yet in a curious sense maintained by what has become known as the New Criminology.[23] There seems to be a great deal of embarrassment about the startling discovery that criminology may not just be a science in the sense of the natural sciences, but a political science and a political instrument to boot. What could we possibly have meant when we said all along that criminal law was an instrument of social control? The embarrassment seems to be further increased by the suspicion that the New Criminology is Marxist inspired. The embarrassment of course goes both ways since the new criminologists also have to recognize that the function of criminal law and sentencing in Marxist societies is not essentially different from that in capitalist ones. The notion of the common good may be different, the means to achieve it are not. And to declare the means as aberrations of some kind of true Marxism only takes the argument from the material into the ideal and we already have a plethora of ideal solutions in this field. The essential political character of criminal law and sentencing nevertheless has to be recognized as the background for any analysis or reform.

THE SEARCH FOR NEW DIRECTIONS

Whether we couch our language in terms of utilitarianism or moralism, materialism or idealism or any other "ism" that a set of beliefs may provide us with, it seems that the possibilities of discourse around sentencing have been exhausted. The last stage was, in fact, the concern with formalism in the 1950s and 60s under the heading of uniformity of sentencing.[24] In 1971 John Hogarth published his study *Sentencing as a Human Process.*[25] As the title indicates, he perceived sentencing not only as a stage in the legal process but one in which the human actor played a decisive role. By differentiating facts, legal criteria and attitudes and perceptions of the decision-maker, he not only explained differences in sentencing patterns but showed the effect varying attitudes and perceptions had on specific outcomes. The proud principle of a government of laws and not of men turned largely into a legal fiction when it came to sentencing. The relationship between fact and law on the one hand and attitudes and perceptions of judges on the other showed itself as being less simple than it had been (and still is) assumed. Beliefs in punishment or treatment, for example, could have paradoxical outcomes; treatment oriented judges tended to give longer prison terms than punishment oriented ones. The implicit reasons (hardly ever explicit) for length of sentence were obviously different. All this is now well known but what for Hogarth was a method of analysis and a way of understanding the sentencing process has become a plan for action: the control of discretion. The consequences of this interpretation and the subsequent trend to eliminate the human factor from sentencing decisions are fully discussed in subsequent papers. There was, however, another lesson to be learned, namely, that the criminal process is a human process from beginning to end. This interpretation expressed itself in a renewed interest in dispute resolution, restitution and compensation, a renewed interest in the victim and the victim/offender relationship.[26]

Thus, the legalistic developments during the past decade based themselves mainly on an anti-discretionary, anti-therapeutic stance expressed in legislative proposals and changes towards determinate and flat sentences and administrative developments such as the abolition of parole. The main determinants were due process and the right to punishment with little or no empirical testing as to how this ideology would affect the criminal process.

The other trend, which may be called a search for alternatives expressed itself in a diffusion of the decision-making process recognizing that judicial sentencing was only part of the story and that many, if not most *prima facie* criminal events, were only selectively dealt with in the formal process and depended on the number of decision-making points in the community, by police and prosecution.[27]

The legalistic trend we have already identified as a return to the classical school of criminology and need not be pursued further in this context. It nevertheless warrants the serious attention it will be given by other papers.

The trend towards alternatives can be summarized in three propositions:

De-criminalization: This can be summarized as "no crime, no sentence." It must be recognized that the ambit of the criminal law has been a continuous historical extension from the one initial offence of parricide. But this extension has now reached unprecedented proportions. For Canada, the Law Reform Commission counted about 40,000 offences outside the Criminal Code to which a citizen is subject.[28] There is now an incipient recognition that the criminal law is an inappropriate instrument for many problems which have been brought within its ambit. Groupings such as those of victimless crimes have been singled out but there are, of course, many other crimes such as those committed between people in a continuing relationship, especially the family or work situation which warrant different approaches. The main difficulty in treating these offences differently is that moral discourse has by now become almost totally associated with criminal law provisions and solutions. There is, therefore, a strong resistance to de-criminalization because "legalizing" is equated with approval. Our dependence on criminal law now outstrips any drug dependence we may have. And although there is some success in some areas, in general, for every offence taken off the books, three others appear. Although not very promising at this point, de-criminalization has to be pursued if we are to remain a free society in any sense of the word, and if there is to be a moral discourse in the community which can increasingly replace autonomous state interventions.

Diversion: What was initially a simple proposition that not every offence needed a trial and a sentence, promises, in the light of due process considerations, to become another control industry. And yet if, for example, one learns that last year in one province, Ontario, there were almost four million charges processed through the criminal division of the Provincial Courts alone and this in a total population of 8 million, it is clear that the criminal process cannot possibly be functional within its traditional framework.[29] Neither can the courts fulfil their mandate of a careful examination of offences and an appropriate and effective apportionment of sanctions.

Selective law enforcement has always been and is increasingly a reality which has not been recognized in traditional criminal law theory leading now to the embarrassment of shoddy, if not unconscionable pre-trial manipulations.

Again, however, we have become so wedded to formal state-sanctioned processes, to authoritative, if not authoritarian decisions, that a development such as diversion is in danger of leading to an extension rather than a contraction of the criminal justice system. Nevertheless, the direction of informal dispute resolution has to be pursued if a sense of community and communal responsibility is not to be totally destroyed.

Holistic view: This third proposition is exemplified by the work of the Law Reform Commission of Canada on dispositions and sentences in the criminal process.[30] The Commission recognized that to look at sentencing without considering decisions made on the community, police and prosecution level, gives a distorted picture of the relationship between sentencing and crime. Equally, sentences have to be considered in the light of actual consequences since the administration of sentences can vary the effect considerably. A prison sentence can be spent in maximum security, a community facility or partially on parole; it can lead to persecution as in the case of some sex offenders, or to special privileges as in the case of some professionals. This is outside the meagre specification of time which is all judges are allowed to make. As the criminal law process has been called discount justice, so the law of corrections has been equated with that of the jungle, out of the reach of the courts in most instances.

The Commission's work exemplifies another aspect of sentencing which may yet be the most important one. There has been a development, even if ever so slow, to shift from principles such as punishment, deterrence and rehabilitation to the principle of undoing the harm done by means such as restitution, compensation and community service.[31] As we have seen previously, sentencing has largely moved during the past century in the direction of attempting to reduce crime in the future. Victims, although constantly mentioned as a justification for the criminal process, have always had only a subservient role, mainly as witnesses, to enable the state to obtain a conviction. They could then go and try their luck in the civil process. Even in countries where both processes are combined, the state had the first claim and victims might get whatever was left over. It is not surprising that one finds in the account of victims that they are twice aggrieved, first by the crime and then by the criminal process.[32]

There is still a great deal of uncertainty about what one may call positive sentences, and yet it is this trend which opens up the most serious possibility for a new direction in sentencing. The concept rests on premises which are much older than the criminal law as we know it, and precedes the framework of discourse we have attempted to sketch. The resistance against this trend is understandable since in the final analysis it amounts to no less than the abolition of the criminal law itself. A cogent argument can be made for such a radical position but it would by far transcend the boundaries of the topic of sentencing. Nevertheless, it should be said that if there is to be a truly new direction in sentencing, it must arise from a different conception of its purpose and function in relation to behaviour and the situations we now call criminal.

The notion on which there seems to be the most general agreement at this time as a focus for criminal law is the notion of harm. On the other side, the notion which seems to elicit the strongest disagreement is the notion of guilt. Harm is, however, not reserved to criminal law, and the very word "tort" means injury, harm and a wrong. We may also remind ourselves that the word "punishment" comes from Greek *poine* which literally means the exchange of money for harm done. Guilt, as well, although etymologically fuzzy in its origin, seems to be derived from Anglo-Saxon *geldan* — to pay. (Gothic, *fra-gildan* — to pay back.) It is well established that the Mosaic dictum of an eye for an eye is not an expression of retribution but a tort concept of no more nor less than the value of the harm done. The very word retribution of course easily delivers its meaning of giving a tribute back, literally and etymologically of paying back. The phrase "to pay back" can, of course, have a civil meaning as well as a nasty one. How it came to be that criminal law was isolated out of the framework of civil law is a long story and still to be told.

Much earlier, and much more basic to law than the concept of guilt is the concept of fault. Fault is a deficiency, a failing in the face of obligations. The concept of fault has been questioned in tort as well as other areas of law for the same reasons as the concept of guilt has been questioned in criminal law.[33] In areas in which responsibilities are diffused in a complex society the attribution of specific fault does not make sense and the burden is more reasonably shared as in the case of no-fault insurance. Fault in areas such as matrimonial disputes is increasingly found to be non-justiciable as in the case of marriage breakdown. There we have moved from marital "offences" which obviously dealt with guilt, to the virtual elimination of considerations of fault in the division of family assets as well as support obligations. Not that there is no guilt or fault involved in these situations — just listen to a marital dispute. But we have to realize that there are limits to what the law can reasonably do. If those limits are over-stepped, the law does not provide solutions but becomes part of the problem.

Many, if not most human interactions, cannot be resolved or even understood by assigning guilt to one party. This is, however, what the criminal law demands. Sanctions are only attached to the offender in the form of a sentence. This does not open up the possibility of apportioning responsibility to offender, victim and circumstances, all of which determine, in one way or another and to varying degrees, the situations we now call offences.

To the contrary, within the criminal law context we are even reticent to assign responsibilities in the form of obligations to the offender. We rather let him languish at great public expense in institutions which clearly fulfill none of the functions we assign to them. They do not rehabilitate, they hardly deter, and we are not prepared in any case to inflict the kind of punishment which would create sufficient terror to be effective. The proponents of corporal and capital punishment have a point; but not even the most ardent ones would agree to the recreation of torture in our society. To think, however, even of death in itself as threatening, only speaks to a society that has forgotten that death is a fact of life. Everyone has to face it and anyone walking out of a doctor's office with a diagnosis of terminal cancer is not in a particularly different situation concerning outcome than one sentenced to death. We also tend to forget that in the same society many more seek death in the form of suicide than inflict it in the form of homicide. Even death has to be associated with terror and degradation to be effective as social control.

It is equally not sufficient to deprive offenders of their liberty and to say that this in itself constitutes the punishment. Stone walls do not a prison make — except for those outside. Inside, life has to go on in one way or another, and with our loss of faith in rehabilitation and our unwillingness to consciously continue to inflict pain once the offender is in the institution, we are only left in a further degrading position expressed in the now often-used concept of humane warehousing.

In the final analysis, a call for new directions in sentencing must lead us to a call for the re-examination of the place of criminal law in the house of laws. What we call criminal law and the jurisprudence supporting it may well be an historical phenomenon whose time has run out. The jurisprudence of sentencing has never been convincing in the first place and certainly is not now. In fact, it is most impressive by its absence. All laws are political instruments; but not all laws are, at least *prima facie* instruments of oppression which the criminal law is — at least *prima facie*. Both the political right as well as the left seem to be agreed at this time that state interference should diminish (if not wither away). It is easy to recognize that the administration of criminal justice has largely become a bureaucratic affair. Offenders are not so much tried as processed, and if one looks at moneys expended on the process one finds that only about one-tenth goes to the courts; the rest is absorbed by the ever-growing bureaucracies of law enforcement and corrections, and even the courts themselves are rapidly becoming bureaucratic institutions.[34]

Revolutions will not perform the task of change for us. They, in fact, tend to produce a special need for criminal law it its most vicious and naked form. This goes for revolutions of the left as well as the right. We must thus turn to evolution and this paper has attempted to trace some of the developments which seem to emerge although they have not yet found their critical form. Other papers on more specific topics will show that there are at least some criteria developing which can assist us in determining whether a claim for a "new direction" is simply a throwback into a realm of discourse and a world from which we have to emerge, or whether it is truly a new contribution to a concept of justice anchored in the kind of human community to which we must aspire.

NOTES

1. There is a fascinating consistency in the etymological development of key terms such as crime, punishment, sentence, guilt, etc. For further elaboration see J. W. Mohr, "Law and Society: From Proscription to Discovery," *The Canadian Bar Review,* Vol. 51, 1973, p. 7.

2. What has started with a romantic historical notion of criminal law, has now become endorsed not only in innumerable articles and books but also in legislation, cases and administrative changes gaining in the process the appearance of a new movement.

3. Cesare Beccaria, *On Crimes and Punishment* (New York: Bobbs-Merril, 1963), p. 10. Beccaria is used here as an example, not only because he has been enormously influential up to the second part of the 19th century, but because he is historically located at the beginning of massive social and political changes which have determined present conceptions and applications of criminal law, and especially of sentencing to a much larger degree than is often expressed in traditional legal history.

4. *Ibid.,* p. 11.

5. Jean-Jacques Rousseau, *The Social Contract and Discourse on the Origin of Inequality* (New York: Simon & Schuster, 1964). It should also be remembered that at the same time Adam Smith gave his lectures on Justice, Police, Revenue and Arms which were later called an early draft of the Wealth of Nations. It was also the time when Blackstone dusted off the Laws of England and gave them an appearance of rational cohesion which upset the young Bentham who saw through this rescue operation but did not (and could not) see that his brand of scientific rationality would have little impact on the nature of criminal law, only on its application in the form of penology.

6. H.L. Packer, *The Limits of Criminal Sanction* (Oxford University Press, 1968).

7. Enrico Ferri, *The Positive School of Criminology* (Chicago: Charles H. Kerr, 1913), p. 7. Both Ferri and Garofalo based their sociological and jurisprudential work on Cesare Lombroso who was a physician, psychiatrist and finally Professor of Criminal Anthropology.

8. Nicholas N. Kittrie, *The Right To Be Different,* (Baltimore: John Hopkins U.P., 1971); W. R. Outerbridge, "The Tyranny of Treatment," *The Canadian Journal of Corrections,* Vol. 10, No. 2, 1968.

9. Michel Foucault, "About the Concept of the 'Dangerous Individual' in 19th Century Legal Psychiatry," *International Journal of Law & Psychiatry,* Vol. 1, February 1, 1978, p. 2.

10. J. Chitty, Esq., *A Practical Treatise on the Criminal Law* (London: Butterworth, 1816). It is instructive to compare theoretical works such as Blackstone's Commentaries and handbooks for Practitioners such as Chitty's. Even the latter are usually still a stage removed from what actually happens in the courts but lend themselves better to analyzing underlying assumptions.

11. *Ibid.,* pp. 750-751.

12. *Ibid.,* p. 1003.

13. *Ibid.,* p. 236.

14. Michel Foucault, *Discipline and Punish* (New York: Pantheon, 1977). The inventiveness of the human mind in devising punishments can best be seen in illustrated editions such as that by Peter N. Walker: *Punishment. An Illustrated History,* (Devon: David and Charles, 1972).

15. Harold Garfinkel, "Conditions of Successful Degradation Ceremonies," *Am. J. of Sociology,* 78, September, 1972.

16. Even in the psychological perspective, expressions have changed from Lomboso's hereditary theories of degeneration or atavism to psychoanalytic theories of repressed childhood experiences.

17. For an exposition of the morality aspects see: G. D. Morton, *The Function of Criminal Law* (Toronto: Canadian Broadcasting Corporation Publications, 1962).

18. *Op. cit.,* note 3, p. 8.

19. Nigel Walker, *Sentencing in a Rational Society* (Penguin Press, 1969).

20. Bruno Cormier, *The Watcher and the Watched* (Montreal: Tundra Books, 1975).

21. *Op. cit.,* note 19, p. 19, emphasis is Walker's.

22. J.W. Mohr, "Imprisonment: A Policy Without Direction," John Howard Symposium on the Future of Prisons, University of Victoria, January, 1979.

23. Ian Taylor et al., *The New Criminology* (London: Routledge, 1973). Other names used are Radical Criminology and Marxist Criminology. Although these are not interchangeable, they can hardly be separated. See for instance the special issue devoted to Radical Criminology — *Criminology* 16/4, February, 1979.

24. Innumerable articles, conferences, seminars and sentencing exercises were devoted to achieve uniformity in sentencing. Studies such as those by Glendon Schubert, *Judicial Decision-Making* (New York: Free Press, 1963); *The Judicial Mind* (Northwestern University Press, 1965), had already shown that judicial decisions could not be accounted for by the legal process but were a function of differing attitudes of judges.

25. John Hogarth, *Sentencing as a Human Process* (University of Toronto Press, 1971).

26. See for instance the two contrasting essays by John Hogarth, "Alternatives to the Adversary System," and Paul Weiler, "The Reform of Punishment" in: *Studies on Sentencing* (Law Reform Commission of Canada, Ottawa, 1974).

27. Brian A. Grosman, *The Prosecutor: An Inquiry Into the Exercise of Discretion* (University of Toronto Press, 1969).

28. *Studies on Strict Liability* (Law Reform Commission of Canada, Ottawa, 1974).

29. *Justice Statistics, Ontario* (Provincial Secretary for Justice, Toronto, 1978).

30. The Commission has issued Working Papers, Background Volumes, Study Papers and Reports to Parliament. The ones most closely related to sentencing are:

Working Papers:	The Principles of Sentencing and Dispositions (# 3 - 1974)
	Restitution and Compensation (# 5 - 1974)
	Fines (# 6 - 1974)
	Diversion (# 7 - 1975)
	Imprisonment and Release (# 11 - 1975)
Background Volumes:	Studies on Sentencing (1974)
	Studies on Diversion (The East York Community Law Reform Project) (1975)
	Studies on Imprisonment (1976)
	Sentencing — Community Participation (1976)
Study Papers:	Native People and the Law (1974)
	Decision to be Slightly Free (1976)
	Fear of Punishment (1976)

Reports: Our Criminal Law (1976)

Mental Disorder in the Criminal Process (1976)

Dispositions and Sentences in The Criminal Process (1976)

31. For a recent empirical study on community service which attempts to place it in the framework of Walker's aims of a penal system see M. Thorvaldsen, *The Effects of Community Service on the Attitudes of Offenders* (Doctoral Thesis, University of Cambridge, 1978).

32. Calvin Becker, *The Victim and the Criminal Process* (Law Reform Commission of Canada, 1976).

33. H.J. Glasbeek, R.A. Hasson, "Fault — The Great Hoax," in: *Studies in Canadian Tort Law,* Lewis Klar (ed.) (Toronto: Butterworths, 1978).

34. Bibliographic Guide: *The Economics of Crime and Planning of Resources in the Criminal Justice System* (Department of the Solicitor General, Government of Canada, Ottawa 1978). Despite a fair amount of literature in this area, it is still difficult to get a good assessment of the distribution of costs in the administration of justice. Statistics Canada, Judicial Division has been working on the problem for several years and issued an Interim Report — Public Expenditures on the Administration of Justice by L. Cardill and P. Reed in May, 1977.

CHAPTER 3

The Dangers of the New Directions in American Sentencing

Nicholas N. Kittrie

INTRODUCTION

Seven years ago when I published my book, *The Right To Be Different: Deviance and Enforced Therapy,*[1] I sought to document the history, accomplishments and hazards of the "therapeutic state." In that book I undertook to explore the modern therapeutic or rehabilitative model of dealing with crime and deviance, as contrasted with the classical penal approach. The classical model was clearly articulated by Italian criminologist Cesare Beccaria in 1764, in his book *On Crimes and Punishments.* According to Beccaria crime was viewed as a product of free will, and to be both just and effective, punishment must be proportionate to the crime. The nature as well as the extent of punishment should correspond to the offense: theft should be punished with fines, acts of violence with corporal punishment and murders with death sentences.

In searching for the origins of the therapeutic approach, I pointed to the leaders of positive criminology, in the second half of the 19th century, such as

Cesare Lombroso and Enrico Ferri. They viewed the offender as the product of deterministic forces — biological as well as social — and considered him more ill than evil. They sought therefore to respond to the offender's individual shortcomings and needs, similar to medicine's response to its patients. Ferri wrote: "The reclusion of dangerous criminals for an indeterminate time is a proposal of the positivist criminal school, since it would be as absurd to say that a murderer should remain in prison twenty years rather than fifteen or thirty as it would to say in advance that a sick person should stay in a hospital ten days rather than twenty or fifty."[2]

Exploring the hazards of the therapeutic model which grew out of positive criminology, I pointed out two major concerns. The first was the uncertain or indeterminate period of confinement imposed by the state under the therapeutic claim. Initially, indeterminate confinement, in the full sense, was made applicable to various segments of the deviant population which were viewed as medical or otherwise mentally deficient objects — the mentally ill, juveniles, psychopaths and drug addicts. The confinement of these groups was to continue until they were certified as cured. Less comprehensive forms of indeterminate or conditional confinement were later extended to common offenders as well. In the latter instances the confinement was for a time ranging from a maximum to a minimum period. The exact term was to be decided at the discretion of the judge, correctional authority or the parole board. The basic premise of the indeterminate term was that all deviant and offender groups required periods of treatment which could not be determined at the time the sentence or sanction was imposed. Instead, the length of social intervention had to depend upon the uncertain progress to be made by the deviant or offender during the period of his treatment or rehabilitation.

My second concern with regard to the therapeutic approach was that under it greater powers were being exercised in the name of therapy than had been allowed under the traditional penal model. I specifically surveyed a number of therapeutic measures (such as sterilization, lobotomies, and shock treatment) which were enforced upon those coming under the therapeutic model. It was evident that under the traditional penal approach such sanctions were not likely to be tolerated.

Reviewing the claims as well as the abuses of therapy, I called, in conclusion, for limitations upon the rehabilitative ideal and for controls upon the discretion of the agents serving the therapeutic model. A therapeutic bill of rights was needed, in my view, as a safeguard against excessive powers exercised in the name of therapy. Such limits upon the therapeutic system were to parallel the constitutional prohibition of cruel and unusual punishment which limits the penal system.

The criminal justice system has moved on in the past seven years and new directions in sentencing have evolved. By and large the new movement calls for a return to the traditional penal approach, for reduced discretion by the agents of the criminal justice system, and a diminution of the rehabilitative ideal.

PRESENT DISSATISFACTIONS WITH SENTENCING

Complaints regarding the state of sentencing in America go back to the early part of the century and cover a broad range of procedural and substantive dissatisfactions. Both the means and ends of sentencing have been criticized: the absence of clear and articulated legislative goals, the delegation of excessive sentencing discretion to the judiciary, a lack of judicial preparation for effective sentencing and an almost total absence of scientific decision-making, heavy reliance upon plea bargained sentences, the total neglect of the victim in the sentencing process, sentencing disparities, offender uncertainty regarding the duration of confinement, the granting of unreasonable discretion to correctional and parole agencies regarding the termination of sanctions, and the absence of effective opportunities for the appellate review of unfair and unjust sentencing.

One must concede the validity of many of the criticisms and dissatisfaction with sentencing as presently practised. The means of sentencing have been severely and rightfully attacked. How can one accept a system of justice under which 90 per cent of all convictions and sentences, and perhaps as high as 95 per cent of all misdemeanor convictions, are the products of plea bargaining? Under the plea system it is often the compromise or bargain struck between prosecution and defense which defines the crime and determines the sentence. Little heed is paid under this system to the independent and objective judgment of the legislature or the court.

Plea bargaining has had its defenders. "In light of the general severity of American penal statutes, the bargained plea is a useful device insuring . . . [not only a saving of efforts for the prosecution but also] that the defendant will be punished while avoiding an unduly harsh penalty," claimed Delmar Karlen.[3] But offenders do not necessarily view plea bargaining as a benevolent experience. The New York State Special Commission on Attica reported:

> What makes inmates most cynical about their preprison experience is the plea bargaining system. . . . Even though an inmate may receive the benefit of a shorter sentence the plea-bargaining system is characterized by deception and hypocrisy which divorce the inmate from the reality of the crime. . . . Almost 90 per cent of the inmates surveyed had been solicited to enter a plea bargain. Most were bitter, believing that they did not receive effective legal representation or that the judge did not keep the state's promise.[4]

It is evident from recent history that the legislatures have failed to articulate the major goals and objectives of sentencing. Should the sentencing emphasis be on condemnation, retribution, general deterrence, specific deterrence, incapacitation, rehabilitation or victim restitution?

Legislatures apparently view such definitions as politically undesirable or difficult. The legislatures, moreover, have tended to grant the judiciary excessive discretion permitting them to impose sentences which range from the most lenient to the most severe, for the very same offenses. The permitted tariff for a serious felony may thus range from probation or a fine to a long period of incarceration. When prisoners compare their experiences they soon discover a shameful disparity of sentencing.

Most judges have little of the background or training needed for the selection and imposition of effective sentences. Sentencing decisions often reflect the personal values of the prosecutor or judge rather than being based on scientific considerations. James V. Bennett, former director of the Federal Bureau of Prisons testified: "That some judges are arbitrary and even sadistic in their sentencing practices is notoriously a matter of record."[5]

Judge Marvin E. Frankel asserted:

> The evidence is conclusive that judges of widely varying attitudes on sentencing, administering statutes that confer high measures of discretion, mete out widely divergent sentences where the divergencies are explainable only by the variations among the judges, not by material differences in defendants or their crimes.[6]

It is complained that sentences are not effectively subject to review or appeal in the United States. Appellate courts, by and large, have stayed away from the responsibility of reviewing sentences and as a consequence, once the trial court renders its decision, the offender has little opportunity to have his sentence reviewed on a higher level.

Said Judge Frankel:

> In the federal court and in some two-thirds of the states, there is in practical effect *no appeal* from the trial judge's sentence. To be slightly technical — i.e., accurate — I mean that a sentence within the prescribed maximum limits cannot be lowered on appeal. . . . most trial judges, for all their protests about the agonies of the ultimate responsibility for sentencing, oppose the idea of appellate review. . . . Lending the most support is Chief Justice Warren E. Burger, who has voiced more than once his opposition to appellate review of sentences.[7]

Frequently, the courts which are usually jealous of the judicial powers relinquish their sentencing prerogatives. By imposing an indeterminate sentence, or a sentence subject to parole, the courts in fact turn over the decision regarding the release date to the correctional authorities or parole boards. By being able to impose a severe sentence, which they know will be curtailed by parole, the courts are said to cater both to the public demand for stiff and vengeful dispositions and to the more reasonable requirements of justice. Yet the sentenced offender remains uncertain regarding the term of his imprisonment. His compelling hope is to convince some prison or parole board that he has become "rehabilitated."

It is plain, as a consequence, that present sentences tend to be person oriented rather than crime oriented. They tend to be based on the individual idiosyncrasies of both the judge and the offender. By and large sentences are not readily predictable. As Judge Frankel has sub-titled his well known book, the present sentencing situation produces "Law Without Order."[8]

Regarding the ends or substance of sentencing similar complaints have been heard. It is complained that there is too much resort to incarceration, producing for the United States one of the highest ratios of prisoners to population in the world. There is the imposition of longer sentences than are utilized in other Western societies. There is too small a reliance upon fines as a substitute to imprisonment. There is an almost total ignorance of the victim or of restitution as a sanction, and finally, there is too little experimentation with short-term and community based corrections.

During the past decade and a half there have been serious efforts in the United States to enrich the substantive content of sentencing. Programs have been set up with the goal of diverting non-serious offenders from the conventional criminal process, trial and sentence. Community facilities have been established to experiment with weekend and night incarceration for offenders who otherwise work and function in the open society. Experimental projects relying primarily upon restitution have been funded and tested. Other dispositional alternatives have been introduced in many communities designed to offer offenders the early benefits of social, vocational and psychological services in a community setting.

It is in the face of these liberalizing efforts, of not too long ago, that the newer directions in American sentencing appear most unexpected and puzzling.

THE DIRECTION OF THE NEW DIRECTIONS

That there are some new directions in sentencing is evident. First there has been the literary preparation of the ground (much like what the French Encyclopedists did for the French revolution). Amongst the intellectual output there has been Dean Robert McKay and the report of the Attica commission,[9] which he headed; Norval Morris writing on Sentencing;[10] Ernest van den Haag's book on Punishment;[11] Marvin E. Frankel's book on Criminal Sentences;[12] Andrew von Hirsch on Doing Justice;[13] The Twentieth Century Fund Task Force report on Fair and Certain Punishment;[14] and the American Friends Service Committee's report on The Struggle For Justice.[15] These writings provided the underlying jurisprudential and theoretical background. Then came the action:[16] Maine abolished parole; other states sought to reduce drastically the discretion of parole boards; California curtailed the indeterminate sentence, under which the Adult Authority exercised the actual sentencing authority; flat sentences were introduced in Illinois; mandatory sentences were advanced in New York; and the proposed Federal Criminal Code recommended presumptive sentencing. A host of other recommendations, proposals and initiatives have also been put forth: sentencing institutes, sentencing councils, appellate review of sentencing and several other related approaches.

The two goals which seem to loom highest on the horizon of the recent American sentencing reforms are: (1) the curing of sentencing disparity; and (2) the reduction of offender uncertainty. These are uniquely American goals. In part these goals seem to respond to prisoner complaints, heard more vigorously during the social upheaval of the late sixties. In part they are based on the search for offender equality rather than individualization. And to a great measure they are responsive to the growing disappointment with the "rehabilitative ideal," a concept introduced into literature by Francis Allen[17] in his effort to describe the therapeutic response to deviance, a response fully documented in my own *The Right to be Different.*[18]

That sentencing disparity exists has been documented dramatically by several writers. In the first place the 50 different American jurisdictions prescribe diverse penalties for the very same offenses. Behavior that can bring a 6-year maximum prison sentence in one state may merit not more than a maximum of six months in another state. But it is not this inter-system disparity which has drawn most attention. What is written about most frequently is intra-system inequities. In most states the penalty schemes established by the legislatures for each specified offense offer a wide range of sentencing options, allowing judges to exercise wide discretion between a low minimum sentence and a very high maximum penalty. In the choice between these options judges have almost total discretion, allowing them to rely on a wide range of unscrutinizable factors in reaching their conclusion.

Within the same court system two different judges with different values are likely to reach widely diverse sentences for similar offenses and offenders. And so reports James V. Bennett, former director of the Federal Bureau of Prisons:

> Take, for instance, the cases of two men we received last spring. The first man had been convicted of cashing a check for $58.40. He was out of work at the time of his offense, and when his wife became ill . . . he became a victim of temptation. He had no prior criminal record. The other man cashed a check for $35.20. He was also out of work and his wife had left him for another man. His prior record consisted of a drunk charge and a nonsupport charge. . . . But they appeared before different judges and the first man received 15 years in prison and the second man 30 days.[19]

Even the same judge may reach diverse sentences for similarly severe offenses, as long as significant distinctions can be shown with regard to the "dangerousness" or rehabilitative potential of the offenders. Thus, the offender and his background sometimes become more important than the nature and severity of the crime.

In addition to the wide range of prison maximums and minimums the legislative mandate often permits judges to place offenders on probation or to impose a suspended sentence in lieu of incarceration. Given variations in social background, education, family and community stability, employability, psychological well-being and predictability of future misconduct, those charged with similar criminal conduct might find themselves subject to widely disparate sanctions.

From the ranks of radical criminology one hears further about manifestations of class bias in sentencing schemes. The sentencing disparity between different classes of offenses, it is argued, is often based upon offender characteristics rather than the severity of the offenses. Specific attention has focused on the penalty difference between street crimes and white collar crimes. Notice has been taken of the fact that the first offenses usually bring the heaviest sanctions while the latter often go unpunished or else are treated more leniently. As a specific illustration of this unjustified disparity between classes of offenses critics have pointed out the essential similarity between larceny and embezzlement. Despite this similarity the two offenses often produce great disparity in sentences due to the different socioeconomic backgrounds of the offenders who come to the attention of the courts.

The uncertainty as to the length of imprisonment adds to the complaints about disparity. In some jurisdictions, well illustrated by California, the sentencing judge had the power to impose a totally indeterminate sentence, with the final decision regarding release being made by a special correctional authority. In other jurisdictions the sentence was stated in terms of a minimum and a maximum (say from five to fifteen years) with the parole board or some other agency exercising the release power. In still other states the imposed sentence was more specific in terms of duration, but earlier release was always envisioned upon the favorable decision of the parole board. It was the progress made by the offender within confinement that was expected to aid the parole board in determining readiness for release from prison. Frequently, it has been alleged, offenders put on masks of rehabilitative interest in order to secure the good will of parole boards. The educational and rehabilitative services within the prisons were thus not permitted to serve their original and legitimate functions of preparing prisoners for re-entry into the community. Instead, they became a sham and a guise for manipulative prisoners.

The movement which has produced the most recent changes in the field of sentencing policy and practice has been based primarily on the concern with the excessive discretion exercised by the courts and the parole agencies, and the resultant unfairness imposed upon the offenders who were deprived of certainty of punishment. The new directions in American sentencing are intended by and large to reduce sentencing disparities as well as to eliminate the uncertainty regarding the terms of the penalties. These goals are sought to be accomplished through the introduction of uniform rather than individualized sanctions. A number of approaches have been designed to accomplish these goals. The most drastic approach is to curtail fully judicial discretion by legislative fiat which establishes mandatory sentences. Under this approach all those found guilty of a specified offense are subject to uniform sanctions decreed by the legislature with no opportunity for subsequent modification by either court or corrections agency.

A less extreme measure for curtailing disparity is provided through the legislative specification of presumptive sentences. These sentences offer a standard tariff for average offenders, with the power granted to the court to either increase the penalty by a limited and specified period (i.e., one or two years) or to reduce it similarly on the basis of a list of aggravating and mitigating factors.

A lesser intervention with judicial discretion is provided by legislation which merely narrows the wide gaps between the currently authorized maximum and minimum sentences. For example: as a substitute for a maximum of 30 years and a minimum of 5 years, for a given offense, the reformers would introduce a maximum of 15 years and a minimum of 7 years. The sentencing court thus retains the power to select a sentence suited for the specified offender, yet within much narrower limits.

While the major trend of the new sentencing movement has been intended to reduce the initial disparity produced by the sanctioning court, the other trend has been directed towards reducing subsequent uncertainties in the confinement term. The most extreme remedy proposed and tried has been the total abolition of the parole board. Under such circumstances the sentencing court would be compelled to impose a definite term of confinement, with very limited possibilities of modification. One option for earlier release in such abolitionist jurisdictions would be through the prison's granting of "good time" under a formula which would be most narrowly constructed. Accordingly, "good time" could be available as a matter of course to all offenders who had not been charged with violations of institutional regulations, without any need for these offenders to go before a parole board which usually exercised broader discretionary powers. Even under reforms which permit the retention of the parole board, a redefinition of the board's authority could severely curtail its discretionary power in order to prevent the arbitrary and unjust withholding of parole releases. By narrowly and precisely defining the requirements for parole release, and by specifying what will constitute "good time" for such purposes, the likelihood of differential treatment and of parole abuse is considerably reduced.

Another approach to the reduction of disparity is one which combines a curtailment of the discretionary power of the judiciary with a reduction in the authority of the parole board. Under this approach, which is described as flat sentencing, the sanctioning court is required to select from amongst the options available to it and to set a "flat" sentence over which parole boards are to have only limited powers. Once a flat sentence has been imposed, the only reduction in the confinement term would be in the form of some narrowly defined "good time" allowance which requires little or no parole intervention.

The cures for disparity and prisoner uncertainty, proposed and introduced in the United States in most recent years, have centered on the measures described above. Still, the effort to reduce disparity and to improve sentencing practices has been manifested in yet different ways. One of the most flourishing developments in the country has been the creation of Sentencing Institutes. In these institutes, sponsored by various judicial organizations, judges gather for short seminars to discuss issues in sentencing as well as to analyze hypothetical sentencing cases. The expectation prevails that such educational and simulation practices will foster common standards and will have a positive and consensus-building impact upon the participants' future sentencing conduct.

In a few jurisdictions (commencing with the United States District Courts in Michigan, New York and Illinois) more formal approaches towards producing sentencing uniformity have been instituted.[20] These courts have created sentencing councils composed of several sitting judges, in order to discuss dispositions in all cases which are subject to the court's jurisdiction. The judge charged with a particular case usually introduces the verdict and the pre-sentence report and these are followed with discussions by the other participants in the sentencing council. Although the councils encourage active interaction between judges, each of whom notes a tentative sentence, the final responsibility still remains with the particular judge who is charged with the imposition of the sentence.

More ambitious proposals for mixed sentencing councils or boards have also been heard in this country. Over the years the argument has been made for the creation of multidisciplinary sentencing boards, on which representatives of the judiciary, as well as representatives of various social, behavioral and educational sciences, would participate equally. Professor Sheldon Glueck of Harvard University wrote extensively on this topic over 40 years ago, claiming that sentencing was too important and difficult a task to be left to judges alone.[21] But few results have followed. Mixed sentencing councils, developed and practiced in several European countries, have been viewed as too costly and time-consuming in the United States.

PERSPECTIVES ON SENTENCING REFORMS

New Sentencing as a Link in an Overall Reform Movement

The current focus on the exercise and possible abuse of discretion by the judiciary and the parole boards are not new concerns in the field of criminal justice. Other branches of the criminal justice system have already come under scrutiny for the same reasons from time to time. One who surveys the history of reforms in American criminal justice over the past half century soon discovers that each of the various branches of the criminal justice system — the police, corrections and even the legislature — have been examined and challenged by reform efforts.

For the longest time the emphasis centered upon the operations of the police. Questions regarding police conformity with constitutional standards and requirements were raised, mostly in the courts, in increasing number since the end of the Second World War. The conduct of the police at the stages of arrest, search and suspect identification have been scrutinized by the courts. These reviews produced an extensive system of checks on police conduct. These consist of intra-agency regulations and practices, as well as inter-agency supervisory measures, as evidenced by the requirement for an independent magistrate for the issuance of warrants or the attorney's required presence during police interrogation. The resultant system regulating police discretion combines rules and regulations formulated by state legislatures, court decisions, rules promulgated by the judiciary and also the self-imposed regulations resulting from the police restructuring of its functions.

While the major emphasis on reforming the police function came in the 1950s and in the early 1960s, it was in the late 60s that the attention of the critics shifted from police functions to the correctional process. Again, activist courts were encouraged to inquire into the conduct of penal institutions in order to ascertain whether the treatment of convicted offenders conformed to the standards required constitutionally. The courts, in large measure, responded to the invitation to review the administrative agencies engaged in the enforcement of the sanctions imposed by the judiciary. In this arena, again, intra-agency controls were not considered adequate and inter-branch checks, through judicially formulated and supervised standards, came into being.

The recent attention centering on the exercise of discretion by the courts in the sentencing area may be viewed as a third stage in the on-going reform movement. More accurately, this could possibly be classified as a fourth stage in the reform movement. The earlier focus on police and corrections, and the current emphasis on the judicial branch have been most evident to the public view. But one should not neglect the lesser yet intense attention which has been directed from time to time to the legislative branch in its fundamental role in criminal justice — the definition of what is and what is not properly within the domain of criminal justice. There has been much writing within the last quarter century on the issues of criminalization and decriminalization. The movement to decriminalize various offenses must be recognized in great part as a reform movement directed towards curtailing the powers and the discretion of the legislative branch.

Reviewing the recent movement designed to limit and to restructure the sentencing discretion of the courts and the parole boards, one would do well to bear in mind the experiences, the outcome, and the lessons of the other reform efforts directed towards the police, corrections and the legislature.

Methods of Reform

To understand the direction and potentials of the new reforms, one must take notice of the methods by which these reform movements are being accomplished in the United States. In the earlier movement to reduce the abuse of discretion and to restructure the operations of the police and corrections, considerable reliance was placed on the constitutional standards applicable to these branches of criminal justice. In particular, with regard to the police functions, heavy emphasis was placed on the protections of the Fourth

Amendment to the United States Constitution which provides "that the right of the people to be secure in their persons, houses, papers, and effects against unreasonable searches and seizures shall not be violated and no warrant shall issue, that upon probable cause." In the effort designed to further curtail discretion and the excessive zeal of the police, reliance was also placed on the Fifth Amendment which imposes the safeguards of "due process of law" and the Sixth Amendment which provides that "in all criminal prosecutions, the accused shall enjoy the right . . . to have the assistance of counsel for his defense."

In the subsequent effort to produce changes and reforms in the system of corrections the reformers once more resorted to constitutional standards. Here they found support in the Eighth Amendment which protects against "cruel and unusual punishment." It was in reliance upon these constitutional safeguards that legal advocates sought and gained judicial intervention in the operations of the police and corrections. Both the "exclusionary rule" and the contempt powers of the American courts became effective tools for judicial supervision of the administrative branches.

The movement to reform the sentencing practices has found little support in the requirements of the United States Constitution. Here, only marginal constitutional references appeared to offer any assistance. Article I, Section 10 of the Constitution provides that no state shall pass any Bill of Attainder. That, over the years, has been interpreted to mean that the sentencing function (or more specifically, the function of specifically imposing sanctions upon individuals or groups) must be exercised by the judiciary rather than the legislature. But there is little else in the Constitution which can serve as a tool for reformers seeking to review the powers and the sentencing discretion granted to the judiciary.

As a consequence, the effort to restructure the sentencing branch of the criminal justice system had to rely on a process of reform quite different from that utilized in the other two areas of criminal justice — the police and corrections. Since reforms could not be directly keyed to constitutional requirements, the earlier avenues of judicial test cases was no longer readily available. Instead, the reform movement had to seek support of a different and broader nature. Support had to be sought from the general public and from the legislative branch. Reform further had to be sought through self-regulation by the judiciary itself.

The Realities of Sentencing

Before one fully assesses either the impact or the dangers of the new directions in sentencing one must take careful notice of the role of sentencing within criminal justice. Much has been written previously about the funnel effect of the criminal justice system. The President's Crime Commission reported in 1965[22] that, of 467,000 offenders apprehended on suspicion of committing Index Crimes, some 177,000 were formally charged, only 38,000 went to trial, and of those, some 30,000 were finally convicted. It is clear that it is only with regard to this latter and smaller number of convicted offenders that the sentencing function becomes applicable. The much higher number of offenders apprehended, charged and tried were never exposed to the benefits or deficiencies of the sentencing stage. "In sum," observed the National Advisory Committee on Standards and Goals in 1973, "only about 8% of those apprehended as suspects were processed fully through the formal steps of a criminal prosecution and trial."[23]

More recent statistics, derived from the 1976 Uniform Crime Reports, tell a similar fragmentary story. The outgoing decade's well financed national campaign for better reporting of crime and more vigorous policing, prosecution and trial resulted in significantly increased activity, but produced little change in the funnel function of the criminal justice process. With regard to Index Crimes (murder, robbery, burglary, aggravated assault, rape, larceny and motor vehicle theft) the 1976 figures again demonstrate the small number of those suspected of crime who reached the sentencing stage. In 1976 some 11,304,777 crimes were reported. That year 2,317,811 suspects were apprehended. Of those 1,046,407 were prosecuted, and as a consequence some 673,983 persons were found guilty as charged.[24] These composite figures indicate that arrests were made in about 20.5% of all reported crimes. Prosecutions occurred in 9.2% of all reported crimes and convictions occurred in a mere 5.96% of all crimes reported to the police.

Consequently, while the reform of the sentencing process is likely to have great and important impact upon those who reach the sentencing stage, it has limited bearing on the much larger number of persons involved in crime. Estimates of total victimization in the United States are as high as 40,000,000 per year. The number of crimes reported to the police in 1976 exceeded 11 million. It is apparent that most of those involved in crime in this country, and most of those who are apprehended and prosecuted, never reach the sentencing stage. The reform of the sentencing stage must therefore be viewed, in great part, for its own value rather than for its impact on the overall criminal justice system in the United States.

Yet the new directions in sentencing must also be considered for their impact upon the facilities now available for the disposition of sentenced offenders. There is space for about 250,000 prisoners in the penal institutions of this country. Given that the average sentence served exceeds two years, approximately 100,000 new prisoners may be incarcerated each year. Even though nearly 700,000 offenders are convicted annually for the relatively serious Index Crimes, it is abundantly clear that not more than 14.3% of these convicts can be accommodated in prison. All others must receive lesser penalties: fines, probation and other alternative dispositions. Any sentencing reform movement must, therefore, be carefully observed for its impact upon convict dispositions. Even the slightest increase in average sentences or in the percentage of offenders sentenced to incarceration is likely to have a dramatic impact upon the prison populations. The new directions in sentencing might thus be intimately connected with the question of the need for more and more populous prisons.

In considering the realities of sentencing in the United States, it is imperative also that we take into account the substantial decrease in the number of traditional dispositions which are available to the sentencing tribunals. Capital punishment has been substantially narrowed, if not practically eliminated, over the past several years as a result of various United States Supreme Court decisions. Transportation was abolished long ago.

Corporal punishment has effectively gone out of existence within the past century. Fines are utilized in a fairly small number of cases, at least in the United States. Only 8% of those convicted are exposed to this type of sentence. The major sanctions utilized at the sentencing stage are by and large probation and imprisonment.

Only in recent years has there been in the United States increased resort to suspended sentences, deferred convictions and a host of other innovative community alternatives in corrections. These alternatives, however, remain quantitatively few and tend to be applied to lesser offenses and offenders. The tendency of most communities is to rely primarily on either probation or imprisonment. Since the new directions in United States sentencing are designed to have little effect on probation, the main impact of the reforms must be measured by the effect they are likely to have on imprisonment and the imprisonment powers of the sentencing tribunals.

THE IMPACT OF THE NEW DIRECTIONS

The new directions are in great part the result of the recent jurisprudential and scientific challenges to the rehabilitative goal. Several research findings have asserted that rehabilitation has failed.[25] Several philosophical commentators have argued that rehabilitation is not an appropriate goal for the criminal justice system.[26] Instead, they have called for "just dessert," and "justice" models for criminal justice responses which are based exclusively on society's need to condemn and to deter those committing offenses against it. These writings have by and large tended to argue that punishment should fit the crime. They have constituted a return to classical criminology which was built on this basic premise. The new movement thus denies the basic premise of positive criminology, that in order to be both just and effective the criminal justice system must be individualized and must seek sanctions and treatment which fit the offender rather than the offense.

It is clear that several of the new directions are designed to increase dramatically the power of the legislature vis-à-vis the courts in the total sentencing-corrections process. Whether such an increased grant of power to the legislature is likely to be beneficial to criminal justice or whether it will adversely affect the field remains uncertain. It is argued that courts remain more flexible and more responsive to changes in the public mood. Legislatures, on the other hand, move more slowly and once certain sentencing standards are established it might be more difficult to have them readily modified to changing needs.

The shift of power to the legislature, it is also asserted, is likely to make the field of sentencing more political. On the legislative level the creation of crimes and penalties — as well as efforts at decriminalization — are viewed as sensitive and complex issues of public policy. There may be reluctance on the part of legislatures to respond with innovation in areas where the judiciary, on a case-by-case basis, can exhibit much more flexible responses. As a case in point, it is argued that with regard to marijuana offenses and sexual offenses between consenting adults, it has been much easier for the courts, in the discharge of their sentencing powers, to take into account the new and changing public attitudes, while legislatures have remained reluctant to modify the laws on the books.

The general argument is also heard that removing sentencing decision-making from the judge to the legislature is faulty from a scientific point of view. It is pointed out that it is the trial judge who is best acquainted with the particular offense and with the particular offender, and, therefore, he is more suitable to make the needed and most effective sentencing decision. Removing discretionary powers from the judiciary and placing it in the legislature would mean the shifting of decision-making to a time and place far removed from the realities of the individual crime and the individual criminal.

Most importantly, the new reforms which seek fixed, determinate and inflexible sentencing would offer few if any incentives and no rewards for the offender's effort at rehabilitation. Indeed, the new reforms deny by and large the right of the state to require or to engage in compulsory rehabilitation. Rehabilitation becomes merely an option of the individual offender, for which he gains very little by way of a reduced sentence or any other benefits from the state.

The new movement raises basic questions regarding the parole function. Under some of the reform proposals parole boards would be abolished altogether. Under other proposals the powers of the parole board would be severely curtailed. Several of the reformers who sought to do away with parole altogether have recently indicated a preference for maintaining the parole board as long as its powers are more narrowly defined. Thus the parole board, which has been viewed originally as one of the important innovations in the move towards individualized criminal justice, may well find itself abolished or curtailed without a fair test as to whether it is capable of reformation.

Other issues have been raised with regard to the new directions in sentencing. Some reformers have argued that the new directions will produce shorter sentences. Others have feared that longer terms in prison are likely to result. The outcome is not certain at this time. But serious concern has been voiced that the new sentencing directions are likely to put more people in prison, due to the fact that the traditional function of the parole board, as a capacity adjustment valve for the correctional system, will be drastically reduced. The feared outcome, therefore, is larger numbers of offenders in prison and the need for increased imprisonment facilities.

Finally, it has been noted that the new directions in sentencing more or less deal little with the judicial power to impose probation in lieu of incarceration. As a result, the key question as to how many and which offenders are to be left as probationers in the community, and which are to be incarcerated, remains an obscure and highly discretionary issue regarding which the new reforms have little to offer.

The new sentencing directions could properly be criticized not so much for their dangers, but as for their misdirection, their inefficacy and their implied promise of unrealistic expectations. The new American reform emphasis appears contrary to the reform agenda of other legal systems. As one reviews the legal systems in Western Europe, the socialist countries and elsewhere, one finds there the following trends: (1) a quest for more popular input into the criminal trial and sentencing, as is manifested in China and in Cuba; (2) greater emphasis upon scientific considerations, classifications and facilities, as is evident in Western Europe; (3) a general effort to reduce resort to traditional incarceration; (4) a general effort to reduce the length of prison sentences; and (5) an effort to introduce innovative and alternative sanctions, mostly permitting offenders to remain in the community settings.

The last of these three goals have been also in evidence on the American scene during the past several years. There has been an effort in the United States to reduce resort to traditional incarceration, to reduce the length of sentences and to introduce alternatives or diversion programs from the traditional criminal trial and punishment.[27] As one looks at the main thrust of the more recent directions in American sentencing one wonders whether the new movement is counterproductive to some of the very goals we sought vigorously to advance not more than a decade ago.

With the new and greater quest for uniformity, the desire for individualized sentencing, which is central to the diversion programs, might easily be quashed. With the emphasis on determinate and fixed sentences, the desire for greater scientific input and classification might suffer. With the pressure for parity an increase in imprisonment and longer sentences might ensue.

Serious questions are being raised as to whether once flexibility and discretion are reduced on the judicial level, there may be a concurrent increase in prosecutorial discretion, which is already excessive.[28] Indeed, plea bargaining can readily replace the flexibility lost through the curtailment of discretion on the judicial level. The fulcrum of discretion might thus move from the open court room and the judge to the prosecuting attorney and his less visible pre-trial endeavors.

The reform movement, in my view, is doomed to failure in its efforts to abolish discretion. Discretion can more readily be expected to be displaced than made extinct. You cannot ban discretion in a democratic society. You must seek, instead, to tame it.

While the major function of the new directions is asserted to be an increase in uniformity and predictability, there is no indication that the new reforms will serve any of the major goals of the criminal justice system. There is no evidence that the new directions will reduce recidivism. Although the argument has been made that deterrence might benefit from the institution of fixed and certain punishments, the small rate of those prosecuted, convicted and sentenced makes this little more than an idle speculation. At the same time it is clear that the goal of rehabilitation will be adversely affected by the new directions in sentencing. The new directions offer no incentive to the offender to participate in any rehabilitative effort. Indeed, the new movement, as we have seen, is founded in part on a total negation of rehabilitation.

The new reforms seek simplistic answers for complex sentencing needs. They assume that mandatory or fixed sentences, uniformly imposed on all those charged with the same offenses, will remove the present disparities. To protect against disparity they would also abolish or curtail parole. I find these directions too narrow. I find them not to be promising enough for the constructive reform of criminal justice. The new directions are a result of an alliance between two opposite groups: one seeking harsher penalties and the other hoping for milder sanctions. But the bond between these two groups is not likely to last. Once this bond is broken, the new formalized and rigid sentencing standards are likely to remain as formidable roadblocks to a restoration of an individualized and humane system of sentencing.

By and large, I concur with the observations previously made by Caleb Foote:

> If the mask of individualization and rehabilitation are stripped away, the basic function of discretion in paroling and sentencing practice is revealed: to adjust an impossible penal code to the reality of severe limitations in punishing resources. By an impossible penal code I refer to the fact that, given economic constraints, full or equal enforcement is totally out of the question. . . .
>
> Faced with these economic realities we have three alternative courses of action. The first is to multiply by five or ten times the size of correctional budgets to make possible implementation of the draconian thirst for punishment which characterizes the majority of the public. . . .
>
> Second would be a comprehensive attempt to introduce equal justice to sentencing by adjusting penalties to the limited supply of punishment resources. This would involve control of prosecutors . . .; sentencing by rule and precedent; massive decriminalization spurred by a recognition that imprisonment was a costly resource to be used only in extreme circumstances; and extensive and imaginative use of non-incarcerative punishments. . . .
>
> Given the political impossibility of treating all like offenders with either equal severity or equal moderation this leaves the third alternative as the likely outcome:
>
> To continue as at present with symbolic punishment, combining excessively severe prison sentences for the few with excessively lenient dispositions for the many, using broad grants of discretionary power at all levels as the mechanism to keep the system in balance.[29]

I think, however, that Foote is too pessimistic. I believe that modest progress is possible. While I believe that a reduction in uncontrolled discretion must take place, the institution of mandatory sentences, flat sentences and even presumptive sentences is not my favorite approach. I would rather see a resort to more flexible solutions and approaches.

It is my hope that the reform movement in sentencing will move on from sterile and mechanical reforms to broader areas of interest. I would much rather see a growth of sentencing councils, composed of scientific experts as well as community representatives. I would encourage the popular input into sentencing, in order to increase public confidence in this institution. I would wish to see judicial self-regulation through sentencing guidelines. I would prefer to see new and effective procedures to permit appellate review of unfair and unjust sentences.

I would also insist on retaining the incentives for the rehabilitative effort. A reform movement which seeks to ban considerations of rehabilitation is retrogressive. Our justice system must offer incentives and rewards to offenders to pursue goals of self improvement. The concept of rehabilitation has become confused and abused, but clearly any effort by offenders to improve their intellectual, vocational or inter-personal skills should be encouraged. The reformers deny this basic and self-evident principle in their pursuit of some absolute concept of equality and justice. I remain opposed to enforced therapy. But I believe that the voluntary rehabilitative goal has not been fully tested — we have never allocated to it the necessary resources. Finally, a concern must be voiced that the new directions in sentencing are producing an undesirable shift and reallocation of power between the three major agencies responsible for the criminal justice system: the legislature, the judiciary and corrections. I am not convinced that granting more power to the legislative branch, in the quest for reduced judicial discretion, operates to improve the operation of the system of justice. It would appear that those who have the greatest and the most intimate access to the offender should make the most important decisions regarding him. And that intimate knowledge rests not so much with the legislature as with the judiciary and the correctional agencies.

These criticisms of the recent reform movement in sentencing should not be taken as an endorsement of present practices. Reforms are needed, especially in light of the symbolic value of the trial and sentence in our society. Earlier we noted that with nearly 12 million Index Crimes reported to the police annually, convictions are secured as charged in a mere 5.9% of all reported cases. The sentencing of such a small sample of the offending population is extremely important and must be treated with the utmost care to maintain the needed public confidence in criminal justice. The reform of sentencing is overdue, but that does not justify the simplistic, regressive and ineffective approaches which currently occupy the main stage of the reform movement.

NOTES

1. (Baltimore: Johns Hopkins Press, 1971).

2. E. Ferri, *Criminal Sociology* (Boston: Little, Brown, 1917), pp. xlii-xliii.

3. D. Karlen, *Anglo-American Criminal Justice* (Oxford: Clarendon Press, 1967), p. 155.

4. New York (state) Special Commission on Attica, *Attica: the Official Report* (New York: Bantam Books, 1972), pp. 30-31.

5. "Countdown for Judicial Sentencing," in *Of Prisons and Justice,* S. Doc. 70, 88th Cong. 2nd sess., (1964), p. 311.

6. Marvin E. Frankel, *Criminal Sentences: Law Without Order* (New York: Hill and Wang, 1973), p. 69.

7. *Ibid.,* pp. 75-78.

8. *Ibid.*

9. *Op. cit.,* note 4.

10. Norval Morris, *The Future of Imprisonment* (Chicago: University of Chicage Press, 1974).

11. E. van den Haag, *Punishing Criminals* (New York: Basic Books, 1975).

12. *Op. cit.,* note 6.

13. Andrew von Hirsch, *Doing Justice: The Choice of Punishments* (New York: Hill and Wang, 1976).

14. *Report of the Task Force on Criminal Sentencing, Fair and Certain Punishment* (New York: McGraw-Hill, 1976).

15. *The Struggle for Justice: A Report on Crime and Justice in America* (New York: Hill and Wang, 1971).

16. Frederick A. Hussey and John H. Kramer, "Issues in the Study of Criminal Code Revision: An Analysis of Reform in Maine and California," in N.I.L.E.C.J., *Determinate Sentencing — Reform or Regression* (Washington, D.C.: U.S. Department of Justice, 1978), p. 111.

17. Francis A. Allen, *The Borderland of Criminal Justice: Essays in Law and Criminology* (Chicago: University of Chicago Press, 1964).

18. *Op. cit.,* note 1.

19. *Op. cit.,* note 5, p. 331.

20. *Op. cit.,* note 6.

21. Sheldon Glueck, *Crime and Justice* (Boston: 1936), pp. 225-226.

22. United States President's Commission on Law Enforcement and Administration of Justice, *The Challenge of Crime in a Free Society* (Washington, D.C.: U.S. Government Printing Office, 1967), pp. 262-263.

23. American Bar Association National Advisory Commission on Criminal Justice Standards and Goals (Washington, D.C: U.S. Government Printing Office, 1973), p. 46.

24. Composites by author, from Kelley, Clarence, *Uniform Crime Reports* (Washington, D.C.: U.S. Printing Office, 1976), pp. 7-33.

25. See, e.g., Martinson, "What Works? Questions and Answers About Prison Reform," *The Public Interest,* Spring, 1974, p. 22.

26.   N. Morris, *op. cit.,* note 10; A. von Hirsch, *op. cit.,* note 13.

27.   N. Kittrie et al., *The New Justice: alternatives to conventional criminal adjudication* (Washington, D.C.: U.S. Department of Justice, 1977).

28.   Albert W. Alschuler, "Sentencing Reform and Prosecutorial Power," in *Determinate Sentencing,* etc., *op. cit.,* note 16, p. 59.

29.   Caleb Foote, "Deceptive Determinate Sentencing," in *Determinate Sentencing,* etc., *op. cit.,* note 16, pp. 138-140.

CHAPTER 4

Sentencing: Legislative Rule versus Judicial Discretion

Donald R. Cressey

Two centuries ago, our forefathers operationalized the idea that undesirable conduct should be described in criminal statutes and then minimized by swift, certain, and uniform punishment of those whose behavior fits the descriptions. Everything was to be reasonable and mechanical. Law-makers were told to stipulate that certain types of conduct are punishable, thus warning citizens that such conduct will be punished in a specified way. Police officers were to detect and apprehend all persons who do not heed the warnings, and prosecutors were to convict them. Then judges were to order the stipulated punishments and others were to impose them. In societies using this machine-like system of deterrence, our ancestors predicted, the undesirability of outlawed behavior will be obvious, and crime rates will therefore be minimal.

This deterrence principle remains as a foundation stone of modern criminal law. Computers were nonexistent when Cesare Beccaria's deterrence argument was translated into legislation by Jeremy Bentham. In retrospect, however, the classical doctrine inherited from these men views judges as mindless computers. The assumption is that law-makers can program a computer with crimes and their punishments, and that then, whenever a defendant is convicted, the machine will simply scan its memory bank until it finds the punishment set down as proper for the behavior displayed by the offender. In this view, judges are really not needed in the sentencing process; their only function is to decide whether an accused person is guilty as charged. The deterrence principle also incorporates the assumption that the computer programmers — the law-makers — will change both the kinds of behavior outlawed and the prescribed punishments whenever the criminal law is inconsistent with changing *mores,* so that the persons being governed will always support the law as it is formally stated.

But if the contemporary debate about sentencing is to be understood, a second important idea underlying contemporary legislation about criminal matters also must be considered. Clearly, our forefathers were convinced of the efficacy of state terror — another name for deterrence. Just as clearly, they soon became convinced that law violations and law violators must be examined individually, and that stipulated punishments must be ignored or mitigated in some cases, depending upon the outcome of the examination. This second persuasion led to the "principle of adjustment" which is another foundation stone of contemporary criminal law.

Classical deterrence procedures were almost immediately perceived as a threat to justice. Thus, it became obvious that if intentionally inflicted suffering — be it the pain of a fine or the pangs of imprisonment — is to be accepted by the recipients and by citizens generally, it must be imposed in quantities suitable to correcting serious deviation without stimulating rebellion. Put another way, our forefathers noted that maintaining the consent of the governed requires the system of punishments for law violation to be accepted as legitimate by those being governed. This means that untempered enforcement of statutes is dangerous, even if the enforcement process does not tamper with the rights summarized by the phrase "due process of law." To maintain the consent of the governed (another name for justice), there must be flexibility, change, common sense, and compromise with reference to the criminal code itself, and with reference to administering the code in specific cases.[1]

For these reasons, the factory-like system of equal punishments instituted by Beccaria, Bentham, and others was soon modified at two points. First, the penalties were fixed within narrow limits, rather than absolutely, making judicial discretion possible. Second, children and "lunatics" were exempted from punishment. Over the years, the range of judicial discretion has broadened: judges and sentencing boards have had a wide range of alternatives open to them. Also, the categories of exempted persons have been enlarged: youths, sexual psychopaths, persons suffering from "diminished responsibility," and others have been handled somewhat as children and lunatics were handled in bygone days.

The essence of the adjustment principle was, and is, that punishments should be individualized, meaning that they should be adjusted to the circumstances of the offense and the character of the offender. Morris Cohen, the distinguished legal philosopher, long ago pointed out that the idea of individualization was but a reassertion of Aristotle's idea that equity is a corrective of undue rigor of law, "a corrective to the injustice which results from the fact that the abstract rule cannot take into account all the specific circumstances that are relevant to the case."[2]

In a search for justice, then, our ancestors gave us criminal law which provides advance notice that convicted wrongdoers will be punished in specified ways, but they also gave us criminal law stipulating that these penalties may be or should be officially mitigated. Evidence of the latter are laws pertaining to pardons, suspended sentences, indeterminate sentences, probation, parole, and diversion. In the last analysis, authorization of judicial discretion — and, more generally, of individualization and adjustment of punishments — implemented penal theory that is in direct conflict with deterrence theory. The deterrence principle — sometimes called the "law enforcement principle" — asks judges and members of the executive branch of government to maximize conformity by swiftly and uniformly punishing nonconformists according to law. But the adjustment principle — sometimes called the "individualization principle" — asks the same personnel to maximize conformity by modifying the law so that it fits individual cases. Accordingly, contemporary criminal law is ambivalent about what should be done with, to, and for criminals.[3] "Almost all the problems of jurisprudence," said Dean Roscoe Pound, "come down to a fundamental one of rule and discretion, of administration of justice by law and administration of justice by the more or less trained intuition of experienced magistrates."[4]

CURRENT LEGISLATIVE TRENDS

In the last decade, the adjustment principle has been severely attacked by American legislatures. The freedom of criminal justice personnel to be wise, compassionate, innovative, and judicious has increasingly been viewed as a rip in the net which law-makers have woven to insure that few felons escape the punishment said to be due them. Legislators are mending this perceived rip by mandating that only the deterrence principle shall be used in the collective effort to minimize criminality. That is, they are acting on the assumption that the quality of justice will be better if judges, police officers, parole board members, and others will stop softening the penalties which legislators have prescribed.

The trend is toward fixed and definite sentences set by legislatures and away from indeterminate sentences set by judges or executives. In some states, new laws have mandated judges to send certain kinds of offenders — especially habitual ones and those using guns — to prison with no possibility of probation. Consistently, parole boards are being abolished or their power curtailed. Further, police officers are being told to improve the ratio of arrests to crimes reported, and prosecutors are being told to stop letting criminals plead guilty to charges that are less grave than the most serious ones that could be brought against them. Finally, a hue and cry is being raised about disparities in the sentences handed down by judges, and hundreds of researchers have been sent out in search of "sentencing guidelines" — sets of rules which prohibit judges from exercising judgment in matters of punishment.[5]

In this quest for efficiency, legislators seem to have forgotten that production-line law enforcement is both undesirable and impossible. The question is whether the law — considered simply as statutes defining crimes, specifying punishments for them, and listing the formal procedures that must be used for dealing with suspects and defendants — can be fair and just. Many authorities, including some Biblical ones, have concluded that it cannot, and the adjustment principle was inserted in criminal law administration for this reason. No social system or organization has ever operated on the basis of formal rules alone, partly because such rigidity cannot be obtained and partly because, if successful, it would result in gross injustices. The exercise of discretion is what puts some humanity, love, charity, kindness, and *justice* into the criminal justice process.

Nevertheless, legislators and their academic supporters are demanding uniformity and efficiency in the processing and punishing of criminals. The image is that of an army at war with criminals. In this army, the legislators are to be general officers whose orders must be obeyed by judges and others of lower rank. Should a general officer command, for example, that every robber must be sent to prison for five years, then it is obvious that any person of lower rank — police officer, prosecutor, judge, parole board member — who lets a robber off with less time is disobeying orders. Moreover, the military style calls for close supervision and inspections, down through a chain of command, designed to insure that the persons of each lower rank are obeying orders. This is the epitome of bureaucracy, and bureaucratization of the courthouse is what mandatory sentencing laws and "sentencing guidelines" are all about.

BUREAUCRACY AND EXPERTISE

Any rank-oriented organization puts emphasis on form rather than substance. The persons occupying high positions initiate rules rather arbitrarily, for the good of the system. This is a means to an end. As each participant follows rules from above, each becomes a cog in a machine that does a job. Authority of rank thus requires "discipline" and "obedience."[6] Participants are required to commit themselves to form and procedure, even if such commitment means a decline of achievement as measured by some other criterion, such as quality of end product. In these circumstances, they cannot excel, and, hence, cannot be rewarded for excellence. Perfect behavior is behavior that is up to standard. For example, a judge who meticulously imposes mandatory sentences set down in individual statutes or in sets of "guidelines" is an excellent judge, by definition. In the mandatory sentencing system there is no possibility for a judge to go beyond what is expected, and judges who do not follow the mandates are denied pay raises, dismissed for incompetence, accused of corruption, or sent to sentencing institutes for education.

Experts are not at home in rank oriented bureaucratic settings. They produce desired services and products individually, and their authority rests on possession of technical knowledge rather than on rank. Their work can therefore be rated as poor, good, or excellent, and a basic principle governing their actions is freedom of dissent. Judges and professors, like artists and scientists, are experts. A world characterized by uniformity and efficiency, brought about by orders, close supervision, and detailed inspections, is repugnant to them. Judges, for example, are convinced that sentencing practices infused with wisdom, intelligence, common sense, judiciousness and other indices of expertise are essential to justice; if they did not believe that, they would not be judges.

In sum, bureaucrats favor regulation, standardization, accounting, and equality. Judges and other experts favor risk, experimentation, and equity — conditions which appear to some as reckless spending, inefficiency, and even inequality.

FREEDOM AND CRIMINAL LAW

The tension between rank oriented bureaucracy and expertise is much more than a mere academic or theoretical concern. The two concepts of proper and efficient organization are actually alternative concepts of political order. Indeed, fundamental human rights are always at issue when political authorities and others debate the question of bureaucracy versus expertise. Are "the people" to be mere parts in a rank oriented bureaucratic machine designed to carry out the wishes of a central power, be that power a dictator or a duly elected representative assembly? Or are they to be viewed as experts who are at liberty to make their own personal decisions until such time as they demonstrate incompetence or dishonesty? The criminal law is the most important arena in which answers to these important questions are sought, and in this arena the issue is conceived as a conflict between the deterrence principle and the adjustment principle.

Note, on the one hand, that every criminal law calls for strict control from above, and, thus, for rank oriented bureaucracy. Because enactment of a criminal law is by definition an attempt to implement the deterrence principle, each is a command issued by law-makers to all persons paid to process suspects, defendants, and criminals. The criminal law, unlike the Ten Commandments, does not prohibit anything. Statutes merely stipulate that whoever behaves in a specified way shall be punished in a specified way. This practice reflects Bentham's conception that citizens should have freedom to do as they please until they have done something wrong. For example, citizens are not forbidden by law to rob one another. Instead, they are merely notified that anyone who robs will suffer the punitive consequences. It is judges and executive branch members who are ordered around whenever a legislature enacts a criminal law.[7]

On the other hand, laws pertaining to the administration of punishments view judges and other criminal justice workers as experts and therefore give them some freedom. As indicated, the adjustment principle is the basis of laws authorizing judges to suspend specified punishments and place offenders on probation. Judges are also authorized to order criminals to serve prison terms within minimum and maximum limits set by law-makers, thus enabling judges to display the characteristics we demand in them — wisdom, expertise, judiciousness. Police officers and prosecutors, too, are allowed by administrative laws and rules to overlook law violations, to "use their heads" and "play it by ear," thus in a technical sense disobeying the legislative mandates stipulating that all known criminals shall be punished. And parole boards, of course, owe their very existence to the fact that legislatures have authorized the executive branch to release inmates from prison when they have experienced only some of the pain specified as appropriate by a legislature, or, within statutory limits, by a judge.

Despite penal laws, then, judges and other criminal justice personnel have had an opportunity to be innovative and creative in the approach to doing justice while keeping the crime rate down. Like private citizens, they have been freed from hierarchical controls until such time as they display criminal behavior or dangerously gross incompetence. But, as I noted earlier, the occupational freedom of judges and executive branch criminal justice workers is now being restricted. Politicians are trying to install nondiscretionary systems in which all personnel are fused into a bureaucratic machine which imposes a fixed amount of pain, determined in advance by a legislature, on anyone who commits a crime. A new breed of researchers who call themselves "policy analysts" and "criminal justice scientists" are helping legislatures implement the deterrence (bureaucratic) principle and to emasculate the adjustment (expert) principle.[8]

Judges are fighting a rear-guard action against such bureaucratization. Perhaps the most outspoken of the judicial resisters is David Bazelon, Chief Judge of the United States Court of Appeals for the District of Columbia, who has warned, "Mandatory incarceration, determinate sentencing, and the like are the first steps in a thousand-mile journey, but in precisely the wrong direction, towards repression."[9] In Massachusetts, a 1975 gun control law mandated a 1-year minimum prison term for anyone possessing a firearm without a permit or identification card. Judges must have resisted, for six months after the law went into effect 328 violators had been arrested but only 24 per cent (78) of them were found guilty, and of these only 36 per cent (28) ended up in jail.[10] More recently, California's Supreme Court displayed some resistance by overturning a statute requiring judges to send defendants to prison when they are found guilty of using guns in committing crimes. The Chief Justice joined the majority but wrote a separate opinion which challenged the anti-gun law on constitutional grounds, saying that the legislature does not have a right to usurp judges' authority to grant probation: "These cases simply represent a traditional protection of the judiciary's constitutionally reserved functions as neutral arbiters in the sentencing process."[11]

FACTORS IN REPRESSION

There seem to be five principal, if overlapping, considerations behind the current trend toward legislative dominance of the judicial process.

One is the general growth of bureaucracy as society has become more complex. This historical development is too broad for detailed discussion here. It is enough to say that it was nourished by considerations of the ability of private contracts to produce and maintain equality. Two centuries ago, as now, businessmen publicly demanded free competition and free contracts and cried out against government interference with them. But in their competition for wealth, they soon discovered that advantages can be secured by government regulations designed to restrict competition. The government thus became a regulator of contracts among businessmen, and soon was trying to regulate these and other contracts "in the public interest," "for the common good," or "for the general welfare." As this practice became commonplace and traditional, it seemed logical to assume that the legislature is the state, that it determines what is in the public interest, and that all government employees are to subordinate their personal interests to those of the state. It followed as a matter of course that the public interest would be served by legislative regulation of the behavior of judges and other criminal justice personnel.

A second and more recent factor is disdain of elitist government procedures which favor the rich and powerful and discriminate against the poor and weak. In modern times, persons securing the most political regulation of their competitors and the least regulation of themselves make the most money and secure the greatest life chances. Inequality thus feeds on itself as the rich secure disproportionate political power, thus increasing their riches. Sponsorship and concordant control of government bureaucracy by "the people" through their legislative representatives is widely believed to be a democratic corrective to such unfair governmental procedures. Political liberals, especially, now believe that if rank oriented bureaucracies controlled the criminal justice process, including the procedures for imposing sentences, the punishments of the rich and the poor, the strong and the weak, would become equal.[12]

Closely related to the second factor is a third — economic rationality. Because legislators ultimately are the collectors and spenders of tax moneys, they must appear to be concerned with weeding out incompetent and dishonest government employees. Historically, such concern for efficiency had a four-step process as its consequence. First, governmental workers were melded into hierarchical structures (bureaux), each designed to achieve some goal deemed by legislators to be in the public interest. Second, the behavior of subordinates was monitored, by means of rank oriented supervisory systems, to insure that they actually behave as they are supposed to behave. Third, instances of deviation, stemming either from incompetence or dishonesty, were taken as evidence that tighter controls must be established and closer monitoring initiated. Fourth, when deviations nevertheless continued to appear, even tighter controls followed.[13] This process is easily observable in the growth and character of executive-branch bureaucracies, including police departments and prisons. Now we are witnessing its application to the judiciary — judges are bureaucratized and told to expect that their sentencing behavior will be monitored from above.

Fear of crime and criminals is the fourth factor in the trend toward employing judges and other criminal justice personnel on a bureaucratic basis rather than on the assumption that they are experts who know their business, and, hence, must be free to make discretionary judgments. Since the early 1960s, legislators and government executives alike have increasingly responded to rising crime rates by trying to insure that citizens are monitored more closely — witness the recent stress on increased surveillance by police officers. They also have reverted to Bentham's 18th-century hedonistic psychology, which stresses the efficiency of terror (swift and certain punishment) in crime control.[14] Both the monitoring response and the punitive response to fear of crime call for crime control by tight bureaucracy. It follows that criminal justice personnel, including judges, must be organized into disciplined troops who insure that every person who chooses to commit a crime will be detected and then punished according to a schedule of punishments set down in advance by the officials at the top, the legislators.

Fifth, it is always true that when achievement of a goal is not measurable, alternative goals — whose achievement *can* be measured — will be substituted.[15] Because the judge's primary goal — to do justice — is an unmeasurable one, it is reasonable to expect substitutes to appear. Although it is not possible to measure the quality of justice in any empirical way, it is possible to measure the number of cases processed, the proportion of defendants committed to prison, the disparities of punishments ordered for seemingly similar criminals, and so on. Legislators, in an heroic attempt at rationality, have recently been assigning measurable goals of these kinds to judges, in keeping with the quest for efficiency mentioned earlier. Doing so lets them avoid the laborious task of determining what the aims of the criminal law are, or should be, and also to avoid the difficulties of trying to measure the effects of their appropriations on the quality of justice.

OBSTACLES TO BUREAUCRATIZATION

Dozens of organizational studies have established that bureaucracies never become as monolithic as the people at the top may wish.[16] The reasons for this failure to achieve perfect rationality in team work are complex, but they all stem from the basic fact that contracts, including those between employers and employees, supervisors and subordinates, never can specify precisely what is to be accomplished in order to satisfy an agreement. As someone has put it, "There always will be cracks in the totalitarian monolith."

I suggested earlier that the prevailing image of criminal justice work pictures a "criminal justice system" in which persons of superior rank control the practices of persons of lower ranks, somewhat as an army general is said to control the practices of sergeants, and sergeants are said to control the practices of corporals. But this image does not square with reality. It is not even a correct portrayal of army discipline. Rather than a "criminal justice system" centrally controlled by legislators (generals), there is only a loose collection of agencies whose personnel often work at cross purposes and in a spirit of competition rather than cooperation. And even in a particular agency — such as a police department or a courthouse — there is a collection of people who persistently make discretionary decisions, ignoring or evading the symbolic sergeants, captains and generals who try to control them. Alper and Weiss[17] have given us an illustrative case from Tewksbury, Massachusetts:

> On June 29, 1975, Bessie Stanton, a 70-year-old woman with a seventh grade education, was arrested in a department store. A security guard noticed that she had a .22 caliber pistol, along with some orange peelings and small change, in a bag she was carrying. She had violated the newly passed Fox-Bentley gun control law which mandated a 1-year minimum prison sentence for *anyone* possessing a firearm without a permit or identification card.
>
> The woman reportedly told the police officer: "I didn't mean no harm. I didn't know about no rule or no law." Her brother later told the court, "She don't read no newspaper, watch no television or listen to no radio."
>
> A few months later Bessie Stanton was found innocent. Although she had clearly violated the Massachusetts gun control law and should have received the mandatory prison sentence, the judge ruled that she did not completely understand her constitutional rights when the arresting officer read them to her.

The fact that cases have such outcomes means that there is hope for justice. The current trend toward bureaucratization of the sentencing process will necessarily stop short of eliminating discretionary decision-making. There are at least three solid reasons why judges will never become the automatons legislators are asking them to be.

In the first place, it is not correct to assume that law-makers want all laws enforced with equal vigor. On the contrary, they clearly recognize that the standards of morality set in concrete criminal laws are adjusted informally as community standards change. Often, the statutes reflect a morality no longer widely prevalent, as in current prohibitions against homosexuality between consenting adults, so that criminality is in effect created by outmoded statutes. In such circumstances, discretionary sentencing practices adjust penalties until such time as the statutes can be modified.

Flexibility which permits members of the executive and judicial branches to adjust the "law on the books" to the "law on the streets" also is acknowledged as a legitimate technique for keeping law norms somewhat consistent with the structural norms associated with age, social class, ethnicity, religion, and so on. So far as "law and order" are concerned, at least, a community is rarely a community. It is a collection of competing interests. Police and judges regularly ignore crimes and stipulated punishments not because they are corrupt, but because they serve on the front line of diplomacy between citizens who want specific laws enforced and citizens who do not. They are diplomats who balance the conflicting demands and claims of interest groups, and who help establish unwritten rules, agreements, and understandings among various segments of society, thus serving to maintain the consent of the governed. It is this diplomatic functioning that makes judges administrators of justice rather than administrators of prescribed punishments. So that law and order are maintained, judges negotiate compromises between those who want a uniform set of crimes and punishments and those who do not. A balance is struck, understandings are operationalized, and a negotiated social order prevails.[18] Legislators, like others, are quite aware that judges help meet a political need for social peace, and therefore must not be transformed into mere agents of coercion.

There also is the matter of money. The fact is that law-makers outlaw so much behavior that one can reasonably assume that they expect judges and others to set priorities. Police officers and judges are in some jurisdictions mandated to "enforce all laws," but there never is enough money to do so. Accordingly, every mandate is qualified with an unwritten phrase, "if doing so does not cost too much." A recent study of New York's 1973 "get tough" law calling for mandatory sentencing of certain drug offenders illustrates this point quite nicely. In two years, New York spent $32 million for court costs and an unknown sum for police and prison expenses to implement this law, but heroin use did not decline, drug-related crime increased, and the risk of imprisonment was lowered. It could be argued, of course, that the law would have been more effective if more money had been poured in, but the study concluded, "It is unlikely that the deficiencies in an existing criminal justice system can be overcome solely by the simultaneous application of tough laws and additional resources."[19] In other words, it is unlikely that any amount of money, manpower, equipment, or power will transform criminal justice personnel into automatons that merely administer the coercive directives of criminal statutes.

There always is a need, then, to decide what is "real" crime and what is not, and to punish the former but not the latter. Meeting this need is a discretionary matter, and law-makers seem well informed of this fact. It cannot be said that they want all laws to be enforced or even that they want specific laws enforced uniformly.

A second reason for doubting that judges will become mere automatons has historical roots. History demonstrates the futility of trying to eliminate discretionary decision-making from the criminal justice process. As a leading expert on administrative law has said:

> Every governmental and legal system in world history has involved both rules and discretion. No government has ever been a government of laws and not of

men in the sense of eliminating all discretionary power. Every government has always been a *government of laws and men.*[20]

Put more specifically, all previous efforts to make judges behave uniformly have failed. The classical school's factory-like system for imposing punishments was immediately modified so that judges could make judgments about punishment as well as guilt. This modification was made, and it will continue to be made, because adjusting penalties to the background of individual offenders and the circumstances of their offenses is essential to justice. As was noted earlier, any punishment which is not accepted by the governed is unjust. In modern times, the judge's function is to modify mandated punishments so that they will be just, and, thus, so that the consent of the governed will be maintained. Procedural due process alone will not accomplish this important function of courts.

Suppose, for example, that a robbery statute called for a mandatory ten years in prison for every person taking another's property by force or threat of force. Merely administering this law, in contrast to modifying it on a discretionary, *ad hoc,* basis, would put in prison for ten years a boy who took a candy bar away from a school chum, a youth who forcibly took a basketball from the kids on the playground, and a man who pointed a pistol at a bank teller and gave the teller a free choice by yelling, "Your money or your life." A measure of freedom among criminal justice personnel permits them to decide what is *really* robbery and to adjust the penalties accordingly, thus preventing widespread rebellion against a government's unjust laws. Uniform administration, directed from above by persons of superior rank, cannot take such nuances into account.

A third reason for doubting that legislators can turn judges into robots is this: All criminal laws actually are quite vague, despite the fact that each appears to be precise and rigorous in its definition of what is outlawed. No law-making body, far removed from the occurrences of behavior "on the street," can say precisely what it is that it wants outlawed and made punishable by law. Criminal law and the so-called "elements" of each crime are necessarily stated in quite general terms.

Consider burglary, for example. One form of burglary — called "first-degree burglary" in some jurisdictions — is a breaking and entering of the dwelling of another at night with intent to commit a felony. Each of the essentials is a legal and seemingly precise "element" of the crime — breaking, entering, dwelling, night, intent, felony. But none of these essentials refers to something real, in the way the word *cat* refers to something real. Consequently, judges and others must decide that a specific incident is or is not *close enough* to what the burglary statute seems to outlaw. Their behavior with reference to determining guilt cannot be made uniform. It is *necessarily* discretionary. Similarly, it is reasonable to expect that "real" burglars (those whose behavior seems close to what the statute outlaws) will always be sentenced to more severe punishment than will people whose behavior is only somewhat described by the statute.[21]

The fuzziness of "criminal intent" is highly relevant in this connection. When an incident looks something like a burglary, judges must inquire about the suspect's intentions: "With what intent did Henry Jones enter the house of John Doe at approximately 11:16 p.m. on the night of April the 6th, last?" In most cases, the only correct answer is, "No one knows." Nevertheless, American judges, at least, are required to determine criminal intent in black-or-white terms — either a defendant had criminal intent or did not have criminal intent — just as they must decide other issues in the either-or terms of criminal law.

In everyday life, governed by common sense, criminal intent is a matter of degree. Some defendants have a lot of it, and others have just a little of it. To judges, who use their common sense to solve either-or problems, a burglar who "really" intended the crime should be sentenced to more pain than one who "sort of" intended it, even if the overt behavior of each was objectively quite similar. We will always have so-called disparities in sentences because the process of making decisions about degree of intent, and sentencing accordingly, cannot be bureaucratized.

Even more productive of discretionary decision-making is the fact that legal tradition requires each suspect and defendant to be found either guilty or not guilty. In the world of common sense, however, some criminals are a little bit guilty while others are very guilty indeed. It also is true that a burglar who is somewhat guilty does not deserve the punishment deserved by a burglar who is "guilty as hell." Judges must, and do, adjust penalties to degree of guilt, for law-making bodies cannot specify in advance a punishment for the infinite degrees of guilt among the criminals committing burglary or any other crime. This means that judges cannot reasonably be expected to perform as computerized robots perform. They necessarily must be given room to use their own common sense.

DISCRETION, LEGISLATIVE RULE, AND JUSTICE

It may be concluded that criminal justice personnel, including judges, actually make law rather than merely administering it, as Justice Oliver Wendell Holmes long ago observed.[22] They do this by giving concrete reality to substantive law. Their decisions determine whether an alleged crime is or is not a crime *for all practical purposes,* not that it is or is not a crime according to legislative standards. Consistently, their sentencing decisions seek disparities based on variations in assessed degrees of *mens rea* and guilt, not uniformities based on general legislative rules. Accordingly, disparities in sentences will never be legislated away.

Holmes made a profound discovery. He noticed that judges select appropriate law to cite as justification for the decisions they reach, rather than basing those decisions on the law.[23] By the same token, it is a worthy hypothesis, at least, that judges *first* make policy (sentencing) decisions about cases, and *then* cite factual characteristics of these cases as justifications for their decisions. Rosett and I found this reversal to be characteristic of prosecutors engaged in so-called "plea bargaining,"[24] as did Neubauer.[25]

Courthouses, like the entire legal institution, are organized as though a policy decision ("What, if anything, should the state do with, to, and for this person?") will follow a factual decision ("Is the suspect guilty of burglary?"). The tension between the deterrence principle and the adjustment principle stems from disagreements about how the policy (sentencing) decision will be made, not from disagreements about the procedures for determining guilt. But it is quite possible that judges, like prosecutors, police officers, parole authorities, and others concerned with sentencing, determine factual guilt only after making a sentencing decision. If this is true, legislators would be well advised to examine the quality of justice stemming from the process, rather than continuing their mindless denunciation of disparities in sentencing and their eager pursuit of justice by bureaucratic rule.[26]

My hypothesis, derived from Holmes, is that judges do not determine guilt by referring to a rule book in the way a visitor to a zoo might refer to a guide book for authority on how to tell one animal from another. Judges are law school trained to look for the "elements" of a crime just as a zoo visitor might look for the "elements" of a hippopotamus. Experience soon teaches them, however, that the consequences of calling an event a specific crime are much more momentous than the consequences of calling an animal by some standard name. Justice is at stake.

Consider burglary again. The traditional assumption is that judges look for the elements of the various grades of this crime, including lesser-included offenses such as trespassing and breaking and entering. According to the deterrence principle, the identified elements are to determine sentencing outcome so that, for example, a person whose crime contained the elements of first-degree burglary (dwelling house at night) receives one sentence, a person guilty of ordinary burglary (any building, any time) receives a lesser sentence, and a person guilty of trespassing receives a still milder sentence. The adjustment principle is based on the same logic but allows mitigation of the punishments stipulated for the three offenses.

Now consider the possibility that judges first decide what the sentence shall be, then pick an offense which is consistent with that decision, and then find the defendant guilty of it.[27] In this sequence a judge might, for example, decide that a college-student prankster who broke into a sorority house with intent to steal a valuable trophy is not "really" a felon who should be sentenced to prison or even stigmatized as a felon and placed on probation. For that judge, but perhaps not for others, the "elements" of burglary are not likely to be present in the case. The same judge might decide that a fine or a few days in jail is an appropriate sentence, in which case he will look in his guide book for a crime calling for a sentence of this kind, and he probably will find trespassing, breaking and entering, malicious mischief, or some other misdemeanor.

One outcome of this procedure for matching sentences with crimes is disparities in sentences. Another outcome is unjust imposition of more severe pain on the poor and weak than on the rich and powerful.[28] To illustrate, the conduct of a "bad guy" (for example, a young, tough, black, male with a prison record) might be called burglary by his judge because the judge wants him in prison, while very similar conduct by a "good guy" (such as a middle-aged, middle-class, well-mannered, white, male with no prior criminal record) might be called trespassing (or no crime at all) by his judge because the judge does not want him in prison. Clearly, the differential outcomes of two such cases is a sign of injustice. Indeed, as I suggested earlier, the recent legislative attack on judicial discretion is based in part on evidence that injustices of this kind are being manufactured in almost all courthouses.

But what is important in the current drive to make judges into robot-like servants of legislators is not the fact that injustice is sometimes produced as judges select crimes to fit sentences. Injustice will always be with us. What is important is the question of whether the apparent reversal of expected procedure regarding crime and its punishment produces more injustice than would strict enforcement of criminal statutes. There is no evidence that it does. On the contrary, it seems obvious that the legislators now implementing the classical school's computerized system for imposing sentences are unwittingly asking for an increase in the amount of injustice in the world.[29]

NOTES

1. In France, Beccaria's ideas were embodied in the radical Penal Code of the Third Brumaire of 1795. Only the question of guilt was left to the discretion of courts. Fifteen years later, it was concluded that this Penal Code had proved completely unworkable, mainly because judges refused to limit their discretion, and it was replaced by the Napoleonic Code of 1810, which provided for judicial discretion. See Alper & Weiss, "The Mandatory Sentence: Recipe for Retribution," 41 *Federal Probation* 15 (1977).

2. M. Cohen, *Reason and Law: studies in juristic philosophy* (Glencoe, Ill.: Free Press, 1950), p. 53.

3. In view of the now-popular claim that rehabilitation programs do not rehabilitate, it is important to note that neither of the two principles says anything about "treating" criminals or otherwise rehabilitating or correcting them by nonpunitive means. The conflict is between uniformity and individualization of *punishment.* To the degree that treatment was viewed as an alternative to punishment, not as a supplement to it nor as disguised punishment, its authorization by law-makers was, like introduction of the adjustment principle, recognition of the need to mitigate, in individual cases, the severe penalties prescribed by statute. Language pertaining to the "individualization of treatment" by probation, parole, and prison workers who have tried to correct, rehabilitate or cure convicted criminals obscured this point. Even if one accepts as fact the now-popular assumption that rehabilitation programs have failed, one cannot logically come to the conclusion that discretionary sentencing practices should therefore be abandoned. See Alper & Weiss, *op. cit.,* note 1. Nevertheless, this assumption is at the base of many arguments for mandatory sentences and the abolition of parole boards. See, for example, Goldstein, "Parole Boards Lose the Prison Keys," *New York Times,* January 7, 1979, reporting on a Governor's Committee which recommended that the state's parole board be abolished in all but name — as has already happened in Arizona, California, Illinois, Indiana, Maine, and New Mexico — and that judges' sentencing decisions be restricted by a set of "sentencing guidelines."

4. R. Pound, *An Introduction to the Philosophy of Law* (New Haven: Yale University Press, 1922), p. 11.

5. Although I stress the current tendency for the legislative branch to try to dominate the executive and judicial branches, it should be noted that the "law and order" movement is by no means restricted to legislators. Some members of the executive branch, especially police officers, are also asking for legislative dominance of judicial processes, probably because they are dedicated to the deterrence principle. As Rosett and I have noted, police and prosecutors have in recent years been catering to repressive law-and-order interests and exploiting fears of crime in order to obtain budgetary support, re-election, and immunity from outside legal interference with their activities. Even the statistical reports of crime have been shaped to serve these political interests. A. Rosett and D. Cressey, *Justice by Consent: Plea Bargains in the American Courthouse* (Philadelphia: Lipincott, 1976), pp. 176-177.

Two quite different conceptions of public service are involved in such controversies. On the one hand, there is the conception appearing some years ago in a proposed Code of Ethics for the employees and officials of Arlington County, Virginia. In this Code, the people are the decision-makers, and government workers must obey their will: "Those holding public office, as servants of the public, are not owners of authority but are agents of public purpose." Perhaps this is what a police chief had in mind when he recently wrote, "When some people advocate the philosophy that a police officer has discretion in the field to arrest an individual or to take him home, they are talking about *discriminatory law enforcement,* which is *police corruption.*": Archuleta, "Police Discretion v. Plea Bargaining," 10 *Police Chief* 78 (1974). But another conception of public service views government employees as experts who should have their own views of their mission and of appropriate policy. It is this conception which leads executive-branch members and elected officials to engage in programs designed to "educate the public." Each of these conceptions has its perils. The first leads to bureaucrats for whom thinking is a painful experience and for whom creativity and innovation are naughty words. The second conception, when implemented, produces government by technocrats, or, perhaps even more dangerously, government by propagandists.

Achieving a balance between these conceptions of public service is a fundamental political problem. See Bendix, "Bureaucracy," in *International Encyclopedia of the Social Sciences;* Editor-in-Chief, David L. Sills (New York: MacMillan, 1968), pp. 201-219. Too much restriction of government workers, including judges, is devastating, but unbridled individualism leads to monopoly, organizational power, and subversion of the very values symbolized by individualism. It is probably for this reason that Kenneth Culp Davis, a noted expert on administrative law, argues that criminal justice is at stake in the United States because there is "unnecessary discretion," not because criminal justice decision-making is necessarily discretionary in character. K. Davis, *Discretionary Justice* (Baton Rouge: Louisiana State University Press, 1969).

6. My discussion of rank-oriented authority and the authority of expertise follows the distinction made by the noted German sociologist and lawyer, Max Weber in *From Max Weber: Essays in Sociology,* H. Gerth and C. Wright Mills (trs.) (New York: Oxford University Press, 1946), p. 246, as elaborated by Talcott Parsons in *The Theory of Social and Economic Organization* (New York: Free Press, 1947), p. 49 and Alvin W. Gouldner in *Patterns of Industrial Bureaucracy: A Case Study of Modern Factory Administration* (New York: Free Press, 1954), pp. 20-24, 187-206. The implications that the distinction has for correctional and court work are spelled out in some detail in Cressey, "Prison Organizations," in *Handbook of Organizations,* J. March, (ed.)(Chicago: Rand, 1965), pp. 1023-1070; and the implications for government financing of scientific research are analyzed in Cressey, "Crime, Science, and Bureaucratic Rule," 11 *The Center Magazine* (Center for the Study of Democratic Institutions) 40 (1978).

7. The basis of such mandates seems to be an understandable desire on the part of legislators to set policy for all branches of government, and then to ensure that policy is followed in practice. In the United States, the federal government has taken a similar position regarding state and local governments. Thus the United States Congress, and federal executives and judges as well, tell governors and mayors what they must do. Generally speaking, the idea seems to be to establish practices and procedures that are uniform and standard, thus ensuring that citizens everywhere receive equal treatment from government officials. The federal demand, in other words, is for state and local bureaucracies.

Rights are a different matter. The laws pertaining to them is negative, telling legislators, judges, and executives what they *cannot* do. The United States Constitution contains two of the best examples of such law. The Fifth and Fourteenth amendments do not mandate that persons behaving in certain ways shall be deprived of life, liberty, or property. They authorize such deprivation by implication, and then specify that the depriving action may not be taken unless there is due process of law.

The law has always been at its best when it recognizes citizens' rights and then enjoins government personnel from interfering with them. Consistently, criminal laws would be greatly improved if they enjoined executives and judges rather than mandating them to behave in specific punitive ways. For example, a burglary statute might read, "Whoever commits burglary may not be sent to prison for more than three years." This statute would be a drastic change from current laws which mandate, for example, that whoever commits burglary shall be sentenced to prison for three years, thus implying that judges and executives are low-level bureaucrats who count cadence to the marching orders given by legislators. The revised law would authorize discretion, the very stuff of which justice is made. With such law, the legislature leaves to the executive and judicial branches, within limits, the task of deciding just what, if anything, shall be done to, with, and for criminals. The work of these personnel is not bureaucratized. Innovation is possible, as is the exercise of ingenuity, compassion, and wisdom.

8. See Cressey, "Criminological Theory, Social Science, and the Repression of Crime," 16 *Criminology* 171 (1978). Platt and Takagi present summaries of recent studies and essays purporting to show that if statutes are given a literal reading, thereby minimizing discretionary decision-making, punishments will increase and crime rates will go down. Platt and Takagi, "Intellectuals for Law and Order: A Critique of the New 'Realists'," 8 *Crime and Social Justice* 1 (1977).

9. Bazelon, quoted by Bennett, "A Bicentennial Inquiry Into American Law," 12 *Trial* 16 (1976). *See also* Bazelon, "Street Crime and Correctional Potholes," 41 *Federal Probation* 1 (1977).

10. Alper & Weiss, *op. cit.,* note 1.

11. *San Francisco Chronicle,* December 23, 1978.

12. See American Friends Service Committee, *Struggle for Justice: A Report on Crime and Punishment in America* (New York: Hill and Wang, 1971); Twentieth Century Fund Inc., *Report of the Task Force on Criminal Sentencing, Fair and Certain Punishment* (New York: McGraw-Hill, 1976); and A. Von Hirsch, *Doing Justice: The Choice of Punishments* (New York: Hill and Wang, 1976).

13. The founders of the classical school of criminology advocated this process for whole societies, not merely for individual bureaucracies. Thus, as my first factor suggests, their deterrence principle calls for a society organized for the common good, for monitoring of citizen behavior and punishment of deviants, and for increased monitoring and increased punishments if persons are not deterred by existing penalties. A. Rosett and D. Cressey, *op. cit.,* note 5, p. 157, have noted that in the United States this historical policy of escalation has become the basis of contemporary calls for increased punitive severity:

> To a considerable degree, the legislature becomes an agent of harshness and the courts become agencies for protecting citizens from harshness. The net effect ... is a rather steady increase in statutory severity for certain crimes. Such legislative action follows an established pattern:
>
> *Step I.* Laws calling for severe punishments are passed by legislatures on the assumption that fear of great pain will terrorize the citizenry into conformity.
>
> *Step II.* Criminal justice personnel soften these severe penalties for most offenders (a) in the interests of justice and (b) in the interests of bureaucracy, and (c) in the interests of gaining acquiescence.
>
> *Step III.* The few defendants who then insist on a trial and are found guilty,

or who in other ways refuse to cooperate, are punished more severely than those who acquiesce.

Step IV. Legislators, noting that criminals by acquiescing avoid "the punishment prescribed by law," (a) increase the prescribed punishments and (b) try to limit the range of discretionary decision making used to soften the harsh penalties.

Step V. The more severe punishments introduced in the preceding step are again softened for most offenders, as in Step II, with the result that the defendants not acquiescing are punished even more severely than they were at Step III.

Step VI. The severity-softening-severity process is repeated.

14. I have noted elsewhere that this trend has been accompanied by a decline of interest in the causes of crime and that policy which eliminates sociological considerations from penal procedure is a characteristic of fascist states, not democracies. See *supra,* note 8. However, it should not be concluded that the motives for recent bureaucratization of criminal justice processes are always nefarious. Max Weber lauded bureaucracy, noting that "the choice is only between bureaucracy and dilettantism in the field of administration." Talcott Parsons, *op. cit.,* note 6, p. 337. In their war on crime, law-makers and others are determined to minimize dilettantism, thereby minimizing deviation by improving efficiency. Nevertheless, limiting the occupational freedom of judges and others produces its own forms of inefficiency, waste, dishonesty, and injustice.

15. Transformation or displacement of goals is a central concern of many sociologists. Three studies that have attained classic status are: R. Michels, *Political Parties* (Glencoe, Ill.: Free Press, 1949); P. Selznick, *TVA and the Grass Roots* (Berkeley: University of California Press, 1949); and S. Lipset, *Agrarian Socialism* (Berkeley: University of California Press, 1950). Earlier analyses of how instrumental values become terminal values are discussed in Merton, "The Unanticipated Consequences of Purposive Social Action," 1 *American Sociological Review* 894 (1936). The transformation process has been studied in hundreds of settings, including institutions for juveniles, law enforcement agencies, courts, and prisons. The classic statement about the effects of statistical measurement on goals and behavior is Ridgeway, "Disfunctional Consequences of Performance Measurements," 2 *Administrative Science Quarterly* 240 (1956).

16. Many of the studies are summarized in J. Thompson, *Organizations in Action* (New York: McGraw-Hill, 1967); F. Katz, *Autonomy and Organization: The Limits of Social Controls* (Philadelphia: Philadelphia Book Co., 1968); and *Handbook of Organizations, supra,* note 6.

17. *Op. cit.,* note 1, pp. 15-16.

18. See Cressey, "Bet Taking, Cosa Nostra, and Negotiated Social Order," 19 *Journal of Public Law* 13 (1970).

19. Joint Committee on New York Drug Law Evaluation of the Association of the Bar of the City of New York and the Drug Abuse Council, Inc., *The*

Nation's Toughest Drug Law: Evaluating the New York Experience (New York, 1977), p. 26. Such studies should, but rarely do, stimulate experiments pertaining to the question of whether the money spent in a quest for increased punishment could have been better spent on something else. For example, if each of New York's drug addicts who stayed off drugs for a week had been rewarded with $100 in cash each Saturday, would the drug problem have diminished? Would handling the problem in this way have cost $16 million a year, plus the costs of arrests, incarceration, probation, and parole?

20. K. Davis, *op. cit.,* note 5, p. 17.

21. In the everyday language of courthouses, the word "cheap" is used to refer to burglaries and other crimes which are not "real" burglaries or crimes, and which, therefore, have little "worth." See Alschuler, "The Prosecutor's Role in Plea Bargaining," 36 *University of Chicago Law Review* 50 (1968); and Cressey, "Doing Justice: The Rule of Law Includes More Than the Statutes," *The Center Magazine* (Center for the Study of Democratic Institutions) 21 (1977).

22. Holmes, "The Path of the Law," 10 *Harvard Law Review* 457 (1897).

23. O. Holmes, *The Common Law* (Boston: Little, Brown: 1881), pp. 1, 27, 36.

24. A. Rosett and D. Cressey, *supra,* note 5, pp. 105-107.

25. D. Neubauer, *Criminal Justice in Middle America,* (Morristown, New Jersey: General Learning Press, 1974), p. 121.

26. See, as an example of the many studies in sentencing disparities, Harris and Lura, "The Geography of Justice — Sentencing Variations in U. S. Judicial Districts," 57 *Judicature* 392 (1974).

27. Brian Grosman's Canadian study, *The Prosecutor: An Inquiry into the Exercise of Discretion* (Toronto: University of Toronto Press, 1969), has, like U.S. studies, shown that most sentences follow guilty pleas rather than findings of guilt, and that most sentences are arranged by prosecutors. Nevertheless, it is true that judges "find" guilt when they affirm sentences arranged by others after guilty pleas have been entered. Furthermore, because judges are responsible for all the sentences of their courts, it is proper to discuss sentencing behavior as though it were their property rather than a property of criminal justice committees made up of judge, prosecutor, and defense attorney. *See* A. Rosett and D. Cressey, *op. cit.,* note 5, pp. 173-175.

28. See Hagan's review of 20 studies concerned with the relationship between defendant's race and severity of sentence, and ten sentencing studies which have employed some index of social class as their independent variable, "Extra-legal Attributes and Criminal Sentencing: An Assessment of a Sociological Viewpoint," 8 *Law and Society Review* 357 (1974). Also see the review by Jankovic, "Social Class and Criminal Sentencing," 10 *Crime and Social Justice* 9 (1978).

29. See the arguments made by Flynn, "Turning Judges into Robots," 12 *Trial* 17 (1976), and P. Nonet, *Administrative Justice: Advocacy and Change in a Government Agency* (New York: Russell Sage Foundation, 1969).

Part 2

SENTENCING REFORM

CHAPTER 5

Reforming Sentencing Laws: A Canadian Perspective

K. Jobson

Imprisonment and its over-use remains the central issue in sentencing policy and practice. It is not suggested here that judges cease using sentences of imprisonment altogether. It is suggested, however, that there are abuses in the use of imprisonment and that one such area of abuse concerns the sentencing of non-violent offenders against property to relatively short terms of imprisonment.[1]

It is further suggested that sentencing reform is not so much a matter of changing laws as changing practice. It is up to the judges, primarily, to bring about reform. Others can point out the apparent lack of rational justification for some types of sentencing practices and the resulting problems this raises in terms of practice, legitimacy of legal institutions and professional responsibility for those involved in the sentencing process. It is the judges alone who, clothed with a wide discretion, choose to exercise the power to imprison. Changing the law so as to restrict the judges in using imprisonment is probably not an effective way of reforming sentencing practice and discretion.

Canadian sentencing laws, as already indicated, leave the courts a very wide discretion in sentencing, and, with rare exceptions, judges are not required to impose sentences of imprisonment. If imprisonment is imposed it is because judges have developed practices of imposing prison terms rather than fines, probation or discharges in certain types of cases. These practices, however, appear to be based largely on historical habit as reflected in previous cases.

When subjected to the scrutiny of the social sciences, analysis within a framework of philosophy of law, or simple empirical observation, some of these sentencing practices appear suspect. In these circumstances past practice probably is not a sufficiently strong peg upon which to hang rational judicial decision-making. The exercise of sentencing power based only on past practice or unjustified assumptions may increasingly appear to be less judicial and more political.

The large number of short terms of imprisonment imposed on non-violent offenders against property, the large costs involved in carrying out these sentences and their apparent lack of reasonable justification, in general, give rise to a central issue in sentencing policy and practice. Will the judges be able to reform these sentencing practices or will they be imprisoned by past images and practice?

At the outset it is well to appreciate that judicial use of imprisonment has its greatest impact at the provincial and local level. Eighty-nine per cent of all persons sentenced to imprisonment never go to penitentiaries but to provincial prisons[2] serving sentences of less than two years. It is not always appreciated that only about ten per cent of these persons are sentenced for crimes of violence against the person.[3] In that sense, the overwhelming majority of persons sentenced to imprisonment in Canada are non-violent offenders.

These non-violent offenders fall into several distinct categories: (1) persons convicted of non-violent offences against property including theft, fraud, false pretences, possession of stolen property, breaking and entering, and possession of housebreaking instruments; (2) persons in breach of probation or parole or who failed to appear on a summons or otherwise as required; (3) persons convicted of offences relating to public law and order, for example, causing a disturbance; (4) persons convicted of possession of drugs (including marijuana) or of being in possession for the purpose of trafficking; (5) persons convicted of driving while impaired or other motor vehicle offences. Of these categories, the non-violent offender against property is by far the largest and accounts for over 60 per cent of all sentences of imprisonment.[4]

Moreover, 80 per cent of all persons sentenced to less than two years receive sentences of six months or less.[5] It is estimated that over 95 per cent of non-violent offenders against property who are sentenced to jail receive sentences of three months or less.[6] Many of these offenders are not "hard core" offenders as commonly assumed. It is estimated that 59 per cent of non-violent offenders against property imprisoned in provincial prisons in British Columbia in 1977 had no previous sentence of either jail or probation, and a further 23 per cent had only one such previous sentence.[7]

This type of sentencing practice does not serve the common good and should be reformed. Whatever can be said in favour of prisons, and, in general there is little, it can hardly be suggested that prisons or sentences of imprisonment are socially useful because of their rehabilitative effects. Common experience shows that prisons do not rehabilitate and those who work most closely with the prisons — wardens, guards and other correctional personnel — freely admit that the prisons lack the capacity to rehabilitate.

Black and Weiler in their survey of correctional institutions in British Columbia in 1975 stated:

> Those who are intimately associated with the two correctional systems have changed their views on the viability of rehabilitation as the prime mechanism to achieve a reduction in crime. All of the psychiatrists, criminal lawyers, ex-convicts, inmates, law professors, and even the employees of the correctional systems indicated to us that there was little or no rehabilitation taking place in the system. Frank discussions with doctors, chaplains, and deputy wardens at Oakalla revealed that in the opinion of these people, the programs and facilities that presently exist in the B.C. Correctional System cannot possibly be viewed as embodying the individualized treatment model and fulfilling the task of rehabilitating prisoners. At best these programs constitute a system of diversions, assist a prisoner in passing the time, and militate against an increase in antisocial, criminal or other deviant tendencies in the inmate that often occur in correctional institutions. In short, these programs can only be expected to "hold the line" against an increase in "criminality," or at best to afford a setting whereby extra-institutional factors can affect the inmate in rehabilitating himself.
>
> In summary then we are of the view that considering the available facilities and in the light of recent criminological scholarship, the individualized treatment model, and the theory that rehabilitation of the offender is the route to the protection of society, is unsound in theory and potentially vicious and counterproductive in practice.[8]

The federal government in its report, *The Role of Federal Corrections in Canada,* in 1977, adopting the view of Norval Morris stated that, "Rehabilitation . . . must cease to be a purpose of the prison sanction."[9] The reasoning behind abandonment of rehabilitation as a goal of the federal prison service is explained in the Report as follows:

> Since the early 1960s, one of the most widely held beliefs in corrections management has been, and still is to a great extent, that the best way to protect society is to "rehabilitate" the offender. The implication of this statement is that the correctional agency is somehow directly responsible for the "success" or "failure" of the offender. It makes the assumption that correctional practitioners are able to change or modify the personality which further assumes that criminal behaviour is somehow an expression of some underlying personality disturbance which requires extensive therapy and treatment before the criminal behaviour ceases. As a correctional goal, these claims have been challanged as being unrealistic, unsubstantiated and unattainable.
>
> . . .
>
> The concept of rehabilitation has raised unrealistic expectations of altering

criminal behaviour. The model assumes that criminality is a form of "sickness" and that the offender's pathology must be "cured" before he will cease to engage in further criminal activity. By implying that the offender is "sick" through causes beyond his control, this approach minimizes the offender's responsibility for his own criminal behaviour. The approach gives correctional practitioners a strong inducement to employ coercion in the guise of humane treatment, and to enforce participation in treatment programs as a requisite to release. To quote C. S. Lewis: "Of all the tyrannies, a tyranny expressed for the good of its victims may be the most oppressive." The resulting distrust among offenders of the institutional treatment program further undermines the possibility of effecting fundamental behavioural change.[10]

The social science research underpinning these conclusions is now well known. Much of it has been done in the United States and summarized in a series of illuminating books and manuscripts ranging from Martinson's arresting conclusion that "Nothing Works"[11] to Norval Morris' more reflective analysis of the purposes of punishment now that rehabilitation is dead.[12] Nor has empirical documentation of the failure of prison and parole been lacking in Canada. The most notable contribution, perhaps, is Irwin Waller's *Men Released from Prison*[13] and Peter Macnaughton-Smith's *Permission to Be Slightly Free.*[14] Waller's book makes it clear that prison fails to rehabilitate and is a general failure in preventing recidivism: ". . . parole . . . is not, . . . nor indeed is the prison itself, effective in terms of the primary aim of reducing the likelihood of future criminal behaviour."[15] Macnaughton-Smith's analysis of parole files showed that society might be just as far ahead without a parole law: it was difficult to show that parole was an objective benefit.[16]

To summarize, rehabilitation is no longer credible as a purpose of punishment. As Clay Ruby points out, the promise of the rehabilitative ideal has proved to be hollow and individual liberty has been imperilled by claims to knowledge and therapeutic effectiveness that we do not possess. No longer can it be said that prison sentences can be justified on rehabilitative grounds.[17]

Can short terms of imprisonment be justified on grounds of deterrence or incapacitation? Both experience and research in the social sciences have led to considerable skepticism about the deterrent effects of punishment.[18] Some studies show that there may be a deterrent effect related to punishment, but it is dependent upon punishment being certain. The same studies show that severity of punishment does not appear to affect crime rates; in other words imprisonment is not likely to be more effective than fines or probation. After an exhaustive review of the research findings on the effects of deterrence, a panel of the National Research Council in the United States last year re-affirmed that the evidence to date does not prove the existence of a deterrent effect.[19] Still, the Report observed it was impossible to say there are no deterrent effects either. Common sense claims that there may be some deterrent effect to punishment and experience suggests deterrence may be more effective in relation to some types of crimes than others. Where the apprehension rate is very low the deterrent effect is also likely to be low. In thefts, the clearance rate is typically around 10 per cent while in break and enter the clearance rate ranges from 16 to 23 per cent.[20] It is clear that the odds greatly favor the offender in these cases, and the conclusion is inescapable: crime rates for non-violent property offences are not likely to be responsive to sentences imposed in courts. Yet in British Columbia in 1972 more than 62.4 per cent of persons convicted of break and enter were sentenced to imprisonment, and 56.7 per cent of these sentences were for six months or less.[21] In other words, out of one hundred offenders engaged in breaking and entering only 17.4 are likely to be convicted; 10.8 will receive a sentence of imprisonment, 6 of these being for six months or less. Considering all of this, the additional deterrent effects of imprisonment over fines or probation is likely to be very small.

Experience also teaches us to be skeptical about the deterrent effects of imprisonment for another reason. Even if certainty of apprehension is high in a given offence category, many offenders probably do not stop to consider the risks. As judges have observed, "Among criminals foresight and prudent calculation are even more conspicuous by their absence . . . There are many types of prisoners who cannot learn even from the experience of punishment, much less from the threat of it."[22]

Skepticism about the deterrent effects of imprisonment have given rise to considerable interest in imposing sentences of imprisonment for their incapacitating effects. "Incapacitation involves removing an offender from general society and thereby reducing crime by physically preventing the offender from committing crimes in that society."[23] The size of this incapacitating effect depends upon the rate at which the offender commits crimes. Naturally, there are difficulties in estimating the incapacitating effect. Some offenders reduce their rate of committing crimes or even stop committing crimes independently of being imprisoned. In some offences, such as some drug offences, it appears that imprisonment does not reduce the crime rate because the imprisoned offender is simply replaced by another person recruited to meet the high demand for the illicit goods. Various studies on the incapacitating effects of imprisonment suggest widely differing conclusions, including the possibility of achieving significant reduction in crime through imprisonment of those criminals who commit a high number of crimes on a yearly basis. Cohen[24] reviewed existing studies on deterrent and incapacitating effects of imprisonment and noted that all of the studies to date rely on important and as yet untested assumptions. She concludes:

(1) Where imprisonment rates are already high, further increases in the use of imprisonment are not likely to add much to the reduction in crime rates;

> (2) Reduction in crime rates through incapacitation is likely to be costly in terms
> of a vastly increased prison population: estimates are that to achieve a 10 per
> cent reduction in index crimes through incapacitation, states such as Califor-
> nia or Massachusetts would have to increase prison populations by 150 per
> cent and 310 per cent respectively; for violent crimes only the projected
> prison population increases are 23 per cent and 57 per cent respectively.[25]

Assuming society is willing to bear the costs of building more prisons in an attempt to reduce the crime rate, and that current estimates range from $80,000 to $120,000 per prison bed as the cost of building new prisons, several difficulties remain with incapacitation as a sentencing policy.

The first problem is that it is unjust to punish a person not on the basis of what he or she has done, but on the basis of what the offender may do in the future. Judges have a long practice of justifying sentences of imprisonment not in terms of the gravity of the particular offence but in terms of the offender's prior criminal record. Sometimes, of course, such terms are justified on retributive grounds as well, but public protection, not just deserts, appears to be the prime concern of the courts. As already indicated there are ethical issues raised by such a sentencing policy,[26] a policy moreover that traditionally has received scant approval in the western world as an appropriate philosophy of punishment. Consider, as an example, imposing a six month sentence for theft of a chain saw where the offender has a lengthy record for minor offences going back over 17 years, is a native Indian and has an alcohol problem.[27] It is likely the offender would commit another property offence before long, but this arises to some extent because of his social and economic background. Putting aside the ethical question of whether an accused person ought to be imprisoned in order to prevent him from some possible future act, do we have the expertise and capacity to predict an individual's future crime rates?

The simple answer is "no." In general, we do not have the capacity to predict accurately which offenders are highly likely to commit further offences.[28] Courts, probation and parole officers and others continue to make common sense judgments in these matters daily, but the validity of these judgments must be closely examined. First of all, such predictions are subject to error, and the greater the likelihood of error the less socially useful is the prediction. Secondly, to imprison someone on a false prediction raises serious ethical problems.

What is known about the possibility of error in predicting who is likely to offend again? First, there is the problem of the "false positives," that is the problem of "imprisoning persons because of a prediction that they will commit crimes in the future when in fact they would not commit any." The error in prediction is high. In one reported study 86 per cent of those identified as violent and likely to commit further offences, did not.[29] In another study, involving parolees, for every parolee identified correctly as likely to commit a crime of violence, 326 were incorrectly identified.[30] In the rather more well-known case relating to Patuxent Hospital, the court found that 421 patients were wrongfully detained in a psychiatric institution and ordered their release. Psychiatric staff opposed the releases of 28 per cent of these patients, predicting that they were likely to commit a further criminal offence. Exhaustive follow-up studies showed that the psychiatric staff were wrong two times out of three.[31] After a careful review of reports and studies dealing with prediction, Monahan[32] concludes that there is clear and convincing evidence that neither psychiatrists nor anyone else is able to accurately predict dangerousness. A similar conclusion with respect to prediction was reached by Peter Mcnaughton-Smith in his study of Canadian Parole Board decisions: the outcomes would not be much different if arrived at by lottery.[33]

There is also some practical experience upon which to draw. The California Parole Commission used prediction tables as an aid in determining which prisoners shall be released on parole. Admitting that it had no capacity to predict who was ready for release in a rehabilitative sense, the Board decided to adopt release criteria based on likelihood of committing further offences.[34] Following this approach a guideline was established consisting of a potential for recidivism factor and an offence severity factor. These factors were projected onto a two dimensional table indicating an offender prognosis rating. In predicting potential recidivism the table relies heavily on prior convictions and prior committals to institutions. Several socioeconomic factors are also used but have a relatively low predictive capacity.

This predictive device appears to work reasonably well in California, but its validity for use in other parts of the country or for use in pre-sentence reports is suspect as the device is vulnerable to changes in the population culture. One of the criticisms of these predictive tables is that weighting of factors to each individual case is sacrificed to general policies relating to protection, deterrence and so on. Other criticisms question the accuracy of the predictive tables and their validity over a long term. There can be no doubt, however, that prediction tables tend to bring greater uniformity and consistency to decision-making. At the present time, considerable thought is being given to adapting predictive tables as a major aid in sentencing at the judicial level.[35]

This move is based on the assumption that although courts may lack the capacity to predict selectively in the individual case, they can predict in the mass. The argument is that crime rates could be reduced by X per cent, for example, if all offenders convicted of a given class of offences were imprisoned for a given term of years. This proposition has also been subject to some analysis.[36]

The studies referred to were done in the United States and focused on FBI

Index Crimes. In one study of juvenile offenders it was estimated that a policy of imprisoning all juveniles convicted of Index Crimes for a period of nine months would reduce the crime for those offenders by one to four per cent.[37]

In a different study Greenberg estimated that if prisons were eliminated entirely index crimes would increase by 1.2 to 8.0 per cent, and that increasing the average prison term from two years to three years would result in a decrease of index crime rates of from 0.6 to 4.0 per cent.[38]

Other studies suggest that the rate of serious crime could be reduced in New York State to one-third its potential level by imposing a 3-year prison term on every offender convicted of a serious offence and making sure there was at least one year and one-half in between convictions.[39] As Cohen points out, one of the problems with such studies is that little is known about the rate at which convicted persons commit crimes; another problem is the assumption that police will be able to increase their apprehension rate, for clearance rates have remained relatively stable over the years; similarly so have conviction rates. In short, the criminal justice system may be relatively inelastic and incapable of bringing about dramatic changes in arrest, conviction and imprisonment rates — and without such drastic changes crime rates are not subject to manipulation through incapacitation.

In concluding her analysis of these studies for the National Research Council Panel, Jacqueline Cohen states: "All authors considered would generally agree that the present incapacitative effect of prison is minimal."[40] It would appear that attempts to increase the incapacitating effects of prison are highly speculative and likely to be very costly. Adoption of incapacitation as a serious goal in sentencing policy would mean adopting mandatory imprisonment for selected types of offences, with all the inequities implicit in that approach; changes in prosecutorial policies and practices in an attempt to increase conviction and clearance rates; and adoption of a billion dollar prison building program.[41] Simply to raise these issues suggests that such a sentencing policy may be unrealistic and carry unacceptable cost implications, both financial and human.

The question of cost is not irrelevant to the administration of justice. Sentencing policies and practices must appear not only to be rational and just but socially useful. If current prison sentences cannot be justified for their rehabilitative, deterrent or incapacitating effects, what is their justification? It appears that the only justification left is that of punishment — retribution or denunciation. Prisons are places of pain and shame. That being the case, what financial and social costs is society prepared to bear simply to impose pain and shame on others by means of using prisons?

An illustration of the cost of imprisonment in non-violent offences against property is given in Table 1.[42] It represents the costs for only one of six correctional divisions in British Columbia.

Table 1

COST OF IMPRISONMENT (NON-VIOLENT OFFENCES AGAINST
PROPERTY)

(Vancouver Island, B.C., 1977-78)

Offence	Average Daily Prison Beds	Sample Size	Sentence* Average Length (days)	Annual Cost (Salary and Non-Salary)	Cost per* Sentence
Breaking and Entering	38.2	193	72.2	$610,459	$3,163
Possession of Housebreaking Instruments	2.2	8	100.3	39,946	4,993
Possession of Stolen Property	11.4	74	56.2	188,221	2,543
Theft (Conversion)	0.3	3	36.5	5,933	1,977
Theft (Over $200)	11.9	76	57.1	184,014	2,421
Theft (Under $200)	7.8	98	29.0	128,091	1,307
False Pretences	5.1	43	43.2	83,893	1,951
Forgery and Altering	3.4	16	77.5	61,221	3,826
Fraud (Food and Lodging)	2.0	20	45.6	33,350	1,667
Fraud (Public)	1.6	16	36.5	30,480	1,905
Total	83.9			$1,365,608	

*Estimated by the author using the data supplied.

The cost of imprisonment in cases of breaking and entering should be considered in the light of recent research on residential burglaries in Toronto. Waller and Okihiro[43] report that the average property loss arising from goods stolen in residential burglaries is approximately $300.[44] The cost of repairing property damaged in breaking and entering generally amounted to less than $50,[45] and related to replacing a broken window pane or damaged door. Commercial burglaries, it is expected, would involve losses of a higher order, although, to a greater extent than in residential burglaries, insurance would likely provide one mode of compensation.[46] Waller and Okihiro report that victims of residential burglaries, generally were not vindictive,[47] and approximately two-thirds of those victims who received no insurance compensation said they would have been willing to settle the incident out of court.[48] Approximately 80 per cent of victims favoured a non-custodial sentence.[49] Non-victims tended to be somewhat more punitive.

Although empirical data is not available for theft and other non-violent offences listed, it may be assumed that the property losses, with the exception of public fraud and forgery, are below those in breaking and entering. With respect to theft under 200 dollars, most of the cases probably arise out of shoplifting where the goods are recovered and where the average value of the merchandise is less than $50.[50]

Is the marginal increase in deterrence or incapacitation afforded by imprisonment over fines or probation economically justifiable? Should some real effort be made in reforming sentencing practices so as to reduce what appears to be an unnecessary and costly use of imprisonment?

It would appear that the determination of which offenders deserve the pain and shame of prisons is largely a moral judgment made by the judge with one eye to past practices and another to the feelings of the community as revealed in the submissions of the Crown prosecutor, letters from private citizens or even newspaper editorials. The judgment at bottom is political, in the broad sense, and not legal. A growing body of research in the social sciences tends to undermine the apparent judicial and objective nature of sentencing decisions and reveals instead the subjective and consensual aspect of those decisions. John Hogarth in his widely recognized work, *Sentencing as a Human Process*[51] showed the relationship between sentencing and judges' personal values and attitudes. Other studies suggest that stressful decisions tend to be made on a consensus basis.[52] Sentencing is a good example, for on being faced with the possibility of imposing imprisonment, a judge might well be expected to seek a consensus decision by asking for advice from the probation officer, Crown counsel and hear representations from the accused. This, at first, seems to be no more than a realistic approach. Yet the consensus approach probably does little to enhance the quality of decision-making where each consultant in turn is responding to institutional pressures or unquestioned practice and where in relation to pre-sentence reports, at least, there is some evidence suggesting that the additional information tends to increase the number of inconsistent decisions.[53] In the United States the current concern to structure or even curtail judicial discretion in sentencing[54] is based in part upon the realization that sentencing is marked by inequitable disparities rooted in judicial attitudes. There the emphasis is to ensure greater equity and equality in imposing prison terms, both as to their length in similar circumstances and as to parole release. The real problem, however, is not equal prison sentences but ensuring that prison sentences in cases of non-violent offences against property are, as a general rule, not imposed at all.

Experience also suggests that sentencing in Canada is not immune[55] to pressure from some parts of the public for more punitive measures. To the extent that judges and Crown prosecutors accede to this pressure and ignore issues of cost, purpose and justice as outlined earlier, sentencing will appear to be "political" and not "legal" and in so doing will lose legitimacy and respect. This risk can and should be avoided. The judge expresses the voice of reason and restraint, and since sentencing ought to be an educative ritual for the benefit of the whole community, the judge ought to address himself in public, in the reasons for sentence, to issues of deterrence, incapacitation and punishment, to the costs and limits of these objectives, and to alternatives to imprisonment that may serve equally well. The public is entitled to a statement, at sentencing, showing that the demand for pain and shame through the prisons has low social utility and is purchased only at a high cost, a cost that is out of proportion, in most cases, to the amount of harm done in the offence itself. It would seem that Crown prosecutors and defence counsel have an ethical and professional responsibility to assist the judge in reforming sentencing practices by addressing themselves to these issues as well.

Society has a right to expect that the knowledge of social sciences be reflected in the sentencing practices of the provincial magistrates' courts — courts where over 80 per cent of cases end in guilty pleas so that these courts, in effect, are largely sentencing courts. Yet to what extent are sentencing submissions based upon false assumptions or unfounded dogmatic beliefs about rehabilitation, deterrence or public protection? Faced with the collapse of the rehabilitative ideal and of the prison itself, how far have Crown prosecutors and defence counsel gone in attempting to present the court with innovative sentencing alternatives? As a spur to finding such alternatives, should it be a required part of the Crown's submission on sentencing to include an estimate of the cost of any proposed prison term? If nothing else, taking account of such data would increase rationality and accountability in sentencing.

The burden of reducing the large numbers of prison terms for non-violent offenders rests, then, with the judges. Such a reduction will necessarily be tempered by the community's level of tolerance, the availability of acceptable sentencing alternatives and the judge's own attitudes. What is the situation in Canada with respect to these three variables, and, is it likely that the courts will reform sentencing practices for non-violent offenders?

While the question poses a theme for a major paper in itself, it is possible to make some tentative observations. First, the community's level of tolerance is probably considerably greater with respect to non-violent offenders than violent offenders, and probably is higher than current sentencing practices reflect. While the community may well feel that offenders inflicting serious bodily injury on others should be sent to prison, the same feeling does not exist with respect to offenders who pose no serious threat to public safety and are a nuisance and an annoyance rather than a serious risk.

In assessing the level of community tolerance a distinction ought to be drawn between tolerance and punitiveness. What a community feels it can live with, considering estimated costs and benefits, is likely to be considerably different from what the various members of the community may demand, in the abstract, by way of punishment. This should not be surprising since similar gaps between realistic assessment and wishful thinking is common experience in all areas of life and law.

It should be noted as well that demands for punishment in the abstract may be motivated largely by the individual's "image" of the crime concerned. He may have the worst possible circumstance in mind and be governed by stereotypes that bear little relation to 98 per cent of offences. On the other hand, victims' reactions are less likely to be governed by the "image" of the crime but focused concretely on actual circumstances. Does this probable difference in perception explain why victims tend to be less punitive that those who experience the crime vicariously?[56]

As already noted, Okihiro and Waller in their recent study of residential burglary, found that victims tended to be less punitive than non-victims. They also noted that insured victims tended to be less punitive than uninsured victims, suggesting that compensation may often remove the sting from the offence — something policy planning personnel in departments of government may be able to incorporate into victim compensation schemes.

It is the writer's experience, as well, in discussing sentencing policy in various communities throughout Ontario, British Columbia and elsewhere, that there has been a widespread recognition, at the community level, and by those working in corrections, that alternatives must be found to imprisonment for non-violent offenders.

Opportunities for communities to assist in the reform of sentencing practices should not be overlooked. Native people's organizations and women's groups particularly may be in a position to assist the court in developing and supervising suitable programs that could serve as alternatives to imprisonment for non-violent offenders. Organizations such as John Howard, traditionally concerned about prisons, should be expected to assist the courts and bar in devising proper alternatives and thereby reducing the jail population. There are those who doubt that the public will accept more non-custodial sentences; these persons point to public hostility to half-way houses proposed for location in particular neighbourhoods. Such hostility has often been noted in the press and is well known to those attempting to reform corrections. Yet a distinction should be drawn between an institution or a facility and a program. A work program as a condition of a probation order, or otherwise, permits the sentenced person to commute from his home. No hostel, half-way house or camp facility is needed. In the absence of a visible physical prison in the neighbourhood, public hostility to alternatives to imprisonment is unlikely to develop. Indeed, it is likely that jail populations could be cut in half with little or no protest from the community. In short, it is unlikely that failure to reform sentencing practices or laws respecting non-violent offenders against property can be blamed on the bogey-man of a "red-necked," intolerant public.

Secondly, as to the availability of alternatives to short prison terms, stiff fines and probation, with or without supervision, could no doubt be used more than they are. Both involve a degree of pain, inconvenience and shame, not only as a result of the arrest and trial but from the sentence as well. It is surprising to see an offender's criminal record printed out and note that his first conviction for theft, for example, resulted in a prison term. Such sentencing practices are more likely to ensure a growth in the crime rate than a reduction. Judges, Crown counsel and probation officers may not be fully aware themselves of the degree to which non-prison sentences could be used. It would be instructive to have a computer print-out of sentences imposed in any given court for any given month to give some understanding of how much scope there is for increased use of fines and probation. It should not be surprising to find, as John Hogarth and others have, that some courts use probation or fines two or three times more frequently than neighbouring courts dealing with similar offences.

Hogarth reported, for example, in 1964 that the range in sentencing practices by judicial district in Ontario for indictable offences was large, with some districts reporting never to use probation and others reporting probation in 43 per cent of cases. The disparity in use of imprisonment ranged from 60 per cent in one district to 4 per cent in another.[57] Jobson, reporting on sentencing practices in Nova Scotia and New Brunswick in 1967, found a wide disparity in use of imprisonment, with one provincial court showing 26 per cent of breaking and entering cases dealt with by imprisonment and another court handling a similar number of cases using imprisonment in 65 per cent of the cases.[58] Disparities in New Brunswick courts in dealing with cases of petty theft indicated once more, large and surprising variation in the use of imprisonment: ranging from 0 per cent in some courts to 75 per cent in another. These practices reflect an elasticity in sentencing practices and suggest the possibility of a large reduction in the use of imprisonment in non-violent offences against property.

Data from 1973 continues to reflect a high use of imprisonment in this type of case. In British Columbia, for example, imprisonment was used in 56 per cent of cases of breaking and entering, 27 per cent of thefts, frauds and false pretences, and 61 per cent of forgeries.[59]

In 1976, of the 3419 admissions of sentenced offenders to provincial institutions in Canada, 68.5 per cent were in relation to offences against property with breaking and entering accounting for 34 per cent and theft, 10.6 per cent.[60] It is difficult to reconcile the above statistics with the often heard judicial comment that no one is sent to jail except as a last resort. The "last resort" in these cases can hardly be the need for public protection since the length of the terms is too short to allow for any significant incapacitating effect. For example, in the Maritime Provinces in 1976, 80 per cent of offenders sentenced to provincial or local jails spent less than 31 days in custody and 22 per cent spent less than five days.[61]

Some appreciation of what the judges have in mind when they speak of imprisonment as a last resort can be gained by examining sentencing decisions. Among the Unreported Decisions, Sentencing, for British Columbia, 1978, are a handful of sentencing appeals including the following randomly selected examples:

Case A

Sentence of two years less a day upheld as appropriate; accused was convicted of breaking and entering a business premises at night; he was 25 years old and had a conviction for theft five years ago.

Case B

Sentence of two years less a day reduced to one year; the accused and his friend were convicted of breaking and entering seven business places in order to get parts to be used in fixing a car; the friend was sentenced to 18 months; accused had a reasonable work record, was on probation for theft but had not been in jail before, and was 18 years old.

Case C

Sentence of six months for stealing a chain saw was upheld in view of the accused's past record; he had spent the last 17 years in jail and out of jail; he had a substantial alcohol problem and lived in a far northern community.

Case D

Sentence of three years imprisonment upheld on a conviction of breaking and entering and possession of a stolen truck from out-of-the-province; accused had a "lengthy" record, was 19 years old, and was said to be a "persistent criminal" from whom the public was in need of protection.

Case E

Sentence of six months definite and 9 months indefinite upheld; accused was 18 years old but had a "lengthy" juvenile record; he was convicted of breaking and entering business premises and stealing $1000 worth of stereo equipment; he was on probation at the time and the court stated that the accused had to be taught a lesson.

Case F

Sentence of six months varied to 3 months to be served on weekends, plus a fine; accused convicted of theft of $600 worth of goods and a truck with which to transport those goods to use in a boat he was building; accused had no prior record, had a good job, was a recent immigrant and had acted "out of character."

Admittedly, an examination of the complete record would reveal additional helpful facts, but even so there is room for substantial disagreement about whether cases such as the above show that all other sentencing alternatives have been tried and that imprisonment is the last and necessary resort. These cases reveal imprisonment being used for a number of reasons: to "teach young people a lesson;" for incapacitating purposes — public protection; and as a means of coping with intractable social problems that manifest themselves in minor crime.

It is suggested, however, that Case D alone should be seriously considered for imprisonment; the accused's record appears to be strong evidence suggesting a need for a measure of public protection, but a protection that should be met only within the limits of a retributive sentence. By contrast, it is doubtful whether courts should absorb into the criminal justice system problems better dealt with by health or social welfare, nor is there much evidence to show that prisons "teach people a lesson." Indeed, if lessons are learned in prisons, we are told by experienced correctional officers and ex-prisoners, that they are usually bad lessons. Nor is it easy to understand why thoughtless and selfish conduct such as that displayed in Cases B, E and F should warrant imprisonment rather than a variation of conditions of probation to include a substantial work order of the kind referred to later. It appears that the trial judge, faced with a breach of probation, and seeing probation as a simple reporting order, felt he must now try the only other alternative — imprisonment. Yet sentencing judges and the Court of Appeal know that the use of imprisonment as outlined above will have little, if any, measurable effect on the crime rate. Granted, a case may be made for the incapaciting effects of imprisonment, particularly in Case D, but, in general, the outside observer can't help wondering whether the high use of imprisonment as outlined earlier isn't largely the result of unexamined past practice and inertia at all levels of what is increasingly a bureaucratic sentencing system — an inertia and lack of innovation that affects the court, the prosecution, defence counsel, police and probation staff alike.

If imprisonment is to be used less frequently in these cases, the only practical alternatives are increased use of fines and more imaginative use of probation orders and community service.

One objection to greater use of fines may be the inability of offenders to pay. Already the default rate on fines is approximately 10 per cent and increased use of fines may increase that percentage. It should be kept in mind, however, that with the growing use of Fine Option programs, offenders who find themselves in default need not go to jail but may elect to work off the fine doing community service at the minimum wage rates.[62]

Probation, too, could be used more extensively through the use of a probation work order, that is to say, as a condition of probation, the offender could choose to engage in a work program, for example, in forestry or fisheries reclamation. Such programs would include tree thinning, planting and other forestry services. It might be objected that such terms of a probation order are unreasonable,[63] but as long as they are consented to by the probationer and as long as he can opt out of the program and come back to the court to have the conditions varied, they should be seen as a rational alternative to the destructive and idle conditions that pervade most jails. In any event, Work Orders should be available as a sentence in their own right. These proposed work orders, presumably, would be along the lines of the probation-work order sketched above, and should be seen as requiring a much more substantial work program than has currently evolved under the community service orders.[64] If Work Orders are to develop as an alternative sentence, they should be kept short, reflecting the short nature of the jail terms they are to replace. Moreover, because the work involved is likely to be arduous, it is suggested that a three month order should be the equivalent of a six month jail term.

To a significant extent, in some provinces at least, the kind of work contemplated here is already being carried out in forestry camps as part of a jail sentence. This shows that there is ample work to be done and appropriate consultations can be carried on with industry and labour to ensure their understanding and co-operation. Organized labour is not likely to be concerned unless such work programs make major inroads into work usually done by the organized work force. With proper planning and consultation potential problems are likely to be avoided.

The advantage of using probation work orders rather than jail terms are several: it reduces the general level of punitiveness; it gets away from the necessity of a physical prison or camp and permits the offender to live at home, retaining a close relationship with his family and community; it encourages the community to take some responsibility in dealing with crime and corrections; in addition, such sentences should be less costly than prison terms.

There is some risk associated with any attempt to reduce imprisonment: the alternative sentencing program will tend to be used by judges not so much as an alternative to imprisonment but as an alternative to existing non-custodial sentences. Experience with probation itself has been disheartening in this respect. Rather than simple suspended sentence without probation in the common law tradition, or adjournments *sine die,* or postponing sentence pending an extended sentencing investigation, more and more convicted persons were put under the public supervision of probation officers: judges tended to use probation as a means of "hardening" sentencing practices while the prison population remained relatively stable.[65]

It appears, then, that there is ample room for decreasing the extent to which sentences of imprisonment are imposed. How likely is it that the lower court judges will reform sentencing practices as suggested? The answer to this question may be found by turning to the courts' past record, to the likelihood of individual judges changing their attitudes to imprisonment, and by examining the nature of the court as an administrative system capable of generating internal pressures for reform and resisting pressures from other parts of the system — probation, police and prosecutors — for increased imprisonment.

The lower courts have an honourable tradition of reform in sentencing that reaches back to benefit of clergy as a means of avoiding the hangman's noose; probation itself; suspended sentence, including a now defunct practice of adjourning *sine die* pending disposition; and, more recently, community service orders, an innovation that developed and spread from the lower courts on Vancouver Island. Yet, side by side with this spirit of innovation and reform, there flourishes another strain of judicial behaviour — a strain characterized by a jealous territorial imperative in sentencing matters and a resistance to suggestions made from outside the courts themselves: witness the response a few years back to a federal Department of Justice initiative encouraging judges to use discharges in marijuana cases. Granted, the courts have every right to safeguard their independence against executive encroachment; yet their response to the federal initiative was intensely conservative. In a similar vein, there is antipathy in the courts to pre-trial diversion — an exercise of prosecutorial discretion designed to permit a social rather than legal resolution of selected non-serious cases that would otherwise be prosecuted. The British Columbia Court of Appeal recently decided that the fact of a prior diversion is reason enough for a sentencing court to refuse to discharge on a later offence. This decision will have the unfortunate effect of discouraging diversion and turning it into a formal part of the criminal justice machinery. It reflects a pre-disposition for legalism, a distrust of social solutions, and a tendency to "harden" penal sanctions.

There may be other evidence that the lower courts are unwilling to reform past practices. For three or four years the courts in Canada have heard proposals from various sources respecting non-violent offenders, similar to the proposal being put forward here, but they have shown little indication of responding to the challenge facing them. Indeed, the courts' response to the proposals of the Law Reform Commission of Canada[66] revealed a combined measure of hostility and indifference. It is not only the lower courts in Canada that have demonstrated an unwillingness to reform practices in this area. Recently, in England, Parliament changed sentencing laws so as to restrict the power of courts to pass terms of imprisonment of six months or less. Parliamentary objectives, apparently, were frustrated by courts simply increasing the number of sentences imposed for more than six months.[67] It may be said that "law and order" was an issue in the recent election in that country and if the courts have increased the length of prison sentences, they have the "people" behind them. To attempt to justify sentencing practices on these grounds, however, is simply to reveal the highly "political" nature of the sentencing process. In the United States, so great is the lack of confidence in the power of the courts to reform their sentencing practices that most proposals for reform currently under consideration call for a greatly reduced scope to judicial discretion in sentencing.

Perhaps one should not be surprised by the courts' apparent unwillingness to change sentencing practices in relation to imprisonment. As indicated earlier, sentencing is a highly individual matter depending in a large part on the basic attitudes and values of the particular judge. It is not a simple matter to change attitudes. The ordinary man is likely to say, "If you can't change the attitudes and behaviour of offenders in an institution with all the high-powered expertise of psychologists and classification officers combined with other state powers and pressures, how can you expect judges or even Crown prosecutors to change their attitudes?"

Behavioural scientists would point out what many people would corroborate from personal experience. Incumbents of an institution such as the court are less likely to change attitudes where those same attitudes are supported outside the institution by a measure of public opinion and where there is no real inducement inside the institution itself to change. There would be less reinforcement for unnecessary and costly use of imprisonment were the public better informed about costs and the limited return that can be expected from imprisonment. In this sense "imprisonment" connotes meanings and gives rise to expectations that are almost mythical to the extent in which they depart from reality. It must be observed that members of the legal profession and the police themselves are in part held captive by these myths and play an important role in reinforcing judicial use of imprisonment. Presumably, however, the judge is aware of the myths. Must he not expose them, or is his role to avoid rocking boats and to steer for calm waters? When assumptions underlying a given set of attitudes or a given use of discretion no longer hold, can an office holder continue to exercise discretion as though nothing had changed?

As an administrative structure the court does not provide much opportunity for institutional direction or leadership in reforming sentencing practices. To begin with, there is no systematic effort to provide the court with the kind of statistical data or its analysis even of an elementary nature as provided, for example, by the Administrative Office of the United States Courts. As a result, the sentencing courts are lacking in one of the first principles of accountability: informed feedback on current practices. Second, there is no provision for promulgation of administrative guidelines by the chief judge of the court to assist lower court judges in reforming sentencing practices. Instead, precedents must be found piecemeal in individual cases taken on appeal. While sentence appeals by either Crown or the accused in indictable offences go to the ten-man Court of Appeal in the province, appeals on summary conviction proceedings go to the County Courts or their equivalents. Thus, sentencing appeals are dispersed. Moreover, the Chief Justice of the Court of Appeal has no traditional or statutory authority to impose his views or leadership on the Court. If reform of sentencing practice is to come about through the Court of Appeal, it must be by way of mutual agreement among the appeal court judges. The weakness of the appeal process can be further measured from the fact that in 1973, for example, out of 71,600 cases dealt with in criminal courts in British Columbia, 443 resulted in sentence appeals; 329 were dismissed, 118 allowed.[68] Recorded appeals against sentence in breaking and entering, theft and other non-violent offences against property, for the most part, reveal terms of 12 months or more, and, generally, cases involving three or more previous convictions. Few sentences of six months or less are taken on appeal. This means that for most offenders sentenced for non-violent offences against property, the wide sentencing discretion in the hands of the trial judge is not subjected to rational, objective review. It survives unscathed, a reflection of express or felt needs of police and Crown prosecutors looking for "deterrence," probation officers at wits' end and looking for a solution to troublesome cases, a community impatient with law breakers, and the courts' own felt need to follow past practices.

On the positive side, judges do meet together from time to time to discuss sentencing matters and express an interest in improving what is being done.

Indeed, it was in an address at such a gathering of County Court Judges that the Chief Justice of British Columbia offered some useful and perceptive comments on the purposes of sentencing.[69] Judged by past experience, however, such meetings are not an effective instrument in sentencing reform. Even more elaborate attempts at reform of sentencing practices, such as Sentencing Councils and sentencing conferences, with experience, have proved to be of limited value in reducing sentencing disparities or in developing reform.[70] It would appear that mere opportunity to consider different approaches in sentencing is not enough to change sentencing behaviour. Perhaps the only institutional response that can be effective in bringing about such change is a risk that the sentence will be upset on appeal. At present, in Canada, for the class of offenders under discussion, that risk is almost nil.

Even if the appeal process could be opened up by way of sentencing guidelines from the Courts of Appeal and a new determination by Legal Aid Societies to appeal sentences involving short terms of imprisonment,[71] sentencing practices are not likely to change unless community agencies and probation staff develop innovative alternative programs for use by the courts. Moreover, until Crown prosecutors change past practices, judges may not be able to resist felt pressures from other segments of the criminal justice system for sentences of imprisonment.

If the courts are unable to reform their sentencing practices they may end up losing a large part of the sentencing business to other legal institutions. It has happened before; where the courts were not able to accommodate their decision-making to the changing social and economic needs of the day, boards and tribunals have been created by the legislatures to deal with specific classes of problems such as Workers' Compensation, Labor Relations, Unemployment Insurance, Compensation to Victims of Crime, and so on. The day of the Sentencing Commission may not be all that distant.

NOTES

1. To emphasize the need for reform of sentencing policy and practice in relation to non-violent offenders is not to belittle in any way the importance of reforming other aspects of sentencing laws. Penitentiary terms, for example, continue to create a major sentencing issue not only because of their greater length but also because of the conditions under which such sentences are served. Penitentiary terms, more so than short terms of imprisonment for non-violent offenders, give rise to more visible abuses of human rights and the rule of law. The destructive effect of penitentiary terms still rings in our ears through the words of the *Report to Parliament* by the Sub-Committee on the Penitentiary System in Canada (Ottawa: 1977, p. 156):

> From the inmate's perspective, . . . imprisonment in Canada, where it is not simply inhumane, is the most individually destructive, psychologically

crippling and socially alienating experience that could conceivably exist within the borders of the country.

2. Statistics Canada, "Statistics of Criminal and Other Offences," 1972, Table 1.

3. *Ibid.* Tables 6A and 6B. In 1972, 11.2 per cent of all prison terms were imposed for offences against the person.

4. *Ibid.* Tables 6A and 6B. In 1972, 61.7 per cent of all persons were imprisoned for "non-violent offences against property" as outlined above.

5. Statistics received from the Department of Attorney General, Victoria, B.C., 1979; see also *Rapport Annuel,* 1977 (Quebec: Department of Justice, Quebec, 1978), p. 52.

6. Estimate arrived at by the writer using the statistics supplied to the writer by the Department of the Attorney General (Victoria: B.C., 1979).

7. *Ibid.*

8. W. Black, and J. Weiler, *Report on British Columbia Correctional Institutions,* unpublished (The Justice Development Commission, Department of the Attorney General, Victoria, B.C., 1977).

9. *The Role of Federal Corrections in Canada,* A Report of the Task Force on the Creation of An Integrated Canadian Corrections Service (Ottawa: Department of the Solicitor General, 1977), p. 29.

10. *Ibid.,* p. 25.

11. Robert Martinson, "What Works? — Questions and Answers About Prison Reform," 35 *The Public Interest* 22-54 (1974).

12. Norval Morris, *The Future of Imprisonment* (Chicago: University of Chicago Press, 1974).

13. Irwin Waller, *Men Released from Prison* (Toronto: University of Toronto Press, 1974).

14. Peter Macnaughton-Smith, *Permission to be Slightly Free* (Ottawa: Law Reform Commission of Canada, 1976).

15. *Op. cit.,* note 13, p. 206.

16. *Op. cit.,* note 14, p. 125.

17. Clayton Ruby, *Sentencing* (Butterworths, Toronto, 1976), p. 13.

18. See Daniel Nagin, "General Deterrence: A Review of the Empirical Evidence," *Deterrence and Incapacitation: Estimating the Effects of Criminal Sanctions on Crime Rates,* A. Blumstein, and J. Cohen, (eds.), Panel on Research on Deterrent and Incapacitative Effects, National Research Council (Washington: 1978), pp. 95-159. See also Fattah et al., *Fear of Punishment: Deterrence* (Ottawa: Law Reform Commission of Canada, 1976).

19. "Report of the Panel," *Deterrence and Incapacitation: Estimating the Effects of Criminal Sanctions on Crime Rates, supra,* note 18, hereafter referred to as the Panel Report, at p. 47:

> Our reluctance to assert that the evidence warrants an affirmative conclusion regarding deterrence derives from the limited validity of the available evidence

and the number of competing explanations for the results.

It is also important to recognize that our reluctance to draw stronger conclusions does not imply support for a position that there are no deterrent effects: the evidence certainly favours a proposition supporting deterrence more than it favours one asserting that deterrence is absent. Furthermore, the Panel is convinced on *a priori* grounds that criminal sanctions do influence at least some criminal behaviour by some individuals.

20. Statistics Canada, Crime and Traffic Enforcement Statistics, Catalog 85-205, annual, 1975, p. 59, for example. Waller and Okihiro, *Burglary: The Victim and the Public* (Toronto: University of Toronto Press, 1978), p. 85, states that the clearance rate for burglary in Toronto was only 10 per cent.

21. Statistics Canada, Statistics of Criminal and Other Offences, Catalogue No. 85-201, Annual, 1972, Tables 6A and 6B.

22. John Farris, "Sentencing" (1975-76) 18 *Cr. L.Q.* 421, at 424.

23. The Panel Report, *op. cit.,* note 18, p. 64.

24. J. Cohen, "The Incapacitative Effect of Imprisonment: A Critical Review of the Literature" in *Deterrence and Incapacitation: Estimating the Effects of Criminal Sanctions on Crime Rates, supra,* note 18, pp. 187-243.

25. *Ibid.,* Table 5, p. 226. Index crimes include homicide, non-negligent manslaughter, rape, robbery. aggravated assault, burglary, larceny over $50 and auto theft.

26. Andrew Von Hirsch, *Doing Justice* (New York: Hill & Wang, 1974), pp. 3, 15. After discussing the large errors made in predicting which offender is likely to commit a further offence, Von Hirsch concludes at p. 26:

> But predictive restraint poses ethical problems . . . moreover one may question whether it is ever just to *punish* someone severely for what he is expected to do, even if the prediction was accurate.

H.L.A. Hart, in *Punishment and Responsibility* (Oxford: Clarendon Press, 1968), p. 25, discusses the problem of increasing the punishment merely for rehabilitative purposes or corrective training or preventive detention, and states that laws or practices permitting a penal sanction that is disproportionate to the offence committed violates principles of justice.

27. British Columbia Unreported Decisions, Sentencing, 1978. In the particular case the Court of Appeal upheld a six month prison term. Such a sentence might be defended on the ground that it is "proportional" to the harm done, and, therefore, justifiable within the parameters of Justice. Nevertheless, the court could also have imposed a fine or probation but in all likelihood was influenced toward imprisonment because of the strong possibility of the offender committing further offences. As Hart pointed out, where sentence is disproportionate to the harm done, justice is violated.

28. John Monahan, "The Prediction of Violent Criminal Behaviour: A Methodological Critique and Prospectus," in *Deterrence and Incapacitation:*

Estimating the Effects of Criminal Sanctions on Crime Rates, op. cit., note 18, pp. 244-269. See also Von Hirsch, *op. cit.,* note 26 at pp. 19-26. Waller, also found that prediction by the Parole Board was open to question: *supra,* note 13, pp. 109-110.

29. E. Wenk, J. Robinson and G. Smith, "Can Violence be Predicted?" 18 *Crime and Delinquency* 393-402 (1972).

30. *Ibid.*

31. H. Kozol, R. Boucher, and R. Garofalo, "The Diagnosis and Treatment of Dangerousness," (1972) 18 *Crime and Delinquency* 371-392 (1972).

32. Monahan, *op. cit.,* note 28.

33. *Op. cit.,* note 14, sections 12 and 13.

34. John C. Coffee, "The Repressed Issues of Sentencing: Accountability, Predictability, and Equality in the Era of Sentencing Commissions," 66 *Georgetown L. Jo.* 975-1107 at 990 (1978).

35. *Ibid.* L.T. Wilkins, et al., *Sentencing Guidelines: Structuring Sentencing Discretion* (Albany, New York: Criminal Justice Research Centre, 1976).

36. J. Cohen, "The Incapacitative Effect of Imprisonment: A Critical Review of the Literature," in *Deterrence and Incapacitation: Estimating the Effects of Criminal Sanctions on Crime Rates, op. cit.,* note 18, pp. 187-232.

37. S. Clarke, "Getting 'em Out of Circulation: Does the Incarceration of Juvenile Offenders Reduce Crimes?" 65 *Jo. of Criminal Law and Criminology* 4, pp. 528-535 (1974).

38. D. Greenberg, "The Incapacitative Effect of Imprisonment: Some Estimates" 9 *Law and Society Rev.* 541-580 (1975).

39. R. Shinnar, and S. Shinnar, "The Effects of the Criminal Justice System on the Control of Crime: A Quantitative Approach," 9 *Law and Society Rev.* 4, pp. 581-611 (1975).

40. *Op. cit.,* note 36, at p. 209.

41. This is an estimate based on the assumption that prison bed space would have to be tripled if incapacitation is adopted as a goal in sentencing non-violent offenders against property.

42. Statistics supplied by the Department of the Attorney General, Victoria, B.C., May, 1979.

43. *Op. cit.,* note 20.

44. *Ibid.,* p. 3.

45. *Ibid.,* p. 30.

46. *Ibid.* Waller and Okihiro discuss insurance as an aid to victims and by implication suggest greater use of insurance would reduce victims' annoyance or anger. Insurance coverage appears to affect the way the victim perceives the offence: pp. 90, 93-96. In only 50 per cent of the cases where goods were taken was recovery made or compensation received: *Ibid.,* p. 47.

47. *Ibid.,* p. 89, 90.

48. *Ibid.,* p. 47.

49. *Ibid.,* p. 90.

50. C. Kehler, T. Lajeunesse, and S. Manning, "Crown Discretion"

(Victoria, B.C.: Faculty of Law, University of Victoria, 1977), unpublished. The study included an examination of crown discretion in minor offences against property during the month of July, 1977. An examination of 73 crown files relating to such prosecutions led to the authors' comment at p. 32:

> What is surprising in the above table is the large number of minor cases — none of the property cases involved losses of more than $200 and no more than 11 could have involved losses in excess of $100. It is surprising to see the number of trivial cases involving losses of $2.38, $1.85, $1.19, $3.53 and so on. In this connection it is worth remembering that even on a Guilty Plea it costs approximately $500 to get a conviction. It is also worth remembering that the provincial courts are so busy that cases involving a preliminary hearing and subsequent trial have to wait up to five months to be disposed of.

51. *Sentencing As a Human Process* (Toronto: University of Toronto Press, 1971).

52. I. Janis, and L. Man, *Decision-Making: A Psychological Analysis of Conflict, Choice, and Commitment* (New York: Free Press, 1977).

53. See, Coffee, *op. cit.,* note 34, 984.

54. Senate Bill 1437, 95th Cong. 2d Sess. (1978). The Bill would require judges to give reasons should a sentence fall beyond prescribed guidelines, provide a degree of appellate review of sentences, and, more controversially, establish a sentencing commission to set up guidelines and ranges of appropriate sentences in classes of offences. For an earlier critical review see M. Frankel, *Criminal Sentences: Law Without Order* (New York: Hill & Wang, 1973). See also Wilkins, *op. cit.,* note 35.

55. It is not unusual for judges to note that there has been an increase in this or that type of offence in passing a higher than usual sentence in a given case. Crown counsel, too, appeal against sentences they feel are too low. Perhaps the most widely known recent case arousing public comment was the decision to sentence a well-known musician convicted on a charge of possession of heroin, to give a rock concert to the blind. Usually imprisonment would be imposed in such cases.

The recent move in British Columbia to build jails for juveniles and to pass the Containment legislation arose in part from pressure from police and some communities outside the metropolitan areas which did not have a variety of social services to deal with troublesome juveniles. Judges, it is reported, withheld sentencing pending the opening of the juvenile jails.

56. Waller and Okihiro, *Burglary: The Victim and the Public* (Toronto: University of Toronto Press, 1978), p. 90.

57. Hogarth, *op.cit.,* note 51, p. 11.

58. K. B. Jobson, "Imprisonment," 4 *Ottawa Law Jo.* 421 (1971).

59. Statistics Canada, "Statistics of Criminal and Other Offences," Catalogue No. 85-201, Annual, 1973, Table 6A.

60. Statistics Canada, Catalogue No. 85-207, Annual, 1976, p. 24.

61. *Ibid.,* p. 19.

62. Fine Option programs are established in Saskatchewan and Alberta and pilot projects are testing out the program in New Brunswick and Vancouver Island. Proposed amendments to the Criminal Code in Bill C-57 would make Fine Options available in all provinces.

63. *R. v. Melnyk* (1974), 19 C.C.C. (2d) 311 (B.C.).

64. Bill C-51 also would systematize the use of Community Service Orders. Currently they are used in B.C., Ontario and some other provinces as a condition of probation.

65. A. Blumstein, and J. Cohen, "A Theory of the Stability of Punishment," 64 *Jo. of Crim. Law and Criminology* 198-207 (1973); D. F. Couineau, and J. E. Veevers, "Incarceration as a Response to Crime: The Utilization of Canadian Prisons," in *The Administration of Criminal Justice in Canada,* Boydell, et al. (eds.) (Toronto: Holt, Rinehart, 1974), pp. 235-255, at 236; Statistics Canada, "Correctional and Institutional Statistics," Catalogue No. 85-207, Annual, 1974, Table 1 and 1976.

66. Guidelines: Dispositions and Sentences in the Criminal Process (Ottawa: Law Reform Commission of Canada, 1976).

67. Graham Zellick, "Foreign Perspective in Parliament," University of Toronto, Faculty of Law, February 2, 1979.

68. *Op. cit.,* note 22.

69. *Ibid.*

70. Coffee, *op. cit.,* note 34, 1048.

71. Legal Aid Societies generally are short of funds to distribute on legal aid matters; consequently, appeals approved for assistance on legal aid tend to be carefully scrutinized with a view to its being not only "meritorious" but likely to be successful.

CHAPTER 6

Reforming Sentencing Laws: An American Perspective

Jack M. Kress

The startling thing about American sentencing is not that *it* is so different from Canadian sentencing, but that there is no *it*. There is no single procedure that can be described as American sentencing. Any discussion of reform of the sentencing laws of the United States must begin with a comprehension of the amazing variation of sentencing structures across the 50 states, as well as the federal jurisdiction — variations in substance, procedure and practice. As fragmented and fractious as the Provinces may be — and I am acutely aware that I am writing at a time of heightened consciousness concerning these issues — Canadians have the signal advantage over Americans of having one criminal code to cover most serious offenses and hence to guide sentencing policies and practices. We do not. There are 50 states, *each* of which has its own distinct penal code *and* code of criminal procedure. There is also a separate federal code, but this has its principal application only in the District of Columbia. Therefore, America is divided into 51 individual and unique penal jurisdictions. Thus, of necessity, this excursion into comparative law can only hope to provide a broad, preliminary introduction to the dominant systems to which most states adhere. Indeed, to make the point sharper, I would note that there is more difference between the criminal procedure of Minnesota and Montana than there is between Quebec and British Columbia (saving, of course, the language spoken!).

Furthermore, even we Americans do not adequately comprehend our national differences in this area, not excepting those whom one would think would know better. I have lectured across America concerning sentence variation and was at first nonplussed when the purely *descriptive* portions of my lectures drew expressions of disbelief. Occasionally, I have lectured to audiences of judges from all over America. The first day of each lengthy session is devoted exclusively to shock recognition of differences; we are all prisoners of our experiences and judges at a session typically spend all day asking how the other judges do things. Certain phrases are heard flying about: "You're kidding!" "I don't believe it!" "Really!" It is only after a day or so of this that judges can come back to discussing worthwhile similarities as well.[1]

Let me give some examples from this American hodge-podge, some of which will be elaborated upon later. Five years ago, a major survey of sentencing procedures[2] reported the following differences in the 51 jurisdictions of America (and this *excludes* Puerto Rico, Guam and the Virgin Islands):

(1) On the issue of determinate vs. indeterminate sentencing:

    (a) at the time of that study, only ten states had generally determinate sentencing patterns (since that time, four to eight more — depending upon definition — have followed suit and that is a trend which I will discuss);

    (b) of the 41 jurisdictions with indeterminate sentencing schemes only 13 allow the sentencing body to set a minimum while the others have it legislatively fixed.

(2) On the issue of whether a defendant will be given *credit,* during sentencing, for time served in an institution awaiting trial:

    (a) 39 jurisdictions grant credit, either statutorily or through case law;

    (b) 12 leave the issue entirely as a discretionary matter with the judge.

(3) Suppose a defendant is convicted of two or more offenses at the same time?

    (a) Some states require the terms to run *consecutively.*

    (b) Some states require the terms to run *concurrently.*

    (c) Most states simply authorize the judge, in his or her discretion, to do either.

(4) Most states have habitual offender legislation, but the practice varies markedly.

    (a) Most states enhance upon the second felony conviction, but others only after the third or fourth.

    (b) Some jurisdictions simply double or treble the potential sentence, while others utilize intricate mathematical formulae.

AVAILABLE SENTENCING ALTERNATIVES

It has been said that sentencing is a numbers game of such complexity that only long-term inmates can understand it. After conviction for a felony, in most American jurisdictions, there is usually a pre-sentence investigation report prepared, although most states allow for the waiver of such a report, even in serious felonies, whereas others require such reports for even less serious misdemeanor offenses. While in particular cases a judge may be forced to impose a mandatory sentence, American judges are usually provided a choice; this choice is, typically, *extremely* broad, even for the gravest of offenses. I will briefly list the major options available, although, of course, not each one is available for every crime in every state.[3]

(1) Unconditional discharge: This sanction is accorded when the mere fact of conviction is considered punishment enough. Although this option superficially appears to be of trivial significance, implying no burden upon a defendant, its most frequent application appears to be a recognition that incarcerations resulting from a lack of required bail funds amount to a real penalty; i.e., this is the typical "time served" sentence where the period spent in jail by the defendant awaiting disposition is eventually considered to be equal to or greater than the punishment justifiably proportionate to the offense.

(2) Conditional discharge: This is a sanction imposed when the panoply of probationary conditions are not considered necessary, but some one or more specific conditions are deemed appropriate. The option of restitution to crime victims is typically handled via this sentence. In highly mobile America, one also finds the modern form of transportation or banishment, popularized in western fiction as "get out of town by sundown!" and affectionately known to local probation officers as "grey-hound parole."

(3) Fine: For a number of culturally based reasons, this sentencing alternative is employed far more frequently in England and Canada than it is in the United States, where it is typically employed only for relatively minor offenses, for certain traffic violations, and occasionally for significant white collar crimes.

(4) Probation: This is far and away the most frequent American sentencing alternative exercised. In terms of serious offenses, approximately four out of every five offenders are sentenced to probation. Unfortunately, for anyone attempting to fathom comparative jurisprudence, the term "probation" has a tremendously varying import across the United States. In each jurisdiction, it implies that some set of probationary conditions are attached, but the range of conditions is wide. A number of conditions are usually looked upon as relatively standard, such as not habituating places frequented by criminals, periodic reporting to a probation officer, and seeking gainful employment. The law

books are rife with examples, however, of uniquely crafted, highly individualized but objectively strange conditions. Among these have been compulsory sterilization, "requiring" volunteer work in hospitals, and avoiding one's family. Beyond this, however, one major difference which bedeviled my own sentencing research at the outset was the major "condition" of probation known as time in jail. Not immune from the cognitive bind myself, I rashly assumed in my early research that the term probation, as employed elsewhere, had the same meaning that it did in my home state of New York. Specifically, I felt it to be the major *alternative* to incarceration, rather than merely one *example* of it! I was sorely disillusioned to learn that, in many states, particularly in the western part of America, the imposition of jail time is a frequently imposed *condition* of probation — and I am not talking of a day or two of so-called "shock" probation, but conditions of six months to one year of incarceration! These "conditions" of probation would in most civilized nations be considered extremely lengthy incarcerative penalties by themselves.

(5) Jail: The American jail has two main functions. It typically holds those deemed innocent until proven guilty, but who cannot put up the bail money required for release. Strangely, this jail population mixes indiscriminately in most American jurisdictions with a second jail population, those convicted of misdemeanors and sentenced to this local correctional facility. Maximum jail sentences in America are typically determinate ones of six months, one year or, sometimes, two years.

(6) Split sentence: This sentence attempts to combine features of both probationary supervision and incarceration. It is a period of jail time, usually no longer than six months, followed by a period of probationary supervision. In theory, it is a sentence best employed for young offenders as a "short, sharp, shock" but its practice seems to belie this message. It is at best uncertain as to whether this is a "softened" form of incarceration or a "hardened" form of probation. Another term for the split sentence is, indeed, "shock probation."

(7) Intermittent sentence: This alternative is even less frequently exercised than the split sentence. It is an option that is intended to accommodate offender behavioral patterns to employment situations. For example, rather than truncate an offender's employment, the judge may sentence the defendant to weekends or nights in jail, thus allowing the defendant to continue his or her employment unimpeded. One practical problem often experienced with this apparently humane alternative has been that, while it accommodates to the *rehabilitative* needs of the given offender, jail officials have complained that it does not accommodate to the *habilitative* needs of their personnel; i.e., it is precisely during nights and weekends when jail staffs are at their lowest and when this "reverse" flow of inmates confuses correctional work patterns.

(8) Youthful offenders: In most states, some specific accommodation is

given to young offenders, although the age limits vary, but all accord exceptional treatment to youngsters. Intensive supervision, anonymity of court records and potential expungement are all aspects of typical youthful offender treatment programs.

(9) Prison: This alternative is obviously the nub of the sentencing dilemma and will be dealt with here at length. Who goes into prison as opposed to who stays out of it is the heart of the moral question of sentencing.[4]

(10) Death: With only one execution in the United States in the last decade, it cannot be claimed that this is a frequently exercised sentencing alternative, but it looks as if it will be a growing one. The United States Supreme Court has given its final approval to a number of death penalty statutes[5] and we appear headed for a resumption of executions all across America. While its statistical impact is relatively trivial its moral significance cannot be understated.

These are the major sentencing options available to judges across America, but their *manner of imposition* has three variations that should also be acknowledged here:

(A) Execution: On the date of sentencing, the alternative is announced and imposed immediately.

(B) Suspended: On the date of sentencing, the specific sentence is announced, but its execution is suspended and the defendant is afforded an unconditional, unsupervised release. This procedure obviously leavens the harshness of many announced American sentences, but the defendant has been forewarned that a fixed Sword of Damocles has been set should he or she fail to perform satisfactorily.

(C) Deferred: This is sort of an unfixed Sword of Damocles, with the erring defendant brought back before the sentencing judge to be sentenced as it were anew, with the full range of options available to the judge at the time of execution.

PRISON

Let us assume that our American defendant has been sentenced to prison. What does the sentence mean? How long will the defendant actually serve in prison? Unfortunately again, for the sake of comparative analysis, the very *meaning* of any given prison sentence varies widely across jurisdictions.[6] First of all, until recently, most American sentences have been marked by a very high degree of indeterminacy, with no effective appellate review and with time actually served in prison governed largely by the parole system. In many states, a very large range lies between the maxima and minima prescribed by law, in some cases a range of penalty from nothing to life imprisonment. In other states, sentences are notionally of a fixed length, but the actual date of release is nevertheless governed by the mechanism of parole, and great variation can result. The term "minimum" typically refers to a date of earliest parole eligibility, while the term "maximum" usually refers to a mandatory discharge date. In the last few years, some popularity has been achieved by what has been called a "flat" sentence, sometime known as a "determinate," "straight," or "fixed" sentence: the judge announces a set time to be served by the defendant without any minimum or maximum. Even here, however, variation occurs, largely because of the concept known as "good time."

The term "good time" refers to a credit allowed against the sentence for satisfactory conduct in prison. It was introduced as an incentive for good behaviour and therefore had to be "earned." Most jurisdictions, however, have by now made good time automatic. That is, this credit is always allowed against the sentence unless it is affirmatively taken away. A number of issues have been raised as to what the criteria for good time should or ought to be. Should it be a reward for good behavior or a subtraction for bad behavior? Should cooperation with authority be treated in this manner at all? In terms of simple computation, some states allow for good time as a reduction against the minimum date of parole eligibility, whereas others allow the reduction only against the maximum possible discharge date. To further confuse the comparative analyst, some states allow it to do *both*. The more usual practice, however, is for the good time to be an automatically earned subtraction from the maximum discharge date.

Having entered the prison, the prisoner's main concern is generally when he or she may leave the prison. There are six methods which may be enumerated:

(1) Mandatory release: After one subtracts the automatic good time from the maximum discharge date, the defendant *must* be released under state law. Because the defendant in such circumstances has "maxed out," the mandatory release is typically without supervision. (In Illinois and some other jurisdictions, however, there is supervision of the mandatory releasee just as if that person were paroled.) [7]

(2) Conditional release: After the minimum amount of time, the defendant *may* be released, with or without supervision. In some jurisdictions, the minimum might be reduced by good time and so it would be a very short period of time.

(3) Parole: Parole is the traditional form of prison release found in most jurisdictions in America. The parolee is conditionally released to community supervision by designated state agents generally known as parole officers. In theory, the sentence of incarceration is regarded as uncompleted and the parolee is treated, in terms of civil rights, largely as a prisoner outside the walls.

(4) Escape: Although it is highly publicized when it occurs, this option is not one frequently enjoyed by prisoners. Indeed, the answer to that criminological conundrum "Does prison work?" would generally be positive if one considered

only the incapacitative function of prison. It is only when one imports notions of rehabilitation into the argument that prisons may be said to "fail."

(5) Pardon: Pardon has not typically been the American way of release from prison, although a number of other nations, such as Italy, Spain and those in Latin America, use the Christmas pardon, or political inauguration commutations, as a frequent means of clearing the prisons. As the movement to abolish parole gathers steam in America, it will be interesting to see whether or not parole is re-invented (or re-disguised?) with a Governor's Pardon Board taking on more and more work. Reputationally, for example, the first state to abolish parole in America, Maine in 1976, had the highest rate of pardons.

(6) Death: No matter what are the complaints about institutional food inside the prison, a relatively healthy regimen appears to be maintained and the overwhelming majority of prisoners are released from prison through other than supernatural means.

Thus, we can see that, in the allocation of serious, prison sentencing power, the court in many states will establish a minimum, which amounts to the least amount of time which the defendant *must be held,* and a maximum, which amounts to the greatest amount of time that a defendant *can be held,* whereas the good time and paroling provisions tend to determine the amount of time which a defendant will *actually* be incarcerated.

SENTENCING STRUCTURES

Nevertheless, even in terms of setting prison terms, there is a significant sharing of authority between the three branches of government in America. While all sentencing authority is in some sense derived from the legislature, typical sentencing provisions may more narrowly be read as dividing effective authority between the executive, judicial and legislative branches. Figure 1 exemplifies the varied patterns that one encounters.

Figure 1

	Minimum	Maximum
Statute	a	b
Judge (or jury)	c	d
Paroling agency	e	f

(a) In some states, upon conviction of a given offense, a minimum sentence is required to be imposed by law, but, within given constraints, flexibility is accorded the judge to set the maximum.

(b) In other jurisdictions, the setting of the minimum will be left either to the judge or the parole agency, but the maximum will be established by statute. This is the provision recommended by the Model Penal Code.[8] For example, under the Model Penal Code, a first degree felony will receive a maximum sentence of 20 years (or life in some circumstances), but the judge is given discretionary authority to set the minimum sentence at one year, ten years, or anything in between. (Because the term determinate sentencing is often confused with flat sentencing, it is perhaps here appropriate to note that a legislature may very well establish a sentence that is *both* mandatory *and* indeterminate: e.g., in Ohio, once a defendant has been convicted of a specific serious felony, a fixed indeterminate sentence — e.g., two to ten years — is established.)

(c) In many states, the judge may set both the minimum and the maximum indeterminate sentence within very broad statutory limits. For example, until recently, a defendant convicted of armed robbery in New York State could be sentenced by a judge to an unconditional discharge, or to probation, or to a jail term, or to a prison term completely indeterminate up until 25 years. Moreover, the judge could allowably set a minimum sentence upon any prison term of up to one-third the maximum amount (i.e., a maximum term of 8 1/3 years to 25 years). In other jurisdictions, the judge may set a minimum sentence, but the maximum will be set by statute. In some jurisdictions, the minimum can be set anywhere up to the maximum amount, thus sharply curbing parole board discretion, but most states include some fractional limitation on the minimum, as in New York, of an amount either one-half or one-third of the maximum allowable sentence.

(d) The most frequent sentence situation in America is for the judge to set the maximum amount within very broad statutory limits, while the minimum amount may be fixed by statute. Another major reform proposal in the United States, the Model Sentencing Act,[9] contains provisions such as this.

(e) In a number of jurisdictions, such as Hawaii, the paroling agency sets the minimum felony sentence.

(f) In a number of jurisdictions, the maximum allowable sentence is established by the paroling agency. In California, before the change in its law of July 1, 1977, the classic rehabilitation model prevailed and sentencing was generally *completely* indeterminate, with the California Adult Authority establishing the maximum sentence for each offender, as well as the date of actual release.

As confusing as this structure may appear to the outside observer, it gets even more confusing because within this structure, states classify some particular offenses differently. For example, in New York and Massachusetts, generally indeterminate sentencing provisions prevail, but, respectively with regard to drugs and guns, mandatory minimum sentences are established in each of those states. In a number of jurisdictions, certain offenses (such as murder) are declared non-probationable, whereas probation is an allowable alternative for all other offenses; predicate felon (recidivist or habitual offender) statutes operate very much in this manner.

THE LOCUS OF SENTENCING AUTHORITY

I have just gone over a complicated morass of descriptive material, but I will turn a bit more normative now in describing the discretionary reality of sentencing offenders in America. Quite obviously, a vast amount of sentencing discretion exists across my country, but it will be useful to place this sentencing discretion in context. As will be clear by now, nowhere in America today is the judge the sole determinant of sanction; rather, there is the unarticulated sharing of the sentencing function which I have described. Before going any further, however, I should draw a distinction between punishment and sentencing. Important as it is, sentencing is merely one additional factor in the quantum of punishment which an offender faces in our criminal justice system. Sentencing will not, for example, more than indirectly relate to predispositional incarceration occasioned by insufficient bail funds. Nor can sentencing directly affect the *quality* of any term of probation or imprisonment imposed — and these human factors *do* matter. Nevertheless, sentencing is a remarkably important stage in the criminal justice process, bridging as it does the fact determination components of the system with those components dealing with the disposition of offenders. We may identify eight actors or institutions that compete with the local trial court judge for effective sentencing authority.

(1) Let me first perhaps surprise you by talking about *juries.*[10] In America, in about 35 states, juries are used for sentencing when the potential sentence is death. Moreover, 13 states today provide for jury sentencing in non-capital cases: primary sentencing authority for all serious crimes rests with the jury in 8 of these states; 4 states restrict the jury's sentencing powers only to certain offenses; and Texas follows the unique procedure of offering a choice of judge or jury sentencing to most offenders. In favor of jury sentencing is the argument of introducing citizen input into an otherwise overly professionalized system which insufficiently accounts for community standards and mores. This argument is interesting but ultimately unconvincing. In urging the abolition of jury sentencing, the 1973 National Advisory Commission on Criminal Justice Standards and Goals contended that "jury sentencing was non-professional and is more likely than judge sentencing to be arbitrary and based on emotions

rather than the needs of the offender or society."[11] This seems a good argument: unguided lay jurors simply cannot reach equitable decisions when they have no baseline information to compare with the individual case before them.

Let me now speak of (2) *probation officers* and (3) *prosecutors.* There is no American jurisdiction that places either the probation officer or the prosecutor in a position of *legal* responsibility for sentencing, but it would be naive and simplistic not to acknowledge the power of either of these offices. Typically, for example, the American probation officer prepares a pre-sentence investigative report and the content of that report is generally quite persuasive, with many judges even asking their probation officers to make specific sentencing recommendations.[12] Statistics reveal that these judges almost uniformly follow such recommendations. As for the prosecutor, the prevalence of plea bargaining in the United States — upwards of 90 per cent in many jurisdictions — confers practical sentencing powers upon many district attorneys.[13] This is particularly true in those jurisdictions where negotiations involve specific sentence promises as opposed to discussions concerning multiple counts or lesser charges; that is, what those researching this field refer to as *sentence*-bargaining, as opposed merely to *charge*-bargaining. The most basic administrative rule possible must be that responsibility and accountability go together as taxation with representation; no controls on the potential abuses of discretionary power are at all possible when the powers are unauthorized in the first place.

Three other institutions that may be said to share in the sentencing power ought to be briefly discussed here also: (4) the *sentencing council;* (5) the *sentencing commission;* and (6) the *appellate courts.* The sentencing council (or panel) is an advisory body usually comprised of two judges assisting a third in seeking to arrive at a consensus disposition, although the third judge retains the ultimate sentencing responsibility.[14] The council mechanism is seen as a means of curbing disparity, but of course only within a limited jurisdiction; seen as quite costly — employing three judges to perform the sentencing chore rather than one — the council idea has not been widely adopted. The sentencing commission is a new concept, established so far only in Minnesota and Pennsylvania; in its present incarnations, it is perfectly compatible with judicial discretion and the sentencing guidelines scheme later described.[15] The appellate courts of America, quite unlike those in Canada and the United Kingdom, have exercised relatively little authority with regard to sentencing decisions. Only a slim body of case law — save in the capital punishment area — exists to guide either the propriety or practice of local trial court sentencing.[16]

(7) I have referred to the *parole board* frequently, but the indeterminate sentence which granted extensive sentencing powers to the parole board is no longer popular. Under the theory of the indeterminate sentencing system, neither the legislature nor the judge set the amount of time a convicted criminal

actually served. That decision instead rested with the state parole board. The Wickersham Commission in 1931 summed up the argument as follows:

> Physicians, upon discovering disease cannot name the day upon which the patient will be healed. No more can judges intelligently set the day of release from prison at the time of trial. Boards of parole [on the other hand] can study the prisoner during his confinement. . . . Within their discretion they can grant a comparatively early release to youths, to first offenders, to particularly worthy cases who give high promise of leading a new life . . . and keep vicious criminals in confinement as long as the law allows.[17]

While indeterminacy is unpopular today, I should note that for some specially designated offenders — such as "sex deviants" or "psychopaths" or even "narcotic addicts" — terms of custody still rest largely within the discretion of state correctional authorities.

Today, indeterminacy, the medical model, and its handmaiden, the parole board are on the wane. Both left and right have denounced the concept, the former contending that the indeterminate sentence is unfair to the defendant, due both to its discriminatory application and its psychological unfairness in terms of uncertainty as to time of release, and the latter arguing that such an offender oriented system ignores the cruel facts of the individual offense. Many have attacked the pragmatic foundation of indeterminacy, arguing that the rehabilitation philosophy that undergirds it has proven a practical failure.[18] Others have attacked the philosophy of rehabilitation in more philosophical terms.[19]

(8) Many of the calls today for mandatory minimum, flat-time, fixed, determinate, or even presumptive sentencing are really calls for legislative dominance over — or perhaps substitution for — the judiciary with regard to the sentencing decision. As I have related to you, mandatory sentencing takes many forms, reserving lesser or greater degrees of discretion to the various non-legislative criminal justice agencies. Depending upon one's point of view, these various mandatory sentencing laws are usually urged as a means of controlling the discretion of overly lenient or overly harsh trial court judges. Proponents have made out a clear and adequate case for the existence of judicial sentencing disparity, but they contend that only a system of punishment exclusively commensurate with perceived offense seriousness can provide equality and even-handedness of treatment. The argument appears to be that equality is impossible to achieve when one simultaneously pursues that noble attempt to tailor-fit the sentence to the personal and social characteristics of the particular offender.

A common purpose of many of the so-called mandatory laws of recent years has been an abolitionist mentality with regard to discretionary authority: Abolish parole discretion! Abolish judicial discretion! The 1977 Uniform

Determinate Sentencing Act in California, as one example, fixes sentences in sets of three time periods; for instance, two, three or four years for burglary; five, six or seven years for second degree murder. That law not only abolished discretionary release, but also went a long way towards destroying the discretion of the judiciary. Under that law, the judge is bound to pick the middle number of these three time periods, unless the judge specifically finds enumerated mitigating circumstances, when he must pick the lower number, or aggravating circumstances when he must choose the higher one.

SENTENCING GUIDELINES

Admittedly, I am biased with regard to the sentencing alternative I am recommending. Together with my colleagues Professor Leslie T. Wilkins and Dean Don M. Gottfredson, I helped invent sentencing guidelines;[20] I also directed, alone, the project which first implemented sentencing guidelines systems in jurisdictions all across America.[21] Before proceeding to make my own case, however, let me quote to you the conclusions of the recent report submitted by England's prestigious Home Office Advisory Council on the Penal System:

> We looked at the various penalty systems current in the different jurisdictions of the United States, and noted in particular the recent legislative moves away from indeterminacy in sentencing towards a more fixed and rigid penalty structure. The system of sentencing guidelines, now making headway in the United States as a compromise between indeterminate sentencing and a system of more or less fixed penalties, was of special interest to us, both because the philosophy of steering a middle course between a wide and a narrow discretion in sentencing was the one which most appealed to us, and because the practical solution of adopting a penalty system based on the existing practice of the courts was that which we ourselves ultimately decided to recommend.[22]

Within America too, sentencing guidelines have advanced from a state of nonexistence only a few short years ago, to what has been described as "the most widely recommended proposal" today.[23] Indeed, there are at this writing *twenty* operational sentencing guidelines projects: thirteen of these have occurred at the state level, with the remaining seven projects conducted in local court systems; a further eleven jurisdictions plan to begin a project shortly.[24] The focus, scope and methodologies of these various sentencing guidelines projects vary, but they each retain the core of the sentencing guidelines philosophy, which is the recognition of the necessity for retaining local trial court sentencing discretion, while simultaneously structuring and guiding the application of that very discretion. Judges do need flexibility in accommodating the realities of the individual case before the bench. Proposals which attempt to fix by statutory law terms of probation and incarceration with regard to the offense of conviction only, are unrealistically rigid and mechanical, unworkable in practice, and philosophically undesirable as being too far removed from the human being who will suffer the consequences of the sentence.

The major problem with legislatively fixed sentences is that they are pre-fixed. There is *a priori* establishment of the "correct" sentence with little or no empirical, factually based support for any sentence handed down. Years before the crime in question occurs, the legislature sets the precise duration of imprisonment for some general class of crime, with remarkably little consideration given to either extenuating or exacerbating factors surrounding the specific case that will actually come before the judge. Indeed, my view is that if the legislature makes its decision based only on theoretical argument and the skimpy factual information it now possesses, it will inevitably draw unrealistic conclusions which will ensure the kind of wholesale discretionary avoidance of the legislative mandate by criminal justice officials which has rendered so many prior reform efforts nugatory.

Primary sentencing responsibility *must* continue to reside with the trial judge, and reform must be based upon a careful review of actual sentencing practices. This explains both the methods of analysis of sentencing guidelines, as well as why I and my colleagues have worked cooperatively to aid local trial court sentencing judges. Sentencing guidelines systems attempt to systematize the way that judges sentence based, *initially,* on historical sentencing patterns; they are not intended to eliminate judicial sentencing discretion, but to regulate disparate decision-making and to operationalize a solution to the problem stressed by Zeisel and Diamond that appellate review of sentencing lacks specificity.[25]

Through the statistical and analytical study of actual cases coming before cooperating trial judges across the nation, sentencing guidelines researchers have been able to extract and examine the underlying characteristics, of both offenses and offenders, which appear to account for justifiable variations in judicial sentencing decisions. We were thus able to examine the underlying factors that are the basis for sentencing decisions and also to determine the relative weights accorded each of these factors by judges themselves. This information was then fed back to local trial court judges so they could, for the first time, consciously articulate and carefully control and monitor their own sentencing policies.

These early descriptive results were next reformulated into what became a series of sentencing guidelines, individually developed for each of the jurisdictions in which we worked. These guidelines provided a model sentence to each trial court judge specifically relevant to the case at hand. Figure 2 is a hypothetical sentencing guidelines information sheet that illustrates the components of the two major dimensions that go into the sentencing decision: the Crime Score and the Offender Score. (The reader should note that the factors and weightings comprising these dimensions have varied sharply in each sentencing guidelines jurisdiction.)[26] Figure 3 suggests a hypothetical array of sentences resulting from various combinations of Crime and Offender Scores.

Figure 2

SENTENCING GUIDELINES INFORMATION SHEET

Crime Score

A. Injury
    0 = Injury
    1 = Injury
    2 = Death   _____ +
B. Weapon
    0 = No weapon
    1 = Weapon
    2 = Weapon present and used   _____ +
C. Drugs
    0 = No sale of drugs
    1 = Sale of drugs   _____ =

Crime
Score

Offender Score

A. Current Legal Status
    0 = Not on probation/parole, escape
    1 = On probation/parole, escape   _____ +
B. Prior Adult Misdemeanor Convictions
    0 = No convictions
    1 = One conviction
    2 = Two or more convictions   _____ +
C. Prior Adult Felony Convictions
    0 = No convictions
    2 = One conviction
    4 = Two or more convictions   _____ +
D. Prior Adult Probation/Parole Revocations
    0 = None
    1 = One or more revocations   _____ +
E. Prior Adult Incarcerations (Over 60 Days)
    0 = None
    1 = One incarceration
    2 = Two or more incarcerations   _____ =

Offender
Score

Guideline Sentence_____

Figure 3

FELONY SENTENCING GRID

Crime Score				
4-5	4-6 Years	5-7 Years	6-8 Years	8-10 Years
3	3-5 Years	4-6 Years	6-8 Years	6-8 Years
2	2-4 Years	3-5 Years	3-5 Years	4-6 Years
1	Probation	Probation	2-4 Years	3-5 Years
0	Probation	Probation	Probation	2-4 Years
	0-1	2-4	5-7	8-10

Offender Score

Even when fully implemented, guideline sentences are in no way intended to be binding or mandatory. The judge, as human decision-maker, will still retain the discretion to override any suggested guideline sentence. However, in such circumstances, particularized written reasons will be required as judges depart from the specific, narrowly drawn guideline suggestion. Moreover, the guidelines system feeds back those very departures into the data base used in constructing the guidelines themselves, thus injecting a continuous element of self-improvement and regeneration into the guidelines. Finally, a sentencing guidelines system provides a unique opportunity to produce rational sentences formulated on the basis of informed judgment about what factors are suitable as determinants of guidelines,[27] together with the best available empirical evidence about the effects of sanctions on criminal behavior.[28]

REFORM: MEANS AND ENDS

By now, the benefits of adopting a sentencing guidelines system have been relatively widely publicized, but I should restate some of them:

(1) Enhancing equity and uniformity in sentencing;

(2) Maintaining judicial expertise and experience in sentencing, while providing each judge with a measure of the collective wisdom of his or her colleagues;

(3) Allowing valid individual differences to be taken into account by the sentencing judge in specific cases;

(4) Providing an excellent training tool for judges just coming on to the bench;

(5) Giving judges — as well as prosecutors, defendants and the public at

large — a clearer picture of what judicial sentencing policy has been, is, and should be, thus providing the opportunity for informed change; and, most importantly to me,

(6) Opening up what has hitherto been a closed system of justice.

Sentencing guidelines should best be thought of as a reform *mechanism.* That is, adoption of a sentencing guidelines system will allow for *informed reform* to occur. Sentencing guidelines systems allow reformers to take specific cognizance of the individually weighted values of particular factors that are involved in the sentencing decision. Let me therefore conclude this essay with a discussion, perhaps a prediction, of the future course of sentencing research and sentencing reform.

Sentencing guidelines systems will allow us to concentrate ever more sharply on the particular factors that affect sentencing, factors which may be (a) as broad as the philosophic concerns of the system itself, or (b) as narrow as pragmatic concerns regarding overcrowded courts or prisons. These factors may relate to (c) the gravity of the specific offense under consideration, or (d) to relatively objective characteristics of the offender, or even (e) to the somewhat more subjective characteristics regarding assessments of the offender's social stability.

(a) Dubiously assuming that we could reach consensus on the goals of sentencing, the logic of various sentencing philosophies could be geared ever more closely to given sets of crimes/criminal characteristics. For example, if a retribution or just deserts logic suggested that sentences had historically been unduly harsh for one crime and unduly lenient for another, then the guidelines based on historical norms could be adjusted accordingly. Or, to take a more complex example, if we looked at a deterrence or incapacitation logic, we might be able to measure crime prevention in an amount that the public would be willing to pay x dollars to prevent, but at the cost of y dollars for prison resources; we could then increase the guidelines if x is greater than y, or concomitantly decrease them if y exceeds x.[29] Similarly, were general deterrence or rehabilitation models to prevail, then different concerns would be raised. The point is that factors that would be considered by sentencing judges would vary with sentencing philosophy. A deterrence model, for example, forces us to cope with the "false positive" problem inherent in risk estimation. A just desserts model forces us to come to grips with measures of commensurate behavior. A rehabilitation model forces us to come to grips with available community resources.

(b) Systemic realities and practical concerns would also be accommodated by sentencing guidelines. Proposed guidelines could, for example, be assessed by projecting their implications for prison populations and court caseloads. Whether or not credit should be given to informers who cooperate with the police or to persons who plead guilty rather than stand trial would, perforce, have to be answered specifically rather than skirted as they are today. The impact and legitimacy of plea bargaining in particular would be quantitatively and specifically measured.

(c) Are legislative descriptions of criminal acts sufficiently specific for sentencing purposes? Is a judge bound by a plea of guilty to consider only aspects of a charge at conviction, or may judges — as most do today — sentence on the basis of the "real" offense as revealed by arrest or pre-sentence reports? In addition to these questions, we will have to describe, far more adequately than previously, the concept of commensurately proscribed behavior.

(d) A host of specific considerations surrounding convicted defendants would no longer be answered in general terms such as "taken into consideration." The very specific detrimental impact of a particular prior criminal history on a given offender would now be known. The difference between prior felonies and misdemeanors, between crimes of a similar or different orientation from the present offense, between an adult and a juvenile criminal history, between convictions and arrests, all of these would now be given specific weighted values and those values would be far more reviewable than ever before.

(e) Should the employment record of an offender be a major mitigating factor as it is so often claimed to be, or is it another illegitimate consideration since it is so heavily race-biased? Should the offender's psychological record or medical record be taken into account? Should the fact of family instability be at all taken into account? Assuming that these social stability indicators are to be considered at all, then guidelines systems will help to provide relatively objective measures of these generally subjective criteria.

The salient point about the various questions raised above is not that sentencing guidelines provides *answers* to them. What a sentencing guidelines system will allow is for the proper *questions* to be asked, so that future sentencing reformers can provide the proper answers.

NOTES

1. Among the materials the judges study at the National Judicial College in Reno, Nevada, is a helpful text: J. M. Burns and J. S. Mattina, *Sentencing* (1978).

2. R. C. Hand and R. G. Singer, *Sentencing Computation Law and Practice* (Washington D. C.: American Bar Association, Commission on Correctional Facilities and Services, 1974). A constructive international comparative guide is G. O. W. Muller, *Sentencing: Process and Purpose* (Criminal Law Education and Research Service, 1977).

3. See also "American Bar Association Project on Standards for Criminal Justice, Standards Relating to Sentencing Alternatives and Procedures" (Approved Draft, 1968).

4. This is my view, but it would be fair to note that others focus on prison length as the most significant sentencing issue. See, e.g., D. Fogel, *We Are the Living Proof* (Cincinnati: Anderson, 1976).

5. *Gregg v. Georgia,* 96 S. Ct. 2909 (1976); *Proffitt v. Florida,* 96 S. Ct. 2960 (1976); and *Jurek v. Texas,* 96 S. Ct. 2950 (1976).

6. See generally, D. Newman, *Introduction to Criminal Justice* (2d ed.) (Philadelphia: Lippincott, 1978).

7. I should note here that most "just desserts" proposals have not really bitten the bullet in terms of convincing the American public that prison sentences should be much shorter than they are as announced today. It is in this respect that they lose any "truth-in-packaging" credibility that they might have had. For example, "Conference of Commissioners on Uniform State Laws, Uniform Corrections Act" (March, 1978 Draft) provides for one day of good time to be granted automatically for each day served; thus, an announced just deserts sentence really is equal to only half of what is announced. *See also,* A. Von Hirsch, *Doing Justice: The Choice of Punishments* (New York: Hill and Wang, 1976); and Twentieth Century Task Force Report on Sentencing, *Fair and Certain Punishment,* (New York: McGraw-Hill, 1976).

8. American Law Institute, "Model Penal Code" (Proposed Official Draft, 1962). Although 17 years old, this proposal still significantly influences informed opinion in the United States.

9. National Council on Crime and Delinquency, "Model Sentencing Act" (1963).

10. See H. M. LaFont, "Assessment of Punishment — A Judge or Jury Function?" 38 *Tex. L. Rev.* 835 (1960); Note, "Jury Sentencing in Virginia," 53 *Va. L. Rev.* 968 (1967).

11. National Advisory Commission on Criminal Justice Standards and Goals, "Task Force Report on Courts," Standard 5.1, Commentary at 110 (Washington, D.C.: Government Printer, 1973).

12. Note, "The Presentence Report: An Empirical Study of Its Use in the Federal Criminal Process," 58 *Geo. L.J.* 451 (1970); C. Clement and B. A. Shapiro, "Presentence Information in Felony Cases in Massachusetts Superior Court," 10 *Suffolk U.L. Rev.* 27 (Fall 1973); R. A. Harkness, "Due Process in Sentencing: Right to Rebut the Presentence Report," 2 *Hastings Constitutional L.Q.* 1065 (Fall, 1975); and S. D. Raymond, "Standardized Presentence Report: One State's Response," 41 *Fed. Prob.* 40 (June, 1977).

13. See generally, J. M. Kress, "Progress and Prosecution," *The Annals of the American Academy of Political and Social Science* 99 (January, 1976); D. Newman, *Conviction: the Determination of Guilt or Innocence Without Trial* (Boston: Little, Brown, 1966); A. Alschuler, "The Trial Judge's Role in Plea Bargaining, Part I," 76 *Colum. L. Rev.* 1059 (1976); J. Bond, *Plea Bargaining and Guilty Pleas* (New York: Boardman, Clark, 1975); and Georgetown University Law Center, *Plea Bargaining in the United States — Phase I Report* (Washington, D.C., 1977).

14. M. Frankel, *Criminal Sentences,* (New York: Hill and Wang, 1973), especially chapters 6 and 7; H. Zeisel and S. S. Diamond, "Sentencing Councils: A Study of Sentence Disparity and Its Reduction," 43 *U. Chi. L. Rev.* 108 (1976); and W. Strauss and L. Bashir, "Controlling Discretion in Sentencing,"

51 *Notre Dame Law* 919 (July, 1976).

15. M. Frankel, *Criminal Sentences* (1973) *op. cit.,* particularly his concluding recommendations. M. Zalman, "A Commission Model of Sentencing," 53 *Notre Dame Law* 266 (1977); and J. C. Coffee, Jr., "The Repressed Issues of Sentencing: Accountability, Predictability and Equality in the Era of the Sentencing Commission," 66 *Georgetown L.J.* 975 (April, 1978).

16. D. A. Thomas, *Principles of Sentencing,* (London: Heineman, 1970); J. D. Hopkins, "Reviewing Sentencing Discretion: A Method of Swift Appellate Action," 23 *U.C.L.A. L. Rev.* 491 (February, 1976); C. C. Blabe, "Appellate Review of Sentencing in Federal Courts," 24 *Kansas L. Rev.* 279 (Winter, 1976); and H. Zeisel and S. S. Diamond, "Search for Sentencing Equity: Sentence Review in Massachusetts and Connecticut," 4 *Am. B. Foundation Research J.* 881 (1977).

17. National Commission on Law Observance and Enforcement (Wickersham Commission), *Report on Penal Institutions, Probation and Parole* 142-143 (Washington, D.C.: Government Printing Office, 1931).

18. W. Bailey, "Correctional Outcome: An Evaluation of 100 Reports," 57 *J. Crim. L.C. & P.S.* 153 (1966); J. Q. Wilson, *Thinking About Crime* (New York: Basic Books, 1975); R. Martinson, "What Works? — Questions and Answers About Prison Reform," *Public Interest* 22 (Spring, 1974); and G. Cole and S. Talarico, " Second Thoughts on Parole," 63 *A.B.A.J.* 972 (July, 1977).

19. American Friends Service Committee, *Struggle For Justice* (New York: Hill and Wang, 1971); J. Q. Wilson, *Thinking About Crime, op. cit.;* N. Morris, *The Future of Imprisonment,* (Chicago: University of Chicago Press, 1974); E. Van Den Haag, *Punishing Criminals,* (New York: Basic Books, 1975); A. Von Hirsch, *Doing Justice: The Choice of Punishments, op. cit.;* and G. Newman, *The Punishment Response,* (Philadelphia: Lippincott, 1978). The most frequently proposed alternative philosophy is "just deserts," which is retribution in present day garb. Reluctantly supporting this philosophy, Leslie Wilkins argued: "It seems that we have rediscovered 'sin,' in the absence of a better alternative," in A. Von Hirsch, *Doing Justice: The Choice of Punishments, op. cit.* "Ou bien, comme diraient mes collègues distingués de la belle province de Québec, "Plus ça change, plus ca reste la même."

20. L. T. Wilkins, J. M. Kress, D. M. Gottfredson, J. C. Calpin and A. M. Gelman, *Sentencing Guidelines: Structuring Judicial Discretion — Report of the Feasibility Study* (Criminal Justice Research Center, 1976).

21. For an overall explanation of sentencing guidelines, its history and its future, *see* J. M. Kress, *Sentencing Guidelines* (in press, 1979).

22. Advisory Council on the Penal System, *Sentences of Imprisonment: A Review of Maximum Penalties* 8 (1978). As I will emphasize shortly, however, the penalty system is only *initially* based on existing practice.

23. Executive Advisory Committee on Sentencing, *Crime and Punishment in New York,* Appendix E at 3 (1979).

24. Criminal Courts Technical Assistance Project, *Overview of State and Local Sentencing Guidelines Activity* (1979).

25. H. Zeisel and S. S. Diamond, "Search for Sentencing Equity: Sentence Review in Massachusetts and Connecticut," 4 *Am. B. Foundation Research J.* 881 (1977).

26. See J. M. Kress, *Sentencing Guidelines in Four Courts* (in press, 1980).

27. In Canada, this might logically, and in large measure, involve an analytical review of relevant appellate court decisions.

28. See, e.g., National Academy of Sciences, *Deterrence and Incapacitation: Evaluating the Effects of Criminal Sanctions on Crime Rates,* (Washington D.C.: National Academy of Sciences, 1978).

29. See Executive Advisory Committee on Sentencing, *Crime and Punishment in New York,* Appendix E.

CHAPTER 7

Towards Sentencing Uniformity: Integrating the Normative and the Empirical Orientation

Aidan R. Vining
and
Cory Dean

TWO APPROACHES TO SENTENCING REFORM: THE NORMATIVE AND THE EMPIRICAL

How should we go about thinking about sentencing reform in Canada?

Currently there appear to be two main approaches to the problem: one primarily normative in orientation, the other more driven by empirical considerations. The former approach tends to be espoused by bureaucratics and lawyers, the latter by academics and social scientists. The former approach — exemplified by the recent deliberations of the Law Reform Commission of Canada[1] — tends to stress what *should* be done about sentencing reform. This is, of course, a worthy goal per se. However, the last decades have taught us that reform, if it is not to be counter-productive, must be solidly grounded in behavioural reality. As Wildavsky puts it:

> When organizations cannot achieve the objectives set for them by others, changes will be sought not in the accomplishments attained but in the objectives expected to be obtained. . . . But why should objectives that most people consider desirable ever be altered? Because bad things happen when organizations are asked to do (a) what nobody knows how to do, and/or (b) what cannot be done at all.[2]

Elsewhere, one of the authors has extensively argued that most of this normative literature on sentencing reform in Canada — especially that dealing with issues of reducing sentencing disparity and discretion — ignores important behavioural realities of the existing criminal justice system, and its incentives and constraints.[3]

Others have chosen to approach sentencing reform from a different perspective — namely the empirical. They seek to move from what "is" to what "should be." This is, in principle, an inherently reasonable approach. Thus, there has been a growing empirical literature on the determinants of sentencing outcomes; both in Canada[4] and in the United States.[5] This literature has come about because of the happy convergence of improved data bases and more sophisticated statistical techniques. The literature has been useful in establishing that so-called "legally relevant" variables such as charge, prior record and criminal status[6] are indeed utilized in the sentencing process. For example Vining (1979a) found that in California five different levels of prior record were relevant, i.e., as the offender's prior record worsened from one level to the next, the sentence increased. These studies have also been useful in demonstrating that obviously inappropriate factors, such as race[7] have an impact on sentencing even after having controlled for the so-called legally relevant variables.

The empirical studies, however, if utilized, can have unfortunate consequences. Empirical research, not unnaturally, tends to be "driven" by the nature of the available data. Unfortunately this has led some researchers to conclude that those variables which can be measured are the most important from a normative or policy perspective. Frequently they are not; they are simply the most measurable.

For example, let us trace the genesis of one unfortunate trend in the literature — that dealing with the role of "legally relevant" variables.[8] The use of this term to describe charge, prior record and criminal status has led some researchers to conclude that they are the *only* legally relevant variables in a normative sense. The result of such thinking, however, can be illustrated from the conclusions drawn by Warner and Renner in their multivariate study of sentencing outcomes in Nova Scotia. They conclude;

> Although the offense and offender variables were important determinants of the sentence, nearly two-thirds of the variance in sentence severity was unaccounted for by these factors. There are three possible explanations for the large portion of unexplained variance:
> First, limitations in the available offense and offender information. However, complete data was available on nine offense and offender variables for 565 cases, which should be sufficient to provide a good indication of the ability of this type of information to predict sentence severity.
> A second explanation might involve limitations inherent in the statistical procedures. But multiple regression analysis is the standard procedure and permits accurate prediction if sentence severity were determined in an explicit and uniform way for all defendants by the predictor variables. To reject this model is to reject the concept that a rationale for judicial decisions is a necessary and an appropriate area for empirical analysis.
> A third reason for the limited success in predicting sentence severity may have been the absence of variables reflecting the behavior and attitudes of judges and lawyers. Our analysis did not include such information, although it seems to be the most likely source of determinants of the unexplained variance in sentence severity. There was indirect evidence for such a belief, given the demonstrated importance of having a defense lawyer, and the absence of conflict in lawyers' sentencing recommendations.[9]

However, we submit that one could plausibly argue for a fourth, and completely different, explanation of the "unexplained variance in sentencing severity." It is quite conceivable that the unexplained variance would be explained by numerous other "relevant" variables, such as various mitigating or aggravating circumstances of the crime — it is obviously relevant whether a robbery was committed with a toy pistol or a loaded sub-machine gun. Other factors might well be around the judge's attitude to punishment (this is different from Warner and Renner's third explanation which relates to judges' beliefs about process).

The result of ignoring these factors leads the authors to conclude:

> Conflict was infrequent in open court, prosecutors, defense lawyers, and judges rarely expressed differing positions on the sentences. Possibly one could argue that the minimal conflict was simply due to the predictability of sentences given the offense and offender characteristics of the case. However,

this approach cannot explain the fact that a large portion of the variance in sentencing decision (62.5%) could not be accounted for by offense and offender characteristics. A more reasonable explanation is that communication, if not agreement (i.e., plea bargaining) accounted for the minimal level of conflict. The sentencing hearing was merely a formal ratification process.[10]

Thus, the authors conclude that because the "offense and offender characteristics" *that they measure* do not account for a great deal of the variance, those offense and offender characteristics could not explain more of the unexplained variance. There is no justification for such a conclusion, yet the sentencing process is characterized as a "formal ratification process" because of the existence of this unexplained variance. But this is not so. Under these circumstances unexplained variance is exactly that — unexplained variance. The slippery path the authors are led down by such reasoning is illustrated by their next paragraph:

Plea bargaining appears to be prevalent, . . . But how prevalent? There is no reliable quantitative answer, nor any way to obtain one, which illustrates the lack of openness and accountability. The courts do not collect empirical data on how and why decisions are made, nor allow access to external persons.[11]

The lack of "quantitative" data, according to them, demonstrates a lack of "openness and accountability." This seems to be an absurd result. The lack of data probably illustrates many things, but at least two things come to mind. First, that there are many issues — and potentially variables — which are normatively "cloudy." While several studies historically have suggested that inappropriate variables play a statistically significant role in sentencing,[12] there are numerous other variables where the normative issues are not at all clear; for example, the imposition of a lighter sentence for those defendants that agree to plead guilty. While numerous commentators have criticized such a practice,[13] the Supreme Courts in both Canada and the United States have either implicitly or explicitly endorsed the practice.[14] Another problematic example is cases where the judge (or judges) impose a more severe sentence where there is a high frequency of a particular offence in a given city or region.[15] Given that these issues have never to any extent, at least to our knowledge, been debated in a parliamentary context it seems harsh to accuse judges in a particular city or province of not formulating such factors.

This example hopefully demonstrates that attempts to extrapolate policy conclusions from empirical evidence, especially shaky quantitative data, is fraught with danger. Indeed, several commentators have concluded that improved bases and statistical techniques will never allow to develop sentencing practices which reduce the existing wide range of discretion. Thus, Carter in a recent study has argued that:

These pages thus challenge the premise that those who do justice *should*, as a practical administrative matter, seek primarily to treat similar cases similarly. These pages also challenge the assumption that we could in fact create an administrative system that achieves ordered or controlled case dispositions, even if we decided to try. Organization theory also provides a basis for challenging the assumption that those who do justice *can* treat similar cases similarly. We shall investigate the possibility that those systems that *are* highly rule-ordered normally operate with "technologies" and in "environments" that provide a high degree of certainty. Perhaps, if the techniques of doing justice were clear and those with whom criminal justice administrators deal behaved predictably, we could create uniform systems of case dispositions. But we shall see that prosecutors, as do other participants in the criminal justice system, operate with "technologies" and in "environments" that pose for them high degrees of uncertainty.[16]

A central hypothesis of Carter's is that order and uniformity are antithetical to "learning." He puts it thus:

> We shall see that in evaluating the decisions of those who do justice, the concept of justice fails to provide useful assessment criteria. It fails because the concept of justice itself embodies two mutually incompatible standards: order and learning. The compatibility arises because the objective of ordered application of law, unquestionably desirable in itself, presents a pragmatic tactical question: What administrative apparatus can achieve it? The conventional administrative apparatus for making behavior uniform — bureaucracy — imposes costs of its own. Specifically, bureaucratic controls can interfere with the alternative conception of justice as learning.[17]

This study will attempt to demonstrate that the search for selective uniformity is not chimerical and that it is currently possible, especially in a Canadian context, to at least partially define what we mean by uniformity. This is, of course, not to argue that questions of data, measurement, conceptualization and normative consensus have reached, or ever will reach, the point where all discretion would be eliminated.

Our premise is that utilizing existing empirical data in developing normative models is likely to be inadequate, and, indeed, seriously misleading. Furthermore, developing normative models "from first principles" without reference to empirically observed statements and behaviour, as we have argued elsewhere, also has serious flaws. We suggest that one approach to remedying the "bias" in empirical research is to more fully elucidate those variables which may be conceptually important but which have not as yet been measured. A subsequent necessary step will be to operationalize these variables and test their substantive importance and statistical significance (Hagan, 1974).

The analysis begins from a premise of one of the authors " . . . that the courts themselves have provided considerable guidance on relevant sentencing principles," and " . . . that future reform should be based on existing knowledge."[18] With the lack of legislative guidance, it has for the most part been up to the courts to develop these principles and criteria in sentencing. But given this lack of guidance and with the wide discretion left in the judges and magistrates, it is not surprising that there is considerable inconsistency in the enunciation of sentencing principles.[19] Therefore, "existing knowledge" must be analyzed and evaluated with due consideration of the possible inconsistencies. As Hogarth points out, some of the inconsistency can be explained by the lack of legislative enunciation of social goals to be achieved through sentencing. Further explanation comes from the courts' shift in emphasis in sentencing.

> In recent years there has been a noticeable shift in emphasis in rationale for sentencing from "looking backward" to the offence for the purposes of punishment to "looking forward" to the likely impact of a sentence on the future behaviour of the offender and in some instances on potential offenders in the community at large.[20]

This focus by the courts on what Hogarth terms as "control of crime" has increased the factors to be examined as the courts have placed upon themselves the burden of predicting the probable effect of the sentence on the offender — by necessity this involves more than a mere cursory evaluation of the offender as an individual.

We suggest that the decisions of the various provincial Courts of Appeal, on appeal against the sentence, are a viable starting point to develop clear, consistent and uniform sentencing principles which should substantially reduce disparity.[21] These decisions are both an important manifestation of how judges actually sentence and what sentences the learned justices think should be given. Thus, they provide a unique synthesis of what is *and* what should be.

Unfortunately, these decisions have not played the central role that they might have in the development of sentencing principles.[22] There are several reasons for this: appeals on sentence do not lie to the Supreme Court of Canada; additionally, the precedential nature of these decisions is hazy, and, one consequence has been that these cases are usually unreported, and this further increases the likelihood that their impact will be diminished.

This paper attempts to demonstrate how a systematic analysis of such cases could provide considerable guidance on sentencing and might provide the basis for legislative initiative. A systematic analysis of such unreported cases is an enormous task; obviously, our study can not be an exhaustive one. Rather we chose a sample of offences that are generally representative of the Criminal Code; namely, robbery, breaking and entering and fraud.[23]

THE EVIDENCE — APPELLATE REVIEW OF SENTENCING IN BRITISH COLUMBIA

For our analysis we chose appeals on sentence in British Columbia between January, 1974 and June, 1978. The cases analyzed included appeals both by the offender and by the Crown. The objective was not in any sense to select a statistically vigorous sample, but rather to construct, in a qualitative manner, a picture of the factors that appellate judges utilize in sentencing. Our broader goal was to see if we could develop a taxonomy of sentencing factors and principles.

There were 103 robbery cases, 76 breaking and entering cases and 40 fraud, false pretence and forgery cases. The information for the cases was obtained from the actual Court of Appeal Registry file used in court by the Court of Appeal Justices, and it is felt that as much information about each case as possible was obtained. The information gathered included the offence, case name, data of the appeal, sentence at trial, sentence as altered, if at all, on appeal, facts of the offence, age of offender, prior record, number of offences (whether several counts or multiple offences), criminal status at time of commission of the offence (whether no criminal status or no probation, on parole, on bail, escaped, etc.), aggravating or mitigating circumstances and whether a guilty plea or a not guilty plea was noted by the court.

A preliminary perusal of the cases suggested that few "types of factors" were involved for all of the offences. These four factor categories are: (1) factors relating to the offence; (2) factors relating to the offender before the offence; (3) factors relating to the offender after the offence; and (4) factors relating to broad societal goals. As we suspect that these four factor categories are generally applicable to most criminal offences, we utilized the factors as our main organizing device; thus, each offence is dealt with *within* these four major categories.

As we shall see, offences which involve a wide variety of fact patterns may require additional sub-categories, such as robbery, but the evidence suggests that these four factors will retain their usefulness for categorization.

Table 1 provides a basic outline of the analysis which is to follow. Each of the three offences is dealt with under the four factor categories. As the Table shows, factors relating to the offence of robbery had to be quite finely differentiated to make sense of the data. Thus robbery had to be broken down into (1) robberies of businesses, and (2) robberies of persons. Robbery sentences imposed on offenders convicted of robbing businesses made greater sense when this category was further divided into offences against banks and other large institutions, and robberies of "small shops." We have attempted to list the elements of each factor — such as degree of violence and use of weaponry — in this order of importance. This was necessarily a very subjective process; our rankings are sometimes based on what we perceived to be the tone of the particular case. As we have mentioned, the first factor related to elements of the offence itself. Under this factor we will deal with robbery, breaking and entering and fraud in turn.

Table 1

FACTORS MENTIONED BY THE B.C. COURT OF APPEAL AS EFFECTING SENTENCE OUTCOME

I   **Factors Relating to the Offence**

(A) *Robbery*

  (1) *Robberies of a Business*

    (a) *Banks and similar institutions*

      (i)   Degree of sophistication

      (ii)   Vulnerability of victim

      (iii) Probability of large number of victims

      (iv) Fact that a hostage was taken

      (v)   Avoidance of actual violence vis-à-vis potential violence

      (vi) Degree of violence

      (vii) "Size of the take"

      (viii) Passive participation

      (ix) Successfulness of the robbery

    (b) *Small Shop Robberies*

      (i)   Degree of violence

      (ii)   Degree of sophistication

      (iii) Use and type of weapon

      (iv) Amount of harm imposed on the victim

      (v)   Vulnerability of victim (in terms of time, place, physical conditions)

      (vi) Number of perpetrators

      (vii) Successfulness of the robbery

      (viii) Passive participation

      (ix) Purpose and need for application of violence

  (2) *Robberies of Persons*

      (i)   Degree of violence

      (ii)   Use and type of weapon

      (iii) Brutality and necessity of violence

      (iv) Vulnerability of victim (in terms of time, place, physical condition)

      (v)   Successfulness of robbery

  (3) *Fact-Neutral Factors Relating to the Offence*

      (i)   Number of counts and multiplicity of offences

      (ii)   Alcohol or drugs

(B) *Breaking and Entering*

  (a) Degree of sophistication

  (b) "Size of the take"

  (c) Type of premises

  (d) Possession of a weapon

  (e) Any application of violence

(f) Sexual implications

(g) Vulnerability of the victim

(h) Knowledge of the premises (breach of a position of trust)

(i) Successfulness of the offence

(j) Passive participation

(k) Number of counts and multiplicity of offences

(C) *White-collar Crimes*

(a) Degree of sophistication

(b) "Size of the take"

(c) Breach of a position of trust

(d) Passive participation

(e) Successfulness of the scheme

(f) Multiplicity of offences and number of counts

(g) Character of the victim

II Factors Relating to the Offender Before the Offence

(a) Age

(b) Sex

(c) Record (violence, developing pattern, etc.)

(d) Responses to previous leniency

(e) Professional criminal

(f) Association with criminal

(g) Criminal status

(h) History, and mental and physical condition of the offender

(i) Impetus of the offence

III Factors Relating to the Offender After the Offence

(a) Effort at rehabilitation

(b) Possibility of employment or training upon release

(c) Assumption of responsibilities

(d) Support of family or others

(e) Attitude and conduct in court and respect for the law

(f) Remorse

(g) Guilty plea

(h) Ability to cope with prison life

IV Factors Relating to Broad Societal Goals

(a) Protection of the public

(b) Deterrence

(c) Punishment

(d) Rehabilitation

I FACTORS RELATING TO THE OFFENCE

(A) Robbery

It is safe to say that the court treats robbery as one of the most serious in the Criminal Code, especially as the maximum sentence is life imprisonment. In dealing with the offence we first examined the cases in four categories, as provided in the Code.[24] The bulk of the cases, 56 of 103, appeared under armed robbery and most of the cases involving sophisticated bank and commercial robberies were contained within this category. The other three subsections involved more crimes in the category of street robberies, muggings, strong-armings, and robberies of occupants of dwelling houses although, of course, these types of crimes certainly were included in the armed robbery category.

There were found to be wider variations of individual sentences in each subsection; the average range of armed robbery sentences was higher than robbery and robbery with violence cases. The armed robbery sentences rarely dropped below two years except where the Court stated that a sentence in a provincial institution would be in the best interests of the offender in light of mitigating circumstances such as young age, lack of prior record, etc. On the other hand, for robbery and robbery with violence convictions, there are a number of cases where the sentence imposed was under two years, especially where there was little or no record. Although there are differences in sentences between the subsections, it was felt that utilizing the statutory subsections to divide the cases would not be particularly useful in analyzing the factors which relate to the commission of the offence.[25] Rather, we adapted fact patterns developed by Thomas[26] to deal with English robbery cases.[27] His classification of fact patterns is summarized in the following statement:

> Description of the general pattern of sentences in robbery will be easier if the cases are divided into five broad categories of fact situation — the large-scale bank raid or wage snatch, the attack on a tradesman carrying takings to the bank or other person carrying a substantial amount of cash in course of business. The attack on a small shop, sub-post office or garage, the house breaking accompanied by violence against the householder, and what for want one of a better term will be called the "mugging" — the attack on a person late at night or in a secluded place, with a view to stealing his wallet or whatever valuables he may have with him. Clearly, these categories merge into each other and the classification will in many cases be an arbitrary one.[28]

We simplified Thomas' scheme by only utilizing two categories: (1) robberies of a business which would include Thomas' first three categories (no cases were found of attacks on tradesmen, etc.); and (2) robberies of a person for their personal belongings which would include also a housebreaking accompanied by violence.

Our examination of the cases suggested that factors described as important in altering sentences varied between these two categories. Dealing first with business robbery, two factors relating to the offence appear to be pre-eminent: the type of business and the degree of sophistication involved in the robbery. The type of business appears to involve a definite "sentence hierarchy" with small shops at the bottom and banks at the top.[29] Obviously the second factor — degree of sophistication — is correlated with the kind of institution, although not inevitably. The degree of sophistication includes consideration of the degree of planning and organization, number of persons involved, premeditation and precision in carrying it out. Inherent in these two factors are considerations relating to offences against the person, which can either mitigate or aggravate the sentence. With respect to mitigation, the Court may look at the degree of planning in terms of whether the object was the avoidance of violence. It would appear that this was a consideration in *R. v. Bilawchuk,*[30] which involved a well-planned armed robbery of shopping centre employees who had the day's receipts: the two perpetrators of the crime received sentences of 9 1/2 months and one year. Similarly, in the English case of *R. v. Gardiner,* cited by Thomas,[31] where the Court reduced a sentence of ten years to seven years pointing out the fact that the robbery was "well planned and executed" with an absence of violence.[32]

However, it is much more likely that a large-scale operation and a large institutional business will aggravate an offence against the person. With a more organized bank type robbery there is, as Ruby points out, greater danger to the public because " . . . they usually involve danger to more than one person, i.e., innocent bystanders and employees."[33] Certainly this factor can go towards explaining the fact that the courts hand out more severe sentences for bank robbery. Also, the vulnerability and probability of persons in banks being robbed is greater than in other institutions because of their susceptibility to being robbed. One factor which appears to have a very serious aggravating effect on the sentence is whether a hostage was taken; this is inherently more likely in connection with a bank robbery. In *R. v. Kandral*[34] and *R. v. Stephen Smith,*[35] the offenders were sentenced to 11 and 12 years respectively. In *Smith,* the Court of Appeal was particularly cognizant of the "premeditation and seriousness of the offence," notwithstanding a minimal prior record and fairly young age, 23. However, even where there is a violent taking of a hostage, the Court sometimes will not be precluded from imposing sentences of less than ten years. In *R. v. Hernstad and Rhodes,*[36] the Court of Appeal dismissed a Crown appeal against sentences of one year and two years' probation for the 19-year-old offender who, with an accomplice, executed a well-organized bank robbery. In the course of the operation, a bank employee was kidnapped at gun point and the bank was robbed of more than $21,000 by the armed and masked offenders while the employee was left tied up. The Court felt a longer term of imprisonment was not necessary for rehabilitation in light of the young ages and lack of record.

The court's definition of the usual range seems to present some problems. The Court of Appeal has not been entirely consistent in stating the usual range for armed bank robberies. Although it is clear that a range can not be narrowly defined and a sentence will vary according to the circumstances; two cases clearly illustrate the inconsistency. In *R. v. Miller,*[37] Taggart J.A. noted the common range for bank robberies as being ten to twelve years. Two weeks later, in *R. v. Owens,*[38] he stated that the norm is seven to twelve years. On the other hand, in *R. v. MacAskill,*[39] Farris C.J.B.C., for an armed bank robbery case, stated, "In the usual case a sentence of twelve to fifteen years would be certainly appropriate and in many cases, it should be more."

In bank-type robberies, consistent with the findings of Thomas, although the use of and degree of violence is an important factor, there is much more focus on the degree of planning. The Court takes note of whether the offender was armed, what type of weapon, if a gun, whether it was loaded, and whether any shots were fired. Thus, in *R. v. Lidal,*[40] the fact that the gun went off during the bank robbery was taken into account in imposing a 10-year sentence. However, violence appears to become much more important where there is a robbery of a small shop or person on the street. On the other hand, absence of planning may be an important mitigating factor in the small shop or person robberies. The "size of the take" also appears to be of limited significance, although it is usually positively correlated with the degree of planning.[41]

Turning to the small shop robberies, an inconsistency problem is confronted from the outset. In general, while it is quite clear that in actuality the usual range of sentences for small business robberies is one to six years (absent extreme violence) and for bank-type institutions, seven to fifteen years.

The Court of Appeal stated in *R. v. Rivera*[42] that "[t]he smaller storekeeper should be entitled to the same protection as the large bank and thus those who prey on the stores must be expected to pay the penalty." In this case, the offender received four years on three counts of armed robbery of drug stores. Occasionally, the courts will impose sentences in excess of the usual range. For example, in *R. v. Urchenko,*[43] an offender with a minor criminal record received what the court described as a "heavy" sentence of 12 years for two armed robberies of service attendants. In *R. v. Irvine,*[44] the offender with a similar record held up a service station attendant at knife-point and received an 8-year sentence. However, these cases fail to give much insight into what is required to take the sentence out of the usual range.

As we have mentioned for "small shop" cases which fall within the usual range, there is an identifiable difference in the relative importance of the various factors relating to the offence as compared to bank robbery. First, the degree of sophistication is less important and the court is concerned more with the degree of violence. Thus, in *R. v. Brown,*[45] the Court of Appeal noted the premeditation and planning in a violent armed robbery of a store, but felt a sentence of two years was appropriate in light of the offender's alcoholism and lack of a criminal record. The amount of violence is the factor most instrumental in positioning the sentence within the usual range. As will be seen with robberies of the person, the Court tends to engage in a detailed examination of the facts to differentiate cases in determining the degree and seriousness of the violence. Of course, the use of a weapon will be an aggravating circumstance varying in importance with the type of weapon and use or lack thereof. The fact of a gun being discharged may not, however, even take the sentence out of the usual range. In *R. v. Lee,*[46] a sentence of five years was imposed on a 19-year-old offender with an atrocious record who, in a night robbery of a hotel, had his 12 gauge shotgun go off in the female night clerk's direction just missing her head. On the other hand, in *R. v.*

Dumbleton,[47] McFarlane J. A. said, "Although there was a question as to whether or not there was an actual striking with the knife, the *mere presence* of the knife, in the circumstances, involves a degree of violence which is important to note."

Certainly the lack of a weapon is a mitigating circumstance in a robbery of a business, but its occurrence is very rare. The fact that the offender has an imitation of a weapon is of little effect where the victim believed the gun to be real. In *R. v. Hapi,*[48] the offender received four years for robbery of $53 with a toy gun. Apart from the use of arms, the court is very conscious of two factors: the degree of violence of harm imposed on the victim, and vulnerability of the victim.[49] As would be expected, grievous bodily harm to storekeepers will be treated severely. This was particularly evident in *R. v. Dellow and Yates,*[50] where a service station attendant was seriously cut by a knife; the offenders received seven and eight years respectively. Again, in *R. v. Schneider,*[51] the Court of Appeal noted the violent manner in which the offender dealt with the female shopkeeper in forcing her to the floor and tying her up, and dismissed the offender's appeal from a 5-year sentence. In addition, the Court almost invariably treats the vulnerability and character of the victim as an aggravating factor. Both the time and place of the offence are relevant here. Night robberies of motel clerks, all-night grocery store or gas station attendants are treated severely as they are usually alone with little protection. Other aggravating factors include those circumstances where the victim is very young or old, or the victim is a female.[52]

It is not entirely clear from cases how the Court treats the fact that the robbery was unsuccessful. In two store armed robbery cases, the Court imposed relatively lenient sentences within the range but there was no comment on the unsuccessfulness and there were other identifiable mitigating factors. Thus, in *R. v. Robinson,*[53] the female offender armed with a loaded .22 calibre rifle attempted to rob a grocery store. She received a sentence of 18 months definite and 12 months indeterminate. The Court of Appeal pointed out that she had created a threatening and dangerous situation and clearly intended robbery but felt that rehabilitation was indicated by the mitigating factors of age and pathetic circumstances.[54] It would appear that there is little, if any, mitigating value for the unsuccessful robbery if one were to remove other mitigating circumstances in these cases.

Also unclear from the cases is the Court's treatment of the offender's participation in the offence. Passive participation in the sense of driving a getaway car or acting as a lookout certainly could be argued as being a mitigating factor. Yet, with a serious crime like robbery its mitigating value on the sentence is likely to be very limited. In *R. v. Hodson,*[55] McFarlane J.A. seems to imply that the offender's passive participation in a violent robbery, although recognized by the court, will have little effect on the disposition of sentence. In this case, in which the offender drove the getaway car for three others involved in a violent robbery of a service station at 2:00 a.m. and received a 4-year sentence, McFarlane J.A. stated:

There was no question that this is the kind of robbery which courts must deal with in a very serious way because of the violence involved. Although the accused did not act violently, he was one of the gang who acted in concert.

The purpose of the application of the violence is an important factor. The application of unnecessary violence was recognized as a highly aggravating factor in *R. v. Penlerich.*[56] The offender was convicted of robbery with violence. The offence took place in a small shop early in the morning with the accused and his accomplice attacking a lone female employee, striking her on the head with a stick, punching her in the face and forcing her on the floor face down. On the offender's appeal, the Court of Appeal dismissed the appeal stating that a heavier sentence could have been applied. McFarlane J.A. stated further,

> There was no need, if the accused wanted to steal the money, to make this attack on a lone woman in the shop . . . a total unnecessary application of brutal violence.

With robberies of persons,[57] as with robberies of small businesses, the usual range of sentences is one to six years, in the absence of very dangerous weapons which the offender threatened to use or used and the absence of unnecessary sadistic imposition of violence. Apart from this, the main differentiating factor is the use of violence and the vulnerability of the victim. Planning and premeditation are very rarely aggravating factors because they are rarely evident. However because of this, spontaneity is not as much of a mitigating factor as it is with robberies of businesses.

Planning and gang organization may become relevant, however, when they are closely related to the degree of violence. Thus in *R. v. Billy and Joachim,*[58] the Court pointed out that the seriousness of an offence which involved two women victimizing a man with the threatened use of a knife was increased because of the element of planning involved, and increased the sentences from four and eight months to nine and eighteen months for the two Indian women, respectively. In *R. v. Sun Kail Szeto et al.,*[59] (three others) the Court of Appeal stated that it was correct for the trial judge to consider information which showed the existence of a gang and their activities, and compare it with the pattern of activity of the four offenders in question, that is, the organized way in which the crime was carried out.

There are three major considerations in assessing the degree of violence: the seriousness of the use of a weapon on the person, the brutality and sadism of the violence applied and vulnerability of the victim. The normal range of these armed robberies of persons appears to be three to five years.[60] However, where there is a serious use of a weapon, such as a knife or razor, resulting in physical harm to the victim, it appears the Court will raise the sentence out of the usual range. In *R. v. Parent and Holyoak,*[61] the offenders received sentences of ten and eight years, respectively, for a crime in which they inflicted serious slash wounds and stabbed a helpless and bound victim in the victim's apartment. The court described the attack as sadistic. Maclean J.A. went as far as saying:

> It was as bad an offence as the court has yet seen in its experience in dealing with criminals of this kind and it is not necessary nor would it be proper to write all the particulars of what was done by each of the defendants.

With cases that involve the absence of a weapon, the focus turns to degree of physical harm and savagery of violence imposed upon the victim. When the attack is less than brutal and vicious and any violence is necessary for the commission of the offence, the sentences were never in excess of four years. Again, though, the unnecessary application of violence will be a highly aggravating factor. Here again the vulnerability of the victim becomes relevant, since the court must enter upon a subjective evaluation as to whether the violence imposed was necessary. As soon as the court regards the application of the violence as being brutal, sentences of five to seven years are imposed.[62]

Although the vulnerability of the victim is closely related to the assessment of the brutality of the violence, it is also an important factor in its own right. The court takes note of the sex, age and physical condition of the victim and the time and place of the attack. However, merely because of the fact that the victim is an elderly person in a disadvantaged state or a woman, where the offence takes place, in a secluded place at night, the court will not necessarily impose a severe sentence where there is an absence of brutality. These facts are likely to have more effect where they are coupled with a brutal attack. Thus, in *R. v. Frank,*[63] the young offender received one year indefinite and one year indeterminate for a robbery of an elderly woman, and in *R. v. MacDonald,*[64] the 30-year-old offender waylaid a woman in a secluded parking lot but merely received a suspended sentence with three years probation. However, in *R. v. Minilowitch,*[65] a brutal attack of a 70-year-old man placed this 26-year-old man in prison for four and one half years, and in *R. v. Bruce,*[66] the offender beat up a 50-year-old woman breaking her shoulder and received four years. Consistent with *R. v. Iwaniw; R. v. Overton*[67] cited by Ruby,[68] the British Columbia courts appear to recognize the special vulnerability of the taxi driver whose occupation makes him vulnerable to attack, *ergo,* sentences should be more severe. In *R. v. Maclean,*[69] the B.C. Court of Appeal reduced a sentence of six years which they felt was appropriate for the circumstances (armed robberies of cab drivers) to a sentence of four years because of the offender's improvement in attitude and commitment to ridding himself of alcohol addiction.

The degree of participation rarely arises in either mitigation or aggravation in these cases, as the accused is usually directly involved in the commission of the offence. It was not mentioned in any of the cases. Usually the court ignored whether the robbery was successful; and because of the seriousness of the crime, the court is unlikely to give this factor much weight. However, in one case the court noted that the offender abandoned his attack when unsuccessful, and this seemed to have a mitigating effect on the sentence.[70] The defendant received a suspended sentence and three years of probation.

Two other factors are often relevant in robbery offences: (1) the number of counts and multiplicity of offences; and (2) alcohol or drugs. It is difficult to determine whether the number of counts and multiplicity of offences have very much effect on the sentence unless the sentences are consecutive rather than concurrent.

The Court is more likely to treat the offences as being in a series, or as part of the same transaction, where the offences are committed within a limited time; the Court then looks at facts of each of the counts but focuses especially on the most important and serious count. Where multiple offences are involved the Court is almost invariably more concerned with the robbery charge because it is usually more important. The rule appears to be that the Courts focus on the most serious count of robbery and merely note the offences or counts committed, usually treating them as elements in the series or as part of the transaction unless they are readily and clearly differentiated groups of counts or offences which should be treated consecutively because of their significant separate importance.[71]

The Court will consider whether alcohol or drugs played any part in the commission of the offence. It is more likely to be evident in robberies of persons and will be considered in relation to the spontaneity of the offence. In a number of cases the Court notes that the accused "became involved through an excessive amount of drink."[72] However, in general, the Court leaves us with little guidance as to the extent of the mitigating effect of alcohol or drugs. Certainly, as in *R. v. Ross*,[73] the Court is unlikely to give much mitigating effect where there is a high degree of violence. In this case the offender received a 5-year sentence for robbery with violence with a 1-year consecutive for assaulting a police officer. On the other hand, in *R. v. O'Brien*,[74] the Court of Appeal reduced a two year less a day sentence to six months for a 21-year-old offender with no record whose only explanation for involvement with three others in robbery with violence was the fact that he had been heavily drinking earlier in the evening.

(B) Breaking and Entering

Turning now to breaking and entering, we can note an important and sharp contrast to robbery cases in terms of factors relating to the offence. For the most part, the Court's analysis of the facts is relatively minor and the Court in its approach is much more concerned with factors relating to the offender.

> In robbery the most significant factors are the nature of the offence, the degree of organization and the extent of any violence used, and the offender's record may often be disregarded as irrelevant; in breaking offences the sentence tends to depend much more on personal characteristics and record of the offender subject to the general principle that the sentence must be in proportion to the

offence for which it was imposed. For this reason, identification of the ranges of permissible sentences is extremely difficult.[75]

Consistent with Ruby's finding,[76] the sentence range in British Columbia was found to be from a suspended sentence to five years imprisonment. The Court consistently concerned itself with the individual rather than the offence. However, where the offence involves a very high degree of premeditation, planning, organization and sophistication, the Court does appear to become less concerned with rehabilitation and emphasizes deterrence. In these cases, factors relating to the offender are given less weight than in the "usual" breaking and entering. In *R. v. Lemire,*[77] leave to appeal was refused by Bull J.A. on a sentence of four and one half years for a breaking and entering of an auctioneer's premises which was described as ". . . a sophisticated, carefully planned and premeditated caper in which a great deal of planning had to be done to accomplish the purpose," with almost $200,000 worth of jewellery and money taken. Bull J. A. still noted the offender's record and age. On the other hand, lack of premeditation and impulsiveness in the commission of the offence will usually mitigate the offence. This is clearly evident in *R. v. Mitchell*[78] in which the 27-year-old offender received a six month suspended sentence for an impulsive breaking and entering in which the offender and another stole primarily food. In assessing the impulsiveness, the Court readily takes into account any evidence concerning whether the accused was on drugs or alcohol.[79]

The value of the amount taken appears to have much more significance in breaking and entering offences than in robbery. The Court of Appeal in most of the cases took note of the value of the goods taken and their treatment of the cases indicates a high take will be an aggravating factor. Additionally, considerable damage will certainly be an aggravating circumstance. This is illustrated by *R. v. Bonner*[80] where the Court of Appeal noted the considerable damage done to a church in a breaking and entering by the offender, and assessed a nine month definite and twelve month indeterminate sentence, notwithstanding the offender was only 17 and had no adult record. The Court examines the premises and appears to treat breaking and entering of dwelling houses more severely than other places which is consistent with the statutory scheme of section 306 of the Criminal Code which provides for life imprisonment for dwelling houses and 14 years for other premises.

Further, aggravating to sentence is the application of violence, bordering on robbery, towards the occupant. In *R. v. Prokopovich*[81] the Court of Appeal upheld a sentence of four years and Bull J.A. stated:

> The violent breaking and entering of a home of an innocent man late at night while his wife and children were sleeping, the brandishing and firing of a firearm, the use of extreme violence in smashing the doors to gain entrance constitute criminal conduct of the most vicious kind.

The case also illustrates the aggravating effect of time (late at night) and possession and use of a firearm. As with robbery cases, the Court in considering dwelling house breaking and enterings will consider the character of the victim. This is illustrated by *R. v. Degoutiere*[82] in which the offender received three years concurrent on two counts for getting into the homes of two elderly ladies by the means of deceitful tricks and stealing while he was there. Also, knowledge of the premises appears to be an aggravating factor in the sense of a breach of trust. In *R. v. Zinna,*[83] the Court of Appeal noted that the accused used his knowledge of his former employer's premises to commit a routine breaking and entering; he received two years. The Court also noted when the offender burglarized the same premises on separate occasions in *R. v. Lindal,*[84] and *R. v. Belegratis.*[85]

As with robbery, it is not clear how the courts treat attempts, but it would appear that there is little mitigating value since in *R. v. Chounard*[86] and *R. v. Shewchuk,*[87] the offenders received three years and two years less a day, respectively, for attempted breaking and entering. The number of offences appears to be more important with breaking and entering than with robbery. The Court of Appeal expressly stated in *R. v. Bryce*[88] that when there are a number of breaking and entering offences committed within a relatively short period, it is more appropriate to sentence the accused to one appropriate term with respect to the worst of the offences and to make the other sentences concurrent. Probably the fact that there were eight counts influenced the Court of Appeal in imposing a 2-year sentence where none of the counts appeared especially aggravated.

(C) White-collar Crimes

Even more so than with breaking and entering, the Court's approach to sentencing for the so-called "white-collar" offences is one directed at the offender rather than at the offence. As Table 1 indicates, there are few relevant differentiating factors relating to the offence, although the cases vary from large scale sophisticated fraudulent schemes involving large sums of money, to relatively minor schemes to obtain relatively small sums of money by forgery or passing of dud cheques. The range of sentences varied from conditional discharge to five years of imprisonment.

The false pretences cases involved mostly cases of passing NSF[89] cheques and false representations to obtain goods from small businesses. Included under the forgery head were cases of forgeries of cheques, licence renewals, and prescriptions, the bulk of which were forged cheques. The fraud cases varied from minor label switchings, to welfare fraud up to major sophisticated schemes to defraud persons, employers, insurance companies and businesses. The fraud offences probably best represent the true "white-collar" crime and the major focus will be on this offence. Certainly the Court is more concerned with examining these factors in fraud cases.

There appear to be three major aggravating factors associated with these crimes: (1) degree of sophistication and planning; (2) the size of the take; and (3) the position of trust of the offender. The lack of premeditation or spontaneity is unlikely to be a mitigating factor with the exception of the passing of an NSF cheque where the accused decides to pass it on the spur of the moment. In *R. v. Prentice,*[90] the Court of Appeal noted the offender's impulsive behaviour but it was unlikely that this had any effect on the sentence as there were 14 counts of passing worthless cheques. Certainly, such an argument would lack conviction in forgery or fraud cases.

The degree of sophistication is very seriously considered by the Court in disposition of sentence. Notwithstanding that the offender has no serious criminal record, the Court will impose substantial terms of imprisonment if there is a highly sophisticated, well-organized fraudulent scheme. Thus, in *R. v. Lewicki,*[91] an offender with a very old, non-serious record received a 5-year sentence for an elaborate mortgage fraud in which he defrauded the victims of over $75,000 over several years. In *R. v. McDougall,*[92] a female offender with an inconsequential record received a 3-year sentence for a "carefully premeditated and worked-out plan" in which she embezzled over $40,000 from her employer. Common fraud, involving considerably less planning and organization rarely resulted in sentences over two years in length. The aggravating impact of the amount realized is also clearly evident in the *Lewicki* and *McDougall* cases, *supra*. When the offender holds a position of trust, it is clear that the factor has an important aggravating impact as shown in *Lewicki, McDougall* and *Menzing,*[93] where the offenders breached the trust of their clients, and employer respectively. In *Menzing,* the Court of Appeal made particular mention of the special position of trust the offender was in.

It appears there are two mitigating factors relating to the offence. Passive participation was noted in *R. v. Usher,*[94] where the Court of Appeal reduced a sentence of six months to three months as the offender's companion was the instigator of a false pretences offence.[95] A small take or unsuccessful scheme may be taken as a mitigating factor, but as in *R. v. Kosdrowski,*[96] it may be overriden by other aggravating factors relating to the offender such as a serious record, drug addiction, and past probation failure. Thus, in this case, a sentence of 18 months was imposed for a relatively minor forgery.

Once again the cases failed to clearly indicate how the Courts deal with the number of counts and multiplicity of offences. Most of the false pretence cases involved more than one count — in general, multiple counts were more prevalent in the forgery and fraud cases than in robbery or breaking and entering cases. In all of the cases, the multiple counts were treated as a series and all sentences were concurrently imposed. In only one case were there multiple offences: *R. v. Dupuis;*[97] here the Court of Appeal did take into account the total money involved. So it would appear that the Court considers the total dollar value of the counts in assessing the seriousness of the offence, rather than merely looking at the most serious count. This seems logical in light of the importance the Court places on the size of the take.

The Court will also sometimes consider the relative importance of the loss to the victim. In *R. v. Birch,*[98] the offender received two and one half years for five counts of passing forged cheques to tradespeople. Farris C.J. stated, "People of the offender's type are serious nuisances, to put it mildly, to tradespeople, and cause innocent people substantial loss. Therefore, the crime should be treated seriously." However, the Court of Appeal felt that the 4-year disposition of the sentencing judge was excessive for the circumstances. Ruby[99] found that the type of victim appeared to have little bearing on the sentence.[100] The Court usually did not mention the factor and it certainly would appear to be much less important than for crimes against the person.

II   FACTORS RELATING TO THE OFFENDER BEFORE THE OFFENCE

The effect of the factors relating to the offender before the commission of the offence (hereafter referred to as pre-existing factors) is obviously difficult to accurately assess. It would appear that these factors, along with those relating to the offender after the commission of the offence, are considered after the Court has studied the factors relating to the offence and attempted to determine an appropriate sentence range for the offence given the factors already considered above. The majority of the factors relating to the offender are mitigating in influence and appear to be consistent with the practice of the English courts as described by Thomas:

> The process by which . . . the length of a sentence is reached involves three main stages. The determination of the general range for the category of offence; the preliminary placing of the particular offence within the range by reference to its intrinsic seriousness; and the calculation for allowances for mitigating factors.[101]

We found that an analysis of factors relating to the offender required an offence oriented basis. The importance and relative effect of the various factors varies according to the seriousness of the offence and the court's attitude toward the offence. We begin with an examination of age of the offender; as Thomas puts it, the youth of the offender is "[w]ithout doubt the most effective mitigating factor."[102] Moreover, the court's consideration of age may not be limited to offenders under 21; in some robbery and breaking and entering cases the Court referred to the mitigating impact of age where offenders were in their early twenties.

Age is of least importance in robbery cases, especially where there is violence. As the Court of Appeal pointed out in *R. v. Nutter et al.:*[103]

> I do not think the ages of persons makes much difference when they are committing these violent crimes. Young men who persist in committing crimes of this sort cannot expect that their ages will be regarded as mitigating circumstances. We are in a period now where, as I have already said, there is a

rash of crimes of violence. This is no time for softness and sentimentality to govern the imposition of sentences for offences of this sort.[104]

The Court of Appeal in two cases noted the trial judge's overemphasis on age and increased the sentences accordingly.[105] On the other hand, one case shows that, notwithstanding *Nutter,* age may have a mitigating impact if coupled with lack of record. In *R. v. Hernstad and Rhodes,*[106] one year in jail and two years of probation was imposed on two youths for a planned armed bank robbery involving a hostage. Even if there is a serious record, age may still be mitigating. Thus, in *R. v. Healy,*[107] a 1-year sentence was imposed on a 20-year-old offender with a serious record for robbery with violence.

In breaking and entering cases, age is often mentioned as a mitigating factor and in a number of cases as the key factor. For example, in *R. v. O'Sullivan,*[108] for a fairly serious breaking and entering of a dwelling house involving theft of a television and camera, a 19-year-old offender with an "unenviable record" had the 18-month indeterminate portion of his sentence removed to leave him with a 18-month sentence. In *R. v. Francoeur,*[109] the Court of Appeal refused to increase the suspended sentence and 1-year probation of an 18-year-old offender for breaking and entering a home in which he was challenged by the occupant. Definite-indeterminate sentences were considerably more frequent for the under 22-year-old offender convicted of breaking and entering offences as was the Court's use of probation coupled with sentences of less than two years. Usually, age was not a factor in fraud cases. In fact, only one of the offenders was under 21 and age was not mentioned as having any effect.

The sex of the offender may also be a relevant consideration, although the courts have said in a number of cases that where a man and woman are equally involved in an offence, the sentences should be the same, assuming similar circumstances; to the contrary, however:

> Nonetheless, it is common practice for sex to be taken into account in mitigation for female accused; one common justification is the existence of minor dependents who would suffer if the mother were to be imprisoned.[110]

Certainly the six robbery cases involving women offenders resulted in sentences which were at the low end of the range, the highest being two years less a day. There were no women offenders in the breaking and entering category. Thirteen of the forty white-collar cases involved women. There appeared, however, to be no discernible difference in the treatment of women where children were not involved. In four cases the Court of Appeal noted that the offender was a mother.[111]

"The one fact that is uniformly relied upon, when available, to assist the court in sentencing is the criminal record, if any, of the prisoner."[112] There appear to be two basic ways of approaching the application of prior record: (1) it can be used either in mitigation or aggravation of the sentence; (2) it can be used only to mitigate the sentence. The latter approach has been expressed as follows:

> The seriousness of the offence . . . creates a ceiling; the sentence must be proportionate to the offence, even where the offender has very many previous convictions. From the initial figure calculated by reference to the seriousness of the offence allowance may be made by way of mitigation for good character, or for modestly good character; but the initial figure remains and the maximum sentence permissible for that particular offence, and any inflation of the sentence beyond that point in view of a particularly bad record is considered incorrect.[113]

None of the cases stated this latter principle, although the Court of Appeal did reduce the sentence in *R. v. Burke,*[114] where an offender with a serious record was charged with breaking and entering; the sentence was reduced from five years to three years. The approach that appeared evident in the cases, although not expressly stated, was one of utilizing a serious record to negate other mitigating factors, thus allowing the sentence to remain near the "ceiling" set for the sentence according to the seriousness of the offence.

An examination of the cases suggested that the appellate court utilized prior record extensively. We identified at least eight classifications,[115] namely: (1) no record; (2) one to five unrelated, relatively minor offences; (3) minor drug, drinking, or driving offences only; (4) past non-serious history (out of trouble for long time); (5) past serious history (out of trouble for long time); (6) somewhat lengthy record but non-serious with no pattern developing nor violence; (7) serious record with pattern developing and possible violence; (8) atrocious with well-developed pattern of propensity to crime and serious and violent crimes. The impact of this prior record is very clearly dependent on the type of offence for which the offender was sentenced. For example, a record of violence in the past will likely have much more impact on a subsequent robbery conviction than on a forgery conviction.

Examining our eight categories, it was evident that as the seriousness of the prior record increased, the sentence increased. The increases, however, did not appear to be constant over all categories of prior record. The impact was clearest when the offender had either very little prior record, or a serious prior record. The serious and no record or very minimal record record categories had ranges of sentences which were much more concise and definable than the moderately serious sentences. For the no record or very unrelated minimal record category, we see a highly mitigating impact on sentence and a resulting sentence near the bottom end of the range. With the serious record, we observe a severe reduction in the mitigating impact of other factors resulting in sentences near the top of the range. However, a moderate prior record has less impact either mitigating or aggravating, and the sentence tends to be determined by other factors.

Turning our attention to the effect of the record on the specific offences, it was evident that as the violence and premeditation increased, the mitigating effect of no record or a minimal record was decreased or eliminated. This is illustrated by *R. v. Kandrul,*[116] where the Court of Appeal upheld an 11-year sentence for an armed bank robbery in which a hostage was taken. The Court noted the lack of record and even stated: "This is only a single lapse unlikely to be repeated." In robbery cases, the Court is primarily concerned with violence in the past record, especially previous robbery and assault convictions. The Court's treatment of the sentence is markedly altered where the accused has been out of trouble for a long time and the effect of the sentence will be dependent upon the seriousness of the past record coupled with the length of time the offender has been out of trouble.

In robbery, co-accused are less likely to be differentiated in terms of sentence on the basis of their record. In *R. v. Uttley*,[117] the Court of Appeal was not influenced by counsel's argument that the appellant received the same sentence as co-accuseds who had much more serious criminal records and who had more culpability in the offence.

With breaking offences, as with our "white-collar" crimes, especially false pretences and forgery, the Court's major focus in assessing the record turns to whether a pattern is developing rather than violence in the offender's past.[118] The mitigating effect of lack of record is less likely to be diminished by other factors relating to the offence, whereas it may be with robbery. A serious record and a developing pattern may, however, override the mitigating effect of other factors such as age.[119] As with robbery, the Court will take into account the fact that the offender has been out of trouble for a long time.

Ruby[120] and Thomas[121] talk of a "jump effect" as a mitigating factor in which the court will reduce a present sentence because the "jump" up from the previous longest sentence was too great. However, the factor was never mentioned by the B.C. Court of Appeal and certainly would appear to be of little mitigating value, especially for violent robbery or even serious breaking or "white-collar" offences, for offenders who failed to benefit from previous leniency.

Related to the examination of the record are three further factors: whether the offender is a professional criminal, whether he is associated with other criminal types, and whether he has improved himself as a result of previous leniency by the courts. Where the court has decided the offender is a professional criminal or has "deeply entrenched himself into a life of crime" with little hope for rehabilitation (taking into account factors relating to the accused after the commission of the crime), the court's primary purpose in sentencing becomes protection of the public. Mitigating factors relating to the accused, such as pathetic family background, are severely downplayed. The court appears to be more severe with crimes against the person. In *R. v. Baker*,[122] the Court of Appeal increased a sentence to eight years as the offender had lived a criminal life since 17, notwithstanding that the offender was only 21 and had a favourable pre-sentence report. The professional "con" man certainly appeared to be at the top of the list for high sentences even for relatively minor false pretences offences; thus, in *R. v. Simmons*[123] the Court of Appeal staunchly refused to consider any efforts at reform by the offender and left the matter to the Parole Board.

Association with criminals was mentioned by the Court in all types of offences and would appear to influence the court's opinion of whether the offender is likely to return to crime. The Court of Appeal also noted gang association frequently, especially when robbery and breaking offences were involved. Of the three factors, the most important appears to be the offender's response to leniency by the courts in the past. In cases where the offender had a previous robbery conviction or other violent crime conviction where the sentence was lenient, there appeared to be a substantial increase for a subsequent conviction of the same type of offence.[124] It was also mentioned frequently in breaking offences. *R. v. Tremire*[125] is illustrative of the court's emphasis on the factor. In this case a youthful offender with only two previous convictions for theft and breaking and entering and who initially received a suspended sentence and one day, on appeal, was sentenced to nine months definite and eighteen months indeterminate.

Criminal status at the time of the commision of the offence is an aggravating circumstance. The five possible states analyzed were probation, parole, escaped, just after release[126] and out on bail. The Court of Appeal frequently mentioned the factor without, however, clearly enunciating any guidelines as to its relative importance. Nonetheless, a few observations can be made. First, notwithstanding an offence was committed while the offender was on probation, the court is not reluctant to impose another term of probation following some sort of imprisonment, especially for breaking and entering. However, young offenders with a non-serious offence and record who breach their probation, often receive an indeterminate sentence to allow the court more control. This desire for control seems to be evident in the Court of Appeal's rejection of one youthful offender's appeal for removal of the indeterminate portion of his breaking and entering sentence for the offence committed while on probation.[127] In *R. v. Byrant,*[128] the Court of Appeal cited the offender's failure on probation as reason in rejecting an appeal against a definite-indeterminate sentence. Offences committed while on parole or after escape would appear to be treated more seriously, but the effect on the sentence was difficult to isolate because the offenders in these cases usually had serious records.

The importance of factors relating to the history and mental and physical condition of the offender is largely dependent on the seriousness of the offence and the record. In general these factors are less significant in mitigation than no record or youth. It is useful first to list a number of the often mentioned factors: work record (may be aggravating or mitigating); disruptive family background (usually mitigating); violent or aggressive propensity (aggravating); low intelligence (mitigating); good reputation and character (mitigating); good family background, not disadvantaged (may be aggravating); personality disorder (may affect where the offender is sent); and educational and vocational ability (usually mitigating). In practice, lack of skill may be aggravating, where the offender is forced to remain in an institution to acquire a skill, or mitigating, where he is released to take training at an outside institution.

Examining these factors in terms of offences, it is evident that these mitigating factors were given much less weight in robbery offences, especially where there was serious violence and/or a serious record. Violent and aggressive propensities along with personality disorders focused the Court on protection of the public and deterrence. If the offence was described as "out of character," the Court, especially in breaking offences, may be willing to impose lenient sentences arguing that a person of this character can be suddenly deterred.[129] However, good character is treated very differently with white-collar crimes. In *R. v. McDougall,*[130] the Court of Appeal cited *R. v. Spiller*[131] for the proposition that a person of good character who can appreciate his wrong and weigh the consequences of his crimes should not be allowed to rely on his previous good character as a mitigating circumstance for this type of crime. However, with a forgery case, the Court's approach may be somewhat less strict; in *R. v. Cavadas,*[132] the offender's good work record and character were the factors which saved him from a penitentiary term.

The Court may also consider the impetus or cause of the offence as a mitigating factor. Mention was made of the causative factor in relation to factors relating to the offence. Some of the more common causative factors include financial difficulties, domestic or emotional crisis, alcohol or drugs, the need for excitement and substantial influence of others. The weight attached to this factor depended on the Court's assessment of the gravity of the offence in relation to the causation factor. As illustrated by *R. v. Chamberlain,*[133] the Court may be impressed by evidence that the offender was, as a result of his difficulties, at the point of desperation, thus leading to an impulsive act. In this case the sentence was a $2,000 fine with two years of probation, notwithstanding an armed robbery of a storekeeper. In *R. v. Thurston and Power,*[134] a day to two months and two years of probation on seven counts of breaking and entering where evidence was brought before the Court that the main catalysts to the offences were financial difficulties and alcohol. In *R. v. Myles,*[135] the Court accepted that welfare frauds were the result of the desperate acts of a deserted mother attempting to survive on an inadequate income.

Perhaps the most complicated factor involves the influence of drugs and alcohol. Partially, this complexity arises because the use of drugs goes to both the circumstance of the offence and the pre-existing state of the offender: few other factors have such a dual role.

Addiction to drugs or alcohol is a factor which may be mitigating, aggravating or neutral. It appears that the courts recognize its importance in assuming the offender's likely behaviour in the future. In all the cases, the courts gave some indication as to how much impact the factor had on sentence. There appeared to be five ways in which the Court viewed the factor, three being mitigating and two aggravating: (1) the sentence may be mitigated to allow alcohol or drug treatment at a provincial institution;[136] (2) drugs or alcohol may represent a partial excuse especially if the offence is out of character;[137] (3) the offender's effort to rid himself of the addiction may also cause the Court to mitigate the sentence to encourage the offender further in his efforts;[138] (4) the factor may lead the Court to increase the sentence with a view to deterrence because of the increased crime associated with the prevalence of drugs in the area;[139] and (5) the factor may point towards a need for protection of the public because of the Court's assessment of the offender's likelihood of future crime to further the habit.[140] Table 2 summarizes the number of cases where drugs or alcohol played a mitigating or aggravating role in sentencing various offences.

Table 2

EFFECT OF ALCOHOL AND DRUGS

No. of Times / Offence	Mitigating	Aggravating	Not Evident
robbery	1	4	19
robbery w/violence	4	7	10
assault w/intent	1	0	1
armed robbery	10	7	39
break & enter	11	12	53
false pretenses	0	0	10
forgery	0	2	12
fraud	0	0	16

III FACTORS RELATING TO THE OFFENDER AFTER THE OFFENCE

These factors subsequent to the offence include consideration of efforts to rehabilitation, employment and educational possibilities upon release, evidence indicating the assumption of responsibility (such as marital status and support of dependents) support of relatives and others, attitude in court, respect for the law, remorse, co-operation with police, a guilty plea and inability to cope with prison life. It appears that the Court of Appeal is not entirely consistent with its treatment of these factors. Although the Court may recognize that these factors should have a mitigating impact, it is not necessarily the case that the sentence will be reduced accordingly. The Court has said in a number of cases that this matter is best left to the Parole Board.

The effort at rehabilitation is probably the most important mitigating factor of any of those subsequent to the commission of the offence. The Court here is looking for positive concrete efforts rather than mere statements of intention. In *R. v. Allred,*[141] the Court ignored the offender's interest in learning a trade. If the offender has a number of problems and there has been no effort at rehabilitation, the Court will infer he is unwilling to improve and unlikely to change in the near future and bring the sentence more in line with the seriousness of the offence; thus, in one case, the Court raised the offender's armed robbery sentence to five years from twenty months and four months consecutive, notwithstanding the offender had no record.[142]

Looking at the mitigating effect of the factor in terms of specific offences, the Court of Appeal was much more willing to reduce a robbery sentence if the initial sentence was either at the high end or low end of range than if the sentence was on the middle of the range, that is, about three to four years. This is probably because of the fact that any significant reduction in the middle range is likely to take the offender out of the penitentiary, whereas with the low or high sentences, the Court can give substantial decreases without changing the nature of the sentence, which should still reflect the Court's assessment of violence and planning. In *R. v. Hodson,*[143] *R. v. Bruce,*[144] and *R. v. Dube,*[145] the Court of Appeal noted the offenders' efforts but refused to reduce the four-years-sentences for robbery with violence. It would appear that the Court was also influenced by the fact that there was unnecessary violence in the last two cases.

Rehabilitative efforts had some impact in breaking and entering cases. In *R. v. Zinna,*[146] a sentence of three years was reduced to two years and would have been less, but the Court felt it would be in the offender's interests to complete a mechanical training course. As for "white-collar" crimes, efforts at rehabilitation are less likely to be relevant for fraud convictions because the offender usually has a minimal record and a previously good character. With forgery and false pretences, efforts are likely to be noted if the problem at which the rehabilitation is to be directed was at the root of the offence. In *R. v. Ballendine,*[147] the offender's treatment of her heroin addiction was central in the Court's reduction of her six month sentence to imprisonment of three days already served, with two years of probation.

The most common type of rehabilitation is an effort by the offender to rid himself of alcoholism or addiction to drugs. The Court here makes an assessment of the real possibility of success and likely will not reduce the sentence for the mere effort. Two pieces of evidence seem to weigh most heavily: involvement in a treatment plan, and the effort to acquire a skill, training or education. Under these cirumstances where the offender had a long prison sentence, the Court of Appeal allowed or upheld substantial reductions. In *R. v. MacAskill,*[148] the Court upheld a sentence of nine years for a serious armed robbery (for which a 15-year sentence would have been appropriate) because the offender was enrolled in a university program and was doing well. In *R. v. Cross,*[149] the Court of Appeal was "willing to bend over backwards" to reduce the offender's sentence from nine years to six years to encourage and stimulate the offender's involvement in a number of educational programs. Even where the initial sentence is less than two years, the Court is not reluctant to reduce the sentence substantially in relation to the initial sentence. In *R. v. O'Brien,*[150] the Court of Appeal reduced a robbery with violence sentence of two years less a day to six months recognizing the offender's enrollment in school. In *R. v. Shaw,*[151] an initial 1-year breaking and entering sentence was reduced to the time already spent of 27 days along with two years of probation. An offender's involvement in prison government was recognized in *R. v. Miller.*[152] In *R. v. Huestis,*[153] the Court of Appeal indicated the possible mitigating value of an effort to move out of the environment in which the offender was constantly getting into trouble.

The possibility of employment or enrollment in a training or educational institution upon release may also be a mitigating factor. The Court of Appeal will take this into account in allowing an appeal for reduction of sentence or in dismissing a Crown Appeal.[154] Not surprisingly, the factor is much less likely to be of value in robbery cases than in breaking and entering cases. In *R. v. Booth,*[155] notwithstanding efforts at rehabilitation by the offender, the Court of Appeal altered an 18-month sentence to 2 years less a day definite and indeterminate. The Court was not persuaded by the fact that the offender had a steady job to go to, in light of the violence associated with the crime. Whereas, in *R. v. Grant,*[156] although the Court felt a two and one half year sentence was appropriate for a serious, premeditated breaking and entering of a dwelling house, the sentence was reduced to the time already spent in custody of six months; the Court relying on the offender's steps taken to improve his education along with a promise of enrollment in a vocational institute upon release. There were similar reductions in false pretences and forgery cases, although again it is not as likely to come up with fraud cases.[157]

The Court favors evidence which shows that the accused is assuming responsibilities, provided they are reasonably attainable for the offender given his financial and emotional condition. This intended assumption of responsibility must be such to indicate that the offender has completely changed his attitude and lifestyle. Apparently in *Huestis,*[158] the mere fact of the offender's caring for his dependent mother, even coupled with his considerable effort to improve himself, were not sufficient to demonstrate the type of change necessary. However, in *R. v. Fox,*[159] the offender's robbery with violence sentence of two years less a day and probation for one year was reduced to one day in jail with three years probation where the circumstances showed the offender was married, expecting a family and prepared to accept the responsibilities of raising a family together with the opportunity for job training. In *R. v. Chase,*[160] the Court of Appeal upheld a breaking and entering sentence of 90 days to be served intermittently on weekends with two years probation where two years would have been appropriate because of the offender's assumption of responsibility for his deaf child. It would appear that the Court makes an examination and evaluation of the type of relationship between the offender and a dependent to ensure that there is a sufficient degree of cohesiveness and sense of obligation so that the responsibility will deter the offender in the future.

For the young offender, the Court is especially impressed by whether there is support from relatives or interested persons. In *R. v. Wilson,*[161] a female offender convicted for armed bank robbery had, since sentence, made contact with her parents and gained their support. The Court expressed the hope that the family would give her the motivation to move away from drugs and reduced her 5-year sentence to two years less a day. Even the support of friends may be relevant when coupled with other factors: *R. v. Chamberlain.*[162] In *R. v. Biggs,*[163] the only reason the Court reduced a 17-year-old offender's sentence from one year to six months was because of the adult sister's commitment to provide supervision and support. The factor is, however, not of much relevance for the so-called "white-collar" crimes. Negative family relations may even end as an aggravating factor, thus the Court, in one case, noted the offender's rejection of his parent's support in increasing the offender's sentence to seven years from three years for armed robbery of a credit union.[164]

The matter of the offender's attitude and conduct in court, the trial and the offender's respect for the law are factors to which it is difficult to estimate the importance the courts attach, because these are largely determined by the trial judge through his observations of the offender at trial.

> There is a serious question as to what weight should be attached to this factor. In *R. v. Simmons,*[165] the dissenting judge relied upon the trial judge's observation that the three accused found their proceedings "humourous and boring" and he characterized their attitude as cynical and a little short of contemptuous and as indicating a complete lack of contrition. The majority, apparently also taking these factors into account, nevertheless lowered the sentence.[166]

The matters were rarely mentioned in the cases possibly indicating their lack of significance. However, in four cases in which a poor attitude in court or a disrespect for the law was mentioned, the Court did dismiss the appeals.[167] The Court of Appeal seems much more willing to take into account the offender's lack of remorse. In *R. v. Dube,*[168] as mentioned earlier, the Court of Appeal recognized the offender's efforts at rehabilitation but upheld the 4-year sentence, pointing out he showed little remorse, his only concern being that he left fingerprints.

The factors of remorse, co-operation with the police and prosecution, and guilty plea are closely related and often occur together. Certainly, co-operation with the authorities is concrete evidence of the offender's remorse. One case demonstrates the importance the factors may place. In *R. v. Piette,*[169] the Court in reducing a 10-year sentence to 5 years, cited as the major reason the fact that the offender after four months turned himself into the police when there was little chance of being caught. In the *O'Brien* case,[170] we see all three of these associated factors operating — the offender was remorseful, co-operated with police and pleaded guilty. In the fraud case of *R. v. Barron,*[171] the Court noted the fact that when the fraud was discovered, the offender readily admitted the offence and gave the required information. Payment of compensation was recognized in both the *Barron* case,[172] and the *Owens* case.[173]

The guilty plea has been held to be a mitigating factor that may be taken into consideration.[174] However the Court, in making its decision, did not consistently mention whether there was a guilty or not guilty plea. In breaking and robbery cases, the guilty plea was only mentioned where there was a decrease in sentence or the sentence remained the same. However, with two fraud cases and one forgery case, guilty pleas were noted notwithstanding an increase in sentence. In the forgery case of *R. v. Dupuis,*[175] the Court of Appeal stated that consideration should be given to the fact that the offender allowed the authorities to clear up several matters by pleading guilty to 9 counts of forgery and 33 related counts, but, in practice, seemed to be little impressed by the plea as it increased his sentence.

Ability to cope with prison life was recognized in two cases as a possible mitigating factor. In the *O'Brien* case,[176] the Court felt that a 2-year less a day prison term would destroy the 21-year-old offender and ensure that he would be into the ways of crime. Certainly, the factor turns on the Court's assessment of the offender's possibilities for rehabilitation and the likely effect of prison on that rehabilitation. The other case was more of an exceptional case. In *R. v. Kennedy,*[177] a sentence of two years less a day was reduced to the time already spent with two years probation because of the effects of incarceration on the offender due to fear of the treatment received by the other inmates in light of the fact that the inmate thought he was a female.

IV   FACTORS RELATING TO BROAD SOCIETAL GOALS

It is often said that the imposition of sentences is one of the more important mechanisms through which society attempts to achieve its social goals. The main difficulty arises from the fact that there is little agreement as to what these social goals are, or indeed should be.[178]

The Court consistently made reference to the broad goals of sentencing, namely: protection of the public, deterrence (both general and specific), rehabilitation and punishment. It appeared that the Court first usually assessed the specific factors we have described, relating both to the offence and the offender, and then applied a general "label," or goal. The Court would then assess the trial judge's overall label and attempt to compare the two. Obviously, where the labels were not congruent the Appeal Court was more likely to alter the initial sentence.

For robbery offences, protection of the public was most often mentioned as being paramount, followed by deterrence, and punishment, with rehabilitation coming into effect where the offender clearly demonstrated that there was substantial potential for rehabilitation. With breaking and entering, deterrence and protection of the public appear most often to be regarded as the first concern, with punishment and rehabilitation following. For "white-collar" crimes, deterrence and punishment appear to be more at the centre of attention with protection of the public a primary concern where the offender has a very serious criminal record with a consistent pattern of these types of crimes or an addiction to alcohol or drugs and rehabilitation.

In many of the cases, the Court merely states that the prime factors are deterrence, protection of the public or punishment without pointing to specific facts relating to the accused or offence. Only where rehabilitation is cited as a significant factor is the Court explicit as to what circumstances were instrumental in turning the Court's focus away from the other three objects. The terms are used loosely and transcend many different types of fact patterns and circumstances relating to the offender. The use of these concepts had limited value in assessing the Court's determination of range for sentences and the aggravating (in the sense earlier discussed) and mitigating effects of factors relating to the offender.

Where protection of the public is stated as being a prime factor, it was evident that the Court was concerned with the seriousness of the offence and to those specific factors relating to the offender which indicate a potential danger to the public, e.g., serious record, anti-social tendencies, severe addiction to drugs and alcohol, disposition for violence, disrespect for the law.

When discussing deterrence, the Court brought in the community's assessment of the seriousness of the crime and its desire to have the incidence of that type of crime decreased.[179] A number of cases included the statements to the effect that there were too many crimes of this nature and therefore deterrence was an important factor, for example: *R. v. Bolton*[180] and *R. v. DePerry.*[181] These statements were accepted merely as indications of the importance to be accorded certain factors without any assessment as to the deterrent effect of the sentence.

Often we were left with the impression that these more general concepts were "shorthand" descriptions of the other three factor sets — they stated a conclusion rather than forming part of the analysis. A robber with a propensity to violence and a serious prior record was often sentenced in terms of protection, deterrence and punishment, while a breaker and enterer with a trivial record would often be sentenced in terms of rehabilitation.

SUMMARY: THE VALUE OF APPELLATE CASE ANALYSIS

Our analysis of these cases led to one fairly obvious conclusion — it is possible to construct a taxonomy of the factors utilized by appellate judges in sentence review. We believe that the few inconsistencies and gaps discovered are just as important as the positive information. Often they highlight areas where the courts have not yet resolved difficult normative problems. As a result of the study we are able to provide a rough guide to some of the sentencing practices of the British Columbia Court of Appeal. Indeed we have prepared a short summary guide.[182] However, it is submitted that such a guide is not the primary output of this study.

We would argue that extensive analysis of appellate sentencing decisions, in all provinces, will encourage the development of sentencing principles that are empirically grounded (that is, judges actually utilizing such factors) and are normatively sound. This is not to say that all will agree with the various appellate courts reasoning or weighting of factors. Rather we would argue that only by a full discussion can the appropriateness or unappropriateness of these factors be decided.

It is our contention that the systematic collection of data on how appellate judges make their decisions will allow us to refute the arguments of commentators such as Carter (described earlier) that order and learning are antithetical. However such an improvement is only realistic if information is collected systematically and presented to judges in a usable form (see Vining, 1979; Gottfredson, Wilkins and Hoffman, 1978), so that we can achieve selective uniformity. Further research in this area should lead to an administrative system that achieves more uniform case dispositions. The factors elicited here should be particularly useful in implementing the kind of sentencing reform "matrix" proposed by Vining (1979). It may also assist those jurisdictions which have attempted, through parole schemes (and which therefore are relatively flexible), to implement selective uniformity to refine the factors utilized to differentiate offenders. It should help empirical researchers to identify and measure variables, which, heretofore, have been reported as unexplained variance.

We believe that it is important to note that the chief impetus of Canadian sentencing reform, as represented by the Law Reform Commission of Canada is not in this direction. Their proposed reforms would give little direction to judges, or appellate courts, on the factors to be considered in sentencing. We do not believe that such reforms will provide learning or order. These reforms would result in the continuation of a highly decentralized and discretionary justice system *without effective feedback mechanisms* which is doomed to go on repeating its mistakes. Rather, our aim should be to encourage institutional learning that is refined enough (that is, recognizes the existence of enough factors) so that the individual is not sacrificed to a God of order.

NOTES

1. See, for example, the work of the Law Reform Commission of Canada, including, *Imprisonment and Release Working Paper 11* (1975); *Studies on Sentencing* (1974); *Studies on Imprisonment* (1975).

2. A. Wildavsky, "The Strategic Retreat on Objectives," *Policy Analysis* (Summer, 1976), p. 500.

3. A. R. Vining, "Canadian Sentencing Reform: Problems and Prospects," 17 *Osgoode Hall Law Journal* (1979).

4. John Hogarth, *Sentencing as a Human Process* (Toronto: University of Toronto Press, 1971); A. Warner and K. E. Renner, *Research on the Halifax Criminal Courts: A Technical and Conceptual Report* (Halifax: Dalhousie University, October, 1978).

5. Henry Bullock, "Significance of the Racial Factor in the Length of Prison Sentences," 52 *Journal of Criminal Law, Criminology and Police Science* 411 (1961); John Hagan, "Extra-Legal Attributes and Criminal Sentencing: An

Assessment of a Sociological Viewpoint," 8 *Law and Society Review* (1974); L. Tiffany, Y. Avichai and G. Peters, "A Statistical Analysis of Sentencing in Federal Courts: Defendants Convicted after Trial, 1967-1968," 4 *Journal of Legal Studies* (1975); Aidan Vining, *The Limits of Individualization: Sentencing Variation and Disparity in California* (Berkeley: unpublished Ph.D. thesis, University of California, 1979a).

6. Hogarth, and Warner and Renner, *op. cit.,* note 4; Vining (1979a), *op. cit.,* note 5.

7. Warner and Renner, *op. cit.,* note 4; Vining (1979a), *op. cit.,* note 5.

8. Hagan, *op. cit.,* note 5.

9. Warner and Renner, *op. cit.,* note 4, p. 91.

10. *Ibid.,* p. 92.

11. *Ibid.*

12. For example race, sex and type of defence have all been empirically analyzed. For reviews of this literature see Hagan, *op. cit.,* note 5, and Vining (1979a), *op. cit.,* note 5. For recent empirical evidence in Canada see Warner and Renner, *op. cit.,* note 4.

13. See especially A. Alschuler, "The Defense Attorney's Role in Plea Bargaining," 84 *Yale Law Journal* 1179 (1975).

14. In Canada see D. Cousineau and S. Verdun-Jones, *Setting Standards for Canadian Criminal Courts: The Case of Plea Bargaining,* S.F.U., 1977, and in the United States see *Brady v. United States,* 397 U.S. 742 (1970).

15. In British Columbia, see *R. v. Hinch and Salanski* (1967), 62 W.W.R. 205 (B.C. C.A.).

16. L. Carter, *The Limits of Order* (Lexington, Mass.: Lexington Books, 1974), p. 2.

17. *Ibid.*

18. Vining (1979), *op. cit.,* note 3.

19. Hogarth, *op. cit.,* note 1; Vining (1979), *op. cit.,* note 3.

20. Hogarth, *op. cit.,* note 1, p. 4.

21. For a more detailed argument on this point, see Vining (1979), *op. cit.,* note 3.

22. *Ibid.*

23. Robbery was chosen as being broadly representative of offences against the person, breaking and entering as broadly representative of crime against property, and offences involving fraud as broadly representative of "white collar" crime (including ss. 324-336 of the Criminal Code). Obviously, robbery includes aspects of both offences against property and offences against the person. Ruby points out that historically in the common law, violence associated with robbery was the most important factor with the aspects relating to property being of only secondary importance. However, as will become evident later in the paper, these property aspects have gained much more importance. Yet, it was felt that robbery was better classified as a crime against the person recognizing the property aspects to the crime (Ruby, *Sentencing*, Toronto: Butterworths, 1976, p. 438).

24. The offence of robbery is broken into 4 subsections under section 302: (a) robbery whereby the offender uses or threatens the use of violence for the purpose of stealing; (b) robbery with violence which can be described as constructive robbery in that the offender steals with the proximate application of violence, that is, violence is not necessary for the commission of the theft; (c) assault with intent to steal; and (d) armed robbery, which requires the offender be equipped with an instrument other than a clenched fist. Section 303 provides that every one convicted of robbery is liable to imprisonment for life.

25. It is recognized that the subsections are more relevant for establishing a conviction for the offence of robbery rather than for providing guidelines for sentencing. The Crown will proceed with whichever subsection it feels it has the best chance of establishing, and not necessarily the one which most accurately describes the facts of the case.

26. D. A. Thomas, *Principles of Sentencing* (London: Heinemann, 1970), pp. 71-169.

27. We should, of course, keep in mind that there is a different statutory scheme in England.

28. Thomas, *op. cit.,* note 26, p. 129.

29. The cases examined involved a wide range of premises including corner stores, small business firms, restaurants, motels, grocery stores, jewellery stores and banks.

30. Unreported, May 3, 1977.

31. Thomas, *op. cit.,* note 26, pp. 130-131.

32. However, two passing observations concerning English cases should be made here. First, as Thomas points out, courts in England seem much less willing to reduce a sentence below seven years where there is a large scale operation.

> Seven years clearly represents the Courts' view of the minimum sentence in normal circumstances for a robbery involving organization and a substantial sum of money, in the absence of violence. (Thomas, *op. cit.,* note 26, p. 131)

Canadian courts seem to be a little more flexible. Second, English bank-type robbery offences tend on the average to be much more organized and on a larger scale than in Canada.

33. C. Ruby, *Sentencing* (Toronto: Butterworths, 1976), p. 441.

34. Unreported, May 13, 1974.

35. Unreported, November 19, 1976.

36. Unreported, March 16, 1978.

37. Unreported, May 14, 1975.

38. Unreported, May 28, 1975.

39. Unreported, October 21, 1977.

40. Unreported, March 3, 1974.

41. The Court of Appeal rarely mentioned the size of the take for a bank robbery. However, of the three cases in which they did and which involved fairly large sums, two were cases in which the offenders received lenient sentences. In *Hernstad and Rhodes, supra,* note 36, the offender received one year of imprisonment and two years of probation, where $21,000 was taken, and in *R. v. Sangster* (December 10, 1976) for an armed bank robbery of $1,825, an offender who was a family man with no previous record received an 18-month sentence. However, a 3-year sentence was increased to seven years in *R. v. Dunstan* (January 30, 1978) where the offender was convicted of robbery of $2,200 from a credit union. Furthermore, the fact that the robbery was unsuccessful or that the offender was not an active participant are of much less importance where the offender is involved with the well-planned bank robbery.

42. Unreported, September 8, 1976.

43. Unreported, January 17, 1974.

44. Unreported, December 3, 1975.

45. Unreported, October 7, 1977.

46. Unreported, February 2, 1977.

47. Unreported, June 14, 1977.

48. Unreported, June 14, 1976.

49. Much of this parallels the discussion concerning robberies of persons.

50. Unreported, October 28, 1977.

51. Unreported, November 18, 1976.

52. *R. v. Schneider, supra,* note 51.

53. Unreported, May 5, 1975.

54. See also *R. v. Harry* (April 16, 1975).

55. Unreported, June 28, 1976.

56. Unreported, January 4, 1977.

57. Within this class we have included muggings, taxicab robberies and housebreakings accompanied by violence.

Robberies of persons as defined above straddle all the four subsections of section 302, although the bulk of the cases are found within robbery, robbery with violence and assault with intent to steal. Of course, there are robberies of persons under the armed robbery subsection with the factor of a weapon being an aggravating factor.

58. Unreported, October 6, 1975.

59. Unreported, February 23, 1976.

60. In some cases the courts will impose a sentence of two years less a day (to allow imprisonment in a provincial institution) where the offender is young and does not have a serious record.

61. Unreported, August 22, 1977.

62. See, for example, *R. v. Price* (June 6, 1974).

63. Unreported, October 16, 1974.

64. Unreported, November 18, 1975.

65. Unreported, December 15, 1977.

66. Unreported, September 10, 1976.

67. (1959), 127 C.C.C. 40 (Man. C.A.).

68. C. Ruby, *Sentencing* (Toronto: Butterworths, 1976), p. 440.

69. Unreported, September 9, 1976.

70. *R. v. MacDonald* (November 18, 1975).

71. See *R. v. Saumer* (March 17, 1977), and *R. v. Magnussen* (May 16, 1977).

72. *R. v. Hance and Johnny* (January 1, 1977); see also *R. v. Ross* (May 25, 1977); *R. v. O'Brien* (November 21, 1977).

73. See note 72, *supra.*

74. *Ibid.*

75. D. A. Thomas, *Principles of Sentencing* (London: Heinemann, 1970), p. 139.

76. Ruby, *supra,* note 64, p. 444.

77. Unreported, June 8, 1977.

78. Unreported, April 10, 1974.

79. *R. v. Cikvar* (March 26, 1976), and *R. v. Marshall* (May 16, 1975).

80. Unreported, June 10, 1974.

81. Unreported, April 19, 1977.

82. Unreported, September 16, 1976.

83. Unreported, May 24, 1977.

84. Unreported, May 8, 1975.

85. Unreported, November 5, 1975.

86. Unreported, January 9, 1976.

87. Unreported, May 11, 1974.

88. Unreported, March 26, 1976.

89. Not sufficient funds.

90. Unreported, March 29, 1977.

91. Unreported, June 16, 1978.

92. Unreported, December 14, 1977.

93. Unreported, February 2, 1978.

94. Unreported, June 12, 1978.

95. This is consistent with reported cases such as *R. v. Hinch and Salanski,* [1968] 3 C.C.C. 39 (B.C. C.A.).

96. Unreported, May 15, 1978.

97. Unreported, February 2, 1978.

98. Unreported, March 8, 1977.

99. C. Ruby, *Sentencing* (Toronto: Butterworths, 1976), p. 450.

100. Citing *R. v. Major* (1966), 48 C.R. 296 (Ont. C.A.), where the elderly victims lost their life savings.

101. D. A. Thomas, *Principles in Sentencing* (London: Heinemann, 1970), p. 36.

102. *Ibid.,* p. 171.

103. *R. v. Nutter et al.* (1970), 7 C.C.C. (2d) 224 (B.C. C.A.).

104. *Ibid.,* pp. 228-229.

105. *R. v. Hope* (June 4, 1976), increased from 2-1/2 to 4 years; *R. v. Lee* (February 28, 1977), increased from 3 years to 5 years.

106. Unreported, March 16, 1978.

107. Unreported, September 27, 1977.

108. Unreported, June 2, 1975.

109. Unreported, January 23, 1978.

110. *R. v. Williams* (1953), 37 Cr. App. R. 71 (C.A.).

111. *R. v. Ahlstrom* (May 20, 1976); *R. v. Frances Philip* (July 8, 1975); *R. v. Barron* (April 26, 1976); and *R. v. Myles* (January 16, 1978).

112. C. Ruby, *Sentencing* (Toronto: Butterworths, 1976), p. 28.

113. D. A. Thomas, *Principles of Sentencing* (London: Heinemann, 1970), p. 39.

114. Unreported, September 9, 1974.

115. In classifying some of the cases, consideration was made of the Court of Appeal's evaluation of the past record, especially where there was no actual criminal record included in the file.

116. Unreported, May 13, 1974.

117. Unreported, November 9, 1977.

118. Although violence may still be a factor, *R. v. Lindal* (May 8, 1975).

119. In one case, *R. v. Johnson* (June 28, 1976), the court felt the offence, in light of a persistent pattern of breaking offences, called for a penitentiary term but reduced the sentence due to the offender's age.

120. Ruby, *op. cit.,* note 112, p. 98.

121. Thomas, *op. cit.,* note 113, p. 182.

122. Unreported, September 30, 1974.

123. Unreported, October 29, 1974.

124. *R. v. Bee* (December 12, 1975).

125. Unreported, November 5, 1974.

126. Just released is, of course, not a criminal state, but the courts tend to treat it in the same way as a criminal state.

127. *R. v. Letkeman* (May 17, 1976).

128. Unreported, March 11, 1974.

129. *R. v. Harrison and Garrison* (September 14, 1977), and *R. v. Falcon* (December 5, 1977).

130. Unreported, December 14, 1977.

131. (1969), 6 C.R.N.S. 360 (B.C. C.A.).

132. Unreported, March 22, 1977.

133. Unreported, February 2, 1978.

134. Unreported, December 5, 1975.

135. Unreported, January 16, 1978.

136. *R. v. Wilson* (May 4, 1977).

137. *R. v. Sangster* (December 12, 1976).

138. *R. v. Johnson* (June 28, 1975).

139. *R. v. Tennisco* (May 12, 1975).

140. *R. v. Urchenko* (January 17, 1975).

141. Unreported, October 30, 1974.

142. *R. v. Hancock* (April 26, 1976).

143. Unreported, June 28, 1976.

144. Unreported, September 10, 1976.
145. Unreported, October 7, 1976.
146. Unreported, May 24, 1977.
147. Unreported, October 14, 1977.
148. Unreported, October 21, 1977.
149. Unreported, January 14, 1975.
150. Unreported, November 21, 1977.
151. Unreported, January 14, 1977.
152. Unreported, May 14, 1975.
153. Unreported, January 20, 1977.
154. *R. v. Waboose* (September 11, 1975).
155. Unreported, December 7, 1976.
156. Unreported, November 19, 1976.
157. *R. v. Chapman* (June 5, 1974).
158. Unreported, January 20, 1977.
159. Unreported, March 24, 1976.
160. Unreported, November 8, 1974.
161. Unreported, May 4, 1977.
162. Unreported, February 2, 1978.
163. Unreported, November 22, 1976.
164. *R. v. Siebot* (January 1, 1978).
165. (1973), 13 C.C.C. (2d) 65 (Ont. C.A.).
166. C. Ruby, *Sentencing* (Toronto: Butterworths, 1976), p. 127.
167. *R. v. Seiferling* (November 5, 1974); *R. v. McNabb and Fillion* (April 18, 1977) ("a matter of having some fun"); *R. v. Fredette* (February 17, 1977); and *R. v. Riches* (November 22, 1977).
168. Unreported, October 7, 1976.
169. Unreported, February 2, 1978.
170. Unreported, November 21, 1977.
171. Unreported, April 26, 1977.
172. *Ibid.*
173. Unreported, May 28, 1975.
174. *R. v. de Haan* (1967), 52 Cr.App.R. 25 (C.A.); *R. v. Johnston,* [1967] 4 C.C.C. 64.
175. Unreported, February 8, 1978.
176. *Supra,* note 170.
177. Unreported, February 2, 1975.
178. John Hogarth, *Sentencing as a Human Process* (Toronto: University of Toronto Press, 1971), p. 3.
179. *R. v. Chamberland (No. 2)* (November 8, 1977).
180. Unreported, October 7, 1974.
181. Unreported, November 1, 1976.
182. Available from the authors. Write to C. Dean, Faculty of Law, University of British Columbia.

Part 3

SENTENCES: OLD AND NEW

CHAPTER 8

Sentencing to Death: The Inherent Problem

E. A. Fattah

INTRODUCTION

Death penalty debates usually focus on its presumed deterrent effect, its
retributive merits, the moral, philosophical and religious arguments for or
against it. Consequently, little attention is paid to the several practical problems
inherent in its application. These problems are frequently obscured by the
emotionalism and sensationalism usually surrounding philosophical debates on
the death penalty, and overshadowed by the hot controversy that characterizes
discussions around the deterrence issue. Deterrence is, no doubt, of great
relevance to legislators and policy-makers in their deliberations on whether to
retain or abolish capital punishment. It is, however, of less pertinence to
sentencing judges and juries whose task is to settle the issue of guilt and to apply
the law as it stands. Arguments about the deterrent effect of capital punishment
may still be addressed by the courts when other issues are examined. They were
addressed by the U. S. Supreme Court in some of its recent rulings on the
constitutionality of the death penalty and by the Canadian Supreme Court in *R.
v. Miller and Cockriell.*[1]

Of more relevance to the judge and jury are the sentencing problems more or
less unique to capital cases, as well as the evidentiary problems raised or
accentuated by the legal provision for the death penalty as a mandatory or a
possible sanction for the crime. For example, does capital punishment have an
inhibitory effect on judges and juries in capital case? Does it, especially if it is
mandatory, aggravate the evidential requirements thus resulting in more guilty
killers being acquitted? Does its abolition secure more convictions? Is it
discriminatory? Is it applied in a randomly selective manner? All these
questions and many others are susceptible to empirical testing and validation.
But the problems the death penalty poses for sentencing are by no means limited
to these ones. Does capital punishment enhance the potential for error? Does it
increase the frequency of insanity pleas? Does it serve any of the modern aims of
sentencing? Is it the only "just" punishment for deliberate killing? Is it
indispensable for demonstrating society's abhorrence to murder? Is it a more
effective deterrent than the alternatives? Is it a cruel and unusual punishment
contrary to the Canadian Bill of Rights? All these are questions in search of
answers and the purpose of the present paper is to provide some information
that may be helpful in finding those answers.

CAPITAL PUNISHMENT'S INHIBITORY EFFECT ON JUDGES AND JURIES

Supporters of the death penalty contend that it is an indispensable means of protecting society against murderers and dangerous killers. This theoretical argument does not take into account empirical evidence suggesting that rather than deterring potential murderers the death penalty exercises an inhibitory effect on juries and judges in capital cases.

Those who are familiar with the administration of justice know that retaining the death penalty, especially if it is made mandatory, reduces the likelihood that indicted offenders will be convicted. In many instances, the jury's reluctance to be responsible for, or involved in, the legal taking of human life overrides all evidence and defys inevitable inferences from undisputed facts. Prosecutors have always complained that the death penalty makes it more difficult to secure convictions and often results in the acquittal of obviously guilty defendants. In an historical article by Mackey[2] judges, legislators, newspaper editors, and others are quoted as asserting the unwillingness of jurors to convict when the penalty is death. Mackey, for example, quotes a writer in a New York journal who claimed, as far back as 1847, that "The law of blood is virtually inoperative. . . . Unpunished criminals were walking the streets because juries would not convict them in capital crimes." When a human life is at stake, he wrote, "It is evident that the minds of jurors become distempered and unsettled and they rush to any conclusion, however irrational and absurd, rather than pronounce the doom of a fellow being."[3] This view simply echoed opinions expressed by legal scholars and law-makers on the Continent. The point was well stated in what is known as the "Rejected Preamble" of Sir Samuel Romilly's Bill of 1808:

> Whereas the extreme severity of penal laws has not been found effectual for the prevention of crimes; but, on the contrary, by increasing the difficulty of convicting offenders, in some cases affords them immunity and in most cases renders their punishment extremely uncertain.

The idea that severity of punishment prevents convictions and results in impunity for the offender was again expressed some years later by the French penal reformer, Charles Lucas, in his attack on capital punishment. Lucas maintained three fundamental principles: (a) that the efficacy of penalties depends on the certainty and proximity of repression; (b) that the certainty is in inverse relationship with the severity of penalties; and (c) that, in this perspective, the death penalty was, of all penalties, the least repressive.[4]

In the introduction to the British Criminal statistics furnished by the Home Office in 1924 it is stated that:

> In consequence of the strong proof of guilt necessary for conviction of crimes punishable by death, the proportion of acquittals for murder is higher than for

most other crimes, and an acquittal in such a case does not necessarily imply
failure to detect the perpetrator of the crime.[5]

And, more recently, the Home Office Statistical Division reported in its study of
murder in England and Wales that:

> The analysis suggests that juries were reluctant to convict of capital murder
> and that they found to be "non capital" a number of offenses which would have
> been classified "capital" if estimates had been necessary.[6]

In the United States the problem was stated before the House of
Representatives of the State of Pennsylvania on January 19, 1834 when
statistics on 238 cases of homicide in Pennsylvania were read into the record of
the House to demonstrate the efficacy of the penalty of life imprisonment in
relation to the death penalty in securing convictions in homicide cases.[7]

In a study published in 1909, Shipley reports some interesting statistics on the
rates of conviction and acquittal in the states that abolished the death penalty in
the 19th century or early in the 20th century. In his comments, Shipley notes
that:

> From the facts already presented with reference to the administration of justice
> before and after abolishment of capital punishment in Michigan, Wisconsin,
> Rhode Island, Maine and Colorado, it seems evident that convictions followed
> murder with greater certainty after life imprisonment was made the supreme
> penalty.[8]

In Tappan's view,[9] there seems to be little doubt that juries are less willing to
convict and prosecutors more ready to take a lesser plea in states where capital
punishment is used. The statistics unequivocally show that the death penalty is
rarely applied in cases where it is applicable. As an example, Tappan quotes the
American statistics for 1950: 1,556 prisoners were received in state and federal
correctional institutions for murder and only 82 were executed. Thus, he
argued, the death penalty "does not fulfill one important condition of effective
deterrence, i.e., a high degree of certainty of application."

One of the more convincing studies was carried out by Barber and Wilson in
Australia and published in 1968.[10] In 1922, capital punishment was abolished in
Queensland after having been in abeyance since 1915. On the basis of statistical
data, the authors set out to test the hypothesis that capital punishment acts as a
deterrent on juries in capital cases. For murder, a comparison was made
between the conviction and execution rates from 1860 to 1914, and between the
conviction rate for murder and that for manslaughter in both the 1860-1914 and
the following "non-hanging" periods. The conviction and execution rates for
rape during the 1860-1899 and 1900-1909 periods were also examined. The data
supported the proposition that juries were less ready to convict a man of murder
when the chances of his being hanged, as indicated by the execution rate, were

high. This conclusion is given further support by the fact that, during the four years from 1896 to 1899 in which no executions were carried out, the conviction rate rose to 55.2% whereas it had been only 35.4% during the preceding 4-year period (1892-1895) when the execution rate had been 43.5%. Barber and Wilson equally found that in each of 11, 5-year periods, except the first and the last (i.e., 1860-1864 and 1910-1914) the conviction rate for manslaughter was higher than the corresponding one for murder. This would tend to support the argument that juries were not only less willing to convict for the capital offence (murder) than they were for manslaughter, but also were, seemingly, more inclined to bring in a conviction for manslaughter when the charge was murder. Furthermore, the data lent credence to the argument that juries were more likely to bring in a conviction for murder than one for manslaughter in murder trials after capital punishment ceased to be operative in Queensland. With regard to rape, it was found that after the execution for rape of the first white man in 1882, the conviction rate for rape underwent a rapid decline. After 1882, juries were most reluctant to convict in rape cases if there was any reasonable likelihood of the convicted man being executed. Indeed, in the two 3-year periods following the last two executions for rape (1884-1887 and 1894-1897), there were no convictions at all for rape while there were 13 and 7 acquittals respectively. Barber and Wilson conclude that the cumulative evidence from their study appears to indicate that capital punishment acted as a deterrent on juries against their convicting for either murder or rape, where the probable consequence of such conviction would be the prisoner's execution.

The findings of the Barber and Wilson study and many others are quite important because they confirm the existence of an inverse relationship between the severity and certainty of punishment. They demonstrate that the menace of the death penalty tends more to protect the guilty murderer through intimidation of the jury, than to protect society through the conviction and execution of dangerous killers. The experiences of Canada and New Zealand both lead to the same conclusion. A speaker in the debate on the restoration of capital punishment in 1950 in the New Zealand House of Representatives commented on the proportion of convictions to acquittals since capital punishment was abolished. He said:

> The total convictions on the charge of murder between the years 1920 and 1941 were 57, while the total acquittals were 17. There was, therefore, approximately one acquittal for every 3.3 convictions. Since abolition of capital punishment, the total convictions for murder have been 41 and the total acquittals 10, approximately one acquittal for every 4.1 convictions. It may be argued of course that there are other inferences — that we have a more efficient police force; that the type of crime is varying but at least the inference I draw is possible that juries are more reluctant to convict on the murder charge when capital punishment is in vogue. Lawyers freely recognize that it is easier to get an acquittal because of the greater scope for defending counsel on the capital charge.[11]

The same speaker compared the percentages of convictions for murder and for manslaughter in cases where persons were initially charged with murder. During the period 1920 to 1941, the percentage of verdicts for manslaughter was 44, and 56 for murder. That is, on conviction on murder charges, the juries brought in almost equal numbers of verdicts for manslaughter and murder. Since 1941 (year of abolition), there has been more certainty of conviction for murder. The percentage of convictions for murder since the abolition of capital punishment has risen to 71, and the percentage of convictions for manslaughter has fallen to 29.

In my own study of the deterrent effect of capital punishment[12] I compiled data on charges and sentences for murder, manslaughter and for other violent offences in Canada during the period 1881 to 1967. The average yearly conviction rate for murder proved to be the lowest among all crimes of violence. While several factors do intervene to determine conviction rates for any particular offence, the hypothesis that the fear of inflicting death deters many a jury from bringing in guilty verdicts in cases where a death sentence is mandatory, seems at least plausible. There were other findings as well lending further support to the hypothesis:

(1) The 5-year period, 1931-1935, witnessed more executions in Canada than any other 5-year period during the past 100 years. During that 5-year period, 45.9% of those charged with murder were convicted while 38.5% were acquitted. Following the wave of executions the rate of conviction dropped in the next 5-year period (1936-1940) to 42.9% and further during the following period (1941-1945) to 37.8%. The rate of acquittal rose to 44.4% in 1936 to 1940, and remained nearly unchanged during the next period at 44.2%. While there may have been other factors responsible for, or contributing to, the drop in convictions and the rise in acquittals, it seems reasonable to assume that the high rate of executions in 1931-1935 did influence the sentencing patterns during the following two periods.

(2) Over the years there has been a steady increase in the conviction rates for manslaughter and a decline in the conviction rates for murder, as can be seen from Table 1.

Table 1

Years	Conviction Rates For Murder	Years	Conviction Rates for Manslaughter
1941-1945	37.8%	1943-1947	41.6%
1946-1950	42.7%	1948-1952	46.1%
1951-1955	35.7%	1953-1957	55.9%
1956-1960	33.0%	1958-1962	76.4%

There are, of course, various explanations as to why the conviction rate for manslaughter has been going up while that of murder has been declining. A distinct possibility, no doubt, is that during the 1950s and 1960s juries were becoming less and less ready to convict on a charge of murder, in particular since prior to 1961, the death sentence was mandatory upon a conviction for that crime.

The fact that the conviction rate for manslaughter was always higher than the corresponding one for murder (the only exception was during the 1930s) would seem to suggest that juries were not only less willing to convict for the capital offence (murder) than they were for manslaughter, but also, were more inclined to bring in a conviction for manslaughter when the charge was murder. The truth of this latter proposition is, however, incapable of precise verification since like the Australian data, Canadian statistics on manslaughter convictions do not distinguish between cases in which murder was the original charge and those where the charge had originally been only for manslaughter.

THE DISPARITY BETWEEN LEGAL PROVISIONS FOR, AND ACTUAL APPLICATION OF, CAPITAL PUNISHMENT

In Canada, up to 1961 when the Criminal Code provisions for homicide were changed, death was the mandatory penalty for murder. Juries were not given any discretion to choose between the death penalty and life imprisonment. The only option left to a jury unwilling to send the defendant to the scaffold was to acquit, bring in a verdict of non-guilty by reason of insanity, or convict for the lesser charge of manslaughter. All this resulted in a great disparity between the legal provisions for capital punishment and the actual application of this punishment. Even when executions were carried out with relative frequency, only a small percentage of those who committed and were charged with murder legally punishable by death, were ultimately sent to the gallows. This led professor Topping to make the following statement in 1952:

> It seems clear that there is an inverse relationship between severity of punishment and certainty of punishment, and that Canadians are suffering under a delusion when they assert that they know how to hang. The net result of the administration of justice in Canada as it relates to capital offences is that murder has become the least risky of any or all the offences which a citizen might choose to commit.[13]

In an attempt to assess the extent to which the legal provision for a mandatory death penalty for murder has been applied in Canada, I compiled statistics for the 80-year period from 1881 to 1960. The 80 years were then divided into periods of five years each. The highest percentage of death sentences to charges (45.9%) was recorded in the period from 1931 to 1935 when a person charged with murder had approximately an even chance of being sentenced to death. The last period, 1956-1960, revealed a low percentage of death sentences (33), the highest percentage of commutations (73) and the lowest percentage of executions (23.8). In other words, during that period, although capital punishment was still the mandatory penalty for murder, a person charged with murder had only one chance in three of being sentenced to death. Once sentenced to death, he had more than three chances out of four of escaping the death penalty. The chances of being executed during that period for a person accused with the capital offence of murder were 8 in 100, a very low probability indeed. If the period is examined as a whole, we find that from a total of 3,249 persons charged with murder, only 634 were actually executed. The percentage of executions to charges was 19.5 meaning that only one charge in five led to an execution, again a very weak probability. These findings not only reveal a great disparity between legal provisions for, and actual application of capital punishment, but they also indicate that the probabilities for actual executions were far from reaching the degree of risk needed for deterrence.

THE DEATH PENALTY AND THE ADMINISTRATION OF JUSTICE

The Standard of Proof and the Relativity of the Concept of Reasonable Doubt

One reason for the particularly low conviction rate for murder when capital punishment is available or mandatory is the evidentiary problems created or aggravated by the death penalty. Every civilized system of justice (if we may call a justice system retaining the death penalty civilized) accepts in many ways the exceptionality of a death sentence and the appropriateness of having higher requirements of due process for death than for other punishments. Harlan, a former Justice of the Supreme Court of the United States, is quoted by Professor Black from a concurring opinion:

> So far as capital cases are concerned, I think they stand on quite a different footing than other offenses. In such cases the law is especially sensitive to demands for that procedural fairness which inheres in a civilian trial where the judge and trier of fact are not responsive to the command of the convening authority. I do not concede that whatever process is "due" an offender faced with a fine or a prison sentence necessarily satisfies the requirements of the constitution in a capital case.[14]

It seems evident, therefore, that the standard of proof required in capital cases is set higher than in other cases, and that evidence required for conviction of a noncapital offence is usually less stringent than that required for conviction of a capital one. Jurisdictions affirm the uniqueness of a death sentence by making special procedural requirements or by setting standards different from the usual ones, for example, by requiring that the defendant in a capital case be represented by defence counsel, by forbidding pleas of guilty to a capital offence, by requiring jury unanimity and/or by providing for automatic appeal or review of the sentence, etc. These standards are intended to protect the rights of the defendant, to ensure a fair and due process and to reduce the probability of error. While such procedural safeguards are undoubtedly desirable whether the sentence is death or life imprisonment, they inevitably result in a lower rate of conviction in capital cases. Furthermore, because a human life is at stake and because of the irrevocability of the death penalty, the notion of "reasonable doubt" carries a particular significance and assumes new dimensions. Making a judgment about the physical facts of a criminal case, whether capital or not is deciding on past events, a reconstruction of what took place at some time in the past. Such a reconstruction can never be a matter of certainty but only one of probabilities. For this reason, the law requires that the guilt of the defendant be established beyond a reasonable doubt. But reasonable doubt is neither an absolute nor constant concept. It is not a quantifiable and measurable standard. It is essentially relative and subjective. The concept of "reasonable doubt" can never be interpreted in the same manner. Its meaning varies according to jurisdictions and from one case to the next. What may be considered beyond a reasonable doubt in a noncapital case does not necessarily constitute sufficient grounds for a guilty verdict in a capital case. Because of the subjective nature of the concept, the assessment of what constitutes a reasonable doubt will inevitably vary with the person required to make the judgment. The same evidence may therefore be judged quite differently by the prosecutor, the defence lawyer, the judge, the member of the jury, etc. And within the same jury various members may differ considerably in their evaluation of the evidence, in judging the credibility of witnesses, the reliability of expert testimony, etc. The late Professor Packer summed it up best when he wrote:

> We traditionally say that the defendant's innocence is assumed and that his guilt must be proved beyond a reasonable doubt. It is useless to try to define "reasonable doubt." What it suggests is not a quantifiable standard but an adjudicative mood. If there is any hesitation, which reflection does not dissipate, in deciding that what "really" happened accords with the legal requirements for finding the defendant guilty of the offence with which he is charged, then the jury must acquit him.[15]

If guilt and innocence were judged by some immutable and unchangeable criteria, and if the validity of evidence were measurable by some kind of mathematically fixed and invariable standard, then the penalty prescribed for the offence would, in all probability, be irrelevant to the final outcome. But this is not and will never be the case. Evidence will always be considered under the "reasonable doubt" rule. And the relativity of the rule will inevitably lead to arbitrariness and capriciousness and will result in the disparity of decisions on guilt and innocence. It will enable latent and manifest biases and prejudices to become operational and to influence the outcome of the justice process.

The Possibility of Error

Opponents of the death penalty argue that there is always a risk that an innocent man will be convicted and hanged. Although this argument is basically correct since such mistakes have occurred in the past, it creates the false impression that judicial errors associated with the infliction of the death penalty are limited to those cases in which the wrong man has been hanged. No wonder then, that the literature devoted to the errors of justice focuses almost exclusively on such cases. Yet the array of potential errors when capital punishment is retained is definitely more extended than the simple possibility of convicting the innocent. Mistakes regarding the physical facts may be the least frequent of all possible mistakes. It is true that in some cases, especially those in which the evidence is purely circumstantial, the factual question may be exceedingly difficult to determine, and this, no doubt, enhances the potentiality for error. In other cases, miscarriages of justice may take place induced by coerced confessions, mistaken identity, frame-ups, denial of due process, etc. More frequent still are the mistakes related to the psychological facts and/or to the interpretation and application of the law. These mistakes are more subtle in nature and therefore more difficult to detect or to establish. Mistakes may occur when decisions are made as to whether the killing was with or without malice, with or without premeditation, whether it was deliberate or reckless, whether the defendant was sane or insane, whether the killing was committed in self-defense (actual or perceived), whether the murder was in the course or furtherance of theft or not, whether the accused was or was not deprived of the power of self-control by reason of provocation, etc. Needless to say, that all these decisions are susceptible to error led Professor Black to state that,

> ... the penalty of death cannot be imposed, given the limitations of our minds and institutions, without considerable measures both of arbitrariness and of mistake.[16]

Paradoxically, the more sophisticated (or seemingly sophisticated) the law on homicide becomes, the more likely are the mistakes. Deciding whether the defendant was sane or insane when committing the crime is less complex than deciding whether he was under irresistible impulse or whether his responsibility was diminished. When the law makes distinctions between different categories of homicide, the judge or the jury have to decide not only whether the defendant has perpetrated the material act of killing, but also on the qualification of the act.

    The range of possible mistakes seems without end. Black argues that mistakes are not limited to the physical facts nor even to the decision on guilt or innocence:

> But the possibility of mistake in the "guilty" or "not guilty" choice does not end with mistake either as to physical or unproblematically describable

psychological fact. The jury is also called upon to pronounce upon mixed questions of fact and law, questions that have puzzled the most astute legal minds. One of these, perennially with us, is "premeditation." Premeditation is very often a defining characteristic of capital murder.[17]

Black also underlines the extreme difficulty the jury may have in answering questions of law:

> Hundreds of . . . questions of law, great and trivial, may be raised and answered in the course of a criminal proceeding, from arrest until the final appeal in the last post-conviction proceeding. Some are obvious of answer. Some are sufficiently difficult that learned judges will disagree on them. Not only the Supreme Court of the United States but the Supreme Courts of the states may and often do divide very closely on such questions, great and small. Yet the answer to the question of law, in a capital case, may decide the issue of life or death for the defendant.[18]

Most of the mistakes outlined above may be described as unintentional errors. In addition, there are the "intentional errors" which are enhanced and augmented by the death penalty. What I mean by intentional errors are those occurring in cases in which the jury comes in with a verdict of "guilty" of some offence lesser than the one strictly warranted by the evidence. Black gives several factors which may account for such a "mistaken" decision: sympathy, doubt of physical "guilt" in the narrow sense, doubt as to the other, less tangible factors going to make up "guilt," and feeling that extenuating circumstances exist, and so on — may motivate this behaviour.

> But the pragmatic fact, visible from the outside, is that the jury, in finding a defendant guilty, let us say, of "second-degree" rather than of "first-degree" murder, is, for whatever reason and on whatever basis, choosing that this defendant not suffer death.[19]

In view of all of the above, it seems clear that if we resume use of the death penalty we will be hanging some people by mistake. Supporters of the death penalty usually respond to the possibility of mistake by three counter arguments. They argue that:

(a) The risk of an error of justice is so infinitesimal that it may be safely ignored. This argument is based as mentioned above on a restrictive view of what is a judicial error.

(b) The possibility of error is an inescapable concomitant of every criminal trial. This is no doubt true. Human justice is not infallible. To be fallible means to make a mistake sometimes. This is not surprising. What is surprising is that we accept to make the issue of life and death dependent on decisions susceptible to a good number of errors.

(c) The risk is one which should be taken in view of the unique deterrent effect of the death penalty. The problem with this argument is that this unique deterrent effect as we shall see later on has not been established and is unlikely to be established.

Jury Selection in Capital Cases

The right to a trial by jury of peers, representing a cross-section of the community is considered one of the most important features of our democratic system of justice. While the right is fully recognized in principle it may not always be fully guaranteed in practice. Many factors may intervene in practice resulting in a biased or prejudiced jury. This becomes particularly serious in capital cases when the jury decision may mean the difference between life or death. The retention of the death penalty makes the selection of a jury extremely difficult and time consuming. In the United States, before the Supreme Court handed out its landmark decision in *Witherspoon v. Illinois*[20] on June 3, 1968, it was becoming increasingly difficult to obtain a jury in capital cases, the reason being that such juries had to be "death qualified" in the sense that to sit on such a jury a person had to first declare under oath that he/she is willing to return a verdict of death if the evidence seems to him to warrant it. If he has "conscientious scruples" against death as a punishment he was subject to "challenge for cause" by the prosecution and excused by the trial judge.[21] Oberer notes that frequently, mere hesitance to vote for a death verdict was sufficient to disqualify a prospective juror. The systematic exclusion of all persons who had religious or moral scruples against the death penalty from jury service in capital cases meant that a capital jury was made up entirely of that part of the population which approves of the death penalty as a sanction.[22] Greenberg and Himmelstein correctly argued that this procedure is a denial of the defendant's right to a jury that is representative of a cross-section of the community and is a denial of a fair trial. The requirement of a true cross-section insures the accused an equal opportunity to benefit from all the attributes people may have so as to prevent any one group from dominating the delicate jury process. The challenge to the "death qualified" procedure before the U.S. Supreme Court came in *Witherspoon v. Illinois*. William Witherspoon was convicted in 1960 of the murder of a Chicago policeman. He was sentenced to death. At his trial, prospective jurors who had scruples against, or objected to, the death penalty were routinely excluded. Witherspoon asked the Supreme Court to reverse his conviction by a non-scrupled jury because the jury selection process was unfair. He argued that since prospective jurors who admit to having scruples against capital punishment are excluded, the result is a "death qualified" jury, more prone to convict than one more representative of the community. The Court reversed the death sentence and held that a sentence of death cannot be carried out if the jury which imposed or recommended it excluded persons who were generally opposed to the death penalty.

Of interest in the *Witherspoon* case is the fact that the petitioner offered empirical support for his proposition, but the Supreme Court rejected the data as "too tentative and fragmentary" to establish conviction proneness; the Court did indicate, however, that it would be receptive to further experimental evidence.[23] Mr. Justice Douglas in a separate opinion argued that no empirical data need be advanced to show that excluding jurors firmly opposed to capital punishment would bias the guilt determining process. He concluded that the "prejudice" is so subtle, so intangible, that it escapes the ordinary methods of proof.[24]

Since *Witherspoon,* several experimental studies have been undertaken to examine the relationship between a potential juror's attitudes toward capital punishment and his proneness to convict or acquit. The evidence strongly implies a need for change in current jury selection procedures since the findings of the studies relate a favourable attitude toward capital punishment and a tendency to convict.[25]

THE DEATH PENALTY AND THE PRINCIPLE OF EQUAL JUSTICE

The Arbitrary and Discriminatory Nature of the Death Penalty

Arbitrary

Opponents of the death penalty argue that it can never be applied uniformly, that it is randomly and capriciously invoked, and that whether it is made mandatory or left to the discretion of the sentencer, it will continue to be inflicted in an arbitrary and selective manner. In the few western countries which still retain the death penalty, its actual infliction every year is restricted to a very small number out of a very much larger number who commit the offence for which it is most commonly prescribed, namely murder. Some murderers are never detected, others are not charged and of those who are indicted, many escape the death penalty through a reduction of charge (frequently as a result of plea bargaining), through jury discretion, through a verdict of "not guilty by reason of insanity," through acquittal or finally, if sentenced to death, through executive clemency.

In the case of *Furman v. Georgia,*[26] one basic rationale explicitly or implicitly underlying all five majority opinions is that the death penalty has been applied in an arbitrary manner and thus constitutes cruel and unusual punishment. The three marginal judges, who concurred with Marshall and Brennan JJ., seemed to be holding (with some variation in reasons and in expression) that capital punishment *as currently administered* violated the American Constitution because of the arbitrary selection of a small number of sufferers — a selection mostly made not on clearly articulated grounds but on the basis of a "standardless" discretion lodged in juries and judges.[27] Mr. Justice Brennan compared the actual execution of those sentenced to death to a lottery system — a system where most of those who are in do not get called:

> When the punishment of death is inflicted in a trivial number of cases in which
> it is legally available the conclusion is virtually inescapable that it is being
> inflicted arbitrarily. Indeed it smacks of little more than a lottery system.[28]

In response to the *Furman* decision, many state legislatures passed statutes to
meet the Eighth Amendment Commands as articulated by the Supreme Court.
The statutes were generally intended to reduce the arbitrariness in the
imposition of the death penalty and to provide a set of standards aimed at
guiding juries and judges as to who is to die. Despite their diversity, they all
attempted to pass the arbitrariness test by some or all of the following:

— making the death penalty mandatory for certain offences;
— providing reasonably comprehensive sets of aggravating and mitigating
  circumstances, the existence of which is to be determinative of sentence or
  weighed in the sentencing determination;
— individuating the judgment through consideration of the character and
  record of the individual offender and of the circumstances of the particular
  offence;
— providing for a case-by-case review of capital sentences, for an appellate
  re-evaluation of the death sentence.

The post-Furman Georgia statute was tested and upheld in the *Gregg* case,[29]
when the Supreme Court upheld capital punishment as not "cruel and unusual
punishment," provided the death penalty statutes "individuate" the sentencing
decision and thereby avoid the admittedly "arbitrary" and "freakish"
imposition of the death sentence against which the Court had ruled in the
Furman case.

Despite the Supreme Court ruling, the new statutes have been severely
criticized. It is argued, for instance, that these legislative attempts to narrow the
range of cases for which execution is authorized, fail to acknowledge the
immense difficulty in drawing distinctions that will effectively control a
contemporary jury when the difference is life or death.[30] Davis notes further
that the identification of aggravating and mitigating circumstances is intended
to avoid arbitrariness by providing legislative guidance in the capital sentencing
process. However, little is required with respect to mitigating circumstances —
the Georgia statute upheld in *Gregg* provides only that the sentencer "consider . . . any mitigating circumstances," and nothing necessarily turns upon a finding that "mitigating" (or aggravating) circumstances exist. With regard to
aggravating circumstances, Davis argues that these statutes do no more than
suggest topics for consideration in the deliberative process.[31]

Arbitrariness is ineradicably inherent in the death penalty. It is not simply a
result of a standardless, unguided or absolute discretion of juries and judges.
Recent decisions of the U.S. Supreme Court may give the impression that the
new statutes, by making the death penalty mandatory other than at the
arbitrary option of the jury and by limiting its application to a narrowly defined
offence, have succeeded in eliminating or reducing its arbitrariness. But

evidently this is not the case. Mandatory death penalty does not eliminate the prosecutor's decision in charging and in accepting a plea, nor does it eliminate the jury's discretion in finding the defendant guilty of a less-than-capital offence. As Professor Black notes, the prosecutor and the jury practically always retain control.[32] Arbitrariness will continue to characterize decisions on who is charged with "capital murder" or "first degree murder" and who is charged with "murder," "second degree murder" or a lesser offence; or who is convicted and who is acquitted, who is pronounced guilty and who is pronounced insane. It will always characterize executive decisions of clemency. Human justice will always be arbitrary and no standards or guidelines, legislative or otherwise, are likely to cure this fundamental and inherent defect. As Professor Black puts it:

> ... the official choices — by prosecutors, judges, and governors — that divide those who are to die from those who are to live are on the whole not made, and cannot be made, under standards that are consistently meaningful and clear, but that they are often made, and in the foreseeable future will continue often to be made, under no standards at all or under pseudo-standards without discoverable meaning.[33]

In his remarkable analysis of the post-Furman statute from Texas, Black convincingly demonstrates that the new statute is far from eliminating arbitrariness. For example, the statute provides that once the defendant is found guilty of a capital offence, the court has to conduct a separate sentencing proceeding to determine whether the defendant shall be sentenced to death or life imprisonment. Following the presentation of evidence, the court is required to submit three issues to the jury, the second of which reads, "whether there is a probability that the defendant would commit criminal acts of violence that would constitute a continuing threat to society." In an eloquent comment on this issue, Black notes that people are to live or die, in Texas, on a jury's *guess* as to their *future* conduct because a negative finding on this second issue precludes death. This, writes Black, is really enough to stamp this section as outside the bounds of civilized law.

The arbitrariness issue did not generate the same legal debate in Canada as it did in the United States, probably because juries in Canada were not given any discretion to choose between the death penalty and life imprisonment since the mandatory sentence for a capital crime was death. Because Canada, unlike the United States, never recognized the jury option as a mode of imposing capital punishment, only the Governor General-in-Council could, in principle, have been guilty of arbitrarily inflicting the death sentence through the exercise of executive clemency.[34]

In his dissenting judgment in *R. v. Miller and Cockriell,* Mr. Justice McIntyre of the British Columbia Court of Appeal addressed the arbitrariness issue holding that clemency despite all precautions cannot be exercised but arbitrarily:

> I intend no criticism of those who have faced the awesome responsibility for the
> decision between life and death when clemency was considered. However, the
> best and most high-principled of men exercising discretion in matters of this
> gravity will apply individual tests, individual ideas and beliefs, and the result
> which emerges will of necessity bear an arbitrary complexion.[35]

Unfortunately, in reviewing the case, the Supreme Court of Canada was not
prepared to accept that the Governor General-in-Council acted arbitrarily in
commuting death sentences.[36] Berger expresses the view that by sentencing the
offender to death or life imprisonment at the discretion of the Cabinet, the
Court is "authorizing" the subsequent application of "individual tests,
individual ideas and beliefs." It is therefore authorizing the Cabinet to apply a
severe punishment in a randomly selective manner. Section 2(b) of the
Canadian Bill of Rights can be interpreted as prohibiting a court "from
relinquishing its responsibility to guard against the authorization of imposition
of executions in circumstances which make the punishment cruel and unusual."
The court, according to Berger, has the duty to preclude this possibility by
declaring the capital punishment sections of the Criminal Code inoperative.[37]

The Arbitrariness of Legal Classifications of Murder

The discussion of the inherent arbitrariness of the death penalty would not be
complete without some words about murder classification. When capital
punishment is retained or reintroduced it is usually restricted to certain
categories of murder but not to others. A proper classification of murder is,
therefore, essential to a non-arbitrary administration of the penalty. This is not a
simple task. In 1953, the British Royal Commission on Capital Punishment
(Cmnd 8932) concluded after an exhaustive examination that "a quest for a
method dividing murder into degrees had proved chimerical."[38] Despite this,
the Homicide Act of 1957 made distinctions between different categories of
murder but soon after its passage, the essential irrationality and the inherent
arbitrariness of the distinctions became quite evident. What else can be said of
an Act which distinguishes murder by firearm from murder by strangling and
murderers who kill to steal from those who kill for vengeance or some other
motive.[39]

Sir Charles Cunningham notes that although the Homicide Act of 1957
retained the death penalty for certain categories of murder, those capital
murders were not necessarily more heinous than other murders nor were
extenuating circumstances less likely to be present in such cases. "In fact," writes
Cunningham:

> capital cases occurring after 1957 were probably judged by much the same
> criteria as those which occurred before that date; but the state of the law meant
> that a man might be hanged for a murder no worse than one for which the legal

penalty was life imprisonment. It is sometimes suggested that the difficulties created by the 1957 Act would be avoided if the death penalty were related not to particular types of murder but the heinousness of the particular crime. Moral obliquity cannot, however, be defined.[40]

Speaking of discretion, Cunningham noted that it is extremely difficult to exercise. However hard those exercising it might try to be both fair and consistent, unacceptable anomalies inevitably result from different courts and different juries taking different views of cases appearing to be similar.

The recent amendment to the Canadian Criminal Code[41] also divided murder into first and second degrees. The philosophy behind this division appears to be that those murders which are most inimical to public order should carry a greater penalty than the others. First degree murder includes "planned and deliberate" murder; murder of certain categories of victims (police officer, police constable, constable, sheriff, deputy sheriff, sheriff's officer, a warden, deputy warden, instructor, keeper, gaoler, guard or other officer, a permanent employee of a prison, etc., acting in the course of their duties); murder committed in the course of certain offences such as aircraft hijacking or attempted hijacking, kidnapping and forcible confinement, rape, attempted rape or indecent assault on a female or a male.[42]

As can be seen from this classification, the determination of the categories of victims or categories of offences is arbitrary and discriminatory. The killing of an on-duty police officer or prison guard constitutes first degree murder, but the same provision is not extended to the Governor General, the Prime Minister, foreign diplomats, nor to highly placed civil servants. The so-called protection provided to prison personnel in the course of their duties is not extended to the inmates. The arbitrary nature of the classification is even more evident in the provision which singles out murder committed in the course of completed or attempted skyjacking, kidnapping, and certain sexual offences. If the act of killing is directed against the victim of rape, attempted rape, or indecent assault it qualifies as first degree murder under section 214(5), but only as second degree murder if it is directed against the victim of robbery or burglary!

Distinctions between murders which are "planned and deliberate" and those which are not have been under attack for many years. Individuals who commit premeditated murders are not necessarily the most dangerous killers and those who commit spontaneous, non-premeditated or impulsive murders are not exactly the least dangerous. Murder, whether planned and deliberate or not is predominantly a family crime. Research findings in Canada and elsewhere indicate that nearly half of all homicides occur within the family and more than three quarters between people who know one another. While many of these killings may be "planned and deliberate" thus qualifying as first degree murders, the offenders involved do not usually pose any significant further risk to society.[43]

Discriminatory

Another problem in the administration of the death penalty is its discriminatory nature. This discrimination is too flagrant to be denied even by the penalty's strong advocates. In his book *Neither Cruel Nor Unusual,* Carrington admits that capital punishment has been applied in a discriminatory fashion against the minorities in the United States. He writes:

> The question of racial discrimination in the infliction of the death penalty looms large. We cannot deny that racial minorities were oppressed and discriminated against in this country for years. In the area of capital punishment, this discrimination was particularly invidious.[44]

The U.S. Supreme Court decision in the *Furman* case[45] declared the death penalty to be cruel and unusual punishment because it has been used in a rare, arbitrary and discriminatory fashion. Mr. Justice Douglas believed that the inherent discrimination against minorities in the death penalty rendered it unconstitutional and Mr. Justice Marshall expressed the opinion that giving juries "untrammeled discretion" to impose a sentence of death was "an open invitation to discrimination."

In the last two decades there has been a growing body of research lending empirical support to the alleged discrimination that occurs in the imposition of capital punishment. The evidence shows that those who receive capital sentences are the poor and the minorities, and this is way out of proportion to the percentages that these groups represent in the total population and to the rate of criminal offences committed by these groups.[46]

Sex Discrimination

Capital punishment is directed almost exclusively against males. Even when one takes into account the difference in the rate of male and female criminality and the fact that women may often act as accessories rather than as perpetrators in murder cases, one cannot fail to ascertain that police, prosecutors, juries and courts are generally less inclined (or more reluctant) to send women to their death than men. Statistical evidence will bear this out. In his study of executions and commutations in North Carolina covering the period of 1909-1954, Johnson found that out of the 660 admitted to death row, only six were females; one white and five black women, of which two black women were executed.[47] Another study conducted in Ohio by the Research Staff of the Ohio Legislative Service Commission[48] revealed, on the basis of court records for the 4-year period (1955-1958 inclusive), that 50 of 336 persons charged with first degree murder were women. Presumably, these women committed crimes which grand juries considered deliberate and premeditated, as reflected by indictments for first degree murder, subject to the death penalty. However, the figures for convictions show that the percentages of men and women charged with first degree murder diverge widely in the progression toward the death sentence.

While nearly 15 per cent of the persons charged with first degree murder were women, no women were admitted under death sentence. Only eight per cent of the 50 women charged with first degree murder were found guilty of that offence, in contrast to 31 per cent of the men.[49]

In Canada, figures reported in the document on capital punishment, published by the Minister of Justice, show that over a 10-year period from 1950 to 1959, 175 males and 5 females were sentenced to death. Forty per cent of the convicted males were executed (71) but only one of the females, that is 20 per cent. In the following six years (1960-1965), 65 males were sentenced to death but not a single female.[50]

Race Discrimination

Racial discrimination takes place at various stages of the legal process but is most discernible at the levels of sentencing and clemency. Several studies carried out in the United States show that blacks are disproportionately sentenced to death even when one controls for variables other than race. Other studies show that a greater percentage of whites than blacks sentenced to death receive commutations to life imprisonment.

The above mentioned Ohio study[51] revealed that more than twice as many white as black murderers received commutations from death sentences to life imprisonment. The compiled figures indicate that a black murderer, once sentenced to death, is much less likely than a white murderer to be saved by commutation. The study confirmed an earlier finding by Charles Mangum[52] who discovered that among those sentenced to death in nine southern and border states, blacks were more likely than whites to have their death sentences carried out in every state.

As early as 1941, Guy Johnson was able to establish for selected jurisdictions in Virginia, North Carolina, and Georgia, that in murder cases the death sentence was disproportionately imposed when the defendant was black and his victim was white.[53] Harold Garfinkel refined and extended Johnson's findings with data from ten counties in North Carolina, by showing that this tendency to impose the death sentence disproportionately in black offender-white victim murders was the cumulative result of differential treatment at each of several stages — indictment, charge, and conviction — of the judicial process.[54]

The 1960s witnessed the accumulation of a body of sophisticated research on racial discrimination in capital punishment in the United States. At the request of NAACP Legal Defense and Educational Fund, Professors Anthony Amsterdam and Marvin Wolfgang designed a study which inquired into every possible ground that a jury might take into account in deciding whether to impose life imprisonment or death for the crime of rape. These grounds included such things as the viciousness of the crime, the prior relationship between the defendant and the victim, the time of the attack, the place of the attack, the number of attackers, whether a simultaneous crime occurred, whether the defendant testified at the trial and every other conceivable factor that might influence sentencing. A team of 35 law students searched the records of 2,500 cases and the results were subjected to rigorous statistical analysis. The likelihood that any factor other than race accounting for the disproportionality in sentencing proved insignificant.[55] In reporting the findings, Greenberg and Himmelstein point out that:

> Race alone stood out as the constant factor in distinguishing cases in which the death penalty was imposed from those in which some lesser penalty was chosen. If the defendant was black and the victim was white, the chance of a death penalty proved high; in all other rape cases, the chance of a death penalty was remote.[56]

Despite overwhelming statistical evidence pointing to the discriminatory infliction of the death penalty on blacks in the United States, American courts have been reluctant to squarely admit that such discrimination exists. In *Maxwell v. Bishop,*[57] the Federal District Court in Little Rock, Arkansas, was presented with evidence showing that a black convicted of raping a white women in Arkansas had about a 50 per cent chance of receiving a death sentence while any man convicted of raping a woman of his own race stood only a 14 per cent chance. Judge Smith Henley thought the difference could be explained on grounds other than race, and contended that the imposition of the death sentence might be due to some factor for which statistical analysis had not been possible or presentable.[58] Commenting on the court's unwillingness to accept the validity of statistical evidence, Wolfgang quotes Michael Meltsner[59] who in his book *Cruel and Unusual* noted that:

> If race were not related to capital sentencing in Arkansas, the results observed in the twenty-year period study could have occurred fortuitously in two (or less) twenty-year periods since the birth of Christ.[60]

As usual, supporters of the death penalty have countered the argument of discrimination by stating that even if discrimination were proven "it would be a mistake to argue that capital punishment should be rejected because some discrimination exists. The proper approach is to remedy the defect, not abolish the system."[61] Unfortunately, the defect cannot be remedied because discrimination is inherent in the death penalty and because of the impossibility of keeping its administration even-handed.

It has been suggested that making the death penalty mandatory or structuring the discretion of the jury would eliminate or at least substantially reduce discrimination. But neither mandatory death penalty nor guided-discretion are likely to solve the problem. Juries will discriminate in convictions just as they have in sentencing. This is what prompted Wolfgang and Riedel[62] to contend that the new standards for judge and jury sentencing under revised statutes (post-Furman) are unlikely to insure that the death penalty is imposed with greater equity. Support for Wolfgang and Riedel's contention comes from a study made on the six states with the highest death row population. Three of these states — Florida, Georgia, and Texas — were classified as states with guided-discretion statutes and included 99 persons under death sentence for murder and felony murder. Louisiana, North Carolina, and Oklahoma were classified as mandatory states and included 123 persons under death sentence. Eighteen variables were used for comparison regarding characteristics of the offender, the victim, the offence and the trial. No significant statistical differences were found between defendants from mandatory and guided-discretion states. Neither the mandatory nor guided-discretion states in the pre- and post-Furman periods showed any significant differences in the percentages of non-white offenders sentenced to death.[63]

If discrimination is inherent in the administration of the death penalty, and I am convinced it is, then doing away with discretion and making the penalty mandatory will not solve the problem. Discrimination, as we all know, is not the result of direct procedural violations of the defendant's right but rather a result of the prejudiced way jurors view the defendant and weigh the evidence against him.[64] Prejudices and biases do not usually operate at a conscious level. They influence people's decisions in a rather subtle and unconscious manner. They intervene into the decisional process at the stage when subjective judgments are made: assessment of evidence; choice between conflicting testimonies; evaluation of psychological facts such as malice, intent, premeditation, insanity; etc. Discrimination results from social attitudes deeply seated in the personalities of judges and juries, attitudes which are an integral component of the judicial process. As Bowers notes:

> As a representative cross-section of the community, the jury can be expected to include those who hold the prevailing prejudices against social or racial minorities. To the extent that such prejudices are widely disseminated and deeply felt, the jury will enter the courtroom predisposed against "socially disfavored" defendants.[65]

Discrimination will continue as long as prejudices and biases exist. It cannot be eliminated unless the whole fabric of society and the whole web of social attitudes are fundamentally changed. And even if racial prejudices against blacks in the United States are eliminated and if male chivalry in Canada is eradicated, human sentiments of sympathy and antipathy, of attraction and repulsion, will continue to influence judicial decisions and to tip the scales of justice against the unattractive, the unsympathetic, the poor and the disadvantaged.

CAPITAL PUNISHMENT AND THE INSANITY DEFENCE

Capital punishment raises in a particularly acute form the question of the insanity defence. Many legal scholars, including Norval Morris[66] and Chief Justice Joseph Weintraub of New Jersey believe that the historic purpose of the insanity defence has been to avoid capital punishment.[67] It makes little or no difference for the protection of society whether the murderer is detained in a mental institution for the insane or incarcerated in a penal institution for convicted offenders. Thus, when the punishment for murder is life or term imprisonment, the outcome of the insanity defence does not carry the same serious consequences as when the punishment is death. In the latter case, the jury's decision on an insanity plea may mean the difference between incarceration and execution, between life and death. When capital punishment is abolished the insanity defence becomes redundant and loses most of its practical importance. The Law Reform Commission of Canada expressed this view in its working paper No. 14:

> For all its theoretical importance, the insanity defence — whatever its form — is now of little practical consequence. Probably as a result of the virtual abolition of capital punishment. . .[68]

When capital punishment is retained, the assessment of the mental state of the defendant at the time of the crime and of his fitness to stand trial become crucial evidentiary issues. In deciding on these issues the possibility of error looms large because the insanity issue is settled not on the basis of objective, hard facts, but on a subjective and frail psychiatric diagnosis. It is true that the final decision on the insanity defence rests with the jury or the judge and they are not bound by the psychiatric evidence presented in the case. But it would be too optimistic to expect the common sense of the jury to make good the deficiencies of psychiatry. As mentioned earlier, judicial errors, contrary to the popular conception, are not restricted to cases in which an innocent person is convicted or a guilty person is acquitted. Because our criminal law recognizes insanity at the time of the offence as an exculpatory condition, we have to acknowledge that a judicial error is made every time an insane offender is convicted or a "normal" offender is declared "not guilty by reason of insanity." The potentiality for such error is enhanced and aggravated by the retention of the death penalty. *First,* capital punishment increases the frequency of insanity pleas and consequently increases the probabilities and the risks of judicial errors. *Second,* although the potentiality for mistake is always present when the question of material guilt is decided, it is much greater with regard to the issue of moral guilt and the moral elements of the crime. *Third,* although the potentiality for error is ever present in any system of human justice, it is much more serious when the life of a human being is at stake. Errors of justice not involving the taking of a human life may always be revoked when the mistake is discovered, though the harm done by imprisonment or labelling is usually irreversible. Capital punishment is not only irreversible it is irrevocable as well.

The great potential for error regarding the insanity defence can be attributed to at least three factors:

(1) the extreme difficulty of reaching an adequate definition of such a complex and relative notion as the concept of insanity;
(2) the limitations of psychiatry and the frailty of the psychiatric diagnosis of insanity;
(3) the difficulty of linking the defendant's mental disease or defect, if such has been diagnosed, to his alleged offence.

The Ambiguity of Insanity Definitions

Defining insanity is not an easy task. The problem is as complex as that of defining "responsibility." Baroness Wootton has repeatedly argued that no satisfactory line can be drawn between the mentally normal and abnormal offenders, that there are no clear or reliable criteria.[69] And in 1968, the late Professor Packer described the issue as the most controversial in the criminal law. He wrote:

> There is no more hotly controverted issue in the criminal law than the question of whether and, if so, to what extent and according to what criteria individuals whose conduct would otherwise be criminal should be exculpated on the ground that they were suffering from mental disease or defect when they acted as they did.[70]

Neither the M'Naghten formula dating from 1843, nor the doctrine of irresistible impulse nor the Durham Test (written by Judge Bazelon of the U.S. Court of Appeals for the District of Columbia in 1954) provide a clear and satisfactory definition of insanity. All of them have been roundly condemned and there is a general agreement that a better, unambiguous definition has to be found. In response to such need, the American Law Institute proposed in its Model Penal Code Draft a new definition of insanity. By 1971, the new ALI test had been adopted by statute in seven American states and by decision in three more.[71]

The Law Reform Commission of Canada noted in its working paper No. 14[72] that the word "insanity" (or insane) appears in 12 different sections of the Criminal Code and has at least four meanings. The Commission argued that inconsistent language makes understanding difficult even where social policy is clear.

The absence of an adequate definition and the lack of proper criteria are compounded by the discrepancy which exists between legal definitions of "irresponsibility" and psychiatric definitions of "mental illness." For judges and lawyers, insanity is a legal standard, for the psychiatrist it is a medical fact. In addition, insanity tests include questions involving elements of law which lay outside the psychiatrist's field of competence. As a result, the psychiatrist may be asked in court to give an opinion in terms of knowledge of right and wrong, or of responsibility and may feel that he is not especially competent to express a view on such matters. The Group for the Advancement of Psychiatry (GAP) cited by Goldstein has stated that test questions call not only for facts which are dispositive of the insanity issue, but also for value judgments which the psychiatrist thinks he has no special competence to make. Goldstein comments that according to this view, the M'Naghten questions do not carry "a precise psychological or psychiatric meaning."[73]

Insanity, then, means different things to different people and the inevitable result is a lack of uniformity and a wide disparity in court decisions on the issue. The ambiguity of the definition and the relativity of the notion open the door to both intentional and unintentional errors. The latter may occur in the application of criteria or in the judgment of symptoms. The former results directly from the death penalty. A jury having doubts about the defendant's guilt, having scruples about the death penalty, or, for some reason, unwilling to send the accused to his death, may find in an insanity plea a way out of this dilemma and may declare the defendant insane despite the lack of strong evidence attesting to the irresponsibility of the accused. In another case, particularly that of a defendant admitting to have committed a whole series of heinous crimes, the jury may deliberately disregard overwhelming psychiatric evidence on insanity in an attempt to rid society of a dangerous insane killer.

The legal provision of capital punishment, then, makes the life or death of a defendant in a capital case contingent upon the imprecise and relative notion of insanity, a notion which is neither susceptible to scientific assessment nor to accurate measurement. In his usual eloquent manner, Professor Black summarizes the situation thus:

> The upshot of the best writing on the subject is that we have so far failed in defining exculpatory insanity and that success is nowhere in sight. Yet we have to assume, unless the whole thing has been a solemn frolic, that we execute some people, and put others into medical custody, because we think that the ones we execute fall on one side of this line, and the others on the other side.[74]

How Reliable Is the Psychiatric Diagnosis

Psychiatry is probably the least developed and the least reliable branch of medicine. This is not meant to be a criticism of psychiatry but simply an acknowledgement of the limitations of psychiatric expertise. The lack of precision and the use of vague terminology which often characterize psychiatric reports do not reflect any lack of professional expertise on the part of the individual psychiatrist, but rather the deficiencies of the discipline and the imperfections of current knowledge of the human mind. A part of the difficulty is, without doubt, attributable to the fact that a large number of mental diseases do not result from organic causes and are not accompanied by physical, recognizable symptoms which would allow an easy and accurate diagnosis.

Quite often, therefore, the psychiatrist has to rely on the defendant's own statements and on behavioural symptoms which are not impossible to simulate. There are, of course, some organically based mental conditions, but they are less often involved in the insanity defence than are the functional psychoses. The absence of a known organic cause for the latter diseases makes it much more difficult to assess whether the condition exists, how long it has continued, etc.[75] The problem is compounded by the lack of a universal psychiatric theory of mental illness. There is no agreed upon nosology and there are no common definitions of notions such as schizophrenia or psychopathy. The relativity of the concepts of "abnormality," "insanity" or "mental disease" makes it extremely difficult in many cases to determine whether a particular individual is normal or abnormal, is sane or insane, or to establish whether or not he is suffering from a mental disease. In his brilliant essay on the insanity defence, Dean Goldstein gives the following explanation of the diagnostic difficulties facing the psychiatrist:

> Diagnosis is an incredibly complex matter . . . Diagnosis is made even more problematic because there is a great deal of disagreement about the diagnostic categories themselves . . . very little can be said with certainty except that there is no sharp line dividing the normal from the abnormal, or the psychotic from the psychopath or neurotic . . . The heart of the diagnostic problem, of course, is that most mental diseases do not have the confirmatory physical evidence which one expects of physical disease . . . The medical man thus becomes a judge of a credibility of his sources and a classifier of the abnormal quality of the acts and thoughts described. He can turn to no physical phenomena which are psychologically neutral. Because most of the concepts of mental illness involve theoretical constructs based upon clues provided by the behavior and the words of the patient rather than upon some identifiable organic pattern, they come to depend for too much upon how the behavior and the words are perceived by the community, by the person making the diagnosis, and upon the purposes for which the diagnosis is being made.[76]

Insanity, then, cannot be reliably diagnosed because (a) inorganic mental diseases are difficult to diagnose; (b) insanity (or sanity) can be feigned, and (c) psychiatric diagnosis is an individual application and a subjective interpretation of a variety of diagnostic techniques. The judge and the jury, composed of laymen, are faced with the formidable task of weighing the psychiatrist's testimony and of assessing the reliability of his diagnosis. The task becomes even more complex when there are, as is often the case, conflicting psychiatric testimonies regarding the defendant's mental state at the time of the offence. A psychiatrist for the prosecution may testify that the mental faculties of the accused were not impaired when he committed his crime, when another psychiatrist for the defence may attest that he was insane. And the lay jury has to find its way through a maze of conflicting psychiatric opinions.

The Linkage Problems

One of the problems associated with the insanity defence is the need to establish that the mental disease or defect existed at the time of the offence. This time linkage is not an easy task. Many of the so-called functional psychoses are cyclical in nature. They oscillate between acute episodes with more or less detectable symptoms and remission phases characterized by an amelioration or disappearance of the symptoms. When an insanity defence is made, the judge or the jury are asked to decide on what the accused was really thinking when he committed the crime, with all the difficulties and uncertainties involved in the attempt to penetrate another man's mind, and to recapture his mental condition as it was in the highly dynamic situation of the crime. This is a process strewn with pitfalls.

> When the psychiatrist testifies at the trial, he is called upon not only to describe the person he examined but also to estimate the mental condition of that person at the time of crime, which may have been months, perhaps years, before. Inevitably, therefore, he must deal in probabilities.[77]

In addition to the time linkage, the Durham Test, originally much acclaimed but now generally abandoned, called for a causal linkage: establishing that the criminal offence was the "product" of the mental disease or mental defect. In his summary of the criticism leveled at the Durham Test, Goldstein notes that the jury was seemingly left entirely dependent upon the expert's classification of conduct as the "product" of "mental disease." The requirement assumed a compartmentalized mind because it implied that mental disease "caused" some unlawful acts but not others. Furthermore, the court deliberately chose to leave the phrase "mental disease" virtually undefined so that the insanity defense might draw upon anything medicine could bring to it.[78]

The unreliability of the psychiatric diagnosis would not be so serious were it not for the confidence that is usually placed in the expertise of the psychiatrists. Given the limitations of psychiatry, such confidence can only increase the possibility of judicial errors. Research on psychiatric evidence shows that psychiatrists are influential in various courtroom decisions and confirms the doubts about the reliability of psychiatric diagnoses. Cocozza and Steadman undertook a 3-year longitudinal study of specific psychiatric predictions of dangerousness and found that although the decision as to the dangerousness of the defendant was a judicial one, in reality it was made by the psychiatrists. In no less than 86.7 per cent of the cases, the psychiatrist's recommendation as to the defendant's dangerousness was accepted by the court. Furthermore, the researchers found that the patients evaluated as dangerous by the psychiatrists were not more dangerous than those evaluated as not dangerous.[79] Faulty decisions based on inaccurate predictions of dangerousness only result in the deprivation of liberty and are usually subject to periodical review. But in capital cases, an error regarding the insanity defence may mean the difference between life and death.

DOES CAPITAL PUNISHMENT SERVE ANY OF THE MODERN AIMS OF SENTENCING?

There is no agreement as to what the goals of sentencing are or should be. But despite wide variations of opinion, five major goals can be singled out as having guided legislators and judges at one time or another: rehabilitation, deterrence, incapacitation, retribution and denunciation. The first three are utilitarian goals while the other two can be regarded as moral imperatives or moral ideas.

Deterrence: Is Capital Punishment a Unique Deterrent?

Despite a sizeable body of literature on the deterrent effect of capital punishment, most debates on the topic still focus on the wrong question. The right question is not whether the death penalty is a deterrent, but whether it is a unique deterrent that is significantly more effective than the alternatives. Until recently, empirical research on deterrence seemed to support a negative answer to the question. Since then, certain studies conducted by some economists, notably Isaac Ehrlich of the University of Chicago, have renewed the debate around the issue. Also until few years ago, the debate was largely an academic one and was rarely raised in the courtroom. In 1976, statistical evidence in support of the deterrence hypothesis was submitted to the U.S. Supreme Court in *Fowler v. North Carolina,*[80] when the Solicitor General tendered an *amicus curiae* brief citing Ehrlich's conclusion that capital punishment deters murder. And in *Gregg v. Georgia,*[81] the Court ruled that "the punishment of death does not invariably violate the constitution" and stated that for many murderers "the death penalty undoubtedly is a significant deterrent." Commenting on the decision, Forst noted that although the Court did not support its belief in the deterrent value of capital punishment with empirical evidence, this evidence was not ignored. The Court stated that: "although some of the studies suggest that the death penalty may not function as a significantly greater deterrent than less penalties, there is no convincing empirical evidence either supporting or refuting this view."[82] Zeisel (1976) has taken issue with this opinion arguing that the evidence about the deterrent effect is, indeed, "quite sufficient" and that the request for more proof is but "the expression of an unwillingness to abandon an ancient prejudice."

Ehrlich's findings[83] which received a great deal of publicity and were circulated by many police forces in the United States and Canada, have been criticized on several grounds. Replications of Ehrlich's analysis revealed that his evidence of deterrence depends upon a restrictive assumption about the mathematical relationship between homicides and executions,[84] the inclusion of a particular set of observations, the use of a limited set of control variables, and a peculiar construction of the execution rate, the key variable.

One of the strong criticisms of Ehrlich's study was his use of time series data for 1933 to 1969 in which homicides and executions were aggregated for the entire United States. The Panel of the National Academy of Science noted that Ehrlich's findings were particularly sensitive to the time period included. This sensitivity results largely from the fact that during 1962 to 1969, executions ceased and homicides increased but no more than did other crimes.[85]

Bowers and Pierce[86] reproduced Ehrlich's analysis but used data from slightly different periods, all beginning in 1935 but each ending in a different year in the 1960s. They concluded that:

> . . . it becomes evident that the so-called deterrent effect of execution risk altogether disappears when the effective time period is foreshortened by dropping recent date points.

Another researcher, Passell used cross-sectional data in various states in the United States from the period 1950 to 1960 and came to the conclusion that there was no reasonable way of interpreting the cross-sectional data which would lend support to the deterrence hypothesis.[87]

A third researcher, Forst replicated Ehrlich's analysis while avoiding the major flaws in Ehrlich's study. For instance, he focused on a unique decade during which the homicide rate increased by over 50% and the use of capital punishment ceased, and examined, as well, changes in homicides and executions over time and across states. His findings did not support the hypothesis that capital punishment deters homicides. He concluded:

> The results of this analysis suggest . . . that it is erroneous to view capital punishment as a means of reducing the homicide rate.[88]

Incapacitation: Is Capital Punishment Needed As an Incapacitating Tool?

In view of the lingering doubts about the unique efficacy of the death penalty as a deterrent, its supporters usually find it easier to advocate it on the grounds of its incapacitative rather than deterrent effect. They argue that the penalty of death has an absolute incapacitating power since it ensures that a person executed for murder will not commit further crimes. This argument would, no doubt, have been a strongly convincing one if: (a) capital punishment were the only means of effectively incapacitating dangerous killers; and (b) if murderers as a group were known to have a high recidivisim rate. But neither of these assumptions is true.

Incarceration is, no doubt, an effective means of neutralizing the dangerousness of murderers and other violent offenders. Studies by Morris,[89] Sellin,[90] Akman,[91] and Buffum[92] clearly show that the hazards involved in prison life are not increased by the abolition of the death penalty. Neither does such abolition result in an increase in homicidal or assaultive behaviour in those penal institutions where convicted murderers are detained. Moreover, it is obvious that those who present the greatest danger are insane murderers. Yet, these murderers are by definition excluded from the possible infliction of the death penalty. By reason of insanity they are not liable to the maximum penalty and nobody is calling for their execution as a way of protecting the staff or the patients of the psychiatric institutions in which they are usually held. Surely if we have found incarceration to be an effective means of incapacitating insane killers we can live with it as a means of incapacitating the "normal" ones.

The argument for capital punishment as a means of preventing the murderer from committing other crimes is further invalidated by the empirical finding demonstrating that murderers as a group have one of the lowest rates of recidivism of any criminal group. Various studies conducted in Canada and abroad unequivocally demonstrate that released murderers behave well and that paroled murderers are among the best parole risks.

In England, the Royal Commission on Capital Punishment stated that information received from nearly all the Commonwealth countries and the United States shows that released murderers in general behave well after leaving prison and in none of the countries is this class of prisoner regarded as particularly liable to misbehaviour on release.[93]

In the United States, studies by Giardini and Farrow,[94] Donnelly and Brewster,[95] and by Stanton[96] reached similar conclusions. In their report, the Research Staff of the Ohio Legislative Service Commission reported that Ohio penal authorities testified before the study committee that for the most part murderers are "model" prisoners.[97] Furthermore, the committee established that the overall success ratio for paroled first degree murder life sentence convicts was 94.1 per cent compared with a success ratio of only 74 per cent for all other classes of paroled offenders.[98] Data collected by *Uniform Parole Reports* and reported in the December, 1967, Newsletter showed that of 1,303 persons convicted of willful homicide, 91.25 per cent had a favourable parole performance during the crucial first 1-year period after release on parole. Further, data showed that 98.31 per cent of those persons had no new major offence convictions during the 1-year period following release. In a subsequent study it was found that from a sample totaling 6,908 persons paroled after conviction for willful homicide during the years 1965-1969 and reported to the UPR, 98.23 per cent (6,786) were successful on parole during the first year following their release. They had no new major convictions or allegations of offences resulting in their return to prison.[99]

In Canada, statistics published by the National Parole Board, and quoted by Sheppard show that from 1920 to 1967, 119 capital offenders who had first had their sentence commuted were granted parole. Only one of the 119 committed a second murder, and was hanged in 1944. Between 1959 and 1967, out of the 32 under death sentence whose sentence had been commuted to life imprisonment and who were later paroled, only one was convicted of another crime, and it was not murder.[100]

Denunciation: Is Capital Punishment the Best Means of Showing Society's Abhorrence to Murder?

Supporters of the death penalty argue that murder is the most abhorrent of crimes, striking at the sanctity of life of which it is the first duty of a law-abiding society to protect. The punishment for this crime of crimes should, therefore, adequately reflect the revulsion felt by the great majority of citizens toward this horrible act. More than any other punishment, so the argument goes, the death penalty marks society's indignation, detestation and abhorrence to the taking of human life. It symbolizes the emphatic denunciation by the community of the crime of murder. Thus, by retaining capital punishment for the gravest crime, the law fosters in the community a special abhorrence to murder.

It is difficult to see how the official killing of a murderer by the state can promote respect for human life. As Baroness Wootton puts it, "to imitate immoral actions does not seem a very sensible way of discouraging them."[101] If one of the major aims of the criminal law is to denounce the crime then this aim can be better achieved by means other than repeating the same act for which the offender has been convicted. The death penalty neither fosters nor promotes reverence for life because its effect on the public mind is one of brutalizing and not of humanizing. It is, regardless of what its proponents say, a mode of vengeance rather than a means of expressing society's disapproval. The brutalizing and dehumanizing effect of the death penalty was well described by the Special Commission established in Massachusetts for the purpose of investigating and studying the abolition of the death penalty in capital cases. The Commission declared that:

> The existence of capital punishment tends to cheapen human life. It tends to encourage both children and adults to believe that physical violence, the ultimate form of which is putting an individual to death, is a proper method of solving social and personal conflict.[102]

This was a reaffirmation of a similar belief held by the *British Select Committee on Capital Punishment*.[103] In recommending abolition, the Committee stated that:

> ... we venture to say that, as in the past, there will come, through the carrying into law of the proposals we are about to make, an ever increasing security and an ever increasing respect for human life. Humanity and security, indeed, will walk hand in hand. And as it is the more humane spirit in our people that makes a more humane penal code possible; so, on the other hand, in humanizing our punishments, we will yet further humanize our people. On the one side, and on the other, humanity will beget humanity, as nobleness enkindles nobleness.

Retribution: Is Death the Only Just Punishment for Wilful Homicide?

Under the retributive view, natural justice demands that the criminal be punished with severity equal to the evil of his crime. Death is, therefore, the only fitting punishment for murder. If vengeance and retaliation were the only goals of criminal sanctions, the principle of "life for life" might be advocated as a proper justification for the death penalty. But retribution is surely not the sole aim of the criminal law and justice can be done and seen to be done without strict adherence to the primitive prescriptions of *Lex Talionis.*

Retribution, as a goal of punishment, has been rejected by philosophers and legal scholars, by judges and by lawyers, by social and behavioural scientists. Plato declared in *Protagoras* that wrongdoers should not be punished for what they have done in the past as this would amount to blind vengeance:

> No, punishment is not inflicted by a rational man for the sake of the crime that has been committed — after all one cannot undo what is past — but for the sake of the future, to prevent, to prevent either the same man or, by the spectacle of his punishment, someone else, from doing wrong again.

The same idea was reiterated, more than 2,000 years later, by Beccaria when he stated that the purpose of punishment is neither to torture and afflict a sensitive being, nor to undo a crime already committed. The purpose can only be to prevent the criminal from inflicting new injuries on his fellow citizens and to deter others from similar acts.

The British Royal Commission on Capital Punishment emphatically dismissed retribution and announced that "modern penological thought discounts retribution in the sense of vengeance." The same report quoted Sir John Anderson as saying:

> I think there would be general agreement that the justification for the capital sentence, as for other salient features of our penal system, must be sought in the protection of society and that alone . . . There is no longer in our regard of the criminal law any recognition of such primitive conceptions as atonement or retribution. We have, over the years, fortunately succeeded to a very large extent, if not entirely, in relegating the purely punitive aspect of our criminal law to the background.[104]

Even the *Florida Special Commission on Capital Punishment* which recommended retention of the death penalty on other grounds, rejected "vengeance or retaliation" as justification for the official taking of life.[105]

Several American courts have ruled that retribution has no place in a contemporary system of criminal justice. The New York Court of Appeals stated in *People v. Oliver* that:

> (T)he punishment or treatment of offenders is directed toward one or more of

three ends: (1) to discourage and act as a deterrent upon future criminal activity, (2) to confine the offender so that he may not harm society, and (3) to correct and rehabilitate the offender. There is no place in the scheme for punishment for its own sake, the product simply of vengeance or retribution.[106]

Justice, even retributive justice, can be satisfied without torture, maiming or the shedding of blood. The argument that a retributive punishment has to be of the same nature as the crime is simply preposterous. None of our current penalties is of the same kind as the offences they punish. We do not burn down the houses of arsonists. Rapists are not raped, assaulters are not assaulted and most property offences are punishable by a prison term. Still these penalties are seen as befitting the crimes and as serving the retributive ends of criminal justice. And, except for some loud voices demanding a return to the noose, nobody is calling for a reversion to a system of justice based on the Talion Law. We can punish criminals, if that is ultimately what we want, without necessarily insisting on avenging the crime by the infliction on the offender of the same harm that he has caused to the victim. Capital punishment, we have to admit, is the last remnant of an archaic, primitive and brutal penal system. It is a vestige of a bygone era, an era during which punishment, either for lack of humanity or alternatives or both, was physical, violent, cruel and irreversible. It is a relic of the past which is not concordant with any of the contemporary aims of sentencing. This is the view expressed by Justice Brennan of the U.S. Supreme Court who in *Furman v. Georgia*[107] declared:

> . . . there is no reason to believe that it (the punishment of death) serves any penal purpose more effectively than the less severe punishment of imprisonment.

CONCLUSION

It may be said that many of the sentencing problems I have discussed are not unique to the death penalty but apply to all other punishments; that they are inherent in every system of human justice. To this, my answer is that it is only with respect to the punishment of death that these problems are likely to cause major and irrevocable damage. As Ehrmann[108] pointed out, "the fact of human fallibility is not a good reason for increasing it. If to err is human, then it becomes all the more important to reduce the probability of errors, especially fatal ones."

By discussing the problems inherent in sentencing to death, I hope to have shown that capital punishment has no place in a perfect system of justice and more important still, that it has no place in a human, fallible, and imperfect system of justice.

NOTES

1. (1976), 70 D.L.R. (3d) 324.

2. P. R. Mackey, "The Inutility of Mandatory Capital Punishment: An Historical Note," in H. A. Bedau and C. M. Pierce (eds.), *Capital Punishment in the United States* (New York: AMS Press, Inc., 1976).

3. *Ibid.,* p. 50.

4. A. Normandeau, "Pioneers in Criminology: Charles Lucas — Opponent of Capital Punishment," 61 *Journal of Criminal Law, Criminology and Police Science* (1970).

5. United Kingdom, *Report of the Select Committee on Capital Punishment* (London: HMSO, 1930).

6. United Kingdom, *Murder 1957 to 1968: A Home Office Statistical Division Report on Murder in England and Wales,* E. Gibson and S. Klein (London: HMSO, 1969).

7. L. D. Savitz, "A Brief History of Capital Punishment Legislation in Pennsylvania" 38 *The Prison Journal* (1958).

8. M. Shipley, "Does Capital Punishment Prevent Convictions?" 43 *New York Law Review* (1909).

9. P. W. Tappan, *Crime, Justice and Corrections* (New York: McGraw-Hill, 1960).

10. R. N. Barber and P. R. Wilson, "Deterrent Aspects of Capital Punishment and its Effect on Conviction Rates: The Queensland Experience," 1 *Australian and New Zealand Journal of Criminology* 100 (1968).

11. New Zealand, Parliamentary Debates, House of Representatives, November 17, 1950, pp. 4334-4335. Also quoted in Appendix six to the Report of the British Royal Commission on Capital Punishment (1953) (London: HMSO, 1950), p. 343.

12. E. A. Fattah, *A Study of the Deterrent Effect of Capital Punishment with Special Reference to the Canadian Situation* (Ottawa: Information Canada, 1972).

13. C. W. Topping, "The Death Penalty in Canada," *The Annals of the American Academy of Political and Social Science,* No. 284 (1952).

14. C. L. Black, Jr., *Capital Punishment: The Inevitability of Caprice and Mistake* (New York: W. W. Norton & Co., Inc., 1974), p. 35.

15. H. L. Packer, *The Limits of Criminal Sanction* (Stanford: Stanford University Press, 1968) p. 137.

16. *Op. cit.,* note 14, p. 24.

17. *Ibid.,* p. 48.

18. *Ibid.,* p. 76.

19. *Ibid.,* pp. 16-17.

20. 391 U.S. 510 (1968).

21. W. E. Oberer, "The Death Penalty and Fair Trial," in T. Sellin (ed.) *Capital Punishment* (New York: Harper and Row, 1967), pp. 220-221.

22. J. Greenburg and J. Himmelstein, "Varieties of Attack on the Death Penalty," 15 *Crime and Delinquency* (1969), p. 116.

23. G. L. Jurow, "New Data on the Effect of a 'Death Qualified' Jury on the Guilt Determination Process," in H. A. Bedau and C. Pierce (eds.), *Capital Punishment in the United States* (New York: AMS Press, 1979), p. 461.

24. 391 U.S. at 523, 531.

25. *Op. cit.*, note 23, pp. 464-467, 483.

26. 408 U.S. 238 (1972).

27. Black, Jr., *op. cit.*, note 14, p. 12.

28. 408 U.S. 238 (1972).

29. *Gregg v. Georgia*, 428 U.S. 153 (1976).

30. P. C. Davis, "The Death Penalty and the Current State of the Law," 14 *Criminal Law Bulletin* (1978), pp. 7-17; Black, *op. cit.*, note 14.

31. Davis, *ibid.*, pp. 10-11.

32. Black, *op. cit.*, note 14, p. 18.

33. *Ibid.*, p. 21.

34. S. Berger, "The Application of the Cruel and Unusual Punishment Clause Under the Canadian Bill of Rights," 24 *McGill Law Journal* (1978), pp. 169, 173.

35. (1975), 63 D.L.R. (3d) 193 at 270.

36. Berger, *op. cit.*, note 34, p. 174.

37. *Ibid.*

38. United Kingdom, *Royal Commission of Capital Punishment, 1949-1953* (London: HMSO, 1953), para. 611.

39. Younger, "The Historical Perspective," in Louis Blom-Cooper (ed.), *The Hanging Question: Essays on the Death Penalty* (London: Duckworth & Co., 1969), p. 8.

40. Sir Charles Cunningham, "Some Practical Considerations," *op. cit.*, note 39, *The Hanging Question*, p. 111.

41. 1974-75-76, c. 105, s. 4.

42. Criminal Code, R.S.C. 1970, c. C-34, s. 214(1)-(5), as enacted by 1974-75-76, c. 105, s. 4.

43. P. Morris, J. Hogarth, E. Fattah and R. Stern, "Bill C-83 and C-84: Some Initial Comments on the Custody and Release Provisions" (mimeographed, 1976).

44. F. G. Carrington, *Neither Cruel Nor Unusual* (New York: Arlington House, 1978), p. 117.

45. *Furman v. Georgia*, 408 U.S. 238 (1972).

46. Bruening, *The Death Penalty and the U. S. Supreme Court* (1975).

47. E. H. Johnson, "Executions and Commutations in North Carolina," in H. A. Bedau, *The Death Penalty in America* (New York: Doubleday, 1964), pp. 452-463. Reprinted from "Selective Factors in Capital Punishment," 36 *Social Forces* (December, 1957), pp. 165-169.

48. Ohio Legislative Service Commission, *Capital Punishment: Staff Research Report, No. 46* (Columbus: OLSC, 1961).

49. *Ibid.*, pp. 61-62.

50. Canada, Minister of Justice, *Capital Punishment: Material Relating to its Purpose and Value* (Ottawa: Queen's Printer, 1965), p. 65.

51. *Op. cit.,* note 46.

52. C. S. Mangum, *The Legal Status of the Negro* (Chapel Hill: University of North Carolina Press, 1940).

53. G. B. Johnson, "The Negro and Crime," *The Annals,* No. 271: 93 (1941).

54. H. Garfinkel, "Research Note on Inter- and Intra-Racial Homicides," 27 *Social Forces* 369 (1949).

55. J. Greenberg and J. Himmelstein, "Varieties of Attack on the Death Penalty," 15 *Crime and Delinquency* (1969), p. 115.

56. *Ibid.*

57. 398 F.2d 138 (1968).

58. M. E. Wolfgang, "The Social Scientist in Court," 65 *Journal of Criminal Law* (1974), p. 244; *id.* "The Death Penalty: Social Philosophy and Social Science Research," 14 *Criminal Law Bulletin* (1978), pp. 26-27.

59. M. Meltsner, *Cruel and Unusual: The Supreme Court and Capital Punishment* (New York: Random House, 1973).

60. M. E. Wolfgang, "The Death Penalty: Social Philosophy and Social Science Research," 14 *Criminal Law Bulletin* (1978), pp. 28-29.

61. W. O. Hochkammer, Jr., "The Capital Punishment Controversy," 60 *Journal of Criminal Law, Criminology and Police Science* (1969), p. 362.

62. M. E. Wolfgang and M. Riedel, "Rape, Racial Discrimination and the Death Penalty," *The Annals of the American Academy of Political and Social Science,* No. 407 (1973); and M. Riedel, "Discrimination in the Imposition of the Death Penalty: A Comparison of the Characteristics of Offenders Sentenced Pre-Furman and Post-Furman," 49 *Temple Law Quarterly* (1976), pp. 261-287.

63. M. Riedel, "Discrimination . . . Post-Furman," *op. cit.,* note 60; M. E. Wolfgang, *op. cit.,* note 58.

64. W. J. Bowers, *Executions in America* (Lexington: D.C. Heath & Co., 1974).

65. *Ibid.,* p. 192.

66. N. Morris, "The Dangerous Criminal," 41 *South California Law Review* 514 (1968).

67. A. A. Stone, *Mental Health and Law: A System in Transition* (Rockville, Maryland: National Institute of Mental Health, 1975), p. 219.

68. Canada, Law Reform Commission, *The Criminal Process and Mental Disorder,* Working Paper No. 14, (Ottawa: Information Canada, 1975), p. 31.

69. B. Wootton, "Morality and Mistakes," in L. Blum-Cooper (ed.), *The Hanging Question* (London: Duckworth & Co., 1969), pp. 13-19.

70. H. L. Packer, *The Limits of Criminal Sanction* (Stanford: Stanford University Press, 1968), p. 131.

71. Stone, *op. cit.,* note 65, p. 230.

72. Law Reform Commission, *op. cit.,* note 66.

73. A. S. Goldstein, *The Insanity Defense* (New Haven: Yale University Press, 1967), p. 101.

74. C. L. Black, Jr., *Capital Punishment: The Inevitability of Caprice and Mistake* (New York: W. W. Norton & Co., Inc., 1974), p. 53.

75. Goldstein, *op. cit.,* note 71, p. 31.

76. *Ibid.,* pp. 34-36.

77. *Ibid.,* p. 30.

78. *Ibid.,* p. 84.

79. J. J. Cocozza and H. J. Steadman, "Prediction in Psychiatry: An Example of Misplaced Confidence in Experts," 25 *Social Problems* (1978), pp. 271-272.

80. 428 U.S. 904 (1976).

81. 428 U.S. 153, 169 (1976).

82. *Supra,* note 79, p. 185.

83. I. Ehrlich, "The Deterrent Effect of Capital Punishment: A Question of Life and Death," 65 *American Economic Review* (1975).

84. J. W. Bowers and G. Pierce, "The Illusion of Deterrence in Isaac Ehrlich's Research on Capital Punishment," 85 *Yale Law Journal* (1975), pp. 187-208; L. R. Klein, B. Forst and V. Filatov, "The Deterrent Effect of Capital Punishment: An Assessment of the Estimates," in A. Blumstein, J. Cohen and D. Nagin (eds.), *Deterrence and Incapacitation: Estimating the Effects of Criminal Sanctions on Crime Rates* (Washington, D.C.: National Academy of Sciences, 1978), pp. 336-360; P. Passell and J. B. Taylor, "The Deterrence Controversy: A Reconsideration of the Time Series Evidence," in H. A. Bedau and C. Pierce (eds.), *Capital Punishment* (AMS Press, 1976), pp. 359-371.

85. Panel of the National Academy of Sciences, *Deterrence and Incapacitation: Estimating the Effects of Criminal Sanctions on Crime Rates,* A. Blumstein, J. Cohen and D. Nagin (eds.) (Washington, D.C.: National Academy of Sciences, 1978).

86. Bowers and Pierce, *op. cit.,* note 82.

87. P. Passell, "The Deterrent Effect of the Death Penalty: A Statistical Test," 28 *Stanford Law Review* (1975).

88. B. E. Forst, "The Deterrent Effect of Capital Punishment: A Cross-State Analysis of the 1960s," 61 *Minnesota Law Review* (1977), p. 764.

89. A. Morris, *Homicide: An Approach to the Problem of Crime* (Boston: Boston University Press, 1955).

90. T. Sellin, "Prison Homicides," in T. Sellin (ed.), *Capital Punishment* (New York: Harper and Row, 1967), pp. 154-160.

91. D. P. Akman, "Homicides and Assaults in Canadian Penitentiaries," 8 *Canadian Journal of Corrections* (1966), pp. 284-299.

92. P. C. Buffum, "Prison Killings and Death Penalty Legislation," 53 *The Prison Journal* (1976), pp. 49-57.

93. United Kingdom, *Royal Commission on Capital Punishment, 1949-1953* (London: HMSO, 1953).

94. G. I. Giardini and R. G. Farrow, "The Paroling of Capital Offenders,"

The Annals of the American Academy of Political and Social Science, No. 284 (November, 1952), pp. 85-94.

95. R. C. Donnelly and C. W. Brewster, "Capital Punishment in Connecticut," 35 *Connecticut Bar Journal* (Hartford: 1961), pp. 39-56.

96. J. M. Stanton, "Murderers on Parole," 15 *Crime and Delinquency* (1969), pp. 149-155.

97. Ohio Legislative Service Commission, *Capital Punishment: Staff Research Report, No. 46* (Columbus: OLSC, 1961), p. 79.

98. *Ibid.,* p. 82.

99. United States, National Probation and Parole Institute, "Parole Risk of Convicted Murders," *Newsletter—Uniform Parole Reports* (December, 1972), p. 2.

100. C. Sheppard, "Towards Better Understanding of the Violent Offender," 13 *Canadian Journal of Corrections* 60 (1971).

101. B. Wootten, "Morality and Mistakes," in L. Blum-Cooper (ed.), *The Hanging Question* (London: Duckworth & Co. 1969), p. 14.

102. United States: Massachusetts, *Preliminary Report of the House Special Committee Established for the Purpose of Investigating and Studying the Abolition of the Death Penalty in Capital Crimes* (Boston: 1958), p. 45.

103. United Kingdom, *Report of the Select Committee on Capital Punishment* (London: HMSO, 1930).

104. United Kingdom, *Royal Commission of Capital Punishment, 1949-1953* (London: HMSO, 1953), p. 17.

105. United States, The Washington Research Project, *The Case Against Capital Punishment* (Washington, D.C.: 1971), p. 26.

106. 1 N.Y. 2d 152 (1956).

107. 408 U.S. 238 (1972).

108. H. B. Ehrmann, "The Death Penalty and the Administration of Justice," in H. A. Bedau (ed.), *The Death Penalty in America* (New York: Doubleday, 1964), pp. 415-434.

CHAPTER 9

The Diversion Controversy

Tanner Elton

INTRODUCTION

The criminal trial and the sentence is without question the most visible and dramatic stage of the criminal process, but it accounts for only a small percentage of the total "dispositions" of those who enter the system. The great majority of those who enter our criminal justice system never find themselves before a judge for sentence, but leave by the many side exits open by the discretionary decisions of police and prosecutors — diversion.

Many commentators have suggested that nothing is really new under the sun and that many of the trends and innovations that are being talked about in relation to sentencing are in reality only recycled notions of the past. That may be so, but there has been at least one change, and that is to our vocabulary. We talk about the system differently using new terms to describe both old problems and recent developments. As a consequence there has developed, with little regard to grammar or pronounceability, a shorthand of criminal justice "buzz-words" which have instant meaning for and often reaction from those working within the system. A few examples would be "team-policing" and "professionalization" for the police; "backlog" and "community based sentencing" for judges; "target-hardening" and "victimization" as applied to crime prevention; and "opportunities model" and "cascading" for corrections officials. But few such words have quite the same "buzz" or raise quite the same depth of feeling as "diversion."

To its proponents, the development of diversion is seen as a necessary response to the inadequacies of our present, narrowly focussed system of justice. For them, diversion offers the potential for more extensive community involvement; a better, more flexible forum for dealing with the collateral problems usually accompanying criminal incidents; a less intrusive method of dealing with certain kinds of criminal problems which will result in less crime and greater public confidence; and (in these days of the shrinking dollar) better cost effectiveness. In brief, diversion potentially offers the best of all worlds. But to its detractors, diversion's potential is seen as a serious threat to civil liberties and as an unnecessary competitor to the courts. It will, they predict, result in a huge parallel bureaucracy; it will increase rather than decrease official intrusion into the lives of Canadians, and it will be costly in terms of money and damage to the credibility of the criminal justice system. Some also suggest that diversion contravenes the spirit and the letter of several sections of the Criminal Code. Briefly, for its opponents, diversion is bad in principle, will not work in practice, and is probably illegal in any event.

Such divergent and strongly held views are the stuff from which controversy is made. I will begin by examining one aspect of the controversy which is uniquely Canadian.

THE PROBLEM OF JURISDICTION

Different groups of people and even nations are sometimes attributed, perhaps unfairly, with certain characteristics on the basis of how they are said to react to a common situation. Show something new to the average American and he would ask, "Can I buy it?"; a German would ask, "How does it work?"; a Frenchman would ask, "Is it good to eat?"; a Scot would ask, "How much does it cost?"; and a Canadian would ask, "Is it federal or is it provincial?" Of late, it seems that questions of constitutional jurisdiction between governments cloud and complicate virtually every area of national concern. The division of powers in the Canadian federal state require that we not only determine what to do but also who can do it. Unfortunately, questions of constitutional jurisdiction often distract attention from the substantive consideration of the proper course of action. Nowhere is this constitutional division and confusion more apparent than in our system of criminal justice which is divided between federal and provincial governments in a way unique among federal states. Virtually every facet of the system, be it policing, courts, law making, administration or procedure, are partly the responsibility of both levels of government.

The jurisdictional intertwining of our justice system makes it much like the famous Siamese twins Chaing and Eng, who had separate minds and personalities but were inextricably linked at the abdomen and shared several vital organs in common. As was apparently the case with Chaing and Eng, our two levels of government can argue and disagree about criminal justice issues, but they can not achieve anything without co-operation. As with those first Siamese twins, some individuality between jurisdictions is possible. Programs can be developed and legislation passed by one or the other without consultations. In this regard it is interesting to note that Chaing was a heavy drinker, while Eng remained a tee-totaler. But, as with our system of criminal justice, unilateral action on the part of one party has immediate repercussions for the other, particularly when they share the same liver and blood stream as did Eng and Chaing.

Diversion and the Constitution

As an integral part of the criminal justice system, "Diversion" raises important questions of jurisdiction between the federal and provincial governments. This was amply demonstrated at a recent federal-provincial conference at which diversion was discussed. In spite of a variety of divergent opinions on substance, the provincial representatives agreed that whatever else it might be, diversion was none of the federal government's business. The reasoning behind this conclusion was quite straightforward: diversion is part of the administration of justice, the administration of justice is a provincial responsibility under the British North America Act, 1867,[1] therefore diversion is not a federal concern. The federal officials were equally adamant that there was a role for the federal government in the development of diversion. Apart from the overall federal interest in encouraging the proper functioning of the criminal justice system, diversion is part of criminal law and procedure which is a federal power in the Act.[2] And there the argument rests.

Unfortunately, it is unlikely that any clear workable demarcation between the two levels of government will be laid down by the courts, as was amply demonstrated in the recent Supreme Court of Canada decision of *R. v. Hauser.*[3] What direction the cases do provide tends to suggest that in most areas of criminal justice there are concurrent or at least complementary powers vested in both levels of government. It appears, then, that there will be no legal resolution to the question of constitutional jurisdiction and the problems will have to be resolved through negotiation between the two levels of government.

Perhaps this is as it should be. Perhaps we need to recognize that jurisdiction in criminal justice is rarely a "yes-no" proposition and that the answer to the question of whether diversion is properly federal or provincial is "yes" in both cases. There is a role for both to play.

Federal and Provincial Roles in Diversion

What, then, are the respective federal and provincial roles? Because diversion must be closely tied to the community and carefully linked with existing social services, its encouragement, monitoring and administration is clearly a provincial responsibility. Much of the personnel involved in diversion programs are either employees of, or closely associated with the provincial government. As well, the provincial Attorney General has responsibility for law enforcement within the province, and his agent, the Crown prosecutor, is often involved in the decision to refer the accused to diversion or to proceed to trial. It follows that diversion programs which affect the flow of cases to court and which largely rely on provincial personnel and resources should properly come under the jurisdiction of the provincial Attorney General.

The federal government also has an important role. Diversion, at least to my mind, is unquestionably a part of criminal procedure — a federal constitutional responsibility.[4] It is interesting to note here that the power of the provincial Crown attorney to stay or re-instigate charges against an accused is not found in provincial legislation but in federal legislation in the Criminal Code, as is the power of arrest vested in police officers who are for the most part provincial employees. In both cases, the personnel and administration are provincial while the powers and procedures are federal. The federal government has and will have in the future an important role to play in the setting of minimum standards and procedures for the operation of diversion. I use "standards" here in the sense of setting out a framework within which the provincial jurisdiction over the administration of justice will operate. An analogy to the operation of the police will perhaps illustrate this. There is no question but that the police are largely under provincial jurisdiction and that it is the responsibility of the provinces and the provincial municipalities to train and administer their police forces. But this administrative responsibility takes place within certain guidelines and standards set out in federal legislation. The Criminal Code empowers the police to arrest, search and seize and outlines the procedures to be followed. The Code sets the standard of "reasonable and probable grounds" that must be satisfied before action can be taken. As well, the Code sets out the standard of pre-exercise review of search warrants by an independent judicial officer, in most instances, a justice of the peace employed by the province. No provincial official would seriously argue that the federal government ought not to set such standards because the administration of the police is a provincial responsibility. In a similar way, there are certain minimum standards needed to govern the administration of diversion programs which will have to be set by the federal government because of the impact of diversion on criminal procedure.

The federal government also has a role to play to ensure a measure of consistency in the application of the criminal law throughout the country. It is in an excellent position to promote experimentation in some areas through funding, to initiate research on criminal justice issues like diversion, and to act as a broker of information and evaluation. This role should not be underestimated despite obvious regional disparities which do exist in Canadian criminal justice and the difficulties created by separating legislation and application. Although not without its problems, Canada is the envy of other federal states because of the single legislative standards established by the Criminal Code.

With a proper understanding and respect for their respective jurisdictions and with adequate consultation, the federal and provincial governments should be able to work together to develop a rational policy on diversion. The question should no longer be, "Who can do it?" but rather, "How can we best do it together?"

WHAT IS DIVERSION? — THE PROBLEM OF DEFINITION AND PURPOSE

Having completed our constitutional detour, let us now consider what diversion is, and what it can be. Diversion has spent its youth in search of an identity. Partly because it was new and was seen to confer instant respectability on all it touched, the term "diversion" has been used to describe a vast array of often very different programs and developments throughout the criminal process. Two examples will illustrate this. A recent document from Great Britain speaks of the "divertible element" in prisons in the context of reducing prison population. And at a recent federal/provincial conference an official voiced concern that "front-end" diversion would kill "rear-end" diversion. In the first case, the report was concerned with crowding in English prisons, in the second, "rear-end" diversion was used in reference to increased sentencing alternatives for judges. Both are important topics in their own right, but neither are properly termed "diversion."

This confusion of terms has been apparent very early in the history of diversion. Although already developed in some other jurisdictions, in Canada the term "diversion" was largely introduced and popularized by the federal Law Reform Commission. In the literature of the Commission the term first appeared in its working paper, *The Principles of Sentencing and Disposition,*[5] followed by another working paper, *Diversion*[6] and a background volume, *Studies on Diversion.*[7] But "diversion" then disappears from the Commission's official language to be replaced by the term "screening." This shift, probably in response to the mounting controversy surrounding diversion, did not help the problem of definition. Initially "diversion" was used generally to describe virtually any initiative or program which offered some kind of alternative to the traditional processes of the criminal justice system. This indiscriminate use resulted in a variety of different meanings, and, consequently, expectations.

An inflation of expectations accompanied the confusion of definition. Diversion was *the* solution, the long awaited panacea for the ills of criminal justice. Diversion was going to increase community tolerance of crime, reduce criminality, empty the prisons and increase social harmony. And all this for less money. It was going to leap entire criminal justice systems in a single bound. Understandably, such exaggerated claims were met with increasing skepticism and hostility, particularly from police and prosecutors. This led, unnecessarily, to the impression in some quarters that diversion would result in dangerous criminals being left at large and serious (redundant) conduct left unnoticed by the courts.

In summary, there is presently not a single, widely accepted definition of diversion in use in Canada, and, as a consequence, there is no common understanding of its purposes or objectives.

The Importance of Definition

The search for a common understanding of diversion should not be dismissed as mere academic quibbling. A clear and common understanding of what diversion is and is not is a requisite first step to the rational development of a policy on diversion, and the development of such a policy is necessary if diversion is to become an integral and permanent feature of our criminal justice system. Continued confusion, with the inevitable disparity of goals and purpose, will result in the haphazard development of programs without proper assessment or guidance. Apart from the obvious administrative and funding difficulties this creates, there is also a potential for injustice. It should be remembered that diversion, for all its good intentions, involves discretionary decisions affecting the lives of citizens, and will require the development of policies and standards to ensure a minimum of abuse and a means of rectification when abuse does occur. Also, it can, and has resulted in serious misunderstandings within the system and with the public.

Diversion in Context

To be understood, diversion must be seen as but one manifestation of a much broader initiative for criminal justice reform. This broader thrust is premised on a principle of restraint whereby the criminal sanction is used only as a last resort and then only to the minimum extent necessary. The demand for more restraint has resulted in pressure to decriminalize or substantially reduce penalties in marginal areas of the criminal law. The general theme of restraint was the major thrust behind the reform of the bail laws. It is largely responsible for the efforts to create more non-custodial sentencing options for the sentencing judge, and is presently the primary impetus in the efforts to reduce prison population. The term "diversion" became synonymous with the entire movement rather than focussing only on the pre-trial procedures for less serious offences.

The above developments and diversion are closely related in that they share the common goal of limiting and controlling the extent to which the criminal process intervenes in the lives of Canadians. They are, however, sufficiently different in practice as to make logical distinctions between them important.

A number of different definitions for diversion have been advanced, any one of which is largely adequate. The value of a definition is not in the actual wording but in the distinctions it makes between diversion and other similar programs. With this in mind, any definition of "diversion" should accomplish the following. First, it should only refer to procedures and programs occurring before trial. That is to say, programs which "divert" a potential accused away from the formal trial process. Once the accused has proceeded to trial any talk of diversion is inappropriate. Programs aimed at increasing sentencing alternatives or efforts encouraging the early release of prisoners, while important in their own right, are not "diversionary." Second, it should clearly indicate that diversion is directed toward less serious offences where there exist opportunities for pre-trial resolution. Such "opportunities" include the relationship between the victim and the accused; whether it was a first offence; the possibilities of restitution or reparation, etc. What is important here is that diversion be clearly indicated as inappropriate for serious or repetitive criminal behaviour. Third, the definition must set realistic goals for diversion. There is much controversy in this area and I can speak for myself only. I feel it is important that the objectives of diversion be expressed modestly and concretely. The objectives should be modest in the sense that diversion not promise more than it can deliver. Such objectives as "restoration of social harmony" or "increased community tolerance" are noble and worthwhile, but cannot begin to be attained through diversion alone. Diversionary procedures may promote such developments, but only as a desired side effect rather than a principal goal. The objectives should be concrete in the sense that they lend themselves to measurement and evaluation. Our national coefficient of social harmony is, to say the least, elusive and beyond quantification. If, in a few years from now, we wish to evaluate the impact of diversion, it will have to be on more concrete grounds.

Bearing this in mind, I suggest that the primary objective of diversion is to decrease the numbers of less serious offences being dealt with in court, consistent with the need for public protection. This objective is in tune with the overall aim of restraint in the use of criminal law and has the advantage of lending itself to evaluation. If it also leads to greater social harmony, so much the better, but the future success of diversion will ride largely on the extent to which diversion programs result in fewer, less serious cases going to court.

Should We Distinguish Between Police and Prosecutorial Diversion?

Having indicated that diversion should refer to the pre-trial phase of the criminal process, should a further distinction be made between police and prosecutorial diversion? Police diversion, of course, refers to the initial decision not to charge, while prosecutorial diversion refers to the decision not to proceed to trial once a charge has been laid. A strong case can be made for distinguishing between the two, although both are clearly important decisions which ought to be made consistently, according to known criteria and subject to some kind of review. Ironically, although there is strong evidence to suggest that in terms of numbers, the most important "screening" decision is made by the police at the time of arrest, most of the efforts to develop a policy on diversion has focused on the decision of the prosecutor not to proceed to trial. Recognizing that there may be important reasons for distinguishing between the police and the prosecution phases of the process, there is clearly a need for more attention and policy development for diversion at the moment of arrest.

IS DIVERSION LEGAL?

To suggest that diversion might be illegal appears odd, given that diversion projects are almost all funded and actively supported by the same government which makes the laws the diversion projects are said to be contravening. Nonetheless, from the very outset questions have been raised about the legalities of diversion generally and certain diversionary practices in particular. There are four questions which consider the more important areas of the legality of diversion. These questions are important more for the general concerns they illustrate than for the resolution of the technical points of law they raise. My conclusion is that it is highly unlikely that diversion programs are in breach of the criminal law. Nonetheless, it would be wise to recognize, in legislation, the existence of diversion and indicate how it fits into our scheme of procedure. The legal questions point as well to the need for a well developed policy on diversion.

First: Is diversion an abuse of process? The concept of abuse of process itself is somewhat questionable in light of the recent Supreme Court of Canada decision in *Rourke v. R.*[8] Abuse of process, therefore, needs to be reviewed to determine its application to diversion. Second: How does diversion relate to prosecutorial discretion? The power to withdraw or stay prosecutions clearly relates to diversion since diversionary programs increase the use of such prosecutorial discretion. The issue, therefore, is whether any legal checks exist in the present criminal justice system to ensure that the discretion exercised by prosecutors will not be abused with respect to persons diverted from the formal trial process. Third: Does diversion conflict with the Criminal Code? There are potentially a number of conflicts between diversion programs and existing provisions of the Criminal Code. These include section 127 (Obstructing Justice), section 129 (Compounding an Indictable Offence), section 305 (Extortion), and section 381 (Intimidation). Fourth: Does diversion create a situation of potentional double jeopardy? This raises the problem of persons who enter into diversion programs but fail to complete them successfully. To what extent does reinvocation of the criminal charge at this point raise questions of double jeopardy? The body of this paper considers the above mentioned areas.

Diversion and Abuse of Process

An important feature of any diversion program is the decision to stay or withdraw charges as part of the diversion agreement with the offender. The "justice official" (usually, one would expect, the Crown prosecutor) retains the right to revive the charge if the offender does not complete the agreed to program. The manner in which charges are reintroduced or the possibility that they can be reintroduced at all may constitute an abuse of process. Such was the conclusion of the court in the case of *R. v. Jones.*⁹ In that case the accused was charged with theft and possession of marijuana. She subsequently agreed to a diversion program whereby she was to complete 40 hours of community service work, write a composition of her experience since her arrest, keep the peace and demonstrate good behaviour. After she completed the community work but before she had written the composition, she appeared in court on another charge. At that time, the charge for possession of marijuana was reintroduced. The court did not proceed on the marijuana charge on the basis that its introduction after the diversion program had been largely completed was an abuse of process. In commenting on the diversion, Mr. Justice Anderson stated:

> The exercise of such a power by the Crown constitutes a direct and unlawful interference with the proceedings of the criminal Courts and amounts to an abuse of process. By means of pressure brought upon the accused, the powers which can only be exercised by the Courts are, in fact, exercised by the Crown.¹⁰

Anderson J. took the view that the diversion process was tantamount to a pre-trial probation order made by the Crown. As such the Crown "sentences" the accused and then acts as judge to determine whether the order has been complied with. He then stated, "In my opinion, the wide powers vested in the executive do not permit the executive to impose administrative sanctions in this way."¹¹ It was not so much the program which was objectionable as it was the threat of reviving criminal proceedings being held over the respondent's head to induce her to comply with the diversion agreement.

The *Jones* decision raises a basic policy question as to whether diversion programs ought to allow the reintroduction of charges if the diversion agreement is not successfully completed. Given that diversion is only going to be used in minor cases, it could be strongly argued that once the decision to divert has been made there should not be the possibility of reviving the charge. The possibility of non-compliance would be the risk taken when the decision to divert was made and the only sanction available would be the likelihood of a person who does not successfully complete the diversion program ever being offered this alternative in the future. It would appear that the increasing demands for a more formal diversion procedure with explicit safeguards is largely premised on the fact that the charges can be reintroduced. Remove the threat of the revived charge and many of the concerns are also removed. This of course is a policy question which must be addressed in the formulation of diversion policy. The legal point, however, is whether reviving the charge in circumstances such as those set out in *R. v. Jones* amounts to an abuse of process. This in turn depends on whether the doctrine of abuse of process is available in Canadian law.

The doctrine of abuse of process has been described as a judicial Bill of Rights.[12] The doctrine vests the courts with an inherent jurisdiction to stay or dismiss actions considered to be an abuse of the judicial process. In Canada its history may be divided into two periods, the first period ending with the decision of the Supreme Court of Canada in *Rourke v. R.*, the second period begins with that same decision.

Before Rourke

The earliest reported Canadian case recognizing such a doctrine in criminal proceedings is the 1886 decision of the Supreme Court of Canada *Re Sproule*,[13] where the court quashed a writ of *habeas corpus* because it had been improperly granted. The judgment of the Court states that, ". . . every superior court, which this court unquestionably is, has incident to its jurisdiction an inherent right to inquire into and judge of the regularity or abuse of its process."[14] However, the case most often cited as recognizing an inherent jurisdiction in the Superior Court to protect its process is the House of Lords decision in the case of *Connelly v. D.P.P.*[15] In that case three of the five judges affirmed the existence of an inherent power to control abuse of court practices and procedures. Lord Morris accepted the doctrine in a more limited fashion stating:

> There can be no doubt that a court which is endowed with a particular jurisdiction has powers which are necessary to enable it to act effectively within such jurisdiction. I would regard them as powers which are inherent in its jurisdiction. A court must enjoy such powers in order to enforce its rules of practice and to suppress any abuses of its process and to defeat any attempted thwarting of its process.[16]

Although the doctrine had been frequently invoked in Canadian courts, its effect was limited. For example, various cases established that the criminal courts could not be used to collect civil debts (*R. v. Leclair*)[17] although other cases (*R. v. Jean Talon Fashion Center Inc.*)[18] have held that it is not an abuse of process to institute criminal proceedings where civil proceedings have already commenced in relation to the same matter. The doctrine was upheld in *R. v.*

Ormerod in which the courts were asked to consider certain police practices. The case states that

> [t]here is no statutory warrant for such a jurisdiction, but that does not mean that a Court is powerless to prevent abuses, be they abuses in the lodging of the prosecution itself or in the establishment of the foundation for the prosecution.[19]

There are other examples in the cases which recognized the existence of the doctrine and applied it to give relief to the accused.

After Rourke

This initial growth and encouragement of the doctrine was severely limited by the Supreme Court of Canada in *R. v. Osborn*,[20] and then dealt what should have been a death blow by its decision in *Rourke*.

Osborn was a case where repeated trials on the same facts were alleged to be oppressive and the issue was whether the court had the power to stay proceedings in such circumstances. The Court of Appeal dismissed the charges against the appellant but was reversed by the Supreme Court of Canada. The Supreme Court, however, did not directly address the issue of abuse of process, basing their decision on a lack of evidence to support the contention of oppression. There was, however, a strong statement by Pigeon J., doubting the existence of such a doctrine in Canadian law.[21]

In spite of the strong implications of *R. v. Osborn,* abuse of process continued to be applied by the lower courts until the Supreme Court decision in *Rourke*. In that case the defence moved for a stay of proceedings because the accused was charged 18 months after the crime had been committed, even though his involvement and whereabouts were well known by the police. In those circumstances he argued that he could not prepare a proper defence and that the delay of the Crown amounted to an abuse of the court process. Again, the appellant's argument succeeded up to the Provincial Court of Appeal but was overturned by the Supreme Court of Canada. The Supreme Court rejected the notion that superior courts had jurisdiction to not proceed in cases where delay in instituting prosecution may have prejudiced the accused's case. Pigeon J., for the majority states:

> I cannot admit of any general discretionary power in Courts of criminal jurisdiction to stay proceedings regularly instituted because the prosecution is considered oppressive. . . .
>
> In my view, the absence of any provision in the *Criminal Code* contemplating the staying of an indictment by a trial Judge or an appeal from such a decision, is strong indication against the existence of any power to grant such stay.[22]

The unambiguous judgment in *Rourke* should have ended discussion of the viability of the doctrine of abuse of process in Canada. But it did not. *Rourke* was a 5:4 decision with a strong dissenting judgment by Chief Justice Laskin which supports the proposition that every court having criminal jurisdiction may use abuse of process to stay proceedings which are oppressive or vexatious. As well, several authors, and, more importantly, several judges, have concluded that in spite of *Rourke* the doctrine continues to exist in Canada. Stan Cohen, for example, in "Abuse of Process: the Aftermath of Rourke,"[23] suggests that there continues to exist a doctrine of abuse of process which could give relief to accused persons improperly dealt with. But in spite of the apparent tenacity of the doctrine, its use in Canada is at best questionable; at worst, nonexistent. It was, however, applied by Mr. Justice Anderson in *R. v. Jones*[24] to give relief to an accused from what the court considered an oppressive diversion agreement.

Mr. Justice Anderson held that the proceedings were irregularly instituted due to the prior diversion agreement between the accused and the prosecutor. This result was supported in the decision of *R. v. Babcock*[25] which also upheld the court's discretionary power to not proceed in instances where an abuse of process has been determined. It should be noted that these cases do not challenge the prosecutor's discretion to stay charges and reinstitute them at a later date as is provided for in sections 508 and 732.1 of the Criminal Code. What it does suggest, however, is that where a diversionary agreement had been reached with the accused and the charges dropped or stayed in consequence, then any attempt to reinstitute them in circumstances where unfairness or oppression could be alleged by the accused could give rise to a defence of abuse of process. If the doctrine of abuse of process continues to be available in Canada, it would appear to be applicable in some diversion cases. It would not, however, result automatically from the reinvocation of the criminal charge after a diversion agreement has been struck, but would only apply where there is evidence of unfiarness or oppression. So, in spite of *Rourke,* in B.C. at least, the doctrine of abuse of process has been applied to diversion programs. Just to ensure total confusion in this area the B.C. Court of Appeal, after *Jones,* in *R. v. Lee Brun*[26] upheld a decision by a Provincial Court Judge not to apply the doctrine of abuse of process on the basis of *Rourke* though he felt that there had been a serious abuse. And the beat goes on.

From the above it appears that although seriously compromised and weakened, abuse of process may still be successfully invoked to contest diversion programs which result in the oppression of an accused.

Quite apart from the legal aspects of *R. v. Jones,* the case raises important policy issues. Most impartial observers would agree that the charge in a situation such as that which gave rise to the *Jones* case, ought not to have been reintroduced. Given the minor nature of the offences involved and the substantial compliance of the accused, reinstigating the charge was unfair. It is therefore important, regardless of the applicability of the doctrine of abuse of process, that minimum guidelines be established for diversion programs to ensure that the content of diversion agreements be not oppressive in view of the seriousness of the alleged offence and that there be clear guidelines as to when and in what circumstances charges should be reinvoked, if at all.

Diversion and Prosecutorial Discretion

Most diversion programs require a decision by the prosecutor to withdraw or stay charges as a result of an agreement struck with the accused. The following paragraphs consider whether the use of prosecutorial discretion in diversion programs creates any legal difficulties.

There is no question that prosecutors now have the power to stay and reinstate charges at a later date (sections 508 and 732.1, Criminal Code). However, the availability of diversion programs adds a dimension to prosecutorial discretion beyond that anticipated in the legislation. The question therefore arises as to what extent, if any, a prosecutor's discretion to divert an accused by withdrawing or staying a charge and his power to subsequently reintroduce that charge if some aspect of the diversion agreement is not completed, is subject to some control and review. The previous section indicated that the doctrine of abuse of process may provide a very limited check against the unfair and oppressive reintroduction of charges by the prosecutor.

Not considered, however, is the case where the prosecution decides to proceed even though a diversion program is available and the accused has expressed an interest and willingness to participate in it. To what extent, then, does the law presently provide for review of the discretion of prosecutors as it affects diversion programs.

The Crown Attorney is an agent of the Attorney General who, in turn, is part of the executive branch of government. Because the authority of the Attorney General derives from the royal prerogative it is not reviewable. As a result, the Attorney General and his agents have exceptionally wide discretionary powers. The availability of diversion programs will enhance this power, and, in effect, allow the Crown Attorney to play both judge and jury.

It is generally agreed that the decision by the prosecution to stay a proceeding is not reviewable. It is an ". . . exercise of executive power entirely outside the ambit of court authority."[27] Nor does it appear that prerogative writs would be effective.

> If it is claimed that the authority for the exercise of discretion derives from the royal prerogative, the courts appeared to be limited to the question of vires in the narrowest sense of the term. They can determine whether the prerogative power exists, what is its extent, whether it has been exercised in the appropriate form and how far it has been superseded by statute; it cannot, it seems, examine the appropriateness or adequacy of the grounds for exercising the power, and they will not allow bad faith to be attributed to the Crown.[28]

In summary, it appears that the courts will not get involved in reviewing the prosecutor's discretionary power except to the extent that such exercise amounts to an abuse of process. As noted earlier, the effectiveness of the doctrine of abusive process to review the discretion of the Crown is still being developed, and may, in light of the recent decisions of the Supreme Court, not even exist at all. Ironically, both Cohen and the Law Reform Commission of Canada[29] considered the doctrine of abuse of process as one means whereby the excesses of prosecutors could be controlled. Given the confused state of the law regarding the doctrine of abuse of process, some form of statutory review procedure would appear in order.

Diversion — Potential Conflicts with the Criminal Code

A number of concerns have been raised that there may be conflicts between diversion programs and existing sections of the Criminal Code. As a result, prosecutors in at least one province were at one time directed not to enter into any diversion agreements on the basis that to do so amounted to the offence of compounding (section 129, Criminal Code). Other concerns have been raised concerning extortion (section 305), and intimidation (section 381) particularly in cases where some pressure is put on the accused to enter into an agreement. As well, it has been suggested that a decision to not proceed when all the elements of the offence exist could be construed as obstructing justice (section 127).

Intimidation

One of the arguments often raised against diversion is that the uneducated or timid offender may be intimidated by the prosecutor and forced into a diversion program in circumstances where he otherwise might have gone on to trial and pleaded not guilty. Such intimidation does not, however, appear to fall within section 381(1) of the Criminal Code:

> Every one who, wrongfully and without lawful authority, for the purpose of compelling another person to abstain from doing anything that he has a lawful right to do, or to do anything that he has a lawful right to abstain from doing, . . . is guilty of an offence punishable on summary conviction.

Section 381 requires many elements, one of which is that the person acts "without lawful authority." It is difficult to assert that the prosecutor is without lawful authority when discussing the possibility of entering into a diversion agreement with an accused. He is certainly without his statutory powers to stay proceedings and reinstitute them or to withdraw the charge. Furthermore, section 381 requires positive acts such as the use of violence, following the person around, etc., which are clearly not applicable to the negotiations prior to entering into a diversion agreement. If violence, the threat of violence or any of the means listed in section 381 were used to compel an offender to enter into a diversion agreement, an action would lie. But it is hard to imagine circumstances in which such "techniques" would be resorted to and it seems fair to assume that short of such excesses that diversion agreements do not come into conflict with section 381 of the Criminal Code.

Extortion

But what about extortion? Could it not be argued that the threat of criminal prosecution could be used to extort an agreement from an otherwise unwilling accused? Section 305(1) of the Criminal Code states:

> Every one who, without reasonable justification or excuse and with intent to extort or gain anything, by threats, accusations, menaces or violence induces or attempts to induce any person, whether or not he is the person threatened, accused or menaced or to whom violence is shown, to do anything or cause anything to be done, is guilty of an indictable offence and is liable to imprisonment for fourteen years.

This is a very complicated section. Many elements are required before the offence is committed. Its applicability would also depend on the nature of the diversion program and the diversion agreements. A brief review of the history of the section and the cases seems to indicate that it would be difficult to apply this section to diversion agreements. First, extortion requires that there be some form of gain or benefit accruing to the person who is the author of the extortion. What would that be in the context of diversion? As well, it appears that most diversion programs presently operating are largely free of the kinds of coercive elements which might possibly give rise to such a charge. It can be concluded, therefore, that section 305 of the Criminal Code is unlikely to be a problem for diversion programs.

However, the relative inequality of the accused person and the prosecutor does indicate the need to outline certain minimum standards to guide officials involved with diversion programs as to the manner in which agreements are negotiated.

Obstructing Justice

Another legal issue which is sometimes raised as a potential problem with diversion is that entering into diversion agreements amounts to an obstruction of justice contrary to section 127 of the Criminal Code. At least in part, this is based on the notion that there is some obligation on officials in the criminal process to proceed to formal charge and trial whenever there is evidence of all the necessary elements of the offence. This notion of a duty of full enforcement is non existent in practice and questionable in theory. If it were to be applied it would have far more serious implications for informal police screening practices and plea negotiations than for diversion programs. Nonetheless, because participation in a diversion program does result in not proceeding with a charge which otherwise could have been laid, the question of obstruction may arise. Section 127(2) of the Criminal Code reads as follows:

> Every one who wilfully attempts in any manner . . . to obstruct, pervert or
> defeat the course of justice is guilty of an indictable offence and is liable to
> imprisonment for ten years.

Is participation in a diversion program a wilful attempt to defeat the course of
justice? The answer is clearly that it is not. Underlying diversion is an attitude of
restraint in the use of the criminal law. It is no more nor less an obstruction of
justice than when police officers do not charge even though the legal elements of
an offence appear to exist or when prosecutors stay or withdraw charges even
though it was possible to proceed to trial. Because diversion programs are part
of the criminal justice system, it could be argued that far from being obstructed,
justice is being served through the use of diversion. As well, the cases seem to
indicate that section 127 requires some kind of overt act amounting to
something more than the agreement contemplated in most diversionary
schemes. As such, it appears that section 127 could not be raised with respect to
diversion agreements.

Compounding Offences

This brings us to the argument that diversion agreements may amount to an
offence under section 129 of the Criminal Code (Compounding an Indictable
Offence). The section reads as follows:

> Every one who asks or obtains or agrees to receive or obtain any valuable
> consideration for himself or any other person by agreeing to compound or
> conceal an indictable offence is guilty of an indictable offence and is liable to
> imprisonment for two years.

It was argued in *R. v. Jones* that entering into diversion agreements
constituted an offence under this section. Mr. Justice Anderson disagreed with
this conclusion, stating as follows:

> I do not think that there is any substance to this contention and that s. 129 is
> only applicable to cases where private persons have "compounded or
> concealed" an indictable offence. The prosecutor has an uncontrolled
> discretion to stay proceedings and the mere fact that he may require as a
> condition of granting a stay that an accused person perform community
> services is not an offence and is not in any wise unlawful or unreasonable. What
> is wrong is to compel performance of those community services by holding the
> threat of criminal charges over the head of the accused.[30]

This is the same conclusion reached by Jeanne Proulx in a detailed study of the
history of section 129 of the Criminal Code and its effect on diversion
agreements.[31] She does note, however, that diversion agreements come very
close to compounding an offence in that they may, in some cases, constitute an

agreement not to prosecute in consideration for the return of the goods or services taken by the accused. This agreement not to prosecute in return for some kind of advantage seems, on the surface, to fall within the offence of compounding. However, the cases on section 129 limit the section to accepting valuable consideration for not disclosing information relevant to substantiating the commission of an offence and would not, therefore, apply to diversion agreements. Section 129 of the Code prohibits bargains in the case of all indictable offences, but this does not mean that it eliminates all types of negotiations between persons involved in an offence against public order. It also seems obvious in terms of the kinds of negotiations entered into with an accused prior to trial that plea bargaining is much closer to obstructing justice than public diversion agreements, yet obstruction has not been raised against such negotiations. However, private agreements not to prosecute have been declared illegal by the courts (see for example *Smerchanski v. M.M.R.*[32]). These cases are not applicable to diversion because diversion agreements are not private for the following reaons: (1) the public laying of the charges avoids the problem of concealment; (2) with respect to the victim, section 129 of the Criminal Code does not constitute an offence because the settlement of the private aspect of the problem, including monetary compensation for injury caused by the act, cannot be regarded as unlawful, valuable consideration. This is because the agreement between parties does not contain a promise not to prosecute. It is the prosecutor who promises not to prosecute and as such that decision remains under his authority, and, as discussed earlier, is not subject to review; (3) there is no agreement to obtain valuable consideration for another person by agreeing not to prosecute, because the discretion is left with the prosecutor. The prosecutor is only agreeing to take the result of such bargaining into account in the exercise of his discretion. The agreement does not involve valuable consideration for him or the victim; (4) one element of the offence, that the public interest not be subject to private interest, is missing.

From the above, one can safely conclude that diversion agreements do not amount to an obstruction of justice by either the victim or the prosecutor under section 129.

Diversion raises many other difficult legal questions, particularly in the area of evidence. I understand that these are presently being considered in great detail by the federal Department of Justice. I suspect that the conclusions of the officials of the Department of Justice will not be unlike those above. There are problems, but none insurmountable if there is the desire to see diversion develop and flourish. This indicates that the ultimate success of diversion is not a question of legalities but one of social policy. If diversion fails it will be due to insufficient policy, not legal problems.

DIVERSION — FINDING ITS NICHE

A new and exciting concept can only remain new and exciting for a relatively short period of time. It then must weave itself into the social fabric or fade away. The future of diversion depends largely on how successfully it becomes integrated into the overall criminal justice system. It must find its niche. For this to happen I feel a number of things must take place. First, in typically Canadian fashion, the federal and provincial governments are going to have to come to an accommodation on the question of jurisdiction over diversion and many other aspects of criminal justice. We presently waste far too much time and energy on the important, but essentially unproductive sorting out of constitutional responsibilities. Second, the legal regime governing diversion must be clarified. Diversion programs cannot thrive in a climate of legal uncertainty. This uncertainty, I suggest, would best be resolved through legislative recognition of diversion in the Criminal Code and by stating in legislation what can and cannot be done through diversion programs. Third, every effort must be made to ensure that diversion focuses on getting people out of the criminal justice system, and that it not result in the opposite. Although there is little data available on this, some of the initial indications give cause for concern that for all its good intentions, diversion can result in more, not fewer individuals in the system. Evaluation, research and close follow-up will be required. Fourth, important decisions will have to be made determining the relationship of pre-trial diversion to sentencing alternatives. Because diversion was developed at a time when sentencing was relatively uncreative and harsh it was seen as a potential alternative to much of the sentencing process. Now, with the introduction of an ever expanding variety of non-custodial sentencing alternatives (e.g., Community Service Orders, Fine Options, etc.) the situation is quite different. It will be necessary to establish criteria for determining when diversion is appropriate, or when it would be preferable to deal with the offender through a guilty plea followed by a court imposed community based sentence. The difference between the two, in terms of perception and consequences, is not great.

The future of diversion, then, depends on the collective effort of governments and individuals to make it work.

NOTES

1. S. 92(14).
2. S. 91(27).
3. [1979] 1 S.C.R. 984.
4. *British North America Act, 1867,* s. 91(27).
5. Canada: Law Reform Commission, Working Paper No. 3 (Ottawa: Information Canada, 1974).
6. Working Paper No. 7 (Ottawa: Information Canada, 1975).

7. (Ottawa: Information Canada, 1975).

8. (1977), 35 C.C.C. (2d) 129 (Can.).

9. (1978), 40 C.C.C. (2d) 173 (B.C.).

10. *Ibid.,* pp. 184-185.

11. *Ibid.,* p. 184.

12. S. Cohen, "Abuse of Process: the Aftermath of Rourke," 39 C.R.N.S. 349, 352-353 (1977).

13. (1886), 12 S.C.R. 140.

14. *Ibid.,* p. 180.

15. [1964] 2 All E.R. 401 (H.L.).

16. *Ibid.,* p. 409.

17. (1956), 115 C.C.C. 297 (Ont. C.A.).

18. (1975), 22 C.C.C. (2d) 223 (Que.).

19. *R. v. Ormerod,* [1969] 4 C.C.C. 3 at 11 (Ont. C.A.).

20. [1971] S.C.R. 184.

21. *Ibid.,* p. 190.

22. 35 C.C.C. (2d) at 145, 146.

23. *Op. cit.,* note 12.

24. (1978), 40 C.C.C. (2d) 173 (B.C.).

25. (1978), 4 C.R. (3d) 105 (B.C.).

26. (1978), 45 C.C.C. (3d) 300 (B.C.C.A.).

27. C. Sun, "The Discretionary Power to Stay Criminal Proceedings," 1 *Dalhousie Law Journal* 482 at 503 (1974).

28. S. Cohen, *Due Process of Law* (Toronto: Carswell, 1977), p. 356.

29. Law Reform Commission of Canada, *Control of the Process,* Working Paper No. 15 (1975).

30. *Supra,* note 24 at 185.

31. J. Proulx, *A Study of the Legality of the Conciliation Project Submitted by the Centre Service Social de Montreal Metropolitain* (1978), p. 42.

32. *Smerchanski v. M.N.R.* (1976), 35 C.R.N.S. 228 (S.C.C.).

Part 4

SENTENCING SPECIFIC OFFENDERS

CHAPTER 10

Controlling Juvenile Offenders: Realistic and Unrealistic Strategies[1]

Jim Hackler

How much do we really know about controlling juvenile offenders? In some areas scientific research has made clear progress, but probably the main contribution of recent research on delinquency prevention is that our knowledge is weak and the tools available to us are not particularly effective. Rather than being unhappy about this state of affairs, perhaps we should look at some of the blessings. In other areas our technology is moving rapidly; so rapidly in fact that we cannot see the consequences very clearly. It is like the pilot who announced to the passengers: "I have two things to report, one bad, one good. The bad thing is that we are lost. The good thing is that we are maintaining a very good air speed."

For those of us who are studying delinquency, as well as those who are trying to respond intelligently to delinquent offenders, we may be more like a pilot in the following situation. "I have two things to report, one bad, and one good. The bad thing is that we *might* be lost, but I am not completely sure. The good thing is that we are going so slow and making so little progress, it will be some time before we are *completely* lost."

This attitude may be seen as condoning a "muddling through" approach to the problem of delinquency, but a more radical stance has its drawbacks. If there is in fact no great *leap* forward, delinquency prevention strategies that continually make dramatic and unrealistic claims may actually become barriers to making modest progress. Therefore, this paper will not seek to discuss elusive, if not non-existent solutions to the delinquency problem. Rather, two diverse strategies are offered: the first would suggest a change in the very fabric of society. The second strategy would deal with the juvenile courts, and although this second strategy falls more easily within our grasp, one should expect only modest returns.

ARGUMENT 1: MOVING THE SKEWED CURVE

Central to the first portion of this discussion is the *shape* of the curve which can be plotted if we look at the percentage of juveniles who engage in delinquent acts on a vertical scale and the seriousness of that delinquency on a horizontal scale. See Figure 1.

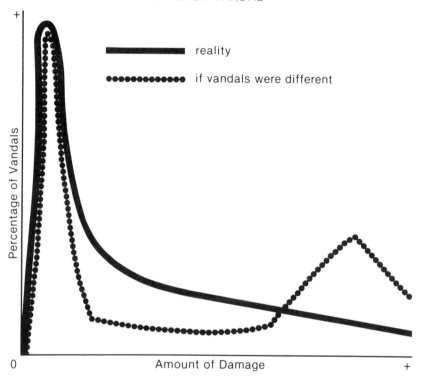

Figure 1
THE FREQUENCY OF JUVENILES COMMITTING VANDALISM
CHARTED AGAINST THE AMOUNT OF DAMAGE COMMITTED
BY EACH VANDAL*

reality

if vandals were different

Percentage of Vandals

0   Amount of Damage   +

* Basic idea from Whitehead and Smart (1972)

Looking at the solid line we would argue that most vandals commit minor acts of vandalism and fit under the hump to the left of the graph. There are a few angels who never do anything wrong, but they are rare and fit close to the zero point of the graph. From the hump, the line tapers to the right with smaller numbers of juveniles committing more serious acts of vandalism. The serious acts become increasingly rare. According to the shape of this curve there is *no* unique population of serious vandals who are particularly numerous who might be a logical target for an anti-vandalism program.

It is also argued that the shape of this curve will remain basically the same for a wide variety of delinquent behaviour. In fact, a similar shape probably exists for most of the deviant behaviour engaged in by people in society in general.

If one looks at the dotted line, instead of the solid line, we might be describing the situation *if* the juveniles who committed acts of vandalism were in fact different from the rest of us. That is, we see a peak on the right side of the chart as well as on the left. In other words, we frequently think of a "problem group" who are in need of special treatment. We realize that many juveniles commit minor acts of vandalism, just as we did when we were young. Of course *we* didn't do anything really bad; our vandalism was just trivial. Many people believe the *real* concern is with those truly destructive juveniles who do large amounts of damage. They are represented by the second, smaller hump in the curve shown by the dotted line.

We could apply this same logic to a number of deviant acts. For example, let us consider drinking. There are a few people who do not drink at all. They appear at the far left of our figure. Most people drink a little and are represented by the tall hump in our curve. These people do not present a problem for our society because their drinking habits do not interfere with their jobs, their driving patterns, or other behaviour that might make them a risk to society. The problem is with those relatively few people who drink a lot, who are out on the right hand side of the graph. If we conceive of the problem in terms of the *dotted* line, our response in terms of public policy is to ignore the group under the hump on the left hand side of the chart and focus instead on the group under the right hand portion of the graph. We assume that if we could only change the behaviour of those problem people, who drink excessively, everything would be all right.

The assumption behind the above thinking is that we can somehow deal with a *portion* of the population while ignoring the rest. Although I may be extending my generalizations too far, I would argue that the shape of the curve for most anti-social behaviour resembles the solid line, and even though the *curve* may move to the right or the left, *the shape remains basically the same.* If this is true, there usually is no special population that can be treated in a unique manner while the rest of us continue going about our business as usual. In terms of effective *policy* strategies, it may be much more meaningful to move the *entire curve* to the left, rather than to focus on one particular portion of that curve.

To return to our example of drinking patterns, if we are concerned about the steadily growing use of alcohol in our society, which we now know is our major drug problem rather than heroin or marijuana, our strategy should be geared toward lowering alcohol consumption for *everyone*. Instead of having cocktail parties at conferences, where hard liquor is a favourite drink, should we try to have a wine and cheese tasting gathering instead? If those of us who drink nine beers during the summer when we are working in the garden can cut that down to six, we move the curve to the left. In other words, an effective program regarding alcohol use would probably have to move everyone's drinking patterns toward the left of the graph.

The point should be obvious. The world is not neatly divided into delinquents and non-delinquents, criminals and non-criminals, alcoholics and non-alcoholics. Instead, there is a large grey area in between. Most boys engage in some delinquency but the majority of them do not persist and do not end up becoming serious criminals. There would probably be general agreement at this point, that a desirable strategy would be to move the entire curve for delinquency over to the left. That is, we should not just be concerned with serious delinquency, but with the entire spectrum. But how could this be done? Let me extend the logic a little further.

Delinquency: Part of the Social Fabric

Is it possible that juvenile delinquency is closely tied to the moral code of the society as a whole? Can we argue that when parents cheat on income tax and corporations systematically commit crimes, juvenile delinquency will remain fairly high? The contention here is that the moral level of a society is woven together; and even though it is a complex fabric, it still forms a whole cloth. The respect for income tax laws, traffic regulations, and laws regarding stealing admittedly evoke different responses from different people, but there seems to be a relationship between violating moral codes among "solid citizens" and delinquent acts among juveniles. Such immoral behaviour would also fit the graph in Figure 1.

Perhaps some types of adult behaviour are more directly relevant to juvenile behaviour. For example, the mother who goes to the hockey games to watch her son play and is yelling, "kill the bastard," should not be surprised if the child is later involved in fighting. Naturally, it is not being suggested that there is a complete one-to-one relationship, but if we generally encourage aggressiveness in sport, business, and every day life, we should expect it to manifest in delinquency as well.

At this point, one might assume that my policy strategy for juvenile delinquency is just for everyone to be better than they are. While that might be theoretically correct, general preaching does not provide a clear strategy for action. Therefore, let me suggest that in order to move this morality curve to the left, we must see if there are certain segments of immoral and illegitimate practices which would be more susceptible to change than others. I will argue that *upper level crime* could be influenced to a much greater extent than *lower level crime,* and by focusing our efforts in that area, we would not only get a better direct return for our efforts, we might eventually have a long-term impact on a whole range of behaviour in society *including* juvenile delinquency. This is not perfunctory Marxist rhetoric. I am not arguing that those in power do nasty things with impunity and criminalize those at the bottom of the social hierarchy. Nor do I excuse crime by the lower classes. Rather, I am saying that particularly in modern democratic societies such as ours, the moral code cuts through the entire society. It may be uneven and interpreted differently within different segments of the society, but the values of the dominant society certainly impinge on most of the other segments.

Systematic self deception that high brow crimes are less damaging to society than low brow crimes: One of the first assumptions is that, somehow, upper level crime is less harmful than lower level crime. Compare the Montreal medical doctor who was able to defraud the medical health care program to the extent of $70,000 with the safe-cracker who specialized in blowing up safes in supermarkets: the Montreal medical doctor was required to pay back $7,000 of the money he stole; the safe-cracker was not treated with the same logic.

When the Ford Motor Company considered changing the design of the gas tanks for the Pinto automobile, it made calculations as to the expenditure involved in paying the court costs for a certain number of deaths and a certain number of injuries. They calculated that it would be cheaper to have a certain number of people die and pay compensation rather than redesign the gas tank for the car. Should the officials responsible for such decisions be held criminally responsible? In the past, we have frequently excused those who have to make such decisions because we felt they could not foresee the future. But this is not the case today. When a large bridge must be built over a river, the number of people who will die in these construction projects can frequently be predicted with surprising accuracy.

This is not to say that it is possible to maintain an industrial complex such as ours without risk to human life. There will be risks, and when cost factors are involved, attempts to reduce those human risks will not go below certain thresholds. The point is that the deliberate actions taken by people in influential positions can be definitely harmful and costly for other portions of the society, and that damage is frequently known in advance. When a lower class person deliberately harms someone to benefit himself, it is a crime. Should we not apply the same standards to the powerful?

But let us go further and compare the consequences of the largest welfare fraud that was ever committed in the United States with other forms of crime. Recently, a woman was able to collect over $200,000 in fraudulent welfare payments in the United States. Naturally, tax-payers should be enraged that someone has stolen so much money. She was sentenced to eight years in prison. By comparison the General Electric conspiracy in 1961, "robbed people of more money than all the other thefts and robberies of that year combined."[2] Some people get very angry about a $200,000 welfare fraud but somehow see "rip-offs" of millions of dollars by corporations as shrewd business. By using a tortuous logic, such individuals deceive themselves that welfare fraud is paid for by tax-payers, but that increased utility bills or food prices which are borne by consumers when some upper level crimes are committed, do not affect people in the same way.

We should not delude ourselves that the 500 million to 1 billion dollars of income tax fraud each year is less costly than other forms of theft. Despite the publicity given to lower level crimes, the pain and suffering, as well as the costs involved, are every bit as great for upper level crime as they are for lower level crime. The fact that those responsible for upper level crimes are frequently several steps removed from the final action does not change the impact on society. Taking upper level crime seriously would be a meaningful first step toward moving our morality curve to the left.

But let us turn to another mistaken assumption. There are a few people who believe that the laws restricting upper level crimes, such as the Combines Investigation Act, Food and Drugs Act, etc., are not as *valid* as other forms of legislation. Our Combines Investigation Act was passed in 1889 and we could probably argue that most corporations would prefer to run legitimate businesses. Sometimes companies rationalize their law violations because other competitors are breaking the law. It would be wiser to see these crimes as we do other crimes, rather than as something different. Usually, we are dealing with greed; the motivation is not greatly different from that which stimulates the burglar.

Selective use of deterrents: To return to the original point: Can we have an impact on upper level crime? While deterrents usually are not particularly effective when applied to most lower class crimes, they definitely work on income tax fraud and upper level crimes. As the news stories of those being prosecuted on income tax charges appear in the newspapers around March of each year, they seem to have an impact on the rest of us as we make out our forms. Of course, it may not be effective if Silverwood Dairies has to pay only $300 after cheating customers on milk for a considerable length of time, nor if Canada Cement has charges dropped through pressures on certain political figures. In fact, the situation becomes even more ludicrous when we see that dominant Canadian companies have to pay nominal fines while reaping rather large profits. When we look at those who have been charged *and convicted* under sections 36 and 37 of the Combines Investigation Act, we see that the average fine levied against dominant companies was $1,887 and against non-dominant companies $350.[3] The most frequent fine was $200 for the dominant companies and $100 for the non-dominant companies. Until 1974, no one had gone to prison under the Combines Investigation Act. During 1974 a small merchant was sentenced to two years for misleading advertising regarding television sets. This was his second offence. We should note however, that Allied Towers, Simpson Sears, and Eaton's have been convicted five times, but no one has been sent to jail.[4] Caltec Citrus Company was convicted of activities which cheated their customers of $1 million. The total fine was $6,000 and the violators got a suspended sentence. Not a bad profit and not much reason for changing the illegal behaviour.

It will be interesting to see whether certain new forms of crimes will be treated as leniently: for example, the piracy of copyrighted films. This is an illegal practice that is arising from the duplication of recently completed films and television programs. These are now copied onto cassettes and sold, illegally, of course, because these were copyrighted materials. As a result, employees from the television program *60 Minutes* were able to purchase illegally taped video cassettes of the film "Superman". One might ask about the impact of such piracy on the total society as compared to other crimes. I am in no position to comment on that, but since the movie studios and others being robbed of certain profits are large and powerful organizations, I doubt that film pirates will simply be brought into court and be subjected to light fines. When powerful people are robbed instead of relatively weak consumers, the penalties will be generally harsher.

The lesson to be learned here is that police action *can* bring about a meaningful impact on certain aspects of deviant behaviour. I predict that police action will be relatively effective against film pirates, because the ox being gored belongs to influential organizations. If the same type of action is taken against other forms of upper level crime, a meaningful deterrent effect would be the result. Basically, those with a stake in society, as most corporations have, can be deterred more easily by traditional social control methods. Those at the bottom end of the social economic scale have less to lose.

The link between upper level crime and delinquency control: Some will say that I have strayed from the topic of juvenile corrections, but I would argue that most of our strategies for dealing with juveniles have made the assumption that there is a target population of juveniles who are somehow different and that our strategies should focus *directly* on them rather than on the larger society. My argument is simply that the curve in Figure 1 will retain the same shape and that actions designed to move the entire moral code to the left will pull more juveniles with it than tactics directed specifically at selected small populations of juveniles. Certain elements within this large body of illegal and immoral behaviour are more susceptible to deterrence than other segments. Upper level crime is susceptible to change and is therefore a much more worthwhile target in terms of practical policy issues. It is absurd to ignore extensive crime and unethical practices among the powerful and expect moral behaviour from juveniles. If we can move the affluent toward the ethical end of our graph, juveniles will probably follow.

What impact does the public trial have on society in general and on juveniles? On the one hand the large fines may represent only a fraction of the money made from the conspiracy. On the other hand, the publicity and possible prison terms could be a determent. More importantly, honest businessmen are reinforced in their efforts to maintain acceptable behaviour. Rather than being viewed as "timid" or "not with it" by their more criminally inclined colleagues and competitors, the courts have reflected the opinion of society in no uncertain terms. It is difficult to assess the impact on children in families that discuss such matters, but there is no reason to believe that moral behaviour in the business world would be excluded from the socialization of juveniles.

Getting the Best Return for our Efforts: When dealing with policy decisions, we have to avoid being trapped by spectacular but relatively rare circumstances. Rather than attempting to develop a sensible strategy for a specific dramatic case, it makes more sense to strive for policies that decrease the likelihood that actions of this serious nature *and* less serious events would occur. For example, I do not have good data on the number of wife beatings in Canada, but 100,000 per year is not a bad guess. Perhaps 1,000 to 2,000 deaths result from these beatings. Some of these deaths are recorded as accidents and others appear under our official statistics as murder or manslaughter. They probably make a significant contribution to the 600 or so murders across Canada each year. If our goal is to cut down on the number of murders, the number of children who are beaten to death by their parents, and the number of children who hire someone to kill their father, we would be well advised *not* to focus on the one per cent of the cases that result in death, but rather to focus on the larger phenomenon of violence in the family which is largely represented by wife beating. If we could cut those 100,000 cases of family violence down to 50,000, we might cut those murders in half.

Notice that something like capital punishment does not touch on the dynamics involved in the violence that we are describing. Even if someone were to demonstrate a deterrent effect, it would still be a poor investment if we were genuinely concerned about saving lives. In the majority of cases, murder and manslaughter are *by-products* of violent situations. Again, working on the larger picture, moving the *entire curve* of violence to the left on our graph in Figure 1 decreases the likelihood that juveniles will kill parents, teachers, or each other.

The same argument applies to the issue of whether those who kill policemen should be subject to capital punishment. That becomes a moral question, and I would like to stay with social policy that yields dividends. If we are genuinely concerned with the lives of policemen, we should decrease those situations that are dangerous for them. Most policemen die in automobiles, just like the rest of us. Secondly, they are killed in family disputes. Rarely, does a "cop killer" gun them down in cold blood. Reducing the risks for policemen in automobiles and in family disputes would also have an impact on minor accidents and on minor injuries, but if policies succeeded in moving *all* of the auto accidents and *all* of the family disputes into a lower volume of activity, one of the by-products would be fewer deaths. Again by moving the entire curve we reduce the acts on the extreme edge of the curve. As you can see, shooting directly at the target may increase the likelihood that one would hit nothing.

Focusing on those who buy stolen goods: My final illustration deals with juvenile theft. Although some juvenile theft is based on thrills, much of it is profitable. The fact that there are adults willing to buy stolen property continues to provide incentives for thieves. In general, we are not particularly harsh on those who possess stolen articles. Should we make greater demands on those who purchase goods to inquire about the source of some of the "good bargains" that sometimes appear? A person who did not check with the police when offered goods at a particularly low price might be viewed as a person who is knowingly purchasing goods that he suspects are stolen. If a larger percentage of the population found that they could be prosecuted for handling stolen goods, the amount of juvenile theft might decrease. Our tendency is to focus on the problem *delinquent* rather than on the problem *adult* who rewards that delinquency.

Summary: Some policies have a very low return for our agencies of social control in forms of reducing delinquency or crime. Capital punishment, crackdowns on prostitutes, punishing drug addicts, and our response to marijuana use reflect policies that yield a poor return on the investment of resources. On the other hand, income tax fraud, focusing on purchases of stolen goods, and corporate crime are illustrations of areas where vigorous crime control practices would yield a much higher return in terms of cutting down on specific types of illegal acts. Since almost all of our *direct* strategies focusing on juveniles have been relatively ineffective, it seems reasonable *to focus on different segments of activity that make up the total business of illegal and immoral activities with the hope of moving the entire morality curve to the left.* The shape of this curve will not change. There will still be individuals on the serious end of the continuum, but strategies that give special attention to that end of the continuum while ignoring the other deviance in society will probably continue to be ineffective. We must drop the assumption that "doing something" to a special group of delinquents will have a meaningful impact on delinquency in society.

ARGUMENT 2: FOCUSING ON THE JUVENILE SYSTEM RATHER THAN ON THE JUVENILE

Focusing on the question, "what should we do with this particular juvenile who comes before the juvenile court," has not yielded tremendous insights. The various alternatives open to a juvenile court judge are frequently not very attractive. Long-range policies, such as those suggested in Argument 1, have little meaning for people who are immediately involved in the juvenile justice system. Assuming that it is difficult to make a dramatic change in a juvenile's life at this stage, is there some way we can modify the criminal justice system so that it accomplishes certain goals more effectively?

The Canadian juvenile court system is complex, there being a great variety of methods of handling delinquent children. While it is unlikely that we would be able to make dramatic improvements, even if we understood the juvenile court system better, policy decisions might be directed more intelligently if we knew the consequences of different court arrangements. Unfortunately, in various jurisdictions at the provincial and federal level in Canada, our fact finding procedures tend to focus on rhetoric more than on empirical evidence. Over the years we have been talking about changing legislation. There was the earlier Young Offenders Act. Then there was the Young People in Conflict with the Law proposal. Now we are talking about another Young Offenders Act. During this period, very little information has been gathered on exactly how our juvenile courts operate. Elsewhere in the world some attempts have been made to understand the informal dynamics of the juvenile courts. In Canada we have many opinions but very little actual knowledge. Finally, in 1979, the Research Division of the Ministry of the Solicitor General has launched a study of juvenile courts in Montreal, Toronto, Winnipeg, and Vancouver. It is unlikely that we will see sophisticated studies of our juvenile courts for some time, but in the meantime we may be able to make use of some of the data currently being gathered by Statistics Canada.

Comparing Juvenile Courts in Canada: We should begin with a note of caution. Most of us are aware of the difficulties comparing cities in terms of crime rates. It becomes even more difficult to make comparisons with juvenile court statistics. If, however, one utilizes our present statistics as indicators of *the way the system operates,* and not as indicators of juvenile behaviour, these data may be useful.

The data in Table 1 will be used to illustrate differences between the juvenile courts in Edmonton and Calgary, and also the potential for using these official data in a constructive manner.

Similar cities — different court strategies: Edmonton and Calgary: Table 1 uses figures related to theft under $200. Instead of using all Criminal Code offences, I have limited myself to the most common crime category, theft under $200. Hopefully, this will minimize some of the differences between the courts.

Table 1

THEFTS UNDER $200: ADULTS AND JUVENILES — 1977 EDMONTON AND CALGARY*

		Edmonton	Calgary
Number of Offences		18,939	13,999
Cleared by Charge		2668 (14%)	3082 (22%)
Adult and Juveniles Charged plus Juveniles Not Charged		3597 (100%)	3859 (100%)
Charges Laid:			
Adult Males		49%	50%
Adult Females		20%	16%
Boys		5%	18%
Girls		4%	14%
Juveniles: Informal		21%	2%
Ratio of Charges:			
Adults/Juveniles	Males	9/1	5.7/1
	Females	2.7/1	1.1/1

*Statistics Canada, *Crime and Traffic Enforcement Statistics* (1979).

We note that Edmonton has approximately 19,000 petty thefts. Calgary has a smaller number, 14,000. However, Edmonton has a smaller number cleared by charge, 2,668, a clearance rate of about 14%, while Calgary has cleared 3,082 by charge, giving a clearance rate by charge of 22%. This might prompt the conclusion that somehow the higher percentage of cases cleared by charge in Calgary is the result of a more efficient police force, but upon further consideration we learn that juveniles are frequently involved in petty thefts and that various police forces and juvenile court systems have different strategies for dealing with juveniles. Hence, one of the first generalizations that might be made concerning Canadian statistics on petty theft is that a low clearance rate might go hand in hand with a strategy for diverting large numbers of juveniles from the court systems. This seems to be the case for Edmonton and Calgary.

In order to get a better picture of the differences between the handling of juveniles in the two cities, Table 1 groups all of the charges laid against all adults and all juveniles plus those juveniles who were handled informally. In the third row we have 100% of the people counted by the police including those juveniles handled in some informal manner. In Edmonton for example, we see that the police "took action" against 3,597 individuals. Note that the number of offences cleared by charge is only 2,668. In other words, more than one person could be involved in a single offence. Of course, one individual could also be involved in several offences.

Our task is to divide the adult and juvenile cases so that we get some idea of how much of the petty theft "business" is handled by the adult court and how much by the juvenile court. In rows 4, 5, 6, 7, and 8, I have distributed the 100% of the cases in row 3 among the adults and the juveniles. We note that for both Edmonton and Calgary, about half of the petty theft business concerns adult males (49% and 50%). Adult females makes up 20% and 16% of the total. When we look at the juveniles, however, we see a noticeable difference. In Edmonton, a relatively small percent of the boys and girls come into court for petty theft (5% and 4%). In Calgary more boys and girls are charged (18% and 14%). The difference seems to come in the number of juveniles handled informally (Edmonton 21% and Calgary 2%). If we go to the last two rows in Table 1 we note that the ratio of charges for male adults to boys is 9 to 1 in Edmonton while it is only 5.7 to 1 in Calgary. For every girl in Edmonton, 2.7 adult females are charged and in Calgary it is 1.1 adult female for each girl. For the petty theft business in Edmonton we can see that the juvenile court handles about 9% of the cases while 21% are handled informally. "Informal handling" probably differs from community to community. Court personnel and other community agencies may or may not be involved. In Calgary, 32% of the petty theft business is handled by the juvenile court while only 2% is handled informally.

We must be careful not to assume that the *actual* practices in the two courts differ markedly. It is quite possible that the handling of a case *within* the juvenile court in Calgary, with greater involvement from the judges, may not result in markedly different results than the type of handling used in Edmonton. At the present time, we simply do not know. In one sense, we have an excellent opportunity for comparing the possible outcomes of different juvenile court strategies. Both cities are similar in size, population make up, social class, and a variety of other characteristics. Theoretically they operate under similar laws.

It would be misleading if one focused on the question, "which juvenile court system is better?" A more meaningful question would be, "what are the consequences for juveniles and for agencies when cases flow through the system in various ways?" Let us now turn to two other cities that display an even more dramatic contrast.

A more dramatic contrast: Regina and Winnipeg: Regina tends to have some of the characteristics shown by Edmonton while Winnipeg has some characteristics that are similar to Calgary. See Table 2.

Table 2

THEFTS UNDER $200: ADULTS AND JUVENILES — 1977 REGINA AND WINNIPEG*

		Regina (juveniles 16 years of age)	Winnipeg (juveniles 18 years of age)
Number of Offences		6,422	18,477
Cleared by Charge		754 (12%)	4191 (23%)
Adults and Juveniles Charged plus Juveniles Not Charged		1316 (100%)	4055 (100%)
Charges Laid:			
Adult Males		35%	29%
Adult Females		20%	17%
Boys		4%	36%
Girls		1%	18%
Juveniles: Informal		41%	0%
Ratio of Charges:			
Adults/Juveniles	Males	10/1	.8/1
	Females	24/1	.9/1

*Statistics Canada (1979): special computer run.

Regina has a low percentage of offences cleared by charged (12%). Therefore, we suspect that a fairly large number of juveniles are handled informally rather than being charged. This turns out to be true (41%). By contrast, Winnipeg has a rather high clearance rate (23%) and therefore we might guess that a high percentage of juveniles picked up by the police are formally charged and brought into court. This is borne out by the statistics. We see that 36% of the petty theft "business" is attributed to boys and 18% to girls. We must take into account, of course, that the age limit for boys and girls in Winnipeg is 18 while in Regina it is only 16. If we wish to compare the two cities more directly, we should reduce the juvenile statistics by 25% in Winnipeg and raise the adults by 25%. Even with such an adjustment, the basic pattern for Winnipeg remains. In addition, from the standpoint of who deals with what type of problem, we can see that the juvenile court in Winnipeg deals with 54% of the petty theft problem. By contrast we might argue that the juvenile court in Regina deals with only 5% of the petty theft problem. Again it would probably be a mistake to jump to such a conclusion. It is quite possible that the juvenile court judge in Winnipeg is *formally* involved in such cases while much of the activity with such youngsters is being handled by juvenile probation officers and others. By the same token, many of the judges in Regina might be *informally* involved in cases while other agencies dealt with these cases in a more direct manner. One might anticipate that in Regina more agencies in the community, and outside the jurisdiction of the juvenile court, would be involved in juvenile matters than in Winnipeg, where one might predict that more of this activity would take place within the context of the juvenile court itself.

The Regina findings are not surprising if one is aware of the Child Welfare model that has been used in Saskatchewan for years. Juveniles are routed directly from the police to child welfare agencies. What we do not understand is whether or not this type of administrative arrangement produces different consequences than some other arrangement.

Looking at the last two rows of Table 2 for Regina and Winnipeg we see that the ratio of charges laid against adults versus juveniles provides a striking contrast. Official statistics suggest that in Regina adult males are ten times as likely to be charged with petty theft as boys and that twenty-four times as many female adults would be charged as girls. By contrast, in Winnipeg slightly more juveniles are charged with petty theft than are adults.

It is important not to view these statistics as either misleading or erroneous. They are indicators of the way in which agencies of social control divide up certain responsibilities. In Regina, and in Saskatchewan in general, diversion programs and alternatives to the juvenile court seem to be available and systematically utilized. In Manitoba, one should not assume that the *activities* are necessarily different, but the jurisdiction of the juvenile court is probably much more comprehensive. Again, the opportunities for comparison could lead us to some useful insights about our juvenile courts.

Conclusion: A potential for understanding court systems: It would be most inappropriate to explain how juvenile courts operate on the basis of the data presented here. Clearly the courts are different, but whether they are different in meaningful or trivial ways cannot be demonstrated by the official data. It does give us some idea of the shape of the funnel at the beginning of the juvenile justice system. The next step is to see what happens further down the line. How many children are placed on probation, how many are sent to institutions? Official statistics can shed some light on such questions, but those who have been handled informally are probably not going to appear in official statistics. Therefore, other data gathering procedures will be needed. Hopefully, some court systems are already recording some of their activities so that we could eventually develop a typology of juvenile courts in terms of the way they are structured in the way in which they respond to certain types of cases.[5]

At this stage, a more meaningful dialogue between researchers and those in the criminal justice system would be important. The city juvenile court systems discussed above contain 3 to 5 judges, a dozen or so court counsellors or probation officers, and a comparable number of police officers. In other words, they are small bureaucracies which could probably be studied fairly easily. My own experience suggests that the people involved in these systems have many insights into what is happening in their community and are quite willing to share those insights with others. Several juvenile court judges and court personnel have expressed an interest in comparing their own court systems with others with the hope that potential changes can be based on knowledge instead of political rhetoric. One should note that the discussions in Parliament and elsewhere about young people in conflict with the law continue while few attempts are being made to gather reliable information about how the systems actually work. It is amazing that governments can spend so much time and money discussing how they will change the juvenile court system while adamantly refusing to gather empirical data about the topic under study. This is sometimes carried to extremes when provinces will not even look at the data they have been gathering themselves.

I hope I have encouraged a few people to look at these data in a different light: as indicators of delinquent behaviour in various parts of Canada, they indeed should be regarded with suspicion; but as indicators of the different ways in which communities organize their resources to respond to juvenile crime, they may be a rough but useful tool.

This approach to juvenile courts is very crude and we should not be content with these types of analyses. Looking at official statistics probably raises questions about juvenile courts without providing many answers. One of the questions which is almost always raised when one discusses juvenile justice is the use of lawyers in juvenile courts.

The Use of Defence Counsel in Juvenile Court: A Researchable Question

Let me note two studies that illustrate the type of research that might be relevant to Canada. One unpublished study in North Carolina offers some interesting findings that seem to be consistent with trends in the rest of North America.[6] The authors point out that during the 1930s and 1940s there was a very noticeable humanitarian and rehabilitative rhetoric concerning juvenile courts, but in North Carolina the juvenile courts were more punitive during this period, at least in terms of institutional commitments, than they are now. I suspect that the recent discussions which suggest that the juvenile court should return to the "crime control model" has not necessarily led to an increase in the use of training schools. Because of some major weaknesses in Canadian statistics regarding juveniles, one can only make a cautious statement that institutions are being used less than they were in the past.[7] In other words, I am inclined to believe there has been a fairly modest but steady application of social science knowledge when it comes to dealing with juveniles. While others may be terribly impatient with those in power for being so stupid, I am inclined to believe that a sort of stumbling progress has been made. The steady use of alternatives to institutionalization, independent of the debates over the "rehabilitation" or "crime control model," is an illustration of this trend.

But a more specific finding coming out of the North Carolina study is that the use of a defence counsel in the juvenile court does not seem to result in fewer commitments to institutions.[8] Another American study of two juvenile courts known as Zenith and Gotham represents one of the few controlled experiments to assess the impact of specially trained defenders in a juvenile court.[9] Cases involving children from poverty areas were randomly assigned to either an experimental group in which they received service of a special defender project or to a control group in which they were either represented by non-project counsel or no counsel. The majority of the children in the control group were not represented by a lawyer.

As in the North Carolina study, there was no evidence that children represented by project lawyers in either Zenith or Gotham had a significantly lower commitment rate than those who were not represented. But commitment rates do not tell the full story. We have to distinguish between specially trained project counsellors, who were probably vigorous advocates, and the climate of the two different courts.

Table 3

THE EFFECT OF DEFENCE COUNSEL ON DISMISSALS, PROBATION, AND COMMITMENT IN TWO JUVENILE COURT SYSTEMS*

	Zenith			Gotham	
	Proj Counsel	Other Counsel	No Counsel	Proj Counsel	No Counsel[1]
		100%			
		39%	61%		
Dismiss	54%	42%	39%	19%	19%
Probation	32%	44%		40%	40%
Commit	8.7%	12.3%		12.6%[2]	4.5%[3]
Denied Charges		53%		36%	

*Stapleton and Teitelbaum, *In Defense of Youth* (1972), Tables II.1, 11.2, III.1, III.2, III.4.
[1] includes 11% with other counsel,
[2] includes all with counsel,
[3] only those with no counsel.

In Table 3 we present some of the data from that study. Notice that there are some basic differences between the Zenith court and the Gotham court. In the Zenith court, those boys who were involved in the control group should be seen in two parts: those who had some other form of counsel, such as a private lawyer or no counsel at all. In Zenith, 61% of the boys in the control group had no counsel at all while 39% did have other counsellors. In Gotham, the boys in the control group had counsel in only 11% of the cases. Therefore, it has been convenient to treat the Gotham control group as having no counsel and compare it with the experimental group which had specially trained project defenders.

Let us first note the first line across Table 3. Project lawyers for Zenith managed to get a 54% dismissal rate for their clients. Other lawyers achieved a 42% dismissal rate, while those receiving no counsel had a dismissal rate of 39%. In Gotham we notice quite a different pattern. The dismissal rate was only 19% with or without counsel. Many more cases were continued, however. This does not necessarily mean that juveniles were treated more punitively in the Gotham court. For example, we note that the percentage of boys receiving probation in Zenith was 32% for those with project counsellors and 44% for those in the control group. In Gotham, both the experimental and control groups received probation in 40% of the cases.

In terms of commitments to institutions, the differences do not vary a great deal. In Zenith, 8.7% of those with project counsellors were committed while 12.3% of the control group were committed. The pattern reverses itself in Gotham with 12.6% of those with projects counsellors being committed while 4.5% of those with no counselor were committed. Clearly, it would be unwise to say simply that having a lawyer makes a difference. *The nature of the court setting* in which lawyers operate may be much more important. With access to relevant data, we should be able to distinguish between the style of various court systems and consequences that result from different procedures.

In the North Carolina study, it is hypothesized that the juvenile court judges sometimes resent the role of the lawyer in their court. While this does not necessarily lead to dramatic differences, it does not seem to result in lighter sentences for those cases who receive counsel. Of course we do not know whether the *presence* of counsel for a few cases tends to change the pattern for the entire court, including those who receive no counsel at all.

Role playing in juvenile court: Here in Canada with the increasing use of duty counsel, a number of dynamic changes may be taking place that are not well understood. However, we could overstate the importance of this new role. In the Vancouver juvenile court, for example, it seemed as if those handling the prosecution for the Crown were also performing many of the functions served by the duty counsel. Given our adversarial mentality, we frequently forget that people may be capable of playing more than one role. Let me describe a case in the Vienna juvenile court which might be revealing.

In Vienna, 15 juvenile court judges perform a variety of roles. Sometimes they are investigating judges for more serious cases, at other times they are sitting on courts that have slightly different jurisdictions. In Austria all juveniles *must* be defended by a lawyer. It is optional for adults. Once I was surprised to see a judge acting as the defence counsel in one case. In this case, the defence counsel evidently did not arrive. The case had been investigated by a judge and then recommended for a hearing. Noting that it would be inconvenient for the mother to return to the court at a later time, the investigating judge said that he knew the facts of the case very well and would be willing to act as defence. I heard later that it was one of the more vigorous and enthusiastic defences that had been given that year.

In the common law system of justice, such a switch in roles is unthinkable; but I suspect this is primarily a limitation of our own mental framework. In other walks of life, we expect people to be able to play different roles and maintain integrity while performing those different roles. The Viennese judge seemed to have no problem doing two different jobs. I think it would be very interesting if all of the juvenile court judges in Canada were to serve one day a week as duty counsel. Perhaps they could do it in a different court rather than in the one where they serve as judge. Would they not get a different perspective on the situation? How would other judges respond to the situation if the duty counsel for that day was a judge on other days?

The basic theme of this argument is that there are a variety of *informal* dynamics that make a difference in the way a court operates. It is hard to compare systematically these operational procedures, but usually we can see basic similarities in some styles of operation that distinguish them from others. These differences cannot be understood directly from the use of court statistics, but if we are clever perhaps we could understand these dynamics without excessively expensive research projects. Let me now turn to a final illustration of an activity which might profitably be examined on the Canadian scene — "bureaucratic convenience."

Bureaucratic Convenience: A Normal and Persistent Phenomenon

In the North Carolina study, when a complaint against a juvenile was made by a juvenile probation officer, the child's chance of being committed was much greater.[10] The authors hypothesized that the commitment may be to some extent bureaucratic rather than either therapeutic or crime preventive. The child who has not played by the rules imposed by the court and his probation officer may be regarded as defying the officer's authority. The officer may seek commitment, partially to shed the responsibility for supervising an unruly child as much as out of the desire to rehabilitate the child or to prevent further criminal behaviour.

There is a tendency to react to a hypothesis of "bureaucratic convenience" as if it were unusual and very improper. I would argue that we should expect to find bureaucratic convenience playing a major role in most bureaucracies. I doubt that we will ever do away with this phenomenon. A more realistic approach might be to analyze the situations and see if bureaucratic convenience can be made more compatible with the needs of the clients and other long-range goals. In other words, we should assume that justice systems are peopled, not by angels, but rather by normal human beings. By arranging our bureaucratic conveniences so that they achieve certain goals, we might be able to bring about a minor restructuring of the juvenile court and still live within the limitations of normal human frailties.

CONCLUSION

I have tried to suggest two radically different strategies that I feel are related to delinquency and its control. My basic assumption is that trying to manipulate juveniles directly has not and will not lead to dramatic changes. Therefore, I have suggested some long-range strategies that might move larger segments of the population in a less deviant direction, and by doing so a reasonable percentage of the juvenile population would be influenced indirectly.

The second strategy was to look at the juvenile justice system itself. Rather than spend so much time drafting new legislation which may or may not have an impact on the actual dynamics of the system, I would suggest that we concentrate on revealing the informal dynamics and then sharing that information across Canada. The goal would not be to devise a "good" system, but rather to offer a cafeteria of choices: ways in which certain things are achieved in different places and what seems to happen when certain procedures are used. For me, the role of research is not to pick the best approach, but instead to provide more alternatives than those presently available. If the cafeteria offers a wide selection of healthful foods, I suspect the consumer will have a better chance of selecting a healthy diet.

NOTES

1. Some court systems may actually not be aware of the data available on their own court system. For example, attempts to gather information concerning the number of juveniles charged or handled informally in Alberta brought confusing responses from the Attorney General's office. Basically, I was told that such information was not available. However, such information has been gathered in the Province of Alberta and had been given to Statistics Canada. It can be found in Table 9 of the recent publication of 1977 Criminal Statistics (Statistics Canada, Crime and Traffic Enforcement Statistics, 1979).

2. Snider, "Corporate Crime in Canada: A Preliminary Report," 20 *Canadian Journal of Crime* 142 (1978).

3. *Ibid.,* p. 155.

4. *Ibid.,* p. 156.

5. See note 1. In other words, many juvenile courts could utilize their own data more effectively than they are at the present time.

6. Clarke and Koch, "Juvenile Court: Therapy or Crime Control, and Do Lawyers Make a Difference?" (unpublished discussion paper, 1979).

7. Hackler, *The Prevention of Youthful Crime: The Great Stumble Forward* (Toronto: Methuen, 1978).

8. *Op. cit.,* note 6.

9. V. Stapleton and L.E. Teitelbaum, *In Defense of Youth: A Study of the*

Role of Counsel in American Juvenile Courts (New York: Russell Sage Foundation, 1972).

   10.   *Op. cit.,* note 6.

CHAPTER 11

Sex Offenders and the Sentencing Process

A. K. Gigeroff

Sentencing anyone, judges frequently tell us, is the most difficult decision that they have to make in a trial and far more trying for them than sorting the evidence and reaching a determination on the question of whether someone is legally guilty or not guilty. Perhaps there are elements at play which make the task of sentencing a sex offender as difficult and perhaps, in some ways, more difficult than sentencing other kinds of offenders. In undertaking the search, perhaps it is better to move freely and scan widely, deliberately keeping a broad focus. Ideas, questions and alternatives towards which we have not given enough attention may be allowed to surface in this way. In taking this approach there is every likelihood that we may miss some elements or overstate others or perhaps speculate on some factor that may not be present in any particular sex offence trial or sentence, but there is something to be said for freedom of search as well as for precision of enquiry. One of the immediate difficulties we have is that judges tend *not* to discuss this sentencing aspect of their work in any personal way and when they do so, it is in a guarded fashion that is quite understandable. It is only through careful listening and looking that one catches small glimmers and often oblique ones of what seems like a human torment. Open, sensitive material from lawyers, police, probation officers and others involved in operating the entire system as it deals with sex offences has not been forthcoming. We need to look widely because adaptations may occur anywhere along the system and can be most significant in terms of how we cope with the overall problem of sex offences or human sexuality in our society. Although sentencing is an important point in the whole system we may be able to move with more flexibility if we do not insist on standing on the one word with one foot.[1]

One unmistakable element that appears to be fairly widely shared by those taking part is the relief that is experienced after a sex trial is over and sentence has been passed. There is a tension level within the court that is not present in cases dealing with property offences or common assault or cases of drunkenness or drugs. The tension is particularly evident in those cases in which children have been used as witnesses. There is often an overriding sense of bad taste, revulsion and offensiveness to the point where the examination of facts becomes slurred and hurried. The detailing of the evidence so common in the courtroom with other subjects becomes almost unbearable with sex offences. The relief experienced on the part of virtually everyone at the end of the case is immeasurable but a very real and palpable thing, akin to "Thank God that's over."

Although the words "sentencing process" contains the notion of "going forward" or "advancing," one senses in some cases the feeling of wanting to clear the subject out of the court, to pass the problem and question of what should be done along the line over to the prison authorities or the probation service or, in rare circumstances where a psychiatric clinic exists which will accept cases, then over to them. One gets the impression too that judges sometimes feel compelled or forced to give a sentence with which they do not feel comfortable and they do so with a sense of frustration because of the absence of a facility or a plan that they think might be a proper and rational alternative.

In a recent case in the Yukon Territories a magistrate refused to sentence a 16-year-old alcoholic who had been charged with property offences either to prison, or to probation or to levy a fine because he concluded after due consideration that none of these alternatives were suitable. He simply adjourned the case *sine die* without doing anything and without setting a date in the future, saying that the boy in his considered opinion needed medical help with his alcoholism and there was none available. His decision forced the problem back into the community for reconsideration of what it will or will not provide by way of services for treatment. The Crown attorney is appealing this decision; nevertheless, the action of the judge has jolted the community and those responsible for social/medical services. One cannot help but wonder when a judge somewhere else will raise the same problem in relation to a case involving a sex offender.

It is part of the theory that we have come to accept that all judges are trained and disciplined so that they do not consider the question of sentencing until legal guilt is established. I think that the question arises in the trial much sooner than that, no matter how much a judge may try to avoid it. I think that the feelings that are raised when the facts are first disclosed during the course of the trial can, and often do, seep over and bleed into the question of sentencing, or in some cases totally swamp the sentencing phase. Defence counsel learn to become adept at attempting to steer cases in front of some judges and to avoid others because of the past reactions they have had in terms of sentencing responses to certain kinds of cases. It is also true that many lawyers avoid dealing with any kind of criminal cases whatsoever, and some would not allow a sex case over very many meters of their broadloomed floor.

There is a drift within the legal profession, difficult to pinpoint and find, an attitude that is something like an oil slick, that one becomes contaminated by the subject-matter of these cases.

Given that the trial and sentencing processes cannot be kept apart and that the former is a powerful factor influencing the latter, I think it is necessary to consider certain aspects of the trial of sex offenders.

All trials as we know them have a great deal of unreality about them but in sex cases the courtroom acts as an incredible filter, a kind of freezing plant, that reduces the evidence regarding the liveliness of sexual encounters into brittle, sharp-edged fragments. The notion of "freeze-dried" comes to mind because the process used in trying a case and the verbalization of the subject has a distorting, shrinking, stiffening awkwardness, and ultimately, a coldness about it. There is an extreme contrast between the subject-matter and the formalism of the setting and the room in which the discussion occurs. It is like being verbally asked to take a bath and wash your private parts in public in front of strangers and to go into more details than that. For almost everyone, sexual activity is a very private thing that, to say the least, is unaccustomed to the glare of legal or any other kind of search lights. The legally trained people who undertake to focus the word search, looking for the significant key words or phrases from which interpretations are to be drawn, are not unaffected in a feeling way about the subject-matter of their search.

For all of us there are different word or subject toleration levels and when that toleration level is crossed, a variety of responses are likely, the most common of which is probably that of shutting off or turning away. This is a very natural process which occurs in lawyers, other professionals and lay people alike. Once that toleration level is crossed the ability to continue to think freely and dispassionately is affected. I think we can note that there is an awareness of the toleration level by the constant laundering of the words that the participants in court feel free to use. The very language in which the laws are written and the manner in which cases are reported are other indications that those involved with the law attempt to blanket over the subject to avoid crossing the toleration threshold.

There is another element of unreality that contributes to the whole masking process: discrepancies exist between the way the case is discussed outside of the courtroom and the way it is presented at trial. A lot of very powerful feelings and attitudes and information gets blocked out before the case enters the courtroom setting. I do not think for a moment that testifying in these cases or reporting the evidence is at all easy for witnesses and counsel. The process of testifying imposes its own strictures so there is one language for the courts and another language, more open and honest used elsewhere. The same thing is true of the lawyers, Crown attorneys, and perhaps even the judges. It is outside of the court that one begins to learn more about how they really feel and think about these cases. There is sometimes a male chauvinism, sometimes a playful ribaldry, that underlines these cases. When one of their own is involved, a judge, a lawyer or police officer, which does not happen often, the shame is enormous.

It is worth remembering that almost all of the persons involved in these trials as police, as lawyers, as judges and as offenders are males. Women are almost never charged as sex offenders. But they are often in the courtroom as victims and witnesses. It is male attitudes towards sexual matters that governs the courtroom scene and plays a very powerful role in how women's testimony as victims is received and understood. It is virtually an all-male event and I am not sure how that factor alone affects the attitudes and judgments involved in a sex trial including sentencing.

A very upsetting factor in cases in which a child has been involved is the child's presence in court. I think there is a genuine concern on the part of everyone present for the welfare of the child, at least during the brief period involving the giving and examination of testimony — the legal system otherwise does nothing helpful for the child either before and after trial. By and large, adults in our society do not talk freely and easily to children about our common human sexuality, even often among family members, and when it comes to doing so with a single child in a room full of adult strangers the process becomes even more strange and strained to the point where it is almost unthinkable, and in fact, largely unmanageable. It is not that it does not happen, it does, but the participants most often are all skating on the edges of their blades. The very subject of child molestation even as an allegation raises a response of horror and its concomitant of anger. It takes a great deal of familiarity with the subject of adult/child sexuality to provide a modicum of real composure and rationality.

It is not only the presence of children or the subject of child molestation that raises the anxiety level in court. It also happens in cases involving sexual contact with animals, sex between family members, excessively aggressive sexual assaults, bizarre uncontrolled sexual acts, public sexuality, deviant sexuality. Each of these in a variety of ways are liable to cross toleration boundaries within the minds of at least some of the legally trained participants and others involved in such trials.

Public interest in the sexual misdoings of others is widespread and frequently the judge recognizing this voyeuristic element, will clear the courtroom. The aggressive and active presence of the press is another disturbing element presenting problems for a presiding judge.

I think it is important to honour the humanity of the judges, lawyers, police and others such as probation officers who participate in the trial process and to admit openly on their behalf, or at least recognize as a possibility for some of them, that they are not usually emotionally, experiencially or mentally prepared for the task that the law and society imposes on them. We are only in the very early stages of progress in the preparation of judges, lawyers, probation officers and police to cope emotionally with the subject-matter of these cases. Most of us received our early sex education on the street but this is not a satisfactory method for the participants in the criminal justice process.

Looking over this whole area I am not at all convinced that the adversary procedure of courtrooms, the very environment of the courtroom itself, the legally trained minds that dominate and in a fashion monopolize the process are at all suitable for the kinds of decisions about sex offenders or sex offences that need to be made. I am not at all sure that either for the individuals who fall into that process, or for society, do we have in our courts a healing process, and I question whether it can ever be made so.

Social agencies have recognized the difficulties and obstacles their clients face in certain kinds of cases that come to their attention, for example incest cases, where the agency would much rather not refer cases for management by the criminal justice system. Cases are being streamed away from the courtroom. So too, police forces in some instances are beginning to exercise more and more discretion in laying charges in certain kinds of cases, often steering cases of exhibitionism and sometimes child molestation to treatment clinics and others for professional help, sometimes under the threat of prosecution unless the accused person consents.

There is a growing recognition that the courts are grossly ill-equipped to respond to the total situation of a sex offence and particularly to the needs of victims, be they children, family members or women who have been through a rape or a rape-like kind of experience. The growing edge of our system seems to be away from the courts, for example with Rape Distress Centres that are established, organized and run by women. There is a broadening social recognition that the courts, the law and the legal process have been all too slow and encumbered to respond to identified needs.

There is also a growing recognition that the courts have in some ways been boxed in. On the one hand there is the lack or inadequacy of treatment facilities for sexual problem cases. On the other is the growing honesty and openness about the sexual expression that occurs in our prisons and the fact that the "treatment" sex offenders receive in prison is more likely to be at the hands of other offenders than of a trained psychiatrist, psychologist or social worker. As we all become more aware of the reality of the prison situation and of our collective guilt in maintaining such a system, the reticence to use that kind of an alternative will increase. The consequences of prison sentence that may involve the sex offender in prison-beatings, murder, anal rape and these kinds of outrages that are countered inside prisons by the total isolation of sex offenders for their own safety, will place greater pressures on judges making these decisions knowing of the possible consequences. The treatment capability for sex offenders within most prison systems is miniscule.

From a much broader perspective I think that we can see a gradual *de facto,* if not also a formal withdrawal on the part of both the courts and the law from involvement in this whole area. Perhaps over a hundred years ago in the Victorian era we witnessed an overreaching in using the law as an instrument for the stringent control of sexual expression in our society. There are long social waves of tolerance and control of human sexual expression and our laws are not always in tune with them.

It was fascinating to follow the evolution of the meanings of the word "sentence" to its root meanings in Klein's Etymological Dictionary. One moves from the meaning of "to go in a certain direction" to "perceive, feel, think, be of opinion." Ultimately the word "sentence" can be traced to "to find out" whence developed the meaning of "to feel". I think that both of those root meanings "to find out" and "to feel" can still be operational and can lead us yet in the right direction. The one "of finding out" will point us in the direction of bringing into the court's decision-making in the sentencing process the information available through forensic and sex research clinics. For example on the one very important question of whether the court is being asked to deal with an incidental or experimental act on the part of a male person or whether the convicted male is firmly committed to an established sexual behaviour pattern, assistance may be forthcoming from the sorting procedures that are being developed and studied in research hospitals. For a court to be able "to find out" about that particular element will be very important to them. And it is not just the courts but other social services and police who need "to find out" much more about what happens in these cases and what can be done about them. Many people "sentence" an accused male person before a judge has the chance.

The other sense of "feel" related to sentencing is equally important for that will lead us in the direction of enquiring further, struggling to understand and becoming increasingly conscious of the feelings of the participants in the decision-making process in relation to sex offenders. In a slow persistent way we must wear away at prejudice which leads to pre-judging of these human events. Judges are not going to be able to do that any better or any faster than any of the rest of us.

Following Klein again one can see the flow and evolution of the word "feel." There is a little humour in relating what one learns about the word "feel" to sex offences because one comes across the early meanings of "to grope, to collide or strike, to pluck or play an instrument, to touch softly, to stroke and to move quickly like an eyelid." So many of those terms apply both to successful and unsuccessful courtships, but I confess it was the last one "to move quickly like an eyelid" that made me think of the wink that begins so many courtships. It is also this very factor of quickness which causes the male so much trouble, moving either too quickly or not quickly enough. Male and female sexuality is not all that well synchronized and it would be terrible to discover that many of the problems we not see in such grim terms in a courtroom arise because the human spark plugs that are set between the sexes have not been set in a happy sequence and that what we all need, males and females alike, is a better tune up. In any event, Klein concludes that all of the words and meanings of "to feel" derived from the base word that meant "to strike softly."

We have been through many phases of striking harshly at sex offenders and we may very well be on the brink of doing so again. However one reads social moods and trends, the signs seem to indicate a popular movement towards calling for a greater harshness for all kinds of offenders. But whether or not we become more punitive there are questions that we should go on asking more than ever. Why are almost all the persons who are punished by the criminal law as sex offenders male persons? Is it only *their* roles in sexual encounters that become obvious and identifiable and is that merely a function of anatomy or body architecture? We are gaining in our understanding of the intricacies of human sexuality, both of the overt and the less easily discernible covert roles. What are some of the causes for the ineffectual, clumsy, inappropriate, wayward male courtship, coupling and sexual expressions? Have we, as Masters and Johnson seem to suggest from their biological and clinical studies, placed too much responsibility for the carrying through of human sexual encounters on the male in everyday life? Is this in part what we have also been seeing reflected in the courtroom? There is the additional irony of words, that with sex offences we have the spectacle of the courts attempting to deal with the hurts and failures of inappropriate courtship. While we are all in the process of finding out, and feeling and thinking our way towards more helpful solutions, perhaps it behooves any court to sentence in a far-seeing, time-honoured sense of the word.

NOTE

1. These comments emerge from the experience of having participated in observing a number of sex offence cases over the years as a defence counsel, as a probation officer and as an informal observer in courtrooms, rather than from a position of formally researched hardware facts.

CHAPTER 12

The Real Crime Problem in America and Sentencing

John C. Ball

INTRODUCTION

As the United States enters the 1980s, it is evident that the nation faces an endemic crime problem which is becoming increasingly serious and unmanageable. Although it is recognized that crime is disproportionately concentrated in metropolitan areas, it is not recognized that professional criminals, i.e., individuals who pursue crime as a livelihood, constitute the core of the crime problem in America.

In this paper, the extent of crimes committed by professional criminals will be reviewed and the fundamental differences between *ad hoc* offenders and persistent career offenders will be discussed. With regard to professional criminals, attention will be focused upon recent research findings pertaining to crimes committed by heroin addicts. These findings pertaining to heroin addicts are particularly significant because they involve the use of a new criminological measure — *Crime-Days* — which provides a means of analyzing the daily and yearly criminal behavior of individuals who pursue crime as a way of life.

Against this realistic background of the nature and extent of the real crime problem in America, the issue of sentencing is considered. It is held that contemporary disagreement as to proper sentencing procedures is due to diverse ideological, sociological and political influences which prevent the formulation of a viable national policy for the criminal justice system.

THE REAL CRIME PROBLEM: PROFESSIONAL CRIMINALS

Although criminologists have recognized for some time that a small proportion of the population commits most of the crimes and that these same persons continue their criminal careers year after year,[1] the solution to this problem remains obscure. One reason that the solution remains obscure is that the public is still unaware of the amount of crime which is continually committed by professional criminals. The public has yet to realize that a small segment of the population (1 or 2 per cent at most) is largely responsible for committing the vast bulk of serious criminal offences.

It is significant to note that this concentration of the American crime problem within a small segment of the population has not changed fundamentally over the past 30 years, although there has been some change in the types of crimes committed. Thus, in 1942 Frank Tannenbaum stated in his "Foreword" to *New Horizons in Criminology*[2] that the fundamental crime problem was what to do with professional criminals:

> Our community has made possible the development of the professional criminal. He does not operate by himself. He is not an individual. He is a member of a group — a group that co-operates for the purpose of making a living by the commission of crimes. The groups vary in size and in the kind of crimes in which they specialize, but they have this in common — that they are more or less loosely organized for a specific purpose, and the purpose varies from the commission of murder to the selling of fraudulent stocks, from the picking of pockets to dealing in vice, from the selling of narcotics to the robbing

of banks. Different in the type of crime committed, they are alike in purpose — the making of a living, the achievement of "success," by illicit methods.

These aberrant individuals may differ in the skills required for the varied operations they indulge in, they may be more or less sophisticated, but on the whole they acquire a common attitude toward society, a common working philosophy, and a common contempt for the ordinary virtues of ordinary men. They live in a specially conditioned universe that, taken as a whole, makes of them professional criminals. The genesis of their attitude is not far removed from that of other, non-criminal elements, but by the time the process of specialization has come to fruition they are full-fledged criminals whose control is one of the basic problems of our society.

Other criminals there are — that is, other men and women who break the law by accident, chance, and mishap — but they are not professional criminals, and they cannot be dealt with, to either their or society's benefit, as if they were criminals in the same sense as the professional group. The sooner we draw the distinction between those who break the law deliberately for gain as a means of livelihood and those who get into the clutches of the law through some personal mishap, the sooner we will be on the route toward a rational criminal law and a rational penal system.

In his appraisal of the American crime problem, Tannenbaum noted the community and peer group influences which nurtured career criminals. His emphasis upon environmental factors helps explain the present concentration of crime within big city slums. Beyond this, however, his emphasis upon the social and attitudinal forces which affect the professional criminal *after* he becomes committed to an illegal way of life seem significant. For the professional criminal learns to eschew the basic values of society and he replaces these with deviant values. He develops in the process "a common contempt for the ordinary virtues of ordinary men."

The distinction between professional and ordinary criminals which Tannenbaum draws is especially apt. For the failure to differentiate between *ad hoc* offenders and persistent offenders has been a major shortcoming of our criminal justice system and society.

THE 1979 STUDY OF HEROIN ADDICTS IN BALTIMORE

In order to delineate in detail the role which professional criminals play in our contemporary crime problem, attention is directed toward one group of career criminals — heroin addicts — and their involvement in criminality.[3] The research findings presented were derived by the author from an on-going follow-up study in Baltimore.[4]

In the present paper, a new measure of criminal behavior is described and employed in an on-going research project. The new measure has been termed *Crime-Days Per Year At Risk*. A *crime day* is a 24-hour period in which an individual commits one or more crimes. The number of *crime-days per year at risk* refers to the number of days per year that an individual has committed crimes, from 0 to 365.

This new measure, Crime-Days Per Year At Risk, is found to have unique analytical power as it permits the calculation of uniform crime rates by years at risk and it is not confounded by multiple crimes committed on a given day. Furthermore, the term Crime-Days Per Year At Risk appears to be an effective procedure for explaining and understanding the extent of serious criminal behavior because it relates the number of crimes committed by individuals to a common frame of reference — times per year.

Definition of Terms

Heroin Addiction. This term refers to the daily use of heroin. (Daily use, or regular use, is defined as use at least four times a week for a month, or longer.)

Crime-Day. A crime-day is defined as a 24-hour period during which one or more crimes is committed by a given individual. Each day of the year, then, is either a crime-day or a non-crime day.

Average Crime-Days Per Year. This measure is defined as the average number of Crime-Days Per Year At Risk for a given individual. The range is from 0 to 365. Thus, an individual with 1,489 crime-days during a 7-year risk period has an average Crime-Days Per Year At Risk of 213.

Years at Risk. Years at Risk is the number of years an individual is "on the street" or not incarcerated. It is calculated on a cumulative basis by subtracting jail or prison time from the years since age at onset of regular opiate use.

Principal Type of Crime. This is the predominate type of crime engaged in by a given individual during his years at risk, as theft (boosting, burglary, etc.), con games, robbery, gambling, drug sales, etc. This principal type of criminal behavior is the most common offense committed from an actuarial viewpoint. It answers the question, what kind of crime does he usually commit? The crimes reported by our sample reflect a broad range of criminal behavior and include: larceny (pick-pocketing, shoplifting, unauthorized use, burglary) robbery, fencing, assault, con games, pimping, soliciting, gambling, rape, abortions, forging, drug dealing, murder, and loan sharking. Mere possession or use of drugs is not classified as a crime in this analysis.

Criminal Career Type. This is the criminal behavior pattern which an individual has followed to date. The two main elements in determining the crime pattern are (a) type of crime and (b) frequency of crime. Examples of crime patterns are: daily theft, daily con games, weekly robbery, weekly forgery, infrequent assault, and so forth. In each case, the crime pattern, or career, is the most common, or usual, offense committed during tbe subject's years at risk and the frequency of commission. Thus, a pattern of daily theft during a 4-year period indicates that the individual had as his common offense theft property and that this was carried on most of the time he was at risk.

The Sample and Interview Schedule

This paper is based on interview data obtained from 243 Baltimore opiate addicts (most were heroin addicts). The 243 male addicts were a random sample chronologically stratified from 4,069 persons listed as known addicts by the Baltimore Police Department between 1952 and 1971. The selection procedure was also stratified by race. Of the 243 subjects, 109 were white and 134 were black. Analysis of cohort and race differences has been undertaken elsewhere.[5]

The initial sample drawn from the police files consisted of 349 individuals, but 57 of these had died by the time of the follow-up interview, 2 were in mental hospitals, 6 were unlocated and 17 refused to participate in the study. Thus, 92 per cent of the sample who were alive and not in mental institutions were interviewed, i.e., 267 of 290 subjects.

Of the 267 addicts who were interviewed, 14 claimed never to had been regular users of opiates, 3 used opiates regularly for only one or two months and the onset of one preceded everyone in the sample by 22 years; these 18 were excluded. In addition, a careful review of the remaining 249 cases revealed that six interviews were invalid because of discrepancies between the self-reports and official FBI records; thus, these six claimed no criminal behavior, but their arrest record listed two or more non-drug offenses. The remaining sample consisted of 243 cases.

Although comprehensive institutional data was collected with respect to the addict sample, the main source of data for the present analysis was obtained through personal interviews. Each of the 243 addicts was interviewed during 1973 or 1974 by specially trained interviewers who were familiar with the Baltimore addict subculture. The interview lasted some three hours and the questions were focused upon six topics: drug use, criminal behavior, work, living arrangements, drug selling and sources of income.

The interview schedule consisted of six parts: (1) Lifetime prevalence of drug use by each drug, dosage and most frequent usage (seven pages, completion time about 30 minutes); (2) History of daily use of opiates. This involves determination of addicted and abstinent periods during risk years of subject's life (three pages, 30 minutes to complete); (3) Pre-addiction history, circumstances of onset of opiate use. Criminal history at time of onset (seven pages, 30 minutes); (4) Circumstances of first regular use of opiates (i.e., daily use for a month or longer). This part included information on criminality for each separate period of regular opiate use or abstinence (10 minutes for each addiction period; seven pages each); (5) Marital history, parental background, juvenile delinquency, military service, treatment history, incarceration history, criminal history (16 pages, 60 minutes to complete); (6) Interviewer's rating of respondent's attitude, appearance and overt responsiveness (one page, five minutes).

Determination of Addiction Status and Crime-Days

The mean age of the 243 males at time of interview was 35.9 years; most of the sample (92.6 per cent) was between 25 and 49 years of age. Since onset of opiate addiction usually had occurred when the subjects were between 15 and 19 years, most of the sample had a post-onset career of 10 or more years (198 had 10 or more years, 37 had 5-9, and 8 had 2-4 years).

Since the focus of the lengthy interview was to obtain detailed chronological data pertaining to the addiction status from onset of regular opiate use to time of interview, each subject was asked to describe in detail his addiction, abstinent and incarceration periods. For the entire sample there were 2,340 distinct time periods enumerated from onset to interview. Of these 2,340 time periods, 1,022 were addiction periods, 488 were abstinent periods, 700 were jail or prison time periods, 52 were hospitalization periods and 78 periods were unclassified because of insufficient data. (These few unknown periods were omitted from further analysis.) In the present paper, attention is directed toward the addiction and abstinent periods as this was the time during which the subjects were at risk (that is, on the street). The incarceration and hospital periods were, therefore, excluded from this analysis.

All subjects had one or more addiction periods. The average length of an addiction period was found to be two years, although longer periods were common. Each subject was asked about his daily and weekly use of specific drugs during each period (dosage, multiple use, times used per day or week). In this manner, each subject's years, months and days at risk was classified as addicted or abstaining from opiates. Inasmuch as addiction was defined as daily use of opiates, the abstinent classification included both times during which lesser amounts of opiates were being used as well as times when other types of drugs were used (such as barbiturates and amphetamines). Eighty-five per cent of the sample had such abstinent periods.

Although periods of addiction or abstinence during the years at risk provided the chronological frame of reference for the interview, additional detailed data was obtained for each period concerning criminal behavior, employment, income, family life and other variables. With respect to criminality, each subject was asked about the number and type of crimes he committed on a daily, weekly or monthly basis for each addiction or abstinent period. These responses provided the basis for determining the number of crime-days, the principal type of crime and criminal career pattern for each subject.

Addiction Status and Criminality Since Onset

After the number of crime-days since the onset of regular opiate use had been coded for each subject, it was possible to classify both his addiction status and criminality during his years at risk. Thus, the following data was coded for each subject: (1) total crime-days while addicted, (2) total crime-days while off opiates (i.e., not using opiates regularly), (3) crimeless days addicted, and (4) crimeless days while off regular opiates. These four statuses were mutually exclusive. When combined, the time in these four statuses was the subject's time at risk.

The most frequent addiction-crime status for the entire sample was that of being addicted and committing crimes on a daily basis; this occurred during 41.7 per cent of the risk period. Next most common was being off regular opiates and not committing daily crimes; this occurred for 34.5 per cent of the risk period. The remainder of the risk period was accounted for by addicted time when crimes were not committed (19.9 per cent) and abstinent time when crimes were committed (3.9 per cent of days).

Table 1

TOTAL TIME AT RISK BY ADDICTION STATUS AND CRIMINALITY FOR 237 ADDICTS

Status While At Risk	Days in Each Status	Per cent of Days in Each Status
1. Crime-Days on Opiates	432,947	41.7
2. Crime-Days off Opiates	40,791	3.9
3. Crimeless Days on Opiates	206,082	19.9
4. Crimeless Days off Opiates	358,304	34.5
Total Days at Risk:	1,038,124	100.0

The total amount of time that this Baltimore male sample spent addicted to opiate drugs since onset of regular opiate use was 61.6 per cent of their risk years. Since their average years at risk was 11.3, they were addicted to opiates almost two-thirds of the time and abstinent somewhat over a third of the time (see Figure 1). Two further points are pertinent concerning their addiction or abstinent status. First, with regard to the abstinence from regular opiate use classification, this status included periods of occasional use of opiates as well as periods of frequent use of non-opiate drugs. Second, it is significant that 85 per cent of the sample had such abstinent periods.

Figure 1
TIME SINCE ONSET ADDICTED TO OPIATES
OR OFF REGULAR OPIATE
USE FOR 237 ADDICTS

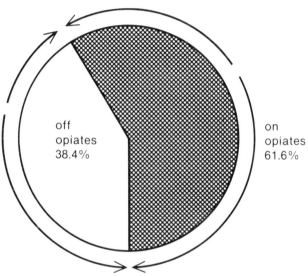

Dr. J. C. Ball
Temple University 1979

Number of Crimes Committed by the 243 Addicts

The total number of crime-days during the risk years for the 243 addicts is tabulated in Table 2. The range in crime-days within the sample was from 0 to 9,450. That is, from no crimes committed by six addicts to 9,450 crime-days accumulated by one addict during his risk years.

Table 2

TOTAL CRIME DAYS FOR 243 ADDICTS

Crime Days	Number of Addicts	Per cent of Addicts
0 (None)	6	2.5
1-99	20	8.2
100-499	31	12.8
500-999	31	12.8
1,000-1,999	54	22.2
2,000-2,999	46	18.9
3,000-3,999	27	11.1
4,000-4,999	12	4.9
5,000-5,999	10	4.1
6,000-6,999	6	2.5
Total	243	100.0

Total crime-days since onset of addiction: 473,738

The total number of crime-days amassed by these 243 addicts during their years at risk was 473,738. This total may be regarded as an underestimate of the total number of crimes committed as multiple crimes during a crime-day were common. It is also noteworthy that most of the crimes reported were for theft and that drug use or possession was not classified as a crime.

The mean number of crime-days per addict during their years at risk was 1,998.9. Thus, the majority of these addicts were deeply enmeshed in a criminal way of life. There were, however, important differences in their patterns of criminal behavior as well as their frequency of committing crimes. The differential frequency is more accurately measured by means of *Crime-Days Per Year At Risk* than by noting frequencies uncontrolled for time at risk.

In order to control for years at risk, crime-days were computed for each person by years at risk (see Table 3). This measure — Crime-Days Per Year At Risk — indicates the average number of crime-days per year during the risk years for each of the 243 addicts.

Table 3

CRIME-DAYS PER YEAR AT RISK FOR 243 ADDICTS

Crime-Days Per Year at Risk	Number of Addicts	Per cent of Addicts
No Crime-Days	6	2.5
Less than 1 per yr.	11	4.5
1-49	35	14.4
50-99	26	10.7
100-149	31	12.8
150-199	32	13.2
200-249	25	10.3
250-299	26	10.7
300-349	28	11.5
350-365	23	9.5
Total	243	100.0

The mean number of Crime-Days Per Year At Risk for the sample was 178.5. Thus, the total amount of time that these Baltimore addicts spent engaged in daily criminal behavior since their onset of addiction was almost half of their risk years. To be exact, they were committing crimes on a daily basis during 45.6 per cent of their years at risk (see Figure 2).

Figure 2
NUMBER AND PER CENT OF CRIME-DAYS
AND CRIMELESS DAYS
WHILE AT RISK FOR 237 ADDICTS

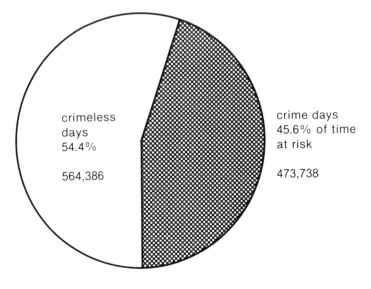

crimeless
days
54.4%

564,386

crime days
45.6% of time
at risk

473,738

Dr. J. C. Ball
Temple University 1979

Criminality by Addiction Status

In order to depict the general relationship between addiction and criminality, the distribution of average crime-days per year at risk was related to the two addiction statuses. The extent of criminality was found to differ markedly by addiction status. Thus, when the subjects were addicted half were committing

300 or more crimes per year (300 crimes to 365 crime-days per year). Conversely, when these same subjects were not addicted, two-thirds committed less than one crime per year during their years at risk. It is evident, then, that a definite relationship exists between addiction status and criminality among these Baltimore males. Thus, 91.4 per cent of their crime-days were also days during which they were addicted. Conversely, only 8.6 per cent of their crime-days occurred when they were off regular opiates (see Figure 3).

Figure 3
ADDICTION CAREER AND CRIMINALITY OF 237 ADDICTS
BY TIME IN EACH STATUS

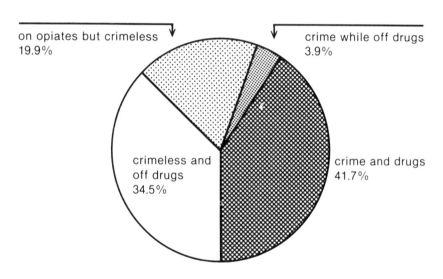

on opiates but crimeless
19.9%

crime while off drugs
3.9%

crimeless and
off drugs
34.5%

crime and drugs
41.7%

TOTAL TIME AT RISK, "ON STREET"

Dr. J. C. Ball
Temple University 1979

Criminal Careers of the 243 Addicts

Each of the 243 addicts was classified as to the common criminal career which he had followed since onset of regular opiate use. These criminal career types were determined on the basis of the principal (most common) type of crime committed, and, secondly, on the frequency of commission — whether daily, weekly or less often. Six of the 243 addicts had committed no crimes during their risk period.

It was found that the 237 addicts who had committed crimes could be classified into nine types of criminal careers (see Table 4). These nine were: daily theft, daily drug sales, other daily crimes; weekly theft, weekly drug sales, other weekly crimes; infrequent theft, infrequent sales and other infrequent crimes. Some two-thirds of the 237 addicts had theft as their principal type of crime. Of these 156 who were career thieves, 41 engaged in daily theft during their year at risk, 58 engaged in weekly theft and 57 in infrequent theft.

Table 4

CRIME-DAYS PER YEAR AT RISK BY ADDICTION STATUS

Crime Career Type	Number of Addicts	Crime-Days Per Year at Risk	Crime-Days Per Year at Risk: addicted	abstinent
1. Theft-daily	41	330.3	347.7	109.7
2. Sale of Drugs-daily	13	328.0	353.2	88.3
3. Other Crimes-daily	7	319.4	341.4	151.0
4. Weekly Theft	58	189.6	280.9	23.3
5. Weekly Sale of Drugs	18	181.1	284.0	27.6
6. Weekly, other crimes	7	201.9	297.0	70.1
7. Infrequent Theft	57	72.4	140.7	7.4
8. Infrequent Sales	14	102.4	260.9	10.5
9. Infrequent, other crimes	22	46.8	108.2	2.3
10. No Crime	6	—	—	—
Total:	243	178.5	248.0	40.8

The selling of drugs was the second most favored type of crime committed by these addicts; 45 were principally engaged in selling drugs, or "dealing." Of the 45 dealers, 13 pursued this crime on a daily basis, 18 on a weekly basis and 14 on an infrequent basis.

The remainder of the sample were engaged in committing other types of crimes on a daily, weekly or infrequent basis. Of these 45, only 7 were engaged in daily crime, 7 in weekly crime and 22 in infrequent crimes. Confidence games, forgery, gambling and procuring (pimping) were the principal types of crime committed by these 45 addicts.

The classification of the sample into nine criminal career types somewhat obscures the fact that many addicts engaged in more than one type of crime during their years at risk. This situation is especially notable with regard to the 61 addicts who were daily criminals. Thus, 55 of the 61 had engaged in theft during their years at risk and 43 had engaged in some dealing, although only 13 had this as their principal daily criminal activity. In addition to theft and dealing — the two most common types of crimes — 33 of the 61 had engaged in other crimes, such as forgery, gambling, confidence games, robbery and pimping. The complete list of all crimes reported by these daily criminals during their years on the street is: theft (this includes shoplifting; "cracking shorts," burglary and other forms of stealing), dealing, forgery, gambling confidence (flim-flam, etc.), pimping, assault, mugging, robbery, armed robbery, and abortion. Lastly, although most of the 61 criminals engaged in more than one type of crime during their years on the street, there still was a marked tendency to focus upon one main, or principal, type of crime, especially theft or dealing. Furthermore, 11 of these 61 males confined themselves exclusively to one type of crime during their years at risk (8 committed only theft, 2 were only drug sellers, one was a confidence man and one a gambler).

The Impact of Addiction Upon Criminal Careers

The extent of criminality among all nine career types was affected by their addiction status. Thus, there was a six-fold increase overall in the number of crime-days per year during addiction as contrasted with the crime rate when abstinent (see Table 4). Rather surprisingly, the proportionate increase in crime-day per year at risk when addicted vs. when abstinent was most marked among the career criminals who engage in weekly or monthly offenses. Thus, for five of these six career types (weekly theft, weekly dealing and three infrequent types) the extent of criminality increased to more than ten times the non-addicted rate. The greatest increase was for the 22 subjects who committed other crimes on a monthly basis — from 2.3 crime-days per year to 108.2 crime days per year. Although the extent of criminality within this addict sample was notably increased when the subjects were addicted to opiate drugs, the non-addicted crime rate was still quite high.

As might be expected, the highest crime rates when not addicted were found among the three criminal career types who had the highest crime rate when addicted (daily theft, daily sales and daily other crimes). In these three career types, the addicts committed from one to three crimes per week when not addicted (for the three career groups, the rates per year at risk were 109.7, 88.3 and 151.0 respectively). In considering the rates of criminality for the nine career types when abstaining from opiates, it seems significant that these nine rates vary more (from 2.3 to 151.0) than do the rates when these same subjects were addicted. In a sense, then, one effect of opiate addiction is to raise the number of crimes committed to a threshold, or support level, and this occurs for all nine career types. Thus, when addicted, 7 of the 9 career types commit more than 260 crimes per year and none of the nine career groups fall below 100 crime-days per year at risk when addicted.

Implication of this Study of 243 Addicts

This study of male heroin addicts in Baltimore found that most of the subjects are deeply enmeshed in criminal careers which often involve the commission of crimes on a daily basis over a period of many years. Secondly, it has been found that the vast majority of these crimes have been committed while the subjects were addicted to opiates. Conversely, the rate of criminal activity was greatly reduced, or even eliminated, when these same subjects were in an abstinent state.

With respect to criminality, it was found that each of the 243 addicts committed an average of 1,999 crimes (i.e., had 1,999 crime-days) and that together this sample was responsible for committing at least 473,738 offenses. (These figures do not include drug use or drug possession offenses.) On an annual basis, this sample of male addicts committed 178 crimes per year from the onset of regular opiate use.

The implications of this study of heroin addicts are far-reaching, for the research findings indicate that a small proportion of the population are actively engaged in committing crimes on a daily basis year after year. Inasmuch as these professional criminals are seldom arrested (far less than one per cent of their crimes result in arrest), both the public and the courts are unaware of the extent and persistence of their criminality. Consequently, both the public and the courts are unprepared to deal with the problem of the professional criminal.

THE PROBLEM OF SENTENCING

The judicial approach to offenders stands in contrast to the endemic realities of big city crime. The judicial emphasis tends to be upon the current offense of a single individual, rather than upon the criminal group, community-wide nature of the problem or national perspective. In many ways, then, the judicial approach to sentencing tends to be clinical and scholastic. Clinically it is concerned with the "correct" treatment, or sentence. It is also scholastic in its emphasis upon formal rules applied within the courtroom argumentation and compartmentalization of thought.

The theoretical and practical issue of determining which system of punishment is most appropriate for offenders has been, and continues to be, a most difficult question to answer.[6] Indeed, the history of criminal law in both Europe and America attests to this difficulty as these laws have continually changed. One need only mention such practices as capital punishment, corporal punishment, transportation of criminals, and use of the penitentiary system to establish that the philosophy and practice of punishment remain as unresolved issues.[7]

Part of the intellectual confusion over the proper function of punishment in society is due to our inability to explicitly state the objective that punishment is intended to accomplish:

(1) Is the goal to fit the punishment to the individual based on the particular crime committed in order to teach him a lesson and, thereby, dissuade him from committing additional crimes of a similar nature?

(2) Or is the goal of punishment to change or rehabilitate the particular offender in a more general sense so that he will refrain from all or most criminal acts?

(3) Or again, is the goal of punishment to serve as a general deterrent to the commission of crimes by the population at large?

The answer to these questions is apparent: we do not know. We do not know (or, at least we cannot agree) what the proper function of punishment in society is because the issue remains beyond the purview of science. Thus, the issues of crime and punishment still, to a marked extent, are not determined by criminological research or historical study. Rather, these issues pertaining to punishment are determined on the basis of ideology, geographical setting (jurisdiction) and personal experiences.

With respect to ideology, the impact of religious and political values upon the criminal law (or punishment system) of particular societies has been widely recognized. Less well understood is the influence of the *zeitgeist* upon the law and its application. How for example, has the "liberal" influence of educational philosophy and the social sciences affected our ideas about punishment and rehabilitation? While consideration of these questions is beyond the scope of this paper, it is pertinent to state that the ideological framework which one brings to this topic usually determines the type of punishment, or sentencing, which will be advocated.

Beyond the influence of ideology, one's geographical locale and role in society are also important determinants of attitudes toward the punishment of offenders. Residence in a neighborhood or city with a high rate of street crime can decidedly affect one's perception of how to deal with criminals. So too can one's role in society: a judge, policeman, teacher, social worker, or criminal are likely to have quite varied beliefs about the efficacy of various types of punishment.

THE RATIONALIZATION OF PUNISHMENT VS. THE REALITY OF CRIME

But all of our efforts at rationalizing punishment (or rehabilitation) may be merely a game in which we delude ourselves into believing that what we do is significant, while in fact it is not. Are we fiddling while Rome burns? Are we engaged in a new scholastic exercise in which the refinements of official punishment are endlessly debated in prescribed courtroom fashion while the vast volume of criminal behavior which threatens the foundation of our society goes unheeded?

What I am suggesting is that metropolitan America has a major crime problem which the present criminal law and judicial system are inadequate to deal with.[8] There are various reasons why the criminal justice system cannot successfully cope with the volume and complexities of criminal behavior in our metropolitan areas. Among the principal reasons are the following:

(1) The legal system is preoccupied with determining the guilt of an individual with regard to a specific illegal act. Thus, crime is not viewed as an ongoing repetitive process, but as a unique event. There is, then, too much attention directed toward *ad hoc* offenders and insufficient resources devoted to dealing with the professional criminal.

(2) The criminal justice system is grossly inefficient: It often is a bureaucratic nightmare. There is a general lack of competent management; there are unnecessary delays and confusion as to courtroom schedules; witnesses and jurors are usually uninformed as to courtroom procedures and their services inadequately appreciated or rewarded; the outcome of the judicial process is frequently unknown by the public because of plea bargaining, delays and poor communication.

(3) The judicial system is preoccupied with the procedures and mechanics of administering the law in courtrooms, while virtually ignoring the reality of the daily crime problem on our streets.

(4) The legal system is unable to deal effectively with organized crime and professional criminals. The law was not established to cope with hundreds of thousands of persons who pursue crime as a way of life.

(5) The United States Government lacks a viable national policy and program to deal with the contemporary crime problem.

CONCLUSION

In this paper, I have suggested that there is a dichotomy between the realities of crime in America and the formal administration of justice. In reality, crime is endemic yet basically unfettered by the criminal justice system. In theory, the judiciary maintains that they should be able to cope with criminals through the court system. It would seem that a crucial first step in controlling the crime problem would involve a resolution of these two diverse viewpoints.

NOTES

1. James A. Inciardi, *Careers in Crime* (Chicago: Rand McNally, 1975); Edwin M. Lemert, "The Behavior of the Systematic Check Forger," in Howard S. Beeker (ed.), *The Other Side* (New York: The Free Press, 1964); Walter C. Reckless, *The Crime Problem* (New York: Appleton Century-Crofts, 1967), ch. 14, "Criminal Careers."

2. Frank Tannenbaum, *New Horizons in Criminology* (New York: Prentice-Hall, 1943).

3. For an overview on this problem, see John C. Ball and Carl D. Chambers, *The Epidemiology of Opiate Addiction in the United States* (Springfield, Ill.: Charles C. Thomas, 1970); and Strategy Council on Drug Abuse, *Federal Strategy for Drug Abuse and Drug Traffic Prevention, 1979* (Washington, D. C.: U. S. Government Printing Office, 1979).

4. David N. Nurco, Arthur J. Bonito, Monroe Lerner, and Mitchell B. Balter, "Studying Addicts Over Time: Methodology and Preliminary Findings," 2 *American J. of Drug and Alcohol Abuse* (1975), pp. 183-196.

5. David N. Nurco and Robert L. Dupont, "A Preliminary Report on Crime and Addiction Within a Community-wide Population of Narcotic Addicts," 2 *Drug and Alcohol Dependence* (1977), pp. 109-122.

6. Panel on Research on Deterrent and Incapacitative Effects, *Deterrence and Incapacitation: Estimating the Effects of Criminal Sanctions on Crime Rates* (Washington, D. C.: National Academy of Sciences, 1978).

7. John C. Ball, "The Deterrence Concept in Criminology and Law," 46 *J. of Criminal Law, Criminology and Police Science* (1955), pp. 345-354.

8. Charles E. Silberman, *Criminal Violence, Criminal Justice* (New York: Random House, 1978), ch. 6, " 'The Insufficiency of Human Institutions': An Introduction to the Criminal Justice System."

Part 5

THE DEFENCE LAWYER'S VIEWPOINT

CHAPTER 13

The Role of the Defence Lawyer in Sentencing

E. L. Greenspan

The role of defence counsel in the sentencing process is, at best, publicized and written about far less than are representations made prior to conviction. Often, in fact, sentencing is simply forgotten in the literature. Criminal law courses at our law schools spend little time on this area. Advocacy courses spend no time on it. How many of us have not, at some time or another, seen another lawyer stand up in court and have to publicly ask his client how old he is and where he lives, before that lawyer can speak to sentence, that being the entirety of his submissions? One United States Federal Court Judge has written:

> It is particularly distressing that many attorneys for the defense, who have proven themselves competent as to the facts and law in the case at trial, display on sentence hardly more than a faint glimmer as to who their clients really are as human beings. Thus it is that they come totally illprepared to advance or meet the vital disclosures which sentencing makes imperative.
>
> Too often it is an appeal in general terms for compassion and empty comment, "You'll never see him in any court again." Then again the plea is that the felonious behaviour of the client should be excused because of his personal weaknesses (drugs, alcohol, sex, other disadvantages).[1]

And yet, although submissions to sentence may not get a fraction of the newspaper publicity that a sensational trial does — that is, unless you are acting for Keith Richards or Leopold and Loeb — nevertheless, the role of defense counsel at sentencing is of critical importance. In fact, when you realize that fully 90 per cent of all persons charged in Canada are ultimately convicted,[2] making submissions for sentence is something a defence counsel is required to do for most of his clients. In addition, almost 70 per cent[3] of all persons charged actually plead guilty so that, in fact, in the majority of cases, speaking to sentence is the only courtroom representation a lawyer will make. What is more, it is to defence counsel that the sentencing judge must necessarily turn for guidance and information. Of all the officers of the court, it is defence counsel who has had, hopefully, the greatest exposure to the person before the court. The United States Supreme Court has suggested that the need for counsel may be greater at sentencing than in the determination of guilt because "there a judge usually moves within a large area of discretion and doubts . . . Even the most self-assured judge may well want to bring to his aid every consideration that counsel for the accused can appropriately urge."[4]

But as important as it is the role of the defence counsel in sentencing is, if not ignored, often simply misunderstood. It is my contention that the role of defence counsel at this stage of the criminal proceedings remains unchanged as an adversarial role — indeed as adversarial as at any stage of the trial. The best statement of the defence counsel's duties was given by Lord Brougham when he represented the Queen in *Queen Caroline's Case*. Threatening to defend his client on an issue that would literally have brought down the Kingdom, Brougham stated:

> An advocate, in the discharge of his duty, knows but one person in all the world, and that person is his client. To save that client by all means and expedients, and at all hazards and costs to other persons, and amongst them, to himself, is his first and only duty; and in performing this duty he must not regard the alarm, the torments, the destruction which he may bring upon others. Separating the duty of a patriot from that of an advocate, he must go on reckless of the consequences, though it should be his unhappy fate to involve his country in confusion.[5]

What he is saying is, let justice be done — that is, *for my client* let justice be done — though the heavens fall.[6] And the statement applies with equal force and effect at the sentencing hearing. And yet this view is shared by virtually no one. The Law Reform Commission of Canada, in its study of restitution, simply makes the comment, "In most cases the procedure during sentencing is not, and presumably should not be, strictly adversarial as at trial."[7] Clive Bynoe, in an article written for the Law Society of Upper Canada, Special Lecture Series instructs us that "The main object of sentencing is the protection of society and it is towards that we all must strive. It is hoped that the best interests of the accused will also in the long run be the best interests of society."[8] The American Bar Association's Project Standards for Criminal Justice discusses the roles of both prosecutor and defence counsel at length[9] but never perceives the role of defence counsel as being what I will suggest to you it is and should be.

There seems to be some feeling that following a conviction defence counsel should consider the interests of society instead of the client. That seems to be what the American Bar Association means when they say "defence counsel should present to the court any ground which will assist in reaching a *proper* disposition favourable to the accused,"[10] and it seems to be a factor in Mr.

Bynoe's approach as well. I cannot agree. Like Mr. Bynoe, I can only hope that the best interests of the accused do result in the best interests of society, but, if in fact they do not, it is not my client who must suffer. I cannot agree that my representations of my client must be affected by considering society's interests — that is not my function. Let justice be done, all right, but *for my client.*

That is not to say that society's interests should not be represented at sentencing — that is, of course, why we have both a prosecutor and an impartial judge. My sole point, at this stage, is that such considerations are not the *responsibility* nor even the *right* of defence counsel. The goal of defence counsel is not a disposition most favourable to society, but one most favourable to the client, and all his efforts must be channelled in this direction. That is why for example:

(1) If I receive a psychiatric report on behalf of a client that is totally unfavourable, I discard it, look for a new report, or, failing that, go to court with none.

(2) I always talk to pre-sentence reporters and direct these very busy people to certain pre-selected persons whom I have talked to in advance and have advised as to what areas they should stay away from and what areas they should discuss. From the point of view of the defence, it is none of the court's business that Johnny's parents are upset with him because he has been stealing money from them for the past six months, and I advise parents that disclosing that fact will not help their son's cause in his trial for indecent assault.

(3) I do everything in my limited power to amend the situation between persons involved in the act of criminality (i.e., victim and accused).

I want to point out, however, that although defence counsel's role remains adversarial, the role of Crown counsel may change at the time of sentencing. The American Bar Association says: "there are aspects of the adversary system which are inappropriate for the sentencing process. The role of the prosecutor, for example, should be significantly different at the sentencing phase."[11] In particular the prosecutor should not make the severity of sentences the index of his effectiveness. In Canada, it is not at all clear that this is the case. The Law Reform Commission of Canada points out that in some provinces it is considered to be improper for the Crown to make a recommendation as to sentence. In other provinces, on the other hand, the prosecutor is viewed as having a very real interest in protecting society and community interests.[12] Although I personally would favour the ABA position, I suppose the danger of not having Crown counsel's submissions for sentencing is that the sentencing judge is not guided by a supposed upper limit of sentence, and, instead of occupying an objective position, may act out of inordinate concern for the community who is unrepresented before him.

But in any case, given my conception of the goal of defence counsel in sentencing, I would now like to look at what that goal entails and how it is achieved. I would like to say immediately that a disposition most favourable to my client does not necessarily mean the least severe sentence. It need not mean that at all. Rather it means finding out, first of all, what are the client's needs. Suppose, for example, your client suffers from an alcohol or drug problem — something serious enough to require a lengthy treatment program. Without that treatment you know your client will simply continue to commit offences, potentially more and more serious. With such an element in the case, you are not helping him by obtaining a result that does not help cure his problem. You do not necessarily have to become a social worker but it is simply common sense that, for example, you are not helping your client by asking for, much less obtaining, a probation order of six months length if a treatment program takes a year and you know that at the end of that six months he will simply drop out and revert to his old ways. In a real life example: a woman was convicted of manslaughter. She had spent most of her adult life in the Kingston Prison for Women. In fact, it was the only home she knew. Her only friends were other inmates of that institution. She actually looked forward to going back there. Faced with that situation, my partner, who acted for her, asked the trial judge that if he were considering incarceration, to sentence her to a penitentiary as opposed to reformatory time, pointing out that she had escaped several times from provincial institutions. She received five years and she was truly happy. So, again, I say, serving your client means purely and simply, obtaining the best result *for your client.* I will not hesitate to agree to a totally unrealistic fine if it is the only way of avoiding jail for my client and if it will not bankrupt him.

Before I come to deal with the creative role of defence counsel in making submissions for sentencing alternatives, it may be trite but nevertheless important to say that the way you frame your submissions to a judge is most important. Getting the judge to accept your viewpoint is what it is all about. That means counsel's credibility with the judge and the Crown is of tremendous importance. For example, counsel should not seek a suspended sentence on a serious rape charge. If you ask for it, the judge will pay no attention to you. To know that, one has got to be familiar with the tariffs of sentencing for the particular offence. No counsel should consider himself bound by these ranges but if any alternative is going to sell itself to a judge, it is necessary to recognize the ranges of sentences for that offence. As well, it is important to know what factors in sentencing will take you to the higher or lower end of that scale — what factors the judge is likely or not likely to consider. Now, there are, of course, a lot of appellate judgments in these areas and it is important to know them but counsel must sit down in each case and list all the possible mitigating and aggravating factors and try to plug them into supporting cases. For example, if the offender's record is more than five years old, obtain the law from Saskatchewan that says your client should be treated as a first offender.

But the representation of your client neither begins nor ends at simply knowing the normal tariff. There is enormous room for a creative approach to sentencing. First of all, I want to look at some alternatives to incarceration. The Law Reform Commission of Canada has pointed out that roughly one in every 1,000 residents of Canada is now serving time in a penal institution, and over

75,000 people are incarcerated each year. The Commission concluded that almost 50 per cent of prisoners in some provincial institutions were imprisoned because they could not pay fines.[13] These are dismaying statistics for, as you know, it is clear that Canada imprisons too many people. But I want to point out again in the words of the Law Reform Commission, "Imprisonment today is seen to be a costly sanction that ought to be used as a last resort."[14] I believe that that defence counsel's submissions to sentence should reflect that position, and that the judge should be reminded of it in the strongest terms. What then are some creative alternatives to incarceration which still remains the most popular sentence with judges? Section 653(1) of the Criminal Code provides:

> A court that convicts an accused of an indictable offence may, upon the application of a person aggrieved, at the time sentence is imposed, order the accused to pay to that person an amount by way of satisfaction or compensation for loss of or damage to property suffered by the applicant as a result of the commission of the offence of which the accused is convicted.[15]

Any doubts that this section was *intra vires* Parliament, involving as it does a civil means of enforcing the order, were removed decisively by the recent Supreme Court of Canada decision in *R. v. Zelensky*.[16] Now this is not by any means a new section of the Code and yet in an analysis done by the Law Reform Commission of Canada of 4,200 convictions from 1967 to 1972, restitution orders were made in exactly six cases — approximately 1/10 of 1 per cent.[17] Certainly, restitution orders are not for every client and certainly the nature of the offence and the amounts of losses involved are factors to be considered, but if the alternative for your client is incarceration, restitution is well worth suggesting. The criticisms directed at the restitution concept have little bearing when an accused person voluntarily accepts it.[18]

But there is another reason for its importance — it is almost trite to say that too many people are involved in criminal offences because they fail to perceive the seriousness of the effects of their actions on others: fraud, vandalism, and theft are prime examples of this. Restitution orders may be beneficial in such cases if only because the client is forced to face the victim, to perceive the injury inflicted and attempt to rectify it. Hopefully, along with greater awareness for your client, will come satisfaction for the victim. And that, after all, is supposedly an often overlooked foundation of our criminal justice system.[19] But unless counsel arranges for this, the judge will not also, and particularly in our lower courts where there is precious little time for a judge to be innovative in sentencing on his own initiative? Counsel's job is to present alternatives to jail, not to wait and hope that the judge will think of it. As counsel you may want to contact the victims of economic crimes or crimes of violence yourself. Initiating contact with victims should not be an area of fear for defence counsel. Try approaching the victim and attempt to resolve the issues, particularly without the impetus of a court order. What better proof of "rehabilitation" can you offer a court than to demonstrate that the victim is satisfied and your client is penitent?

Coming back to restitution, it need not be paid in dollars only. A recently developed practice has arisen in some provinces of coupling a community service-order with a period of probation. That is, the offender is required to perform a certain number of hours of labour either for the victims or for some other part of the community as part of his probation. Naturally your client has to be willing to do it before you suggest it, but it is clearly of benefit to society, and that, of course, is an approach a judge may find difficult to ignore. A recent example of this occurred in Windsor, Ontario where a doctor was convicted of impaired driving arising from a traffic accident which resulted in a fatality. The doctor offered to perform, without compensation, a research project needed by a particular hospital in the area and that suggestion was ultimately accepted by the court in lieu of a prison sentence.[20] His Honour Provincial Court Judge Nosanchuk fined the accused and ordered him to perform, as a condition of probation, 300 hours of community service work, and in his reasons for judgment described the purpose of the work order as follows:

> The purpose of the project . . . was that the work orders would be on projects that were of tangible benefit to the community and would meet community needs. It was felt that offenders would be encouraged to use skills which would benefit the community and which the community could see being used for the common good. The use of a community service order would be to provide a framework within which offenders, who would otherwise be imprisoned, could in some manner repay the community in a positive way for the harm they have caused.[21]

In one case I was involved in I discovered that a group of handicapped people might not be able to go on a bus trip to eastern Canada for three weeks because there weren't enough counsellors available. I was acting for a boy who could have received a substantial reformatory term, but because his service as a counsellor was offered to the court, with the full approval of the organizers of the trip, jail was avoided. The whole purpose of the role of defense counsel is to so limit the trial judge's discretion that only alternatives to imprisonment will be considered.

Up to now, I have been discussing specific alternatives to incarceration. I would like, for a moment, to talk about things you can do for clients in general. Given what I have said already about the rate of convictions for criminal offences in Canada, it makes a great deal of sense to be thinking about that potential conviction right from the beginning, whether or not you think your client has a defence. You are not helping your client if, six months or a year down the line, he is convicted and he has done nothing during that interval to convince anyone the offence will not be repeated. That is why I suggest, when your client first walks into your office, you think about what you can do to mitigate the situation if your client is ultimately convicted. If there is an alcohol or drug-related problem, refer your client to a treatment program, and do not wait until the court orders it at sentencing. The initial interviews should focus on social problems and future plans; if your client needs pyschotherapy — start it; if he needs psychological assessments — obtain it; if he needs counselling — refer him or do it yourself; if his relationship with his parents has deteriorated — repair it. Surely one of the most positive factors in the *Keith Richards* case was that Richards, long before he ever pleaded to the possession of a large amount of heroin, had commenced and was proceeding satisfactorily through a treatment program. If your client is unemployed, impress upon him or her the importance of getting a job. Again, you should not wait until after he or she is convicted because, after all, if you are trying to impress a judge that your client does not need the court or a jail cell to be rehabilitated, it is not too convincing if your client has done nothing to show that there is no need until the date of conviction — the date the law finally caught up with him. There is an element of social work required here, but as an advocate looking out for your client's interest — looking *ahead* for your client's interests — is what is at issue. It is imperative that the lawyer knows the available community agencies that may help the client.

In one case I acted for a lad who had committed a number of breaking and entering offences from one end of Metropolitan Toronto to the other (21 to be exact). He was using a drug, "speed." His parents were fed up with him and threw him out of the house.

I spent hours with the parents trying to bring them back on their son's side. With their help, I got the boy into the House of Concord, run by the Salvation Army north of Toronto. The institution expected to have my client for two months. Because of numerous upsetting incidents at the House of Concord caused by my client, I kept adjourning the case and after one year and three months, between living at his home and working and staying at the House of Concord, when things were well with my client, we pleaded guilty before a judge who quite coincidentally happened to be a director of the House of Concord, and the lad got probation. He had cured his drug problem, restructured his entire life, all before the court was called on to impose sentence.

This is what I call "constructive delay," for delaying the resolution of a case can be a very effective means of affecting sentence. Now, that is a potentially controversial statement to make. Defence counsel are vilified for delaying trials, seeking adjournment after adjournment, clogging the court system with cases that drag on literally for years. The Chief Justice of Ontario, Mr. Justice Howland, in January of this year (1979), indicated the following in his Annual Report on the Administration of Justice:

> The most serious problem in the administration of the courts at the present time, is, I believe, the problem of the continuous adjournments in the provincial courts, the fixing of peremptory dates for trial and then finding that counsel are unable to proceed. The result has been that the work of the courts is disrupted and the public are seriously inconvenienced because the witnesses have to be sent

home and subpoenaed again at public expense for trial at a later date. I realize that as far as possible an accused should be entitled to be represented by counsel of his own choice. The courts endeavour within reason to accommodate counsel whose services are in heavy demand. On the other hand the judiciary cannot permit trials to be delayed for protracted periods of time, particularly where the accused is in custody, nor can it permit the work of the courts to be disrupted at considerable public expense and inconvenience. It is an urgent problem and its solution requires the assistance of the judges, and of Crown and defence counsel.[22]

I do not, of course, quarrel with those words. I would never suggest to you that delay should be utilized improperly to wear the Crown attorney down or to frustrate the victim, in the hope that Crown witnesses will vanish or die. It is, under Ontario rules of practice, unethical to do so.[23] Nevertheless, used properly and legitimately, and I want to emphasize those words, time is an important tool in the sentencing process — if my "break and enter" lad had pleaded guilty soon after his arrest; abandoned by his parents; a heavy speed user; with 21 charges and no prospects or hopes, he would have received a stiff term of incarceration. However, if a guilty plea is being considered, time may work both for and against you. On one hand, a court may be persuaded to mitigate sentence by a prompt and clear admission of guilt — a sign of penitence, I suppose. On the other hand, where a question of rehabilitation or recidivism arises, a quick plea of guilty will hardly assist you to respond to those concerns. How can a court be persuaded that the client has changed their ways when only a week or a month ago they were committing the particular offence now before the court? It is clear that our courts have recognized the importance of positive conduct and circumstances on behalf of the client arising after the offence, but it is particularly evident that they have, by the way appellate courts consider sentence appeals, analogously relied on post-sentence reports.[24]

So, first of all, make use of the system by constructive delay if it is to your client's benefit. On the other hand, be aware of the provisions of Criminal Code section 465(1)(f) which allows you to bring forward proceedings "before the expiration of the time for which the accused has been remanded." If there has been a favourable change in your client's circumstances or if there is a need to dispose of the charge prior to the date of trial, speak to the investigating officers and the Crown about bringing the case on earlier. In short, use the procedural sections of the Code to regulate the proceeding in your client's favour. Again, I stress that this be done within our ethical limitations.

Earlier, I briefly referred to the pre-sentence report, probably the only input seen to be objective in the sentencing process. Because of its objectivity or at least, assumed objectivity, it is viewed with great weight by the judge. As such, it is vitally important for the client that the probation officer preparing the report be directed to sources of positive information. The defence counsel should not be afraid to get involved in the preparation of the report and should not wait until it appears in court already completed.

> Overall, as probation investigators are likely to have substantial case loads and hence little time for other than routine investigation, counsel can be extremely helpful in supplying data which might otherwise go unnoticed. Counsel should, of course, be wary of taking over the interview, developing an adversary relationship with the investigator, or so forcefully intruding that any picture of the client is obscured by counsel's own personality. Counsel can assist his client in appropriate cases, in producing character references, copies of which should be sent to the presentence reporter. Such letters may assist in righting an imbalance, one resulting from so much attention to the crime that little is given to the "offender."[25]

I see nothing wrong with this. The police are consulted by the pre-sentence reporter. They will disclose all their suspicions of other unproved, sometimes unfounded allegations. I believe the defence counsel has the duty to make certain that all the positive things that can be said, are said. Counsel's name will appear as a source of the pre-sentence report. There is no hiding it. Taking a pre-sentence reporter to lunch may be more beneficial to your client than discovering a 1952 precedent where a like offender got a fine instead of five years in jail.

The last area which I would like to touch on briefly is the very important role that has emerged for a defence counsel after sentencing where a term of incarceration is involved. Temporary absence programs and release programs have created an additional and very important role for counsel. All material, data and information creating a good case for release can be prepared by counsel and given to the proper authorities to expedite your client's early release.

In conclusion, my point throughout this discussion has been that the role of defence counsel remains adversarial — the ultimate goal being to achieve the best result for your client — no more and no less than that. When we as lawyers forget that, we do our clients a grave disservice and the system itself suffers as well. I can only refer you once again to Lord Brougham's words:

> To save that client by all means and expedients, and at all hazards and costs to other persons, and amongst them, to himself, is his first and only duty; and in performing this duty he must not regard the alarm, the torments, the destruction which he may bring upon others.

That is the kind of advocacy that I would want as a client, and the kind that I believe I am ethically bound to provide as a defence counsel.

NOTES

1. Cooper, "*The United States v. Unterman:* The Role of Counsel at Sentencing," 13 *Crim L. Bull.* 101 at 113.

2. *Report of the Canadian Committee on Corrections,* p. 48.

3. At least, according to a study conducted by Dean Friedland and referred to in his book *Detention Before Trial* (University of Toronto Press, 1965), p. 89.

4. *Carter v. Illinois,* 329 U.S. 173 at 178 (1946).

5. *Trial of Queen Caroline* (1821), referred to in Freedman, *Lawyers' Ethics in an Adversary System* (Indianapolis and New York: Bobbs-Merrill, 1975), p. 9.

6. *Ibid.,* p. 8.

7. Law Reform Commission of Canada, *Restitution and Compensation,* Working Paper No. 5, p. 11.

8. Bynoe, "The Guilty" (Law Society of Upper Canada Special Lectures, 1969), p. 167.

9. American Bar Association Project on Standards for Criminal Justice, *The Prosecution Function and the Defense Function* (Draft edition, 1970).

10. *Ibid.,* p. 285 (emphasis added).

11. *Ibid.,* p. 132.

12. Law Reform Commission of Canada, *The Principles of Sentencing and Dispositions,* Working Paper No. 3, p. 20.

13. Law Reform Commission of Canada, *Imprisonment and Release,* Working Paper No. 11, p. 6.

14. *Ibid.,* p. 6.

15. Technically, this section refers to "compensation" as opposed to "restitution" which appears in, *inter alia,* s. 663 (2). The concepts are virtually identical and I have used simply "restitution" to refer to both.

16. (1978), 2 C.R. (3d) 107 (S.C.C.).

17. *Op. cit.,* note 7, p. 10.

18. See, for example, Klein, "Revitalizing Restitution: Flogging a Horse that may have been Killed for Just Cause," 20 *Crim. L.Q.* 383 (1978).

19. See, for example, the comments of the Law Reform Commission, *op. cit.,* note 12, p. 19.

20. *R. v. Draisey* (Ont. Prov. Ct.), referred to in "Decision on Sentencing," 20 *Crim. L.Q.* (1978), p. 443.

21. *Ibid.,* p. 444.

22. Reprinted in *The Law Society of Upper Canada Gazette,* Vol. 13, No. 1, p. 8.

23. See The Law Society of Upper Canada, *Professional Conduct Handbook,* Rule 8, p. 22.

24. See s. 649 (2.1) of the Criminal Code, as enacted by R.S.C. 1970, c. 2 (2nd Supp.), s. 13, which is simply permissive in allowing a judge to consider time spent in custody prior to sentence. The practice is, however, that such time should be considered. See *R. v. Wooff* (1973), 14 C.C.C. (2d) 396 (Ont. C.A.), and *R. v. Goodale* (1974), 21 C.C.C. (2d) 471 (Ont. C.A.).

25. Kuh, "Trial Techniques: Defense Counsel's Role in Sentencing," 14 *Crim. L. Bull.* 433 at 435.

CHAPTER 14

Sentencing Laws: A Practitioner's View

Morris Manning

In the public perception, the imposition of sentence is the goal of the process of criminal justice. To the student of the legal process, however, the determination of guilt is the preoccupation. The task of the criminal defence lawyer is to pre-empt the criminal process so that the client need never face sentencing. Crown counsel is supposed to be trained not to seek conviction, but to present fairly and objectively the case for the prosecution. He cannot do so if a thirst for punishment lies behind his case. The primary role of the judge in the criminal process sitting as a trier of fact, is to determine what evidence is admissible, and, on this carefully refined set of facts, according to principles sanctified by their evolution through time, pronounce the accused to be guilty or not. He must then impose sentence, a task equally judicial in nature. The judge, in Anglo-Canadian law, like Crown and defence counsel, is not trained in sentencing. While the imposition of sentence is clearly an essential part of our system of criminal justice, it is equally clear that a broad range of rationales lie behind it. These may be deduced from the case law, but they are not stated in statute. The fervour of the thousands from the Portuguese community who marched on the Legislature of Ontario after the murder of Emmanuel Jacques in Toronto two summers ago demanded peremptory justice for the accused in the form of Biblical retribution. The court and its sequestered jury had to go through the paces of cool consideration of facts and what some would decry as technicalities, in order to overturn the presumption of innocence and impose a mandatory life sentence on the party found guilty. At that point and only then, the combination of legislative and judicial wisdom fashioned the sentence to suit the crime as found. This simplistic overview of the system leads to the question of what correspondence, if any, is there between the retributive passion of the public, and the cool conclusion of the public's agent for justice, the criminal court?

Some theorists affirm that after all is said and done, the sentencing function of the courts satisfies the urge for retribution experienced by a wronged party. The imposition of sentence expresses society's view that certain acts ought to be punished. Although the British Columbia Court of Appeal[1] stated in 1967 that the punitive motive for a criminal sentence does not mean vengeance or retribution, the Law Reform Commission of Canada asserted in 1976 an important interest in retribution:

> We still need to do something about wrongful acts: to register our social disapproval, to publicly denounce them and to reaffirm the values violated by them.[2]

In addition to asserting a retributive motive to sentencing, that Commission reflects what the British Columbia Court of Appeal saw as the function of punishment: the assertion of the gravity of an offensive act. In so doing, a criminal penalty shifts from punishing an individual to declaring a code of behaviour to the general public. As will be discussed *infra*, this raises a question as to how this judicial yardstick of moral behaviour is to be fashioned as well as the question of why we allow judges to have a non-answerable legislative function. In this sense a sentence denounces certain behaviour. Denunciation, a close cousin to retribution, is another classic rationale for the imposition of penalties on the criminally culpable. It speaks to the general public more than to the individual offender. Retribution and denunciation have for those who advocate and administrate them, symbolic and practical purposes.

The symbolic statement is clear: "We disapprove." In the retributive sense, a criminal penalty warns other potential offenders, "this could happen to you too." Thus while a penalty will satisfy the retributionist goal of landing "just desserts," it acts to deter the offender and all others against future criminal acts.

Insofar as the imposition of sentence may not only "even the score," and denounce certain behaviour, but also reduce the future incidence of criminal behaviour, sentencing serves a "practical" or utilitarian purpose. Those subscribing to the utilitarian view of sentencing believe that the symbol of society's disapproval will be taken to heart as a practical guide to behaviour by others who, absent the expectation of punishment, would indulge in criminal behaviour.

The more modern view of sentencing attempts to borrow from the disciplines of psychology and sociology, and intends not only deterrence of potential offenders, but reform of criminal characters. This view shifts its focus from the offence to the offender. The trend to better the offender, and not merely protect society, has emerged in the last century. Unlike the retributive sentencer, the reformist takes a compassionate view of the offender. Rather than saying "you have done wrong and now you will pay for it;" the reformist says, "you have done wrong and now we will teach you how not to do so in the future."

Here are four rationales for sentencing: retribution, denunciation, deterrence, and reform of the offender. Acting as an umbrella for all of them is a final factor which must be seen as the primary function of the entire system of criminal justice: the protection of society whether by retribution or reform, deterrence or denunciation. The agency of the system of criminal justice serves the society as a whole for its benefit, rather than leaving justice to be done among individuals. Regardless of whether the prevailing theory sees criminals as amenable to behavioural change, or simply requiring physical deterrence; and regardless of society's shifting focus from the offence to the offender as the object of the criminal law, society as a whole is seen to benefit by the sentencing of those adjudged guilty of criminal acts. And this is what the courts say in exercising their powers[3] and in interpreting the power of the legislators in relation to the criminal law.

Leaving the question of *why* we vest our judges with power to impose sentence, let us look at the powers the courts have to achieve these various goals.

In Canada, the criminal law power lies exclusively with the federal government, by virtue of section 91(27) of the British North America Act. It was not until well after Confederation, in 1892 that a Canadian criminal code was enacted. This was no small achievement, in view of nearly 60 years of effort in England, at that date, to codify the criminal law, and with no success. One commentator praises the transition from common law to codification of offences in these words:

> The maintenance of order in a state and the suppression of deviant behaviour do not require substantive laws. . . . Substantive criminal law assumes importance only when individual freedom is valued as highly as the maintenance of social equilibrium. A law which marks the boundaries of acceptable conduct to the citizen also defines the power of the agencies of social control.[4]

In this view, Canada moved toward a demarcation between individual behaviour and social control before Great Britain did so. By codifying the common law, much of the discretion which lay in the judge's interpretation of precedent was removed by the single voice of the nation's elected representatives. In fact, great discretion remained in the judiciary, at least in the matter of sentences. The application of this discretion, already referred to in relation to the rationale of sentencing, will be examined in detail further on.

The federal power to create criminal law did not exhaust the legislative field. Each province is responsible for the administration of justice and correctional programs. While penitentiaries are within the federal jurisdiction, institutions for reform are the provinces' responsibility. Judges too are appointed by both federal and provincial decree. There is in Canada an intricate weave of provincial and federal powers concerning the criminal law. More significant in this paper's context is the mix of law made by judges and law made by elected legislators.

Codification of the criminal law was an important step in delimiting a judge's power in sentencing, yet no guidelines were given at the time of codification; a situation not yet remedied despite the power base remaining the same.

Until the nineteenth century the criminal law in Britain was defined by many scattered statutes and common law. It represented the monarch's power to proscribe and punish certain acts, for the purpose, according to one scholar,[5] of maintaining peace among his subjects. By the nineteenth century, the statutes and case law representing this royal power had proliferated to such a degree that, like other jurisdictions, a codification of the criminal law was due and needed. Louisiana had recently prepared a penal code by Livingston. Macaulay had drafted a penal code for India. The French penal code (Code Penal) stood as another example to the Commissioners first appointed to codify the criminal law for Great Britain, in 1833.[6] The deliberations of the Commissioners and their successors continued through the century, and while England still has no exhaustively criminal law, the Commissioners work influenced and indeed gave rise to codifications of the criminal law in other places.

Canada was one of these other places. By its constitution, the powers concerning criminal justice were split between the provinces and the federal legislators. The federal government passed a codified criminal code in 1892, only 25 years after Confederation had empowered it to unify the Canadian criminal law. The Code drew heavily upon the work of one of the foremost British Codification scholars, Sir James Fitzjames Stephen. It set out types of offences, types of sentences, and the procedures for their trial and imposition. It was amended by the Dominion Parliament in subsequent years. The most notable revision came in 1953-54, after the patriation of the Supreme Court of Canada. The new Code replaced the 1892 legislation. It contained roughly one-quarter of the number of sections that the old Code contained. A consequence of this is the lesser specificity with which the new law guides judges in imposing sentence.

While the goals of the convicting process are defined and codified, the goals of the sentencing process are not. These must come through the case law to mark the exercise of sentencing powers. Some say that this is proper:

> The statute law of Canada has of necessity provided little guidance for the judicial officer who seeks an answer to this question (what is the goal of the sentence)[7]

It is submitted here, however, that the lack of legislative guidance in the matter leaves an improper amount of discretion in judges, purportedly in exercise of sentencing powers. In the absence of sufficient legislative definition, Parliament effectively delegates its constitutional power concerning the criminal law to the judges. This is not a desirable state of affairs as it leaves legislative powers to those not answerable to an electorate and also leaves them power to fashion their own standards of behaviour.

However, the composite of present laws and the practice under them indicates how the legislators might prudently exercise powers properly theirs.

They must put into law what is now determined by judges with neither mandate nor training to do so. What follows is an examination of the powers which judges possess by law, and how they apply them. A comparison of them will reveal the legislative changes necessary, in order to close the gap between what is in the law books and what the judges have improvised.

The codification of offences included a section incorporating common law offences. The Code purports to be exhaustive in setting out which form of punishment might be imposed. Originally, a sentence could be served through imprisonment, payment of a fine, undergoing whipping, or following the terms of a probation order. Since then, whipping has been eliminated from the Code, and the device of conditional or absolute discharge has been added. Hard labour may no longer be a condition of imprisonment. The unhappy point lies in the fact that apart from these deletions the only change in legislative guidelines to the judiciary has been the absolute and conditional discharge. We have come a very little way since 1892. While the sentencing judge cannot specify any other form of punishment (Code, s. 5(1) (*b*)) it will be seen that in addition to the law-makers and the courts, various administrators shape the sentence in ways the first two groups cannot.

The following summary compiled by a judge of a provincial appellate court shows the orders that may be made on sentencing.

(a) *Absolute and Conditional Discharges*: A discharge cannot be given if the offence is one for which a minimum sentence is prescribed, or if it is punishable, in the proceedings commenced against the accused, i.e., the proceedings in respect of which he is found guilty: *R. v. Sampson* (1975), 23 C.C.C. (2d) 65 (Ont. C.A.) by imprisonment for fourteen years or life: s. 662.1(1). If a conditional discharge is given, a fine cannot be imposed: *R. v. Leonard* (1973), 11 C.C.C. (2d) 527 (Ont. C.A.). If the judge proposes to give an absolute or conditional discharge, he should make a finding of guilt but not convict the accused: *R. v. McInnis* (1973), 13 C.C.C. (2d) 471 (Ont. C.A.). If, however, the judge convicts the accused, this does not preclude him from giving a discharge: *R. v. Sampson, supra.*

(b) *Probation*: The court can impose probation if one of the following sentences has been given: (1) suspended sentence: s. 663(1)(*a*), (2) a fine: s. 663(1)(*b*), (3) imprisonment for a term not exceeding 2 years: s. 663 (1)(*b*); *R. v. Nutter et al.* (1970), 7 C.C.C. (2d) 224 at 227 (B.C.C.A.); *R. v. Callaghan* (1972), 9 C.C.C. (2d) 125 (B.C.C.A.), (4) an intermittent sentence: s. 663(1)(*c*). Probation can be imposed with a fine, *or* with imprisonment, but not with a fine and imprisonment: s. 663 (1)(*b*); *R. v. Smith* (1972), 7 C.C.C. (2d) 468 (N.W.T.); *R. v. Blacquiere* (1975), 24 C.C.C. (2d) 168 (Ont. C.A.). The term of probation cannot exceed 3 years: s. 664 (2)(*b*).

Conditions in a probation order must not be imposed as punishment, but to secure the good conduct of the accused and to prevent the repetition by him of the same offence or the commission of other offences: *R. v. Ziatas* (1973), 13 C.C.C. (2d) 287 (Ont. C.A.); for example, it is improper in a probation order to provide that an accused will not apply for unemployment insurance: *R. v. Caja and Billings* (1977), 36 C.C.C. (2d) 401 (Ont. C.A.).

Restitution or reparation to the victim may be ordered in a probation order: s. 663(2)(e). Such an order must, however, be based on the accused's ability to pay and be related to the actual loss or damage sustained: *R. v. Dashner* (1974), 25 C.R.N.S. 340 (B.C.C.A.), and see also *R. v. Groves* (1975), 26 C.C.C. (2d) 468 (Ont. Prov. Ct.). In ordering restitution or reparation, the court cannot delegate its judicial function to the parole officer; hence, a term of a probation order that requires reparation to be made from time to time as directed by the probation officer until a certain sum is paid is invalid: *R. v. Shorten* (1975), 29 C.C.C. (2d) 528 (B.C.C.A.).

Probation should only be imposed where the offender needs, and will respond to, continuing supervision. If probation will serve no purpose, it should not be imposed; the probation authorities should not be burdened with cases where nothing can be accomplished.

(c) *Fine*: If an accused is convicted of an indictable offence punishable by imprisonment for 5 years or less, and for which no minimum term of imprisonment is provided, he may be fined in addition to or in lieu of any other *punishment.* If a minimum term of imprisonment is prescribed, he may be fined in addition to but not in lieu of *imprisonment:* s. 646(1).

If an accused is convicted of an indictable offence punishable with imprisonment for more than 5 years, he may be fined in addition to but *not,* in lieu of any other *punishment:* s. 646(2). A probation order is "any other punishment"; hence, if an offence is punishable with more than 5 years, the accused can be sentenced to probation *and* a fine: *R. v. Desmarais* (1971), 3 C.C.C. (2d) 523 (Que. C.A.); *R. v. Johnson* (1972), 6 C.C.C. (2d) 380 (B.C.C.A.). However, since a suspended sentence is not a form of punishment, but a suspension of punishment, the court cannot suspend sentence *and* impose a fine for an offence punishable with more than 5 years: *R. v. Agozzino,* [1970] 1 O.R. 480 (C.A.); *R. v. Pawlowski* (1971), 5 C.C.C. (2d) 87 (Man. C.A.); *R. v. Johnson, supra.* To avoid the provisions of s. 646(2) a nominal sentence of 1 day together with the real punishment, i.e., the fine, is often imposed.

Subsections (3) to (11) of s. 646 provide for the giving of time for the payment of a fine and committal for the failure to pay. Section 646(10) contains a special provision for young offenders (i.e., not less than 16 and not more than 21 years of age); it provides that such an offender is not to be committed for failure to pay a fine until the court obtains and considers a report concerning his conduct and means to pay.

(d) *Suspended Sentence*: For an offence, other than one for which a minimum punishment is prescribed, the court can suspend the passing of sentence: s. 663(1)(a). If the passing of sentence is suspended, the court must impose a probation order. In suspending sentence, the court should not indicate to the accused the precise sentence which will be imposed if he fails to meet the conditions prescribed in the probation order: *R. v. Sangster* (1973), 21 C.R.N.S. 339 (Que. C.A.). A sentencing judge should not say, therefore, "I sentence you to 5 years imprisonment which is suspended," but only, "I suspend the passing of sentence." If the accused breaches his probation, the court which suspended sentence is the only one that has jurisdiction to deal with the breach: *R. v. Graham* (1975), 27 C.C.C. (2d) 475 (Ont. C.A.).

If the Crown wishes to have the probation order revoked and sentence passed on an accused whose sentence has been suspended, an information on oath is not required; however, the accused must be given reasonable notice in writing of the Crown's intention to take such proceedings, and the notice should state clearly the nature of the proceedings, the grounds upon which the Crown intends to rely in support of the application, the nature of the order sought, and the hearing date: *R. v. Tuckey* (1977), 34 C.C.C. (2d) 572 (Ont. C.A.). If the accused is also being sentenced for an offence committed while he was on probation, the sentence for the new offence and the sentence for the offence on which sentence was suspended must be concurrent: *Ex parte Risby* (1975), 24 C.C.C. (2d) 211 (B.C.); *R. v. Oakes* (1977), 37 C.C.C. (2d) 84 (Ont. C.A.).

(e) *Intermittent Sentence*: If the sentencing tribunal imposes a sentence of imprisonment, not exceeding 90 days, it may order that the sentence be served intermittently: s. 663(1)(*c*). If an intermittent sentence is imposed, the court must order probation.

(f) *Imprisonment*: If a sentence is for 2 years or more, or if sentences aggregate 2 years or more, the accused must be sentenced to imprisonment in a penitentiary: s. 659(1); however, it is not necessary to name the penitentiary: the Penitentiary Act, R.S.C. 1970, c. P-6, s. 13(1). Unless otherwise ordered, sentences imposed at the same time are deemed to be concurrent: *R. v. Duguid* (1953), 17 C.R. 370 (Ont. C.A.). If a sentence is not made consecutive to a sentence then being served, it will be concurrent to that sentence: *R. v. Woodward*, Oct. 24, 1972, Ont. C.A. (unreported).

If an accused who is already subject to two or more consecutive terms of imprisonment is sentenced to a term of imprisonment consecutive to the term then being served, the sentence is consecutive to the entire term of imprisonment not just the sentence presently being served: *Re Dean and The Queen* (1977), 35 C.C.C. (2d) 217 (Ont. C.A.).

If an accused is mentally ill, the court cannot direct that he serve his sentence in a mental hospital. The proper procedure is to sentence him to "————— years imprisonment in a penitentiary with the recommendation that such sentence be served at the (name the mental health centre) for such period of time and upon such terms as may be agreed upon between the Mental Health Authorities of the Province of ————— and the Penitentiary Service": *R. v. Deans* (1977), 39 C.R.N.S. 338 (Ont. C.A.).

(g) *Life Imprisonment*: When a life sentence is imposed, an accused is sentenced to life imprisonment with normal eligibility for parole: s. 669(*c*). He must be sentenced to a penitentiary: s. 659(1)(*a*). A fixed sentence cannot be made consecutive to a sentence of life imprisonment: *R. v. Sinclair* (1972), 6 C.C.C. (2d) 523 (Ont. C.A.). It has been held in England that it is desirable that a life sentence should be concurrent, not consecutive, to another fixed sentence: *R. v. Jones,* [1962] A.C. 635.

(h) *Imprisonment for an Escape*: A sentence for an escape can be made concurrent or consecutive to the remanent: s. 137(1) as amended by the Criminal Law Amendment Act, 1977. A prisoner can be sentenced to penitentiary for an escape even if the time to be served is less than 2 years: s. 137(1); *R. v. Gaddie; R. v. Purdy* (1956), 114 C.C.C. 65 (Ont. C.A.).

(i) *Dangerous Offenders*: The Code defines what is meant by a "dangerous offender": see Part XXI as introduced by the Criminal Law Amendment Act, 1977. A dangerous offender may be sentenced to detention in a penitentiary for an indeterminate term: s. 688. An application to declare a person a dangerous offender must be made before sentence for the offence for which the accused has been convicted. The National Parole Board is required by s. 695.1(1) to review after three years, and not later than every two years thereafter, the condition, history, and circumstances of the offender to determine whether he would be granted parole.

(j) *Firearms:* The Criminal Law Amendment Act, 1977 has made a number of changes in offences involving the use of firearms and offensive weapons. Some of the more important are the following: Section 83 of the Code creates a new offence of using a firearm in the commission or flight after the commission of an indictable offence. The sentence for the offence, which has a mandatory minimum term, is to be *consecutive* to any other punishment for an offence arising out of the same event or any other sentence to which the offender is subject at the time. Section 98(1) provides that if a person is convicted (a) of an offence in which violence against a person is used and for which the offender may be sentenced to 10 years or more, or (b) an offence under s. 83, the court *must* make an order of prohibition, in the case of a first offender for 5 years and in any other case for 10 years, for having in his possession any firearm, ammunition or explosive substance; the period runs from the release from imprisonment. Section 98(2) is similar to former s. 95(1). By s. 98(2) where a person is convicted of an offence involving the use, carriage, possession, handling or storage of a firearm or ammunition or of an offence, other than one enumerated in s. 98(1), in which violence against a person was used, the court has the discretion to make an order of prohibition for a period not exceeding 5 years after release from imprisonment.

(k) *Compensation, Restitution or Forfeiture:* An order for forfeiture is authorized by ss. 446, 446.1 and 447, compensation by s. 653(1), and restitution by s. 655(1) of the Code. A compensation order should only be made in clear and simple cases where no great amount is at stake. In most situations, the appropriate court to deal with these issues is the civil court: *R. v. Kneeshaw,* [1974] 1 All E.R. 896 (C.A.). Similarly, a restitution order should only be made in uncomplicated cases, i.e., not involving difficult questions of law as to title to property, or goods of substantial value: *Stamp v. United Dominions Trust (Commercial) Ltd.,* [1967] 1 Q.B. 418.

Dealing for a moment with some of the above powers it will be seen that the reported case law leaves much to be desired in the practical work-a-day world of the criminal justice system. For example, while the power to give discharges is there, it is seldom imposed. The reason for seeking it is to be able to have a clear record and to have no "conviction," yet some judges privately admit that that is precisely why they do not grant it. Probation is too often only given where the individual will "respond" to after care of this kind. Thus, the judge becomes dependent upon the probation officer's report. If it says he will respond, I will impose probation, if not, I will not. Consider, however, the predicament of the accused who doesn't get along with the interviewer, or who although having testified and maintained his innocence, is reported not to be a good risk for probation because he has not admitted his guilt. These situations are not discussed in the case law yet are part of the process.

The suspended sentence deserves a place by itself as it is here that the greatest potential lies for reform in our present system. Why shouldn't we develop a system whereby a suspended sentence is imposed automatically in most offences. Whether the goal of the system be rehabilitation of the offender or protection of society, both can be achieved. The accused knows he must be reformed and stay out of trouble or he will be sentenced to a period of incarceration. Society is monitoring him (thus achieving some degree of probation) by having him report and deal with its agents, and, hopefully, work with him to achieve real reform of the individual.

For a few offences, a judge has no leeway in imposing sentence. First degree murder means life imprisonment without eligibility for parole until 25 years of the sentence have been served.[8] A verdict of second degree murder leaves the judge with discretion only to increase from ten years the number of years which must be served prior to eligibility for parole.[9] Importation of narcotics bears a minimum sentence of seven years incarceration.[10] Impaired driving offences carry a series of minimum penalties, which are greater for subsequent offences.[11] Otherwise, the penalties for indictable offences are set out as maxima in relation to each offence defined by the Code. Where it is not set out, the maximum term of imprisonment may be five years.[12] Summary conviction offences are punishable by a fine of $500 or six months imprisonment, or both.[13] An indeterminate term of imprisonment may be imposed if an accused person is found, upon application, to be an "habitual criminal".[14] Finally, an accused person found to be not guilty by reason of insanity will be ordered held in strict custody in a place named by the judge, "until the pleasure of the lieutenant governor of the province is known."[15]

These are the "guidelines" given to the sentencing judge. Let's be practical, however, and realize that these guidelines are judge-made principles set in the most part, by appellate courts, paid lip service to by lower court judges and seldom really applied. Seldom does a trial judge, hearing many cases per day, compare and analyze sentences and legal principles. More often than not, by pressure of time and circumstance, he makes a quick judgment call looking only at the parameters of what he has heard, what the evidence has been and what is the range permitted by the section of the Code. The judge is not, however, to be blamed. Parliament has failed to define standards or to set guidelines to assist the courts and has forced the judges to look to after-care workers, other judges' opinions and to themselves in order that they come up with the "right" sentence. While the substantive offences and procedures are exhaustively defined by the legislators, and although the Code states that:

> a person who is convicted of that offence is not liable to any punishment in respect thereof other than the punishment prescribed by this Act or by the enactment that creates the offence.[16]

the fact remains that the administrators alluded to earlier affect the actual sentence. These administrators fall into two groups. Probation officers will prepare pre-sentence reports, supervise the terms of probation, if it is imposed, and determine where and how a term of imprisonment will be served. The Parole Board determines how much of the term of imprisonment will actually be served, and what the terms of early release will be.

The pre-sentence report affects the judge's disposition in sentencing. The report is confined to the background, the character, and the circumstances of the accused, it should not attempt to deal with the facts surrounding the commission of the offence.[17] The use which the judge may make of the report is somewhat limited: he may only apply it to his choice of penalties allowed by the Code. He may not prescribe the institution where imprisonment shall be served, and cannot supervise the terms of probation he may set out. Those functions fall to the probation officer. Having regard to the fact that most probation departments are overbooked, not trained to be objective fact gatherers and underpaid, one can question the quality of their reports. While one can and sometimes does contest the statements in the reports, the tenor of an unfavourable report sits in the back of the judge's mind and because the reporter is an "objective" third party, the judge relies heavily on him.

How does a judge determine an appropriate sentence? A reading of case law and practical experience in the courts shows that if judges choose to rely on other judges (by way of following precedents or persuasive authority in other jurisdictions) they often choose those decisions which must accord with their own views. Here again one finds little consistency. The "tariff" or appropriate range of sentence as established through the cases is often referred to by scholars and judges. The application of the tariff in determining sentence is no individualized measure but rather represents the generally accepted "price" of proscribed behaviour. Checklists of proper considerations may be compiled from the cases on sentencing. The individual must be foremost, according to some; others stress the offence. One case states simply that proper sentencing requires a careful consideration of the aims of sentencing.[18] Such a direction can only lead to confusion, as the aims of sentencing range from retribution to rehabilitation. Even if one accepts the protection of society as the overriding goal of the sentence, the limited power of the judge in imposing a sentence, and his limited training in how to protect society makes the attainment of this goal illusory. Indeed, the judicial nature of determinations of sentence may be questioned. A judge of the Ontario Court of Appeal finds it necessary to point out to his brother judges that

> The sentence hearing is as much a part of the trial as the proceedings leading to the verdict. It is not an interview or a conference, and it should not be conducted as such.[19]

When even the judges must be admonished that sentencing is part of their judicial function, one must be concerned about the factors in the process which make it seem otherwise.

How is it, then, that judges seem so "out of their element" in imposing sentence? To answer this question, we need look no farther than the other actors in the sentencing process: the legislators and the administrators. Colin Howard, an Australian authority on the criminal law set out his framework for examining the question of dissatisfaction with judicial sentencing:

> The two most general criticisms of the judiciary are that their sentences are less uniform or consistent than they ought to be, and that they make too little allowance for individual variations between offenders. It is to be observed that these two propositions are inconsistent with each other, for a policy of fitting the sentence to the offender rather than to the offence necessarily produces sentencing decisions which appear to be unpredictable when put in tabular or statistical form. At this level, therefore, dissatisfaction with judicial sentencing does no more than reflect uncertainty or disagreement among its critics as to the function which the sentencing tribunal should be serving.[20]

Thus Howard brings us back to our original inquiry as to the purpose of sentencing.

A survey of recent cases illuminates the inquirer as to the motivation of judges in sentencing. One may occasionally find their views on the question, of "what is the purpose of sentencing." Three sets of examples are used to illustrate what is distilled from the many cases read.

Let us start with the story of a crafty car dealer, who pulled some scam together to sell more cars by having financing available for the entire purchase price.[21] He was charged with fraud, and upon conviction, a $500 fine was imposed on him for each of the 15 counts. This is a penalty aimed at the offender. Other cases of corrupt or fraudulent behaviour, decided during that period of time, indicate that the principal factor to consider in imposing sentence is general deterrence. Now, while others tempted to enter into similarly deliberate and sophisticated enterprise (falsifying invoices to the bank) may be convinced that there would be no gain to be had from such activity, in the face of such fines, the most apparent message from the sentence is "an eye for an eye, a tooth for a tooth." Classic retribution. It is not even modified to restitution, but rather the society claiming its just desserts. The string of 15, $500 fines stands as a modern day lash for each wrongdoing. If it can be characterized as deterrent rather than retributive surely it is individual, not general.

But what happens when the wrongful behaviour is more clearcut, the method simpler, albeit cruder, and the victim more clearly defined? In the car financing fraud, it is difficult after the fact, to identify the victim. No one actually loses property, someone profits and the car purchaser and financer both get what they want. In the case of the financer the bank probably has a right to more money, but it certainly isn't losing money. The penalty imposed reflects retributive motives. With the simpler crimes against rights of property, a different pattern of sentencing emerges. The offence is different. As pointed out about, the person who loses out in a theft situation is pretty easy to determine. Ontario statistics show that about twice as many get charged with theft under $200 (27,228) as with frauds (14,954).[22] It is clear on examination of recent sentence cases for theft that although the maximum penalty available on procedure by indictment for theft under (two years) is rarely imposed, a jail term commonly accompanies conviction. Where there is a victim, a sentence reflecting deterrence is imposed. The number of sentences of 23 months, and the number of appeals whose purpose is clearly to reduce a sentence to 23 months indicates that a live consideration in imposing sentence is the institutional destination. In sending these lesser property offenders to provincial institutions, the judges stress rehabilitation. The incidence of jail terms is remarkable, where the amount in question is less than $200, the victim plainly identified, and the sophistication of the method negligible in most cases. Why send these offenders to jail, instead of fining them as with the fraudulent actor? Why not effect restitution if the sentence deprives the convicted person of money? There must be different motivation in sentencing these two crimes, though they often involve similar amounts of money, and no violence.

Some cases[23] suggest that this range of jail term is imposed to achieve individual deterrence. Appeals to reduce sentence may win where undue emphasis is placed on general deterrence. The use of 23-month sentences indicates a desire to place these individuals in provincial institutions, where rehabilitation rather than sheer protection of society is stressed. In one case, the judge clearly chose a provincial institution in order to protect a convicted person who had just been released from a term under the Lieutenant Governor's warrant.[24]

One might conclude that the purpose of sentencing this type of offence is to achieve individual deterrence with a view to rehabilitation and re-entry into the community. Incarceration in a provincial institution is the answer.

This creates a sharp contrast beside the sentences meted out for different purposes in cases of fraud. There, the penalty is directed at the offender quite personally, and for no purpose but the sake of punishment, takes money (not time) from him.

Another pair of contrasting rationales for sentencing similar crimes may be found in cases of indecent assault. In one case, the Crown won its appeal to raise a suspended sentence to a jail term, for a man whose offence consisted in removing his female victim's panties. Despite his good community standing, incarceration was necessary to achieve general deterrence. For another Ontarion in good standing with his community, a suspended sentence was raised to a jail term for his first offence. He forced an act of fellatio at knife point from a 14-year-old boy. In that case, the protection of the community and the expression of the community's abhorrence of the act in question were stated to be the court's motivation. It was the Ontario Court of Appeal both times, although differently constituted.[25]

Neither offence was violent; both were sexual crimes. The sentences differed. One called for an example to be made of the offender: to deter the general incidence of the offence, he had to go to jail. The other required jail to protect society, and express its collective revulsion. Thus while the offending act and the resulting penalty are similar, the nexus differs. All men must be deterred from committing the act of sexual assault on a female; in the case of the man whose object of sexual assault was male, we express revulsion through the law.

A third case confirms the differing rationales. A scout master of previous good behaviour was sentenced on appeal to a jail term. He had been convicted of assault with intent to commit buggery, in relation to his cub scouts. The reason for imposing the term, by the Ontario Court of Appeal, was once again to reflect society's view of the acts. Might one deduce that where the victim of the untoward sexual act is male, as is the offender, society sends him to jail to express its disgust; while such male behaviour toward a female elicits the symbolic signal to others not to follow? Such is the distinction between denunciatory sentencing and sentences for general deterrence.[26]

The third set of examples I would like to take illustrates again the awkward manoevring which judges undertake in order to exercise the limited flexibility of their sentencing power. Judges will urge early release, or no incarceration, if rehabilitation is the goal of sentencing. Individual deterrence is served by a term in a provincial institution. General deterrence, and the rare occurrence of retributive sentencing stress the need to protect society and denounce the actor; they impose heavy deprivation of time and money. These are the sentences which seem to fall upon those convicted of marijuana possession: first offenders are rarely imprisoned, but upon subsequent offences, the purpose and type of sentence changes.

The rationales seem to range, in proportion to the available disposition:

— Rehabilitation calls for early release or no custody, for best re-entry to the community.
— Individual deterrence results in a term of under 23 months, thus in a provincial institution.
— General deterrence seems to be ascribed where rehabilitation is not a consideration, where a record indicates little hope of individual deterrence. Incarceration, often in a federal institution, is the result.
— Denunciatory sentences are attached to moral crimes, such as illegal homosexual behaviour.
— Finally, sophisticated crime is paid for on sophisticated terms: money. As with the fraud case, and other instances where a substantial fine is imposed, it may be the most suitable way of impressing the wrongdoer. It looks like straight retribution.

What then do the judges try to achieve with their sentencing powers? Colin Walker's spectrum of rationales appears through the cases showing motivation for sentence: rehabilitation, and deterrence, and on occasion, denunciation and retribution. And, according to the classic case on sentencing, *Wilmott,*[27] all are in the name of society's protection.

An interesting recent example of the "spectrum" approach is seen in *R. v.*

Belanger.[28] There a 17-year-old was charged with having sexual intercourse with a female person not his wife under the age of 14 years. He was sentenced to three years in the penitentiary. The girl was 12 years old and became pregnant. The appellant's statement was to the effect that he did not force the intercourse. The court in reducing the sentence adopted the following statement of Lord Justice Lawton in *R. v. Taylor:*

> This Court now has the task of deciding how the law should be administered. It is clear from what the trial judge said that there is doubt amongst many, at the present time, as to what is the proper way of dealing with these cases. What does not seem to have been appreciated by the public is the wide spectrum of guilt which is covered by the offence known as having unlawful sexual intercourse with a girl under the age of 16. At one end of that spectrum is the youth who stands in the dock, maybe 16, 17 or 18, who has had what started off as a virtuous friendship with a girl under the age of 16. That virtuous friendship has ended with their having sexual intercourse with one another. At the other end of the spectrum is the man in a supervisory capacity, a schoolmaster or social worker, who sets out deliberately to seduce a girl under the age of 16 who is in his charge. The penalties appropriate for the two types of cases to which I have just referred are very different indeed. Nowadays, most judges would take the view, and rightly take the view, that when there is a virtuous friendship which ends in unlawful sexual intercourse, it is inappropriate to pass sentences of a punitive nature. What is required is a warning to the youth to mend his ways. At the other end, a man in a supervisory capacity who abuses his position of trust for his sexual gratification, ought to get a sentence somewhere near the maximum allowed by law, which is two years' imprisonment. In between there come many degrees of guilt. A common type of offender is the youth who picks up a girl of loose morals at a dance, takes her out into the local park and, behind the bushes, has sexual intercourse with her. This is the kind of offence which is normally dealt with by a fine. When a man in his twenties, or older, goes off to a dance and picks up a young girl, he can expect to get a much stiffer fine, and if the girl is under 15 he can expect to go to prison for a short time. A young man who deliberately sets out to seduce a girl under the age of 16 can expect to go to detention. The older man who deliberately so sets out can expect to go to prison. Such is the wide variety of penalties which can be applied in this class of case.[29]

Brooke, J.A. then went on to state:

> This case is at the low end of the spectrum. We think the learned trial Judge was wrong in saying that he could not consider a non-custodial sentence and in the circumstances, this was a proper case in which to suspend sentence and place the appellant on probation. The whole proceedings from the arrest, public trial and conviction of this young man would be a substantial deterrent to those of his age group in the community. Besides there is also a deterrent value in probation for in the event of its breach the appellant may once again find himself before the Court. Having regard to his background it would have been quite appropriate to place him on probation. In our view, in these

circumstances the appeal must succeed, the sentence is reduced to time served and a term of probation of one year.[30]

How do the judges dispense these different modes of protecting society? Their options are few: federal penitentiary; provincial institution; the institution resulting on a Lieutenant Governor's warrant; or probation. The extent to which the judge may determine conditions of probation is limited: that is the task of after-care workers, at least, this is so according to the theory of rehabilitation. This is the domain of social workers and psychologists and other specialists. It is not the judicial task. The judge merely names the forum: for rehabilitation, place the subject in social care workers' hands; to deter either the individual or the general incidence of the act, place him in the heavy-handed care of corrections custody; to restrain dangerous offenders, whose past record leaves no credible notion that the penalty will result in changed lifestyle, incarcerate him in federal, maximum security penitentiary. And where appropriate, slap the wrists of the offender in an exhibition of "making somebody *pay*" for his wrongs. Fines, restitution and community service may be attendant features on a probation order which the judge may prescribe. If a jail term is imposed the judge may tinker with the span and location of the sentence. The judge's ruling will determine whether a sentence of incarceration must be served continuously or intermittently, consecutive or concurrent to other terms, and at what time application for early release may be made. On verdicts of second degree murder, the judge is obliged to solicit although not to follow the recommendation of the jury. He is not required to solicit or follow a pre-sentence report. In one case, a sentence was reduced upon introduction on appeal of fresh evidence: a pre-sentence report which had not been made available at trial. In many cases the judge will not consider the pre-sentence report.

There is no requirement on the judge to follow the recommendation of either Crown or defence counsel. Thus the curious result may sometimes obtain, that both Crown and defence counsel will recommend a sentence, which the judge overrides. This is an exercise of judicial independence, said the court in *R. v. Simoneau*.[31] Yet, if the Crown counsel represents the public interest and the defence counsel represents the accused's interest, whose interest does the judge represent, premising that both counsel are equal to their tasks?

So the judge's mission in sentencing is to protect society, and along this basis range the available modes for doing so: rehabilitation, deterrence (general and individual), denunciation and sometimes retribution. Despite these lofty goals, the determination of the appropriate goal and how to achieve it is made with rather crude tools. A judge needn't listen to a social worker's pre-sentence report, but if he determines that a social worker could rehabilitate the offender to the community, then the judge must deliver the offender to probation and have no say in how the rehabilitation shall be had. That area, after all is the social worker's domain. As the motive for penalty travels down the spectrum through deterrence towards retribution, the judge gets to determine with more certainty what happens to the offender. Deterrence of the individual's behaviour is carried out through provincial institutions, with the goal of changing the offender. A judge still surrenders the convicted person to social workers, in expressing the desirability of reforming the person. Probation is used as a deterrent also. But when reform seems a naive goal, and the offender takes courts and crime as part of his lifetime, the power of the sentencing judge is greatest — a sentence of years' incarceration in maximum security institutions, or punitive and exemplary fines are imposed.

Clearly then the task of the judge is not to fashion rehabilitative programs, but to mete out terms of punishment. Rehabilitation is the domain of the social care worker. This is not to say that rehabilitation is not a proper motive for a judge to ascribe to sending someone to a provincial institution, or to prescribing early release on probation. Where Parliament most clearly wants judicial discretion and independence in sentencing is in determining the location, duration, and degree of penalty. After that, it is not the judge's responsibility.[32]

Thus, it can be seen that the judges task is not only not easy, it is next to impossible. Despite the lofty statements in the case law, each court and each judge seems destined to apply its own views. The luck of the draw or the fall of the roulette wheel ball may determine what length of time a person spends incarcerated. Consider the bold facts in many appeals where sentences similar to "12 months definite and 6 months indeterminate" are varied to "6 months definite and 12 months indeterminate" as the result of an "error in principle." Is a change in the appellate court really the result of any "error" let alone one of principle? Is it really a matter of new evidence which was not before the trial judge? Or is it really a matter of three judges instead of one; a matter of quiet consideration with a different kind of caseload; or a matter of an appellate court not falling into a pattern of imposing a tariff. In this area of law we must get away from this type of speculation and we must relieve the judiciary of this responsibility and have those who should be setting the guidelines assume their proper role.

The legislature must hold the ultimate responsibility for sentencing laws. As we have seen, the motives behind sentencing change as society does. Only the legislators are directly responsible to the electorate, and that is the only guarantee, ephemeral as it is, that the process of the criminal law will allow justice. Society's mode of protecting itself through the criminal justice system has certainly changed through time (the most marked recent trend to rehabilitation), but it is the legislators who must instruct the judges how to reflect that in the daily courtroom reality.

Quite properly, the legislators have not assigned the task of rehabilitation to the judges. With the rising prominence in the "corrections" field of rehabilitators, one nearly loses sight of the judge's role. The judge determines the shape of deterrent and other non-rehabilitative penalties.

It is Parliament that must set standards for judicial exercise of sentencing power. It is submitted here that the Criminal Code provides inadequate guidance in the area, and that as such, Parliament is leaving an unduly unfettered discretion to its appointees, and the appointees of the provinces, on the bench. In order that the federal government execute its part of the task of maintaining peace throughout Canada, it must inform the judges and the people by statutory decree of the goals of sentencing and appropriate means of achieving them. The prominence, in the field of criminal justice activity, of after-care workers, in the execution of the provincial mandate to administer justice as defined by the federal government, blurs the distinction between the federal justice function, and the provincial corrections programs. The rehabilitative bent of the last century has judges second-guessing social workers and psychologists. Judges are not trained for this, and have indicated their awareness that supervising the prisoner upon conviction is not a judge's task. That belongs to the provincial authority, the rehabilitator. In the judicial exercise of the sentencing power, a judge applies legislative standards to the individual. So little does the judge influence the conduct of the sentence, that they may not even specify the location of imprisonment. Only the duration of imprisonment, or the sum of monetary penalty, or its suspension may be determined by a judge.

Despite considerable judicial attention to the possibility and suitability of devoting rehabilitative measures to the offender, the cases and the theory show that in the last resort it is still the "tariff" — the "going rate" — which is taken as the most appropriate manner of measuring sentence.[33]

Let us return to Colin Howard's statement of the most common criticisms of judicial sentencing.

> Sentences are less uniform or consistent than they ought to be, and . . . they make too little allowance for individual variations between offenders.[34]

Against the background of the preceding analysis of the case law and the judges' powers, one observes that the lack of uniformity may result from a preoccupation with fitting the sentence to the offender through methods of which the judge is not properly seized; and that the insufficient individualization may be due to the rigid case law of the tariff.

Howard's further observation was that the criticisms he cites are inconsistent with each other. This is also reflected in the judges' stated reasons for sentence: they are often inconsistent. This indicates that imbalance in imposition of what stands for the unified criminal law. Once again, one returns to the legislators as the source of a remedy. Unify the criminal law, codify the case law! The cases confirm what the proper considerations are: protection of society through rehabilitation of the offender, deterrence of the offender's repeated behaviour, deterrence to others, and retributive or denunciatory sentencing. A pattern emerges from the cases defining the appropriate penalty. These should be expressed by the legislators in the positive criminal law.

A scheme for reformed laws on sentencing would incorporate the following principles:

(1) In cases where the desire to rehabilitate offenders is pre-dominant, and the "tariff" shows no imprisonment, Parliament should prescribe a suspended sentence. The purpose of the suspension of execution has been described as "to avoid the bad influence of a short-term prison sentence on a person considered capable of improvement."[35] This is precisely what the cases attempt for first offenders for minor property offences.

(2) For subsequent violations in the first category, and where rehabilitation is no longer a consideration, the sentences move into a sliding scale of years of imprisonment. The number of years will attempt to juggle such factors as provincial or federal institution, and the effect of automatic remission. However, judicial attempts to control factors after the fashioning of a sentence is improper. Where rehabilitation is no longer a consideration, as with continuing offenders, Parliament should impose mandatory penalties, foreclosing the possibility of suspension of sentence.

(3) The duration of imprisonment or probation, or the amount of a penalty are, as we have seen, most properly the judges' domain. Yet even here unification into statute is desirable. Again, the case law creates a strong precedent. It should be ratified by legislation, enacted by those who have the mandate to create Canada's criminal law. A reformed law on sentence would narrow the legislated range of penalty. For example the Criminal Code presently structures the penalties for driving with more than 80 milligrams of alcohol in the blood:

> S. 236(1) Every one who drives a motor vehicle or has the care or control of a motor vehicle, whether it is in motion or not, having consumed alcohol in such a quantity that the proportion thereof in his blood exceeds 80 milligrams of alcohol in 100 millilitres of blood, is guilty of an indictable offence or an offence punishable on summary conviction and is liable
>
> (a)   for a first offence, to a fine of not more than two thousand dollars and not less than fifty dollars or to imprisonment for six months or to both;
>
> (b)   for a second offence, to imprisonment for not more than one year and not less than fourteen days; and
>
> (c)   for each subsequent offence, to imprisonment for not more than two years and not less than three months.

This type of range could be applied to the drug offences in the Narcotic Control Act, and resolve the glaring inconsistencies which occur there. The penalty section now permitting up to seven years imprisonment for simple possession of a narcotic results in such anomalies as three months imprisonment for a Manitoba youth possessing a few grams of marijuana, and a sentence of community service for a rock star in possession in Toronto of 22 grams of high quality heroin. Justice would surely be seen to be done if that penalty section elaborated somewhat on appropriate measures under it.

(4) Finally, a statutory statement of the goals of sentencing would be a progressive innovation in the Canadian criminal law. While the traditional

form in Anglo-Canadian law has shunned such explanations of purpose, the American experience shows that once in place such statements of intention are well-used in the courts, and assist uniformity in interpreting and applying the law. Recent Canadian statutes show a tendency to break with tradition and make such statement, e.g., Canadian Human Rights Act, 1976-77, (Can.), c. 33, ss. 1 and 49; Environmental Protection Act, 1972, Vol. 2 (Ont.), c. 86, s. 2; proposed Evidence Code of Law Reform Commission of Canada, s. 1.

This paper urges the statutory expression of the goals of sentencing, and real statutory guidance to judges in the imposition of sentence. The case law virtually says it all now; the Criminal Code is a mere outline on the matter. The legislators have the mandate to create the law; the judges do not.

Legislative language sanctioning the use of suspended sentences for first offenders, with mandatory penalties to be served thereafter would remedy many of the ills we have noted in sentencing. A student of the suspended sentence describes it in most desirable terms:

> In a general climate of penal and penological thought which leans towards restoring a sense of responsibility to the individual's social behaviour, the suspended sentence . . . is a valid and sound method of non-institutional reaction against crime, based on consideration of the personality of the offender.[36]

NOTES

1. *R. v. Hinch and Salanski,* [1968] 3 C.C.C. 39, 43, 44 (B.C. C.A.).

2. Law Reform Commission of Canada, *Our Criminal Law* (Ottawa: Queen's Printer, 1976).

3. *R. v. Wilmott,* [1967] 1 C.C.C. 171 (Ont. C.A.); *R. v. Nutter* (1970), 7 C.C.C. (2d) 224 (B.C. C.A.); *R. v. Thompson* (1953), 107 C.C.C. 237 (B.C. C.A.).

4. D.A. Thomas, "Form and Function in Criminal Law," in P.R. Glazebrook (ed.), *Reshaping the Criminal Law* (London: Stevens and Sons, 1978), p. 21.

5. Nigel Walker, *Crime and Punishment in Great Britain* (Edinburgh University Press, 1965), p. 45.

6. Rupert Cross, "The Reports of the Criminal Law Commissioners (1833-1849) and the Abortive Bills of 1853," in Glazebrook, *op. cit.,* note 4, p. 7.

7. J.C. McRuer, "Sentencing," 3 *Can. J. Con.* (1961), pp. 207, 213.

8. Criminal Code, R.S.C. 1970, c. C-34, s. 218, as re-enacted by 1974-75-76, c. 105, s. 5.

9. Code, s. 670.

10. Narcotic Control Act, R.S.C. 1970, c. N-1, s. 5(2).

11. Code, s. 234, as amended by 1974-75-76, c. 93, s. 14.

12. Code, s. 658.

13. Code, s. 722.

14. Code, s. 688, as amended by 1976-77, c. 53, s. 14.

15. Code, s. 542(2).

16. Code, s. 5(1)(*b*).

17. "Decisions on Sentencing," *R. v. Rudyk*, 17 *Cr.L.Q.* (1974-75), pp. 347-349.

18. *R. v. Anderson* (1970), 1 C.C.C. (2d) 228 (Man. C.A.).

19. L. Houlden, "Sentencing" (unpublished paper, February, 1978).

20. Colin Howard, "An Analysis of Sentencing Authority," in Glazebrook, *op. cit.,* note 4, p. 411.

21. *R. v. Dekker Chevrolet-Oldsmobile Ltd.,* [1978] 4 W.W.R. 569 (Alta. Prov. Ct.).

22. Provincial Secretariat for Justice (Ontario), *Criminal Justice Statistics for Ontario, 1977,* Table 2.4.

23. *R. v. Cruikshanks* (1977), 22 N.S.R. (2d) 704 (C.A.); *R. v. Blackler* (1978), 2 W.C.B. 116 (Jan. 16, 1978, Ont. C.A.); *R. v. Lapointe* (1978), 2 W.C.B. 119 (Jan. 16, 1978, Ont. C.A.); *R. v. Champagne; R. v. Boudreau* (1978), 2 C.R. (3d) S-15 (Ont. C.A.).

24. *R. v. Hannigan* (1978), 2 W.C.B. 119 (Jan. 17, 1978, Ont. C.A.).

25. *R. v. Laurin* (1977), 2 W.C.B. 11 (Nov. 4, 1977, Ont. C.A.); *R. v. Pearse* (1977), 2 W.C.B. 11 (Nov. 21, 1977, Ont. C.A.).

26. *R. v. Webster* (1978), 2 W.C.B. 328 (May 2, 1978, Ont. C.A.).

27. *R. v. Wilmott,* [1967] 1 C.C.C. 171 (Ont. C.A.).

28. *R. v. Belanger* (1979), 46 C.C.C. (2d) 266 (Ont. C.A.).

29. *R. v. Taylor* (1977), 1 W.L.R. 612 at 615.

30. *R. v. Belanger, supra,* note 28, at 268-269.

31. *R. v. Simoneau,* [1978] 3 W.W.R. 461 (Man. C.A.).

32. *Supra,* note 31.

33. See generally: D.A. Thomas, *Principles of Sentencing* (London: Heinemann, 1970); Nigel Walker, *Sentencing in a Rational Society* (New York: Basic Books, 1971); Rupert Cross, *The English Sentencing System* (London: Butterworths, 1975).

34. *Op. cit.,* note 20.

35. Marc Ancel, *Suspended Sentence* (London: Heinemann, 1971), p. 43.

36. *Ibid.,* p. 72.

Part 6

THE PRACTICE OF SENTENCING

CHAPTER 15

Sentencing Guidelines: A Judicial Viewpoint

E. M. Culliton

For the past few decades we have been experiencing a rapidly changing social order: a social order in which there are new concepts of moral and social values; in which there are changing concepts of legal obligations; and in which there is a social rather than a purely legal approach to the administration and enforcement of criminal law. This changing social order must be recognized, and part of this recognition must take the form of changes in the law to meet the requirements of our new and complex society.

Within such societies there exists substantial concern that disrespect for the law is growing; that disrespect being evidenced by an increasing crime rate, by protests involving violence to persons and destruction of property and by open defiance of public and police authority. The causes of such behaviour are as complex as the society in which they occur, but there is a substantial segment of the public which feels that the courts have contributed and are contributing to this disrespect. It is contended that sentences imposed by the courts are too lenient, that lenient sentences are both a licence and an encouragement for individuals to continue a life of crime. There are, on the other hand, those who argue that the criminal law is out of step with the times, that the entire penal system is a failure and that harsh and severe sentences are causing recidivism.

While these conflicting views relate to only one facet of the administration and enforcement of criminal law, these conflicting views cannot be ignored. They raise the whole question of the sentencing process, a question which is of continuing concern to the public, the Bar, to trial judges and particularly to judges of appellate courts.

The discussion of this question involves two distinct areas. First, a full review of the whole sentencing process to determine whether it is sufficiently effective, either in the deterrence of crime, or in the reformation or rehabilitation of the offender, and, if not, what alternative process could or should be adopted. This is an area in which lawyers, laymen and academics may pursue their studies and pronounce their views uninhibited by the restrictions which necessarily flow from the responsibility inherent in the judge's requirement to apply the law. While the judiciary have views, and probably strong views, as to the value of a particular type of punishment it is usually prudent not to express them publicly. To do so may raise in the mind of the offender or in the minds of the public, the suggestion of bias in the judge. A judge must always remember that laws are passed by Parliament and court's function is to interpret and apply the law and not to legislate. That does not necessarily mean the law is static, because it is encumbent upon the judge to apply the established law to new and changing situations. Generally speaking, however, judges should adhere to the admonition of Lord Loreburn: "A Court of law has nothing to do with a Canadian Act of Parliament, lawfully passed, except to give it effect according to its tenor."[1]

The second area in discussing sentencing is what guidelines should the courts follow under existing law so as to make an effective contribution to the criminal process, in terms of the protection of the public and the reformation and rehabilitation of the offender? This is the area with which members of the judiciary, from a practical standpoint, are primarily concerned. Both for trial and appellate courts there is no problem more important and more difficult than the determination of an appropriate sentence. This is the case because in the imposition or the review of a sentence the freedom and liberty of the accused person are involved.

While sentences are imposed by trial judges, the Court of Appeal in each province is the court of last resort in sentence appeals. Parliament has not only declared the provincial Court of Appeal to be the court of last resort in sentence appeals, it has also given to that Court an almost unfettered discretion in the disposition of such appeals. There is some difference of opinion among judges of courts of appeal as to how that discretion should be exercised. There are those who say, that in a sentence appeal, the court of appeal should interfere rarely; that sentencing is primarily the responsibility of the trial judge and the judges of the court of appeal should only interfere with the sentence if it shocks their sense of justice. There are others who say that in carrying out its obligation to consider the fitness of the sentence appealed against, the court has a duty to go into the matter fully and vary or alter the sentence imposed to what it believes to be a fitting and proper sentence, and that in so doing, its discretion is unfettered. This latter view has been adhered to by the Saskatchewan Court of Appeal for many years.

In considering sentence appeals, there rests upon the Court of Appeal two primary duties:

(1) that of establishing the principles to guide the trial courts of the province in the determination of an appropriate sentence. In this field the Court must, from time to time, review these principles and determine the changing emphasis to be placed upon the various factors, in accordance with continually changing moral and social concepts;

(2) that of disposing, in a practical way, of the appeals which it is required to consider.

The Court of Appeal of Saskatchewan, in a number of decisions, has set out what it believes to be the principles to be followed by a trial judge in the determination of an appropriate sentence: punishment, deterrence, protection of the public and the reformation and rehabilitation of the offender.[2] Not all of these principles are given equal weight. The real problem in sentencing is deciding which factor is to be emphasized in a particular case. As pointed out in these judgments,[3] the concepts of retribution, deterrence and denunciation are being displaced as dominant factors in the determination of an appropriate sentence by those factors which will best reform and rehabilitate the offender, for in that reformation and rehabilitation lies the best protection of society. In the final analysis, however, the emphasis to be placed upon a particular factor depends upon the circumstances in each case.

Courts of Appeal, like courts of first instance, are facing constantly increasing caseloads. In the Province of Saskatchewan, in 1951, the total number of criminal appeals, including appeals in respect of both conviction and sentence, was 51. In 1979, the total number of appeals will be approximately 500 — a ten-fold increase since 1951. This increase has taken place in a province where there has been little or no change in total population during that period. No doubt the same general situation prevails in the other provinces of Canada and in the states of the United States.

In Saskatchewan, the Court of Appeal has developed a simple and informal manner of hearing and disposing of criminal appeals. This is both possible and necessary because 90 per cent of the appellants appear in person, presenting their appeals without the assistance of counsel. This places upon the Court the responsibility of seeing that the appellant is accorded all of the rights to which he is entitled under the law. As well, this necessitates complete preparation by the Court before the appeal is heard.

Each month a Judge of the Court of Appeal is appointed judge of the month. One of his main duties is to summarize every criminal appeal perfected for appeal during that month. In so doing the information or charge is checked to see that it properly charges an offense. Where an election is required the information is checked to see that the election has been given and has been properly endorsed. If the appeal is in respect of sentence and the record discloses that the offence is charged in a manner that renders it invalid, or where there has been a failure to endorse the election, the Court of its own volition converts the appeal into one against conviction and quashes the conviction. If, on the other hand, it is an appeal in respect of conviction and after perusing the record the Court feels that justice requires the appellant to be represented by counsel, the Court will appoint counsel for him.

The Criminal Code provides that an appeal in respect of sentence can only be heard with leave of the court or of a judge thereof. In Saskatchewan, an individual appellant is never denied leave to appeal — such appeals are never disposed of on the ground of refusal of leave. There are in my view, sound reasons for taking this position: (1) It requires the same amount of work and study to determine whether leave should be granted or refused as it does to hear the appeal. Thus why not hear the appeal? (2) The appellant may not understand the refusal of leave and consequently he might feel he had been denied a right to which he was entitled. (3) A notice of appeal filed by an individual is usually lacking in reasons, reasons which become apparent only when the appellant appears in person and enters into a discussion with the Court in support of his appeal. (4) When the appeal is disposed of on its merits, the appellant knows the real reasons for the Court's decisions. (5) The record does not necessarily disclose all of the facts which the Court should know. Such facts become apparent when the appellant appears.

There is another policy followed and adopted by the Saskatchewan Court of Appeal. Although the Supreme Court of Canada has held that on a prisoner's appeal in respect of sentence, the Crown may apply for a greater sentence, the Saskatchewan Court of Appeal will not entertain such an application by the Crown. The Court does not think an appellant should feel not only that his appeal may be dismissed, but also that there is a danger his sentence will be increased.

When the appellant appears in person he is treated as any other individual exercising a legal right. He is usually nervous and may find it difficult to speak. The Court does everything possible to make him feel comfortable and to convey to him that it is sympathetic and understanding of his problem. He is allowed as much time as he needs to present his case. If his appeal is dismissed he is told why. While the Court may counsel and advise the appellant, it never engages in harsh and critical comment.

Both in the imposition of sentences and in the disposition of criminal appeals, the Court must show compassion and understanding. If the trial judge or the appellate court is convinced that the offender really intends to change his ways, the Court should make every effort to assist him. This may be done notwithstanding that the particular offence and the record of the accused, judged by traditional standards, would indicate that nothing should be done. The Court of Appeal has done this on many occasions and has supported trial judges who may have done the same thing. For example, there were two boys in Moose Jaw, brothers, each of whom began their involvement with the law at the age of 16 years. Their mother had died when they were quite young and they were being raised by their father. He did his best but was unsuccessful in keeping them out of trouble.

The older boy, from the time he was 16 years of age, was almost constantly in jail. He had appeared before the Court of Appeal on two or three occasions. Finally when he was 19 years of age he was again before the Court appealing his sentence of two years less one day. When he appeared I said, "Well, . . . what do you think the Court can do for you now?" He replied, "I want a chance to change my ways. I want to go to Technical School at Saskatoon and take a course relating to forestry and to do that I will have to be there about the middle of August." I said to him, "Will the school accept you if you are available at that time" and to this he replied, "Yes." I then asked him, "How are you going to live while attending school?" He replied, "The Department of Social Welfare will provide for my room and board." I then told him that the Court would look into the matter and advise him of its decision in a short time.

Crown counsel was asked to check with the Technical School and the Department of Social Welfare to determine whether the representations made by the appellant were correct. In a few days Crown counsel advised the Court that the school was prepared to accept the appellant and the Department was prepared to take care of his maintenance. The Court then reduced the sentence to time already served to enable the appellant to be released immediately and to complete his arrangements to attend school.

Nothing further was heard about the appellant until about two years later when his younger brother appeared before the Court. I said to him, "What do you want the Court to do for you?" He replied immediately, "The same thing as you did for my brother — you remember him do you not?" I said, "Yes, and how is your brother getting along." He said, "Fine — he finished his course and got a job in Northern Saskatchewan and has not been in trouble since." In these circumstances, the Court had no alternative but to grant the same consideration to the appellant as his brother had received. The result has been that since that consideration was shown by the Court neither of these boys have been in trouble.

This example is cited to support my view that neither a trial judge nor an appellate court should hesitate to take a calculated risk when satisfied that by so doing there is a reasonable possibility the offender may change his way of life. There should be no hesitation to do so even though in the particular case it seems that traditional practices and usual yardsticks are being overlooked. Nothing gives the Court greater satisfaction than to feel it has made some contribution to the reformation of an offender.

Both in the imposition of sentence and in the disposition of criminal appeals, the courts may well be advised to review, to some extent, their traditional approach. I fully subscribe to the report of the Canadian Committee on Corrections, which said:

> The Committee sees the overall end of the criminal process as the protection of society and believes that this is best achieved by an attempt to rehabilitate offenders in that society is given long term protection at least expense in human values and material resources. The Committee believes that traditionally punishment has been overstressed as a means of crime prevention yet it does not deny the necessity for punishment as a sanction and it accepts that in some cases the person may be so dangerous as to justify his segregation from the community for periods up to the whole of his life.[4]

Reformation and rehabilitation of the prisoner should be the primary purpose, both of the sentencing process and of penal institutions. Accepting this premise does not mean that there are not cases where the protection of the public requires that severe sentences be imposed or that there are not cases where deterrence requires a similar disposition. Fortunately, however, the cases in which this is required encompass only a limited number of offenders, and usually in those cases that requirement is so self-evident as to cause no real problem. If, however, courts are to give increasing effect to the principles of reformation and rehabilitation, in the broad spectrum of criminal punishment, this will require a departure from the traditional approach. There must be less emphasis on punishment, retribution and vengeance and less emphasis on deterrence. Fundamentally, punishment must be more closely related to the individual than to the crime. Parliament must have intended that courts would do so when it amended the Criminal Code to give to the court wide powers in the fields of suspended sentence and probation.[5]

In recent years some progress has been made in the area of sentencing. Amendments to the Criminal Code provide for absolute and conditional discharge and the serving of sentences intermittently.[6] These are steps in the right direction. Courts should not be hesitant to resort to these means of the disposition of criminal offences if circumstances are such as to justify so doing.

In the imposition of sentences on young offenders, care must be taken not to make the sentences too long. It must be remembered that to a 16-year-old, one year is a long time and five years is a lifetime. There is always the danger too, that time will be viewed by the trial or appellate judge in the light of his own experience rather than through the eyes of the young offender. Time should be considered as viewed by the offender otherwise the sentence, rather than being one which will contribute to the reformation and rehabilitation of the offender, may break his spirit.

Two further sentencing issues require comment. At times we hear a great deal of criticism of the Parole Board. Notwithstanding this criticism I am convinced that the Board has done an excellent job, carrying out its work conscientiously and effectively. It is truly a safety valve for harsh and unreasonable sentences. It has been a dominant factor in the reformation and rehabilitation of many offenders. We seldom hear of its accomplishments but often of its failures. Any reasonable assessment of the work of the Parole Board can only lead to one conclusion, that in carrying out its duties some failures are inevitable. Only by doing nothing would such failures be eliminated. No sensible person expects the Board, or its members, to be infallible in their judgment. In the final analysis the Parole Board should be judged by successes and not by its failures. When so judged it has established a record of achievement resulting in both protection to the public and in the reformation and rehabilitation of many offenders. It should receive our full support.

There are people who advocate that the court of last resort in sentence appeals should be the Supreme Court of Canada. It is argued that only in this way can there be uniformity of sentencing across Canada. There are several objections to this proposition: In the first place, there is the very practical objection that the Supreme Court of Canada cannot possibly assume the additional work that would result from jurisdiction in sentencing appeals. In the second place, the establishment of uniformity of sentences across Canada is neither possible nor advisable.

It is recognized by all knowledgeable people that there cannot be a uniform sentence. The sentence for the same offence will vary greatly depending upon the circumstances. An excellent example of this are the sentences imposed for manslaughter. As well, conditions vary so much from province to province that, of necessity, this variation will be reflected in the sentencing process. The problem is entirely different in areas where there are organized crime syndicates, from that which arises, where courts are concerned primarily with local residents. These differences can be properly recognized on the basis of provincial jurisdiction. Within a province, however, there must be a proper rationalization of sentences imposed for the same or similar offences. This can be achieved and the responsibility for so doing lies with the provincial court of appeal. If there is a marked difference between sentences imposed for the same or similar offences within the provincial jurisdiction, if the court of appeal is unable to rationalize the reason for that difference, it has the obligation to either increase or decrease the sentence to achieve that rationalization. In my view, the courts of appeal have done this, being concerned primarily with the situation existing in their own province. This practice I am satisfied has served a good purpose and should not be disturbed.

In conclusion: the judicial approach to sentencing should be one of compassion and understanding; all doubts should be resolved in favour of the offender; reformation and rehabilitation should be the main target of a sentencing process. Nevertheless, while a judge should be compassionate and understanding, he must not lose sight of the fact that the whole criminal process is for the protection of the public and that the criminal law must be administered and enforced to attain that purpose and at the same time, maintain the confidence and respect of the public.

NOTES

1. *A.G. Ont. v. A.G. Can.,* [1912] A.C. 571 at 583.
2. *R. v. Kissick* (1969), 70 W.W.R. 365; *R. v. Morrissette* (1970), 12 C.R.N.S. 392.
3. *R. v. Kissick* and *R. v. Morrissette, supra,* note 2.
4. Canadian Committee on Corrections (Quimet Report, 1969).
5. Criminal Code, R.S.C. 1970, c. C-34, s. 663, as amended by 1972, c. 13, s. 58; 1974-75-76, c. 93, s. 81, and s. 664.
6. *Supra,* note 5, s. 662.1, as enacted by 1972, c. 13, s. 57 and amended by 1974-75-76, c. 105, ss. 20, 80.

CHAPTER 16

Sentencing the Individual

E. M. Hall

The courts as we now know them, of whatever level, are civilized society's substitute for the naked power of force. Without the courts we would have chaos and mob rule, with mob law and mob punishment. There can be no substitute for properly constituted courts. Abraham Lincoln stressed this when he said in 1837: "There is no grievance that is a fit object of redress by mob law."

It is in fulfilling the sentencing function that the courts are expected to represent the most civilized facets of today's society; to be just and humane; and to temper man's inhumanity to man. In this essential role of being the ultimate arbiter in sentencing, the court, representing civilized society, is itself often on trial. Accordingly, in sentencing the individual the judge must have the capacity, the resources, and the time to weigh the circumstances of the individual standing for sentence. There must be no blind justice. Whatever place the effigy of the blindfolded goddess may have had in portraying that justice is "no respecter of persons," the blindfold should not be present when the judge comes to passing sentence. Justice must at this stage have both eyes wide open, with a clear, calm vision of all who then stand for sentence. She must be fully aware of the individual with all his or her flaws and/or virtues and possibilities for good or evil.

So much for generalities. It would be well if, in the public estimation, these principles or practices were universally or generally accepted, but, unfortunately, such is not the case. Many people today are questioning what the courts do in the way of sentencing; it is being said that the courts are too lenient with individuals who transgress. This questioning or criticism is a fact and it is becoming clear that we are faced with a growing demand for harsher sentences; by virtue of what goes under the name of "Law and Order" consequent upon the rise in crime in so many quarters. It is a strange phenomena that while great strides have been made in improving the health and economic security of people, crime continues to plague the nation. This failure on the part of society to lessen the incidence of crime impairs the joy of living; lives and property are rendered insecure; the peace is frequently disturbed and some persons are subjected to degrading and terrifying criminal acts, hence public concern.

There will be little, if any, disagreement about this description of the problem of the lawlessness of this era. But, in respect of a cure for or an amelioration in conditions, opinions will and do differ. Men and women of goodwill seek a solution, either through tougher laws and sentences or changes in existing laws and sentencing procedures, and here I sense a growing demand for harsher sentences as though harsher sentences will benefit the victim or his or her dependents. Undoubtedly, the injury to the victim is very real. Provisions to indemnify the victim or his or her dependents have been slow in coming and are yet very inadequate. But the real question is: Can we visualize compensation to the victim as demanding harsher punishment to the individual offender? It is difficult to see an equation in this connection. The two concepts are really unrelated.

So what should courts do in today's situation? Society must be aware that the cause the courts and judges serve is "Justice."

How are individuals to be dealt with? There cannot be the same punishment imposed upon all offenders regardless of their background; their circumstances; their intelligence; its effect on their means of livelihood or family situations. That would be treating unequals equally. Accordingly, punishment must be assessed on individuals, upon the specific person then before the court. The whole concept of making an individual an example to others is fallacious. The public must of course be educated to obey the law, but that education cannot occur at the expense of a specific individual. Nor should the concept of punishment involve punishment in the moral sense. The court cannot equate itself with any form of divine purpose in the reformation of a sinner. The law does not punish sinners as transgressors of the moral law; it punishes those who have been convicted of breaching the code or lawfully enacted statutes. There are a multitude of sins that are not unlawful by statute.

Can society find some middle ground between revenge, retribution and harshness on the one hand and undue leniency on the other? It must be accepted that there are some crimes for which substantial punishment is indicated, such as where the offender presents a danger to society having regard to his past record, or where the offense is one of murder or rape, or the taking of the law into one's own hands and the use of a dangerous weapon to such end, or in hijacking and kidnapping and the like. There are, of course, offences where Parliament or the Legislature has opted for a minimum sentence or penalty. The judge has no option there to impose any sentence below the minimum. It then falls to the parole authorities to deal with those offenders, mitigating in some measure the lot of such prisoners where the circumstances warrant by weekend passes, and other alternatives.

But there are numerous offences where clemency and alternative forms of punishment are indicated. Canada has a reputation for sending a greater proportion of its convicted offenders to prison than any other Western country, except the United States. It is frightening to observe that the majority of those so sent to jail are the poor and native people or Métis, and those in great numbers because they cannot pay the fines imposed and so must serve a term in lieu of payment. All who are so sent to jail are individuals, but in the manner of being committed are dealt with *en bloc.* The system says to them — you are poor; you are a native or Métis; you cannot pay the fine imposed, so off you go to a place euphoniously called a place of correction. That sounds better than saying off you go to jail. We all realize that there is no correctional element in these short sentences. Various alternatives are being experimented with. Native court attendants are filling an important role but the problem is a vital societal one which will not go away until the social conditions that create the problem are remedied.

Some judges have developed the policy of treating all offenders convicted of similar or identical offences alike. This is a practice which should not be condoned. It is the offender, not the offence which should dictate what penalty should be imposed in the circumstances. The court must stand firm in dealing humanely with wrongdoers — young or old; native or alien; white or coloured — all as individuals. Revenge or retribution are no part of a court's function. We can and are entitled to have law and order but not at the expense of justice to the individual.

CHAPTER 17

Sentencing in the North

C. F. Tallis

The Northwest Territories are characterized by a small population scattered over vast tracts of land. The population can be broken down into one-third Indian, one-third Innuit and one-third white. Most of the native population live in relatively small settlements scattered along the sea coast. Historically, the location of these settlements was dictated by shelter from the climate, availability of food, trading posts and so on. In recent years, however, there has been a relocation of some of these settlements as resource development has cut across the traditional pattern. Exploration for the acceleration of resource development, combined with the differences to be found in the social background of each of the three groups found in the Northwest Territories, forms the arena in which the criminal justice system must operate.

In dealing with the question of sentencing, courts in the Northwest Territories cannot overlook the fact that society has the basic roots of these three cultures. When the common law was transplanted into Canada it proved to be very flexible but native people, whether Innuit or Indian, had their own system of laws, tribunals, penalties, and, in effect, their own justice system. Furthermore, such cultures did not have jails. This was a new concept introduced from the white man's world. It continues to be little understood by many of the elders in the Indian and Innuit communities. Consequently, a great deal of consideration is given to the possibility of imposing a non-custodial sentence with terms of probation or community service orders. With approximately 50 per cent of the population being 18 years or younger this is particularly important. In the case of youthful first offenders custodial sentences are generally avoided.[1]

With regard to the question of community service orders, a real effort is being made to carry out the spirit of a statement made by the federal Minister of Justice in 1977:

The community service order which requires offenders to carry out work or perform some service of benefit to the community for a fixed number of hours, is of particular interest. It is a positive, inexpensive approach to dealing with offenders which has the advantage of providing some concrete repayment to the community.

The offender is a part of the community, and in a sense, its product. Just as he has a responsibility to the community, to obey its laws and contribute to its good, the community must assume some responsibility for him, to ensure that he understands his role and appreciates the implications of contravening the rules. Community service orders provide a valuable way of reinforcing this notion of mutual responsibility which should not be underestimated.

Community service orders are already being used in some provinces as part of probation orders and there is evidence that they are most effective. We hope to assist and encourage further use of this approach by offering some legislative guidelines which will enhance its status under law.

There are some constraints inherent in the community service order sentence. It must not be seen as a cheap source of workers which would upset the labour community, not as some form of slavery. Any legislation would have to provide that such orders be possible only upon the consent of the offender. Other factors which will need to be considered include the availability of an appropriate program, and the court's satisfying itself that the offender is a suitable person for such an order.[2]

No less important to the sentencing process in the North are the more localized cultural conditions. Greater contact with southern institutions has affected many northern settlements. This intrusion from the South has created problems and the fact that the contact is not coming in a uniform manner greatly adds to the difficulties. Some settlements are almost unchanged, with the residents living as their ancestors did. On the other hand, there are settlements where the way of life has suffered an almost complete metamorphosis. In between these extremes, there are settlements showing various degrees of change.[3]

Perhaps my approach in trying to deal with offenders who are in the process of bridging the gap between two distinct and different cultures can be illustrated by referring to a summary of the case of *R. v. Naukatsik:*

Rape — youthful offender — appropriate sentence. R. v. Naukatsik (N.W.T.S.C.), Tallis, J. December 20, 1977. *Age:* 19(m). *Facts:* On September 10, 1977, N, who was attending vocational school in Fort Smith, went to a dance. At the dance he met a female classmate, E, and eventually they left the dance together in the company of another couple who gave them a ride to the residence of Ms. E. When they arrived at Ms. E's residence, N and E got out of the car, and before arriving at the door of the residence, N threw E down and raped her. E sustained no bodily injury. Upon arrest a breathalyzer test was given to N and the results showed 140 mg of alcohol per 100 ml of blood. N had no recollection of the event but pleaded guilty to the offence and took the stand on his own behalf. *Special considerations:* Both N and E are Innuit. N had left home owing to his parents' heavy drinking, but since leaving home had developed a drinking problem of his own. A psychiatric report filed with the court indicated that there was no reason to doubt N's statement that he did not remember the events, as N had at an earlier age been a glue sniffer, resulting in problems of loss of memory on occasion. N was a wrestler and had made much progress in both athletics and his education. *Decision:* Although rape is a very serious offence, the court must also be mindful that where youthful offenders are before the court the sentence imposed must not only vindicate the law but also must not "crush or destroy the hope of rehabilitation." Having regard to the physical and mental capabilities of N, as well as his genuine remorse in having committed the act, a term of one year's imprisonment is appropriate. In addition, one year's probation with the following terms: (1) N shall report to a probation officer; (2) N will seek and maintain employment and/or attend educational upgrading; (3) N will obtain alcohol counselling as directed by the probation officer; (4) N will notify the probation officer of any change of address or employment.[4]

To many this would seem to be a lenient sentence but under the circumstances and particularly after the accused gave evidence after a plea of guilty, I was persuaded that a traditional southern sentence would be excessive.

On the other end of the scale, courts are now encountering situations where the accused of native background are quite sophisticated and well educated. They operate in the same or a similar manner as other offenders and accordingly the sentences reflect this fact. Furthermore, people in the smaller communities are now becoming much more knowledgeable with respect to their rights. Complaints of rape, attempted rape and assault causing bodily harm come before the court much more frequently. It is not uncommon for Innuit and Indian women to now bring divorce actions when just a few years ago they would have had no idea of their rights.

As time goes by I can see our sentences becoming more conventional and perhaps similar to those imposed in other jurisdictions. In some areas we have tended to impose much harsher sentences, particularly in the field of drug trafficking. It has been necessary to do this because restrictions on liquor imposed in many of the communities has opened up a drug market which is being exploited by southern traders and sophisticated natives within the community. The advent of drugs is viewed with alarm by the elders. Accordingly, in this type of situation, sentences have been imposed within the same ranges as are imposed or upheld by the Alberta Court of Appeal and the British Columbia Court of Appeal.[5]

Apart from the incidence of drug trafficking, the Northwest Territories is still in the fortunate position of having little if any organized crime. The serious crimes such as murder, manslaughter and rape are usually connected with the consumption of liquor. As time goes by there will undoubtedly be an increase in commercial frauds and similar crimes. In such cases I can see sentences being imposed and upheld in the range of conventional sentences for such offences in other parts of Canada.

In conclusion, sentencing in a multi-cultural society can not afford to be rigid and monolithic. This is equally the case where a society is going through a period of rapid social change. In the Northwest Territories both of these factors are present and this makes flexibility in sentencing practices imperative.

NOTES

1. *R. v. Beacon and Modney* (1976), 31 C.C.C. (2d) 56 (Alta. C.A.).

2. R. Basford, "A Creative Strategy for Criminal Justice," a speech delivered at the 1st National Conference on Diversion (Quebec: October, 1977).

3. See the discussion of these local disparities in Mr. Justice W. Morrow, "The Role of the Court in Opening a Frontier," a speech to the Humanities Association Dinner (University of Calgary: October 20, 1976); *id.* "The General Administration of Justice in the Northwest Territories," a speech to the Faculty of Law (University of Ottawa: January 20, 1977).

4. "On Sentencing," 20 *Crim. Law Quarterly* (1978), pp. 290-291.

5. *R. v. Covlin* (1976), 1 Alta. L.R. (2d) 123 (C.A.); *R. v. Lima,* August 15, 1978, N.W.T.S.C. (unreported).